Racialism, Drugs, and Migration

Racialism, Drugs, and Migration

CONTEMPORARY ISSUES IN LATIN AMERICA AND THE CARIBBEAN

First Edition

Edited by Virginia Ochoa-Winemiller, PhD

New Jersey City University

Bassim Hamadeh, CEO and Publisher
John Remington, Executive Editor
Gem Rabanera, Senior Project Editor
Celeste Paed, Associate Production Editor
Emely Villavicencio, Senior Graphic Designer
Stephanie Kohl, Licensing Coordinator
Natalie Piccotti, Director of Marketing
Kassie Graves, Vice President of Editorial
Jamie Giganti, Director of Academic Publishing

3970 Sorrento Valley Blvd., Ste. 500, San Diego, CA 92121

Contents

SECTION III

Introduction

AS REGIONS, BOTH Latin America and the Caribbean have historically overcome many social, political, and economic issues that transformed their countries and people (See Figures 0.1 and 0.2). A multidisciplinary approach is needed to contextualize and critically reflect on the internal impact of these problems and the role that the global community has played in generating and/or resolving some of them. Nevertheless, the origins, complexity, and overarching effects of many of these issues have remained largely misunderstood. This anthology aims to provide an overview of three topics critical to historical and modern Latin America and the Caribbean: racialism, drug-related activities, and migration.

An overview of both ethnicity and race is critically important to understanding multiculturalism, creolization, cultural hybridity, representation, identity, and population mobility in both Latin America and the Caribbean. Usually perceived as mixed and spared from racial and ethnic conflict, instead these regions had a conflicting history of contentious policies and cultural attitudes that contextualize current cultural and social changes as well as population mobility. European conquest and colonization introduced the ideology and politics of race or racialism to the Americas. Slavery and peonage became the conducive agents to control a Native and African population already devastated by war, disease, and relocation. Those who could not flee resisted by selectively incorporating the new and the old to create a hybrid cultural landscape that has managed to preserve many African and Native cultural traits. As such, cultural resistance was the force challenging oppression and the aftershocks of the European enterprise of colonization. After independence, the political agenda of nation-building aimed toward homogeneity. New identities such as *Mestizo*, *Ladino*, and *Creole* emerged as the preferred means of representation of a mainly mixed but whitened urbanite population. *Indio*, *Negro*, and *Mulato* became othering categories for an impoverished and uneducated population singled out by skin color, an outdated Native culture and lifestyle, and the burden of servitude. Although slavery had ended and the state recognized the rights of Natives and Africans, racism and discrimination still prevailed. In modern times, descendants of both Natives and Africans have been constitutionally recognized as minorities with cultural and, in most cases, land and resources rights. At the same time, economic neoliberalism and pseudo-democratic political ideologies

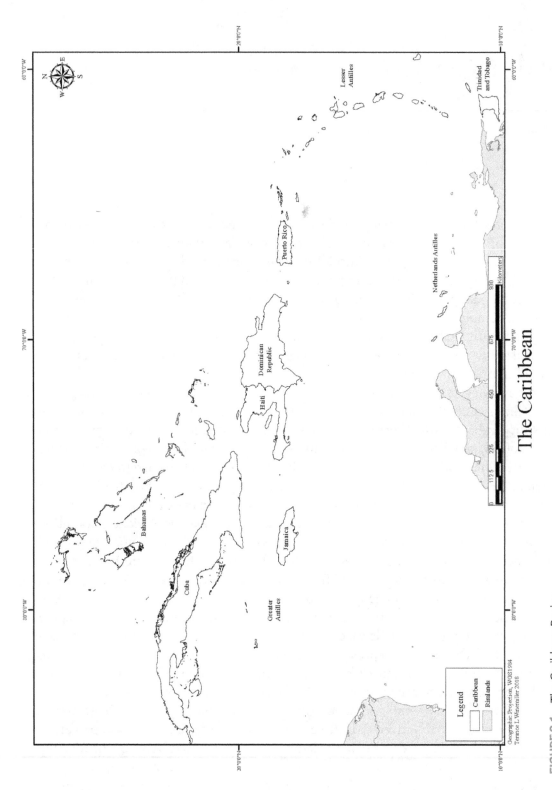

FIGURE 0.1 The Caribbean Region

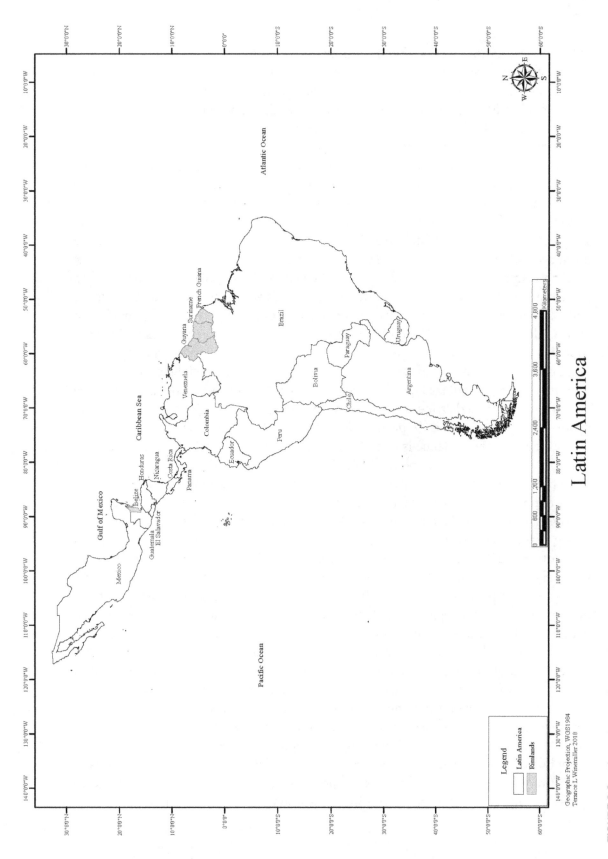

FIGURE 0.2   The Latin American Region

in Latin America and the Caribbean continued to highlight the need to integrate these minority groups and merge them with the state national identity. For the most part, the success of this state-supported nationalistic agenda has been based on the overall rejection of Garifuna, Maya, and Nahuatl ethnic identities and subsequent replacement with "mestizo" national labels such as Belizean, Guatemalan, or Mexican. Furthermore, the unrelenting forces of globalization have accelerated culture change, threatening the preservation and authenticity of Native and African legacies that, along with revamped forms of racialism, are leading to current waves of casual and covert racism, culture appropriation, land and resource seizures, ethnocide, and genocide.

Latin America is a crucial geographic zone for drug production and trafficking. The Andean countries of Colombia, Peru, and Bolivia are the world's main cocaine producers, while Central America, Mexico, and the Caribbean have become the principal corridors for transporting drugs into the United States and Europe. As a result, the countries of the region have suffered various consequences of drug trafficking and U.S.-led eradication and interdiction efforts commonly known as the War on Drugs. The failure of the War on Drugs program has been evident by its inability to suppress both the supply and demand of cocaine, heroin, and methamphetamines. Drug production and trafficking areas have led to an upsurge of violence, corruption, impunity, erosion of rule of law, and human rights violations caused by the emergence of powerful organized crime groups and drug cartels. As a result, more than 60,000 people have died in Mexico in prohibition-related violence since 2006 (Krache, 2013). Today, drug-related violence is one of the main push factors driving migrants from Central America to Mexico and the United States.

In the last 30 years, Latin America has transitioned from an immigrant to an emigrant region. Most of these migrants come to the United States, but the direction is slowly changing to include Europe and Asia as new destinations for the migrant flow. Today, Latin American immigrants represent about 53% of the 38 million foreign-born residents in the United States (Passel & Cohn, 2009). Historically, the demand for low-wage labor in the United States has been a constant force driving migrants searching for economic opportunity. However, the composition of Latin American and Caribbean migration is changing rapidly to include a more diverse population in terms of gender, education, skills, and socioeconomic status. Another persistent issue in immigration continues to be the integration of the migrant population into dominant U.S. society. Historically, policies, opportunities, and barriers to successfully integrate Latino migrants have been shaped by factors such as economic depression, the war on drugs, and terrorism. In recent times, public opinion polls, the media, and academic studies continue to indicate a rise of discontent and intolerance toward Latino and Caribbean migrants in the United States. Driven by economic depression, social anxiety, and a xenophobic political rhetoric infused with threats of deportation, immigration is at the center of an increasingly hostile sociopolitical climate and must be examined to assess its impact for past and future immigrant generations and to understand the opportunities and barriers associated with the successful integration of Latin American immigrants into U.S. society.

This anthology aims to contribute to the discussion of racialism, drug-related activities, and migration issues in Latin America and the Caribbean, both in and outside the classroom. The underlying principle behind the selection of readings and their organization is the inclusion of multiple disciplinary approaches and voices to the current debates surrounding these regional and global issues. By incorporating multiple voices, the goal is to encourage civil discussion, critical thinking, and reflection rather than rote memorization. To aid the reader's exploration of this textbook, readings are organized by topic, with each section including pedagogical tools such as keywords, topic-related questions, and additional suggested readings to follow up on the topic.

REFERENCES

Krache, M., (2013) Think again: Mexican drug cartels. *Foreign Policy*, 203: 30–33.

Passel, J., & Cohn, D. (2009, April 14). *A portrait of unauthorized immigrants in the United States*. Pew Research Center. https://www.pewresearch.org/hispanic/2009/04/14/a-portrait-of-unauthorized-immigrants-in-the-united-states/

Ethnicity and Racialism

LATIN AMERICA AND the Caribbean are regions shaped by ethnic and racial conflict. Throughout their history, indigenous and Afro Latin American populations had been the target of racialized politics and discriminatory attitudes from Ladino elites concerned with building homogenous and progressive nations. Ladino and Mestizo elites argued that, for the most part, indigenous and Afro-Latin Americans' attempts to become autonomous nations in full control of their resources and economic future have only fueled violent uprisings and the fragmentation of the nation-building plan. Instead, these groups were encouraged to discard their ethnic and racial identities and fully embrace the state-sponsored national character. Today, the outcome of such efforts is the prevalence of issues related to identity, self-representation, and visibility among the Native and Afro-Latin American population.

The readings in this section present a sequential overview of several aspects of ethnicity and racialism by focusing on examples from Guatemala, Mexico, and Brazil. Readers will learn about the role of ethnic and racial identity in increasing political visibility and the development of both local and global social movements. Grandin's (2000) article discusses the role that political and economic alliances between the Maya K'iche elites and the Ladino population played in the formation of the modern Guatemalan nation and identity. The Maya views on race and nation were incompatible with the Ladino notions of assimilation and progress, leading to violence and genocide since the 1950s. Johnson III (2007) focuses on identity and visibility as two relevant issues that Afro-Latin Americans must face in politics. The lack of neutrality in state census has limited societal representation of Blacks, hindering their political participation and ability to improve socioeconomic conditions. Focusing on the Zapatista movement, Kueker (2009) addresses Mexico's racialism issues and indigenous social movements resulting from their participation on a global economy. The rise in 1994 of the *Ejercito Zapatista de Liberación Nacional* (EZLN), a Maya indigenous movement aiming to resist colonialism and neoliberal economic reforms from the Western world, is presented as an example of the struggles that these groups still face today. Triggered by the signing of the North American Free Trade Agreement (NAFTA), the EZLN perceived the treaty as an "assault" to indigenous customary tradition of communal land tenure—a neoliberal death sentence to their way of life. Julie's (2012) article is the last in this section, addressing the myth of Brazil as a racial democracy, an invented tradition designed to incorporate Afro-Brazilians into White public space. Under this tradition, *Samba* and Carnival became politically correct mnemonic devices of heritage and *Brasilidade*. Nevertheless, the myth failed and Brazil turned into a racial hierarchy riddled with prejudice and racism and where identity became a subjective self-assessment.

KEYWORDS

Africans, Afro Latinos, autonomy, Black women's network, Brazil, Carnival, *castas*, *comunidades indigenas*, Congresses of Black culture, Cuba, Ecuador, ethnicity, EZLN, Guatemala, global south, indigeneity, *Indios*, informal racial discrimination, *K'iche*, *macehualization*, *Maya*, *Mestizos*, Mexico, miscegenation, *Mulatos*, national identity, naturalization, patronage, political activism, poverty, race, racial categories, racialism, racial democracy myth, racial hierarchy, racial quotas, Samba, scientific racism, social inequality, transnational advocacy networks, violence, *VisBrasil*, White supremacy, Zapatista movement.

Regenerating the Race

Race, Class, and the Nationalization of Ethnicity

Greg Grandin

The Ladinos and Indians are two distinct classes; the former march ahead with hope and energy through the paths that have been laid out by progress; the latter, immovable, do not take any part in the political and intellectual life, adhering tenaciously to their old habits and customs.
—1894 Guatemalan National Census

If today all we can do is contribute to progress by cultivating the earth and transforming raw material into useful products, then, when the moral atmosphere of the republic permits us to develop our natural faculties, we will be able to cultivate the intelligence of our children and contribute to the social and political revolution of the country. We yearn for the regeneration of the Indians in order to obtain the civil and political equality that is the basis of democracies.
—1894 K'iche' petition

GUATEMALAN CAPITALIST DEVELOPMENT allowed for an intensification of ethnic identity, even as class divisions were forming. While this phenomenon helps outline various possible forms ethnic relations could take under the coffee regime, it does not explain how individuals took advantage of these possibilities to make sense of their world. The next two chapters will explore how Quetzalteco K'iche' elites used the political and cultural resources at their disposal to redefine ethnic identity to fit changing times. Historians and anthropologists have assured us repeatedly that nineteenth-century Indians had only the most distorted and rudimentary understanding of nations, territorial boundaries, governing philosophies, and national visions. Further, scholars often lament that, until fairly recently, Indians left no written record to describe their society and culture. This is not so for Quetzalteco K'iche's.

They not only produced a wealth of accounts in their dealings with the local and national state but also erected monuments, constructed buildings, and founded institutions from which their faith in progress and commitment to the Guatemalan nation can be measured. K'iche' elites, in effect, were able to marshal the forces of modernity to develop an identity that was highly modern—that is, historically self-conscious as a subject class in the process of cultural and economic transformation. They were, in the words of Marshall Berman, in a "state of perpetual becoming."[1]

Paradoxically, new liberal ideologies provided K'iche' elites new justifications for their continued caste authority. With the dissolution of the city's agricultural ejidos and Guatemala's transition to coffee capitalism, the authority of principales came to depend on their power to regulate the use of forest and pastureland and on their efforts to become the political representatives not just of Quetzalteco K'iche's but of all the nation's Indians. This chapter will explore how the simultaneous efforts of K'iche' elites to distance themselves from *and* to speak on behalf of poorer, rural Indians produced contradictory interpretations of race, progress, and nation—interpretations that both emerged from and helped shape communal, municipal, and national political relations.

A POSITIVE ANTINOMY: THE ABOLITION OF THE MUNICIPALIDAD DE INDÍGENAS

With the privatization of municipal land came a change in the way Quetzaltenango's ethnic relations were configured. Municipal politics were no longer, primarily, a contest between castes over city resources. As such, K'iche's gradually traded their political autonomy for a role in what became a single municipal body. Yet rather than signaling a loss of political influence, in important ways the political authority of K'iche's grew.

Perhaps chastened by the fate of the preceding generation of municipal authorities, Ladinos did not immediately attempt to abolish the indigenous cabildo after 1871. In fact, K'iche' principales quickly took advantage of the liberal victory to demand that the office of indigenous gobernador be terminated. During the colonial period, as we have seen, gobernadores were generally the most compromised of the K'iche' authorities, using their close ties with Spaniards to enrich themselves and prevent popular unrest. Carrera's restoration of the position, rather than marking a restitution of indigenous autonomy, institutionalized the interdependence of the gobernador and Ladino officials. Immediately following the liberal revolution, principales, acting in the name of the común, complained of abuses committed by the city's two previous gobernadores, José María Paz and Antonio Cajas.[2] The principales demanded that the two be made to account for their handling of community funds. Barrios himself intervened in the dispute and ordered that the office of gobernador be abolished and that its authority devolve to the indigenous alcaldes.[3] In exchange, the principales offered to use

FIGURE 1.1.1 Municipalidad Indígena, 1886. In William Brigham, *Guatemala: Land of the Quetzal.*

FIGURE 1.1.2 Municipalidad Indígena, 1894.
Photograph by Estudio Piggot y Lesher, courtesy of cirma.

FIGURE 1.1.3   Combined Ladino, K'iche' municipality, c. 1920
Photograph by Tomás Zanotti, courtesy of cirma.

the funds misappropriated by Paz and Cajas to buy guns for the new regime. For a brief period, the removal of the gobernador freed principales from the direct control of Ladino elites.

K'iche' authorities did, however, eventually lose their formal political autonomy as Ladinos gradually initiated procedures that would incorporate the indigenous municipal structure into their own. In 1879, the Ladino municipalidad proposed a plan to the minister of government. It was imperative to end the dual system, the Ladinos argued, because there existed a "positive antinomy" between the legislation of the liberal republic and "*monárquica costumbre*" (monarchical practices).[4] Rather than doing away with the K'iche' cabildo "altogether, leaving Indians with nothing," Ladinos proposed that the K'iche's be made to attend Ladino sessions and that a Ladino secretary be appointed to oversee their affairs.[5] In addition, Indians were to assume greater responsibility on city commissions. This, the petition concluded, was the most prudent way of "assimilating the two classes." Throughout the 1880s and 1890s the plan was put into effect. In 1882, the jefe político, Barillas, ordered that a single treasurer be appointed for the two bodies; in the late 1880s, indigenous authorities began to attend Ladino sessions and to serve on municipal commissions; and finally, in 1894, the dual system came to an end with the abolition of the indigenous cabildo.[6]

By this point, however, indigenous political autonomy was little more than a fanciful facade. Carrera's restoration of corporate indigenous protections provided K'iche's with a space in which they could politically and economically regroup, but it could not break the complex social and political relations that bound Quetzalteco Indians and Ladinos to each other. As we have seen, starting deep in the colonial period, Indians had grown to rely on Spaniards and then Ladinos to pursue their interests and maintain their authority. This reliance cut across class and privilege. In 1870, for example, Saturnino Pisquiy, complained to the ministro de gobernación (minister of the interior) that the K'iche' alcaldes were abusing their power by forcing him to serve on cofradías.[7] In 1873, a poor indigenous women, Gregoria Soch, went to the Ladino justice of the peace to seek protection from her abusive K'iche' husband.[8] In 1882, Basilio Tzum, an illiterate indigenous swineherd, signed over power of attorney to a Ladino lawyer in his land struggle with another K'iche'.[9] And in 1895, Tomás Pac, a wealthy K'iche' landowner, complained to the Ladino alcalde that he was being harassed by the indigenous authorities to show title to his land.[10]

The divisions caused by increased political participation—what Rodolfo Pastor has described as the macehualization of indigenous politics—continued throughout the nineteenth century. In 1879, Gregorio Morales was charged with attempting to convene an unauthorized cabildo vote, and in 1881, 88 K'iche's complained that the election for the indigenous municipality, in which 113 voted, was invalid because they had not been informed of the time or place of the balloting.[11] In the 1881 case, both sides complained to the Ladino jefe político that their opponents did not have the political caliber needed to lead the común: "They do not have the character of principales," said the representative of one faction, while a spokesman for the other charged that "disgracefully, there are in our class men who aspire to rule who are good for nothing."[12]

As in other pueblos in this period of liberal state consolidation, social tensions forced competing factions to rely increasingly on the language of community to justify their claims.[13] In 1871, José María Paz, for example, dismissed his detractors as only three Indians "claiming to speak in the name of the pueblo."[14] But in a context of weakening political authority and growing class stratification, indigenous leaders increasingly had to call on the Ladino state to back up their claims. This produced the apparently contradictory effect of deepening community identification while reinforcing the power of the state. The liberal state did not arrive unexpectedly in communities in 1871; it was invited in.

But despite the deepening dependence on Ladino authority, the power of indigenous authorities in some ways increased. The privatization of land removed the common terrain that had bound K'iche's in a field of reciprocal rights and obligations.

To be sure, patriarchal relations continued through cofradías, debt, and kinship. K'iche' authorities still, at times, defended their poorer counterparts.[15] Yet relations of deference and obligation gradually weakened as expectations of subsistence rights withered away. The power of principales became much more directly tied to the punitive function of the state. Revenue collection provides an example. In the past, a good part of the community treasury had been raised through the sale of the communal harvest (siembra de la comunidad), the production of which entailed the mobilization of communal labor. Now, in contrast, the majority of K'iche' revenue was collected through fines and fees. In 1876, for example, of the 1,050 pesos taken in, 712 represented fines or money paid to commute prison sentences.[16] The majority of these sentences were for drunk or scandalous behavior. K'iche' authorities also fined more serious infractions such as assault and domestic violence.

As the city grew, Ladinos came to rely to an ever greater extent on indigenous authority. This reliance was explicitly acknowledged when, in 1895, the Ladino alcalde, upon naming a number of K'iche's to act as *jueces* (judges or heads) of municipal committees, admitted "that the commissions of ejidos, roads and forests should be given to various Indian councilmen because they are the ones who can best carry out the functions ... above all making sure that the forests are not cut down or destroyed."[17] The position of *juez de ejidos* would remain under K'iche' control until the 1960s. That same year, K'iche's were also put in charge of both the electrification and vaccination committees so that they could combat the "general preoccupation among the Indians that their [electricity and vaccines] application is dangerous."[18] Further, although the Municipalidad de Indígenas was abolished in 1894, principales brokered a deal ensuring that the third alcalde and six councilmen in the now single municipality would always be a K'iche'.

K'iche' authorities used their political power to build an extended network of patronage throughout the city and its environs. After 1895, the third alcalde, who also functioned as the third justice of the peace, had at his disposal a large corps of auxiliary alcaldes throughout the municipio. In 1899, for example, he had under his authority forty-nine employees, all K'iche's, including twenty-five alcaldes auxiliaries, twelve forest sentries, and eight night patrollers.[19] By 1910, this number of auxiliaries had increased to 137.[20] Into this century, individuals remained obligated, under penalty of fine or imprisonment, to serve as instructed by the indigenous municipales. In exchange for their services, these auxiliary alcaldes were granted usage rights to land. José María Pac, Serapio García, and José María Orozco were granted twenty-three cuerdas in exchange for acting as forest sentries.[21] Further, the cofradía system continued to be regulated by indigenous authorities. After 1894, the third alcalde was responsible for authorizing and supervising the *entregas* (transferences of cofradía goods and authority) of successive *alcaldes de cofradías*. This authority extended to the poorer cofradías of the rural *aldeas* (hamlets).[22] After Jorge Ubico replaced the position of elected mayors with appointed municipal *intendentes* in 1935, the responsibility for regulating the cofradía system passed to the K'iche' authority in charge of ejidos.

As construction boomed in the region, the power of K'iche' authorities to conscript labor increased. The third alcalde provided weekly work gangs of between thirty and forty indigenous men to maintain the cemetery, build roads, clean the streets, work in the municipal quarry, or attend to other urban needs.[23] The majority of these workers, reflecting the class composition of the city's geography, came from the rural aldeas and cantones. A chronic labor shortage empowered the indigenous alcalde to requisition men from other municipalities, ostensibly outside his jurisdiction, with the authority of the jefe político.[24] By 1912, the third alcalde was communicating with his counterparts in the coffee region and helping to capture escaped colonos.[25]

As private contractors, indigenous elites could use their political connections to secure lucrative deals with the city, which, in turn, helped develop labor relations among K'iche's. Agatón Boj, for example, served in a number of positions in the municipality, becoming the third alcalde in 1900. His son, Enrique, served as regidor in 1903 and 1909. In 1906, Boj won the contract to reconstruct the facade of the municipal theater (see fig. 1.1.4), destroyed in the 1902 earthquake, and, in 1907, he was hired to

FIGURE 1.1.4   Inauguration of the new façade of Quetzaltenango's municipal theater built by Agatón Boj, 1907. *Photograph by Tomás Zanotti, courtesy of cirma.*

build the pantheon crypt of president Manuel Estrada Cabrera.[26] Estrada Cabrera was a former Quetzalteco mayor with whom Boj undoubtedly had had previous dealings. By 1907, Boj was the largest employer in the city, with over fifty workers, all K'iche', on his payroll. Another K'iche', José María Citalán, who served as regidor in 1899 and alcalde in 1907, signed a four-thousand-peso contract in 1905 to build part of the city's new hospital.[27]

The end of formal K'iche' autonomy, then, brought about new forms of indigenous authority that rested more on the power of the state than on communal norms of reciprocity. But while Indians seemingly went along with the political changes, they acted swiftly to retain their cultural authority. To do so, they had to redefine the nature of community.

FOR THE REGENERATION OF THE RACE

In January 1894, confronting the abolition of their cabildo, 107 K'iche' principales sent a petition to the municipal council. The petition is so remarkable, so unexpectedly sophisticated, that it could easily be dismissed as a singular yet anomalous instance of the capacity of Indians to say what elites want to hear—except that it was followed by a series of writings and actions that attest that this was no mere subaltern parroting of elite key words. Written by the indigenous alcalde Santiago Coyoy in a clear, sure hand and exact formal Spanish, the petition makes a plea for increased representation in what would become the single municipality:

> It pleases us to send petitions to vecinos, who for their rectitude and for their truly liberal principles, and for the fact that they have always shown respect for the special character and needs of aboriginals (*aborígenes*), cannot do less than receive our demand with the attention it deserves.
>
> You desire (*vosotros deseáis*) the political advancement of our race, because you are convinced that we contribute to the realization of the progress of the *patria*. And if today all we can do is contribute to progress by cultivating the earth and transforming raw material into useful products, then, when the moral atmosphere of the republic permits us to develop our natural faculties, we will be able to cultivate the intelligence of our children and contribute to the social and political revolution of the country. We yearn for the regeneration of the Indians in order to obtain the civil and political equality which is the basis of democracies. To beat down, ridicule, scorn the Indian, to remove him from the public realm (*alejarlo de la cosa pública*), to restrict his rights, will not, señores, bring about his advancement. That the Indian knows the interests of the collective; that he defends them; that he learns how to administer them; that justice is heard. This is the desire of this petition.

Señores Concejales: As you well know, Quetzaltenango is, at the very least, composed of two-thirds Indians, all lovers of work, all absolutely respectful of their authorities. But, despite all this, Indians lack real representation in the ayuntamiento. The families of Los Alisos, Pacajá, Chichiguitán, Chicalajá and other municipal hamlets do not possess sufficient Spanish to formulate their demands or defend themselves *in voce* before the justices of the peace, that is to say, where they do not permit the intervention of lawyers. What is the result of this? Some would say that the lack of a judge who speaks the K'iche' dialect would be an incentive for Indians to learn Spanish. It would force them to quickly learn, but at the cost of being unjust. It would be inhuman.

In summary, what we ask for ... is that the third alcalde, the second syndic, and that six councilmen ... be, *precisamente*, Indígenas. Also, we ask ... that there be in this city a judge for Indians and that he always be an Indian.[28]

When the Ladino municipality stonewalled, the K'iche's sent their petition directly to the president, who approved their request.[29]

Led by an emerging class of indigenous urban artisans, Quetzalteco principales fashioned an alternative nationalist discourse in the last half of the nineteenth century. This indigenous nationalism was based on a notion of citizenship predicated on property rights. For perhaps the first time, K'iche' elites did not identify themselves as principales but rather as indigenous property owners, the a priori qualification for any claims made within a liberal political framework. Considering the economic benefits that increased commodification brought to many of the K'iche' artisans, traders, and farmers, this is not surprising. But as Guatemala underwent rapid economic and political transformations, a simple embrace of liberal notions of property would not be enough to ensure and legitimize their complex and contradictory cultural, political, and economic positions. What was needed was an alternative discourse that linked the national to the cultural.

The pressures of agro-export capitalism unraveled the closely knit relations of reciprocity that invested principales with their communal authority. In order to continue to receive the benefits that their role as caste elites brought them, indigenous authorities needed to develop an ethnicity that was intimately connected to the progress of la patria. Unlike Ladinos who tended to view nationalism and Indian ethnicity as mutually exclusive (and to whom the progress of the nation depended on the suppression of the Indian), Indian elites argued that these concepts were mutually dependent, that one could not go forward without the other. In their view, regeneration of the Indian would lead to civil and political equality, which was the basis of a democracy. Their alternative nationalism served a dual purpose. By linking the progress of the nation to cultural renewal, they justified their position of communal authority to the local and national Ladino state; and conversely, linking ethnic advancement to the progress of the nation served to legitimize to other Indians their continued political power. Of course, this ideological maneuver would not be enough to ensure the perpetuation of their political power. They therefore asked for, and received, the institutionalization of their role as cultural and political brokers within the new liberal state. Now, more than ever, it was state sanction rather than communal deference that warranted their authority.

But this emerging identity did more than just provide rhetorical support for principales as they attempted to straddle an increasingly commodified community and an ever expanding nation-state. K'iche' elites shared, at least outwardly, many of the liberal assumptions regarding progress, civilization, education, and economic prosperity. Yet while K'iche's and Ladinos traversed much the same terrain, the moral boundaries of the nation that principales attempted to establish were not coterminous with those imagined by liberal elites. Where K'iche' elites drew the line, so to speak, was "race." Although they accepted much of the racist, ascriptive features of Ladino nationalism (e.g., that the Indian was corrupted and needed to be regenerated), K'iche's categorically refused to accept the Ladino equation of race and class, which grew increasingly powerful as Guatemala became transformed into a coffee-producing nation.

Under Carrera, in the middle of the nineteenth century, a liberal elite indigenismo had begun to emerge.[30] Like its Mexican counterpart, this new ideology (which was little more than Creole nationalism) had colonial roots.[31] It would reach its nineteenth-century apogee, as it were, under the presidency of José María Reina Barrios (1892–98), and much of the language K'iche's deployed in the above petition, and others like it, freely circulated among Guatemalan intellectuals and politicians during Reina Barrios's tenure. The years 1893 and 1894 were particularly lively for debates regarding the role of Indians in Guatemala's political economy.[32] Intellectuals, politicians, and finqueros engaged in heated discussion, much of it opportunistic, surrounding the effects of the mandamiento on indigenous communities. In October 1893, Reina Barrios announced the official end of the draft beginning 15 March 1894.[33] These debates pulled forth the latent tendency on the part of Ladinos to collapse class with ethnicity and, in keeping with the new role of Indians as semiproletarianized coffee workers, to associate indigenous culture with hard, demeaning labor.[34] The more charitable of these writers would blame the Spaniards: "¡El Indio! Oh, since the first day of the conquest ... a slave by birth, a beast of burden."[35] With a liberal sleight of hand in which class was eclipsed in the hopeful glare of progress, Indians were "destined to disappear."[36]

There were, of course, variations on this theme. Throughout the 1890s, the economic boom provided by coffee allowed for a somewhat more generous and imaginative vision of Indians' place in the emerging nation than had been previously expressed.[37] Among reformers and intellectuals who seriously thought about the issue there was no consensus about what exactly constituted "progress." Regeneration, a word increasingly bandied about, could hold "material, intellectual and moral" content.[38] For the more critical and thoughtful thinkers, such as Antonio Batres Jáuregui, the advanced nature of pre-Columbian civilizations was proof that Indians, although now corrupted and decayed, were redeemable and could participate as active members in "public life." Batres was particularly critical of both the mandamiento and liberal land laws. Yet even Batres, who hoped that some aboriginal "innocent customs" could be retained, believed indigenous culture was ultimately destined to disappear.[39] Exhibiting a decidedly Lamarckian faith in generational improvement through education, technical training, and contact with national society, Ladino reformers believed that Indian ethnicity needed to disappear for the nation to progress:

> We need to give Indians the means to leave their communal system; their common and unchanging dress; their barbaric diet of *totopoxte* (large corn tortilla) and chili; their antediluvian languages; their rural, primitive, and rustic homes. In a word, Indians need to be removed from their manner of being—immutable and oriental. It cannot be doubted, then, that Indians are very able to develop their civilization and promote progress. It will not be the present generation of *aborígenes* ... but the new generations, young and flexible, will adjust to the demands of the new century. See ... how pueblos full of Indians now are confused with the rest of the Ladinos. Just a few years ago in Jocotenango, there existed a large number of *aborígenes*, dressed like Indians, speaking their primitive language. Today the children of these Jocotecos are nearly all masons and have left their *condición de indios*, becoming Ladinos, losing their language and dressing like ordinary people.[40]

Although they appropriated much of the rhetoric regarding race and regeneration, K'iche' elites rejected both the equation of indigenous culture with class and the belief that this equation would disappear with progress and civilization.

Previously, indigenous authority and power were predicated on the maintenance of social distance between commoners and elites. This distance, owing to the relative homogeneous nature of the rural highlands, took place for the most part within pueblos. But with Guatemala's transformation to agro-export capitalism, it was no longer sufficient for Quetzalteco principales to establish and reproduce a social distance only within their own community. Wealth from coffee was produced from the labor power of tens of thousands of debt-laden Indians. In the national political discourse, culture was increasingly conflated with class; more and more, to be Indian was to be an impoverished seasonal worker.

But Quetzalteco K'iche' artisans, merchants, and farmers were not coffee pickers. To escape the conflation of class and ethnicity, yet retain their cultural authority, principales needed to do three things. First, as they became increasingly assimilated into what was deemed Hispanic culture—in language, in dress, in occupation, and in urban lifestyle—these city K'iche's had to embrace a racial definition of indigenous culture so as not to lose their ethnic identity. Ironically, they were less equivocal than Ladinos about the racial content of ethnicity: one could adopt as many defined Ladino traits as possible and still remain indigenous.[41] Second, by assuming the role of promoters of "*la raza indígena*," they sought to distance themselves not only from impoverished or common Indians within their community but from all Indians throughout Guatemala. For the K'iche' elite it was a short rhetorical step from claiming the role of defenders of the impoverished, Spanish illiterate K'iche's from their own city's hinterland, as they did in the above 1894 petition, to speaking on behalf of all Guatemalan Indians. In the mid-1890s, they began to use a phrase that would appear repeatedly in their written works: they claimed to speak not just on behalf of "Indians of Quetzaltenango in particular" but for those of the "indigenous class in general."[42]

It is important to note here that the desire of urban K'iche's to distance themselves from more impoverished Indians was not just a question of status or maintenance of privilege. The loss of cultural symbols associated with exploitation—dress, sandals, and the like—was also a matter of survival. At the turn of the century, Quetzaltenango was still a place where poor Indians could be conscripted off the streets without notice and forced to carry freight to the coast, and where a peasant coming in from his field could be nearly beaten to death by city police for openly carrying a machete.[43]

Finally, as a result of their own complicated class position as large landholders and labor contractors, K'iche' elites had to account for economic changes in cultural terms. Thus Santiago Coyoy, who himself owned a large tract of land within the municipal boundaries and had a dozen indigenous peons indebted to him, could thank the president, with little sense of irony, for "the abolition of forced labor that was demanded of Indians by rich Ladinos who have agricultural farms."[44]

THE PROGRESS OF A SOCIETY: THE ESTABLISHMENT OF THE SOCIEDAD EL ADELANTO

Indian elites rejected the notion that education, economic progress, and hard work would lead to the *assimilation* of the Indian, as many Ladino elites had advocated. For K'iche' principales progress would entail the *regeneration* of the Indian. In 1894, K'iche's institutionalized this hope in the foundation of the Sociedad El Adelanto—an association "composed of Indians to work for the regeneration of the race and the material progress of the city."[45] Modeled on the guilds and mutual aid societies popular throughout Latin America at this time, the sociedad, which exists to this day, primarily promoted education and civic activities during its first decades of existence: it established schools, supported modernization projects, and participated in cultural and political events.[46] One requirement for membership was that each *socio* (member) had to set an example for other Indians and enroll his children until the age of fourteen in school. Indians may have lost a degree of political autonomy with the abolition of their cabildo, but the establishment of the sociedad would ensure the continuation of their cultural and social power. To highlight the continuity between the abolished Municipalidad de Indígenas and El Adelanto, the city's third alcalde, who was always K'iche', was often a recent president of the society.[47]

The society was founded by over sixty "indigenous principales of the city."[48] Although members were drawn from various sectors of the K'iche' population, a majority of the founders shared a number of social characteristics.[49] Nearly all of those about whom information exists lived in the city's center and owned homes in one of the four barrios. With the exception of one who, judging by the one hundred mules he owned, probably made his living as a teamster and four who possessed a large number of sheep and cows, all seemed primarily to be either artisans or merchants who balanced their trade with subsistence and commercial agricultural production. While a few of the founders, such as Santiago Coyoy and Marcos Cojulún, possessed exceptionally large amounts of land, and others, such as Tranquilino Morales, possessed very little, the majority owned medium-sized plots of fifty to two hundred cuerdas on which they grew wheat and corn.

The foundation of El Adelanto echoes the growth of "friendly societies" or trade clubs in early-nineteenth-century England,[50] where legal dissolution of guilds combined with the beginning of the industrial revolution to threaten the status and privileges of skilled artisans. E. P. Thompson writes that closed artisan societies became popular with the skilled tradesman, who was equally "concerned with maintaining his status as against the unskilled man as he was in bringing pressure upon the employers."[51] These efforts to preserve privilege took place within the parameters of an emerging working class. In Guatemala, by contrast, similar efforts occurred within the boundaries of ethnicity. The artisan founders of the Sociedad El Adelanto were not threatened by technological innovation or a rationalization of labor. Industrialization would not come to Guatemala until decades later, and when it did, its effect on artisans was partial and incomplete. What did threaten the K'iche' tradesmen was the national equation of race with proletarianization. They thus founded the sociedad to promote a vision of Indian ethnicity that was not bounded by class. It is noteworthy that few of the exceptionally wealthy K'iche' landowners, such as Silverio Coyoy and Tomás Pac, participated in founding the society; for that matter, they rarely seemed to involve themselves in city politics. The importance of ethnic revival and caste power may have been more urgent for the city's middle indigenous bourgeoisie, whose members, perhaps, had less confidence in the power of the market to ensure their prosperity.

For these K'iche's, the continued ability to mobilize communal resources may still have been an important factor in their successful participation in a commodified economy—hence their interest in cultural revindication. A number of the founders still rotated their community service between cofradía obligations and municipal offices, thus underscoring the permeable line between political and cultural authority.[52] Perhaps not coincidentally, a number of the original founders of the sociedad, such as Agatón Boj, Benito Reyes, and José María Pisquiy, went on to become some of those K'iche's who increased their property holdings (see chap. 5). Further, the membership of the sociedad included both wealthy K'iche' contractors, farmers, workshop owners and merchants, and more humble artisans and wage workers, thereby suggesting that K'iche's used membership in the society itself to maintain patronage relations weakened by commodification.

Although throughout the first half of the twentieth century both wealthy and poor K'iche's joined El Adelanto, since its inception its leadership has always come from the ranks of the former. José Santiago Coyoy López (1861–1906) and Joel Agatón Boj (1848–1915), for example, were two of the most active members in the sociedad and in city politics. As noted before, Boj benefited from the changes brought about by Guatemala's transition to coffee cultivation and not only increased his landholdings in the last years of the nineteenth century but was able to parlay his political influence into becoming the city's most important construction contractor and largest employer. Although Santiago Coyoy was listed in a census as a mason, he made his living mostly as a merchant and wheat and corn farmer. As we have seen, he owned a number of large farms on which upward of a dozen indigenous colonos resided. His economic production was complemented by that of his wife, Micaela Pisquiy de Coyoy, who was a prominent market vendor. Coyoy was the alcalde when the K'iche' cabildo was finally done away with in 1894, and he was instrumental in both brokering the deal that allowed for more indigenous participation in the Ladino municipality and founding El Adelanto, whose first president he became. Prior to 1894, Coyoy served twice as regidor. Following the unification of the municipalities, he went on to be elected two more times as K'iche' alcalde, in 1897 and 1904. Both Coyoy and Boj served as alcaldes of two of the city's most prominent cofradías—Coyoy of the Cofradía Santísimo in 1900 and Boj of the Cofradía Santo Entierro in 1893.

THE MEANING OF REGENERATION

The complicated linkage between the economic, political, and cultural power of the principales is captured in one of the first acts of the sociedad. In 1894, El Adelanto commissioned the construction of a monument honoring Guatemala's president, Reina Barrios, to thank him for abolishing the mandamiento (see fig. 1.1.5). Upon hearing of the monument, and apparently for the first time of the sociedad, Quetzaltenango's jefe político sent a letter to the Ladino alcalde, asking him for information:

> I have learned that the señores regidores Indígenas have organized a sociedad. These same Indians have asserted that the monument on the road to Almolonga is being raised to celebrate the liberation of the Indians. I want you to find out what the real purpose of this sociedad is, because these señores still do not know what the regeneración de la raza Indígena means.[53]

The mayor dispatched the chief of police to the monument site, where he found four masons commissioned by the "regidores Indígenas ... who were made to believe

FIGURE 1.1.5   Monument commemorating the "liberation of the Indian," 1894. *Photograph by Daniel Wilkinson.*

that they were working on a municipal project."[54] "With this pretext," the chief of police went on, "masons were employed who should be used on works of true urgency."[55] Despite the jefe político's continued protest, the work was completed, and, by a presidential decree, the sociedad was established.[56]

K'iche' principales used the political tools available to them—in this case their ability to mobilize labor and funds—to articulate their new, more expansive ethnic identity, as discussed above. That the monument was erected to thank Reina Barrios for ending the mandamiento—a law to which none of the principales (and probably few if any common Quetzaltecos) were subject—emerged from their efforts to assume the role of representative of all Indians, and hence avoid the association of class with ethnicity. That *regeneration* was a contested word likewise reflects the divergence between K'iche' and Ladino visions of the nation's future.

As recent work exploring the cultural processes of state consolidation makes clear, elite unity or cohesion cannot be the starting point for examinations of hegemony.[57] These studies loosen the tight moorings that bound ideas to class position and replace, as Stuart Hall puts it, the "notion of fixed ideological meanings and class-ascribed ideologies with the concepts of ideological terrains of struggle and the task of ideological transformation."[58] These theories likewise have been concerned with delimiting these terrains of struggle so that understandings of ideology do not slip off into an "unsatisfactory discursive notion which implies total free floatingness of all ideological elements and discourse."[59] The battlefield of ideational struggle, therefore, is best described as a "field of force" in which different social groups "read" competing interpretations into *common* social referents.[60] Thus the word *regeneration* had different meanings for the K'iche' elites and the Ladino jefe político, whose job description was literally to "achieve the assimilation of the indigenous class into that of the Ladinos."[61]

Differential access to social power allows political blocs to form and allows those blocs to impose their reading as the dominant interpretation. The ideological and political maneuvers that went into the K'iche' elites' construction of the obelisk are particularly obvious examples of this process.[62] But the crucial point here—which is key to understanding what took place in Quetzaltenango and Guatemala—is that these battlefields contain more than two opposing armies. To understand republican Guatemala as a nation defined *primarily* along ethnic lines is to buy into the racialist assumptions that sought to reduce Guatemala's complex colonial legacy into two competing camps. Struggles within the field of force (that is, history) need instead to be understood as complex alliances of interests and ideologies that are often, but not always, based on class position. It is through these engagements that social identities, ideologically simplified, emerge.

The political tension caused by the interaction of a consolidating state and a regional elite allowed K'iche' principales, as they had in the past, to strategically play non-Indian elites off against each other. Ladino officials, in their efforts to prevent the construction of the monument and the establishment of the sociedad, tried to contain the ability of K'iche's to mobilize political resources for cultural ends. They argued to national authorities that the building of the monument was both a waste of much needed labor and revenue and an abuse of the municipal positions. Santiago Coyoy responded by personally inviting the Ladino municipales to attend the inauguration of the monument. Even though the stone was "not yet polished," the K'iche's rushed to ensure that the monument's unveiling would take place on President Reina Barrios's birthday. Coyoy took the opportunity to remind the Ladinos that the Sociedad El Adelanto had been approved by Reina Barrios himself and to counter charges that he and his fellow K'iche' regidores were abusing their public power for private ends. Coyoy's response captures the combined private and public nature of principal power: "As municipal councilmen, we have nothing to do with" the sociedad.[63] It was as private citizens, however, that these same councilmen just happened also to serve as its officers.

FORESTS, PASTURES, AND THE CONFLICTED TERRAIN OF HEGEMONY

Following the liberal triumph, the extension of cultivation and increased demands for wood and pasture combined with the rapid privatization of municipal property to create new levels of conflict and confusion surrounding land use. These conflicts—which took place among individuals, between the municipality and individuals, and between the city and surrounding pueblos—often had to do with competing types of production. In 1879, the K'iche' Bartolo Ventura and his two mozos were accused by Gregorio Andrade of damaging his corn plot with their sheep.[64] In 1892, the indigenous authorities claimed that Tomás Pac and Pioquinto Guzmán expropriated municipal forest and destroyed trees in order to plant potatoes.[65] And throughout the 1880s and 1890s, the town of San Mateo fought off the expansion of Quetzalteco agriculture onto land it claimed as its forests.[66]

Quetzalteco K'iche' elites attempted to mediate these conflicts, using new national forest regulations to buttress their authority. During this period the liberal state became increasingly concerned with the rapid deforestation under way in the nation's most populated areas. In 1891 a national forest code was enacted, followed a year later by departmental regulations.[67] The new codes, which declared forests to be an "integral part of the wealth of the nation," effectively nationalized municipal wood-land, defining all land belonging to the state or municipalities "that are covered with trees for construction, firewood, carbon, and other common uses" as national forests.[68] The codes forbade the cutting of young or green trees and ordered all municipalities to carry out reforestation projects. Seed banks and nurseries were to be established, and individuals were to plant seedlings along property-dividing lines and roads. Pasturing of animals on municipal property was to be limited, and anyone extracting wood from forests was required to plant five seedlings for each tree cut.

The K'iche' authorities vigorously applied these codes, often using the language embedded in the regulations to defend their actions "to protect the general good of the population." Repeatedly, the indigenous municipal officials, through their corps of forest sentries and auxiliaries, prevented what they considered violations of the new regulations. In 1895, they accused Julián Tay of trying to bribe a guardabosque into letting him cut trees and pasture his sheep on municipal land. In 1896, a number of indigenous alcalde auxiliaries confiscated a mule and the cut wood it was carrying from a poor K'iche' "mozo," claiming that he extracted it illegally.[69] And in 1894, the Municipalidad de Indígenas ordered Macaria Cajas to allow vecinos to extract wood for personal use from land that both she and the municipality claimed as their own. Again, these conflicts strengthened the power of the local state, since both sides appealed to the Ladino municipality to support their case. In the land conflict mentioned in chapter 5, Tomás Pac, confronted with a surveying commission headed by Santiago Coyoy (his "enemy," as he put it), went so far as to ask the Ladino authorities to name somebody to the commission "that is not an Indian," arguing that he would never get a fair ruling from the indigenous authorities.[70] The K'iche' municipales responded by stating that as Indians "nobody can have better knowledge of the ejidos than we do."[71]

Aside from whatever political power the enforcement of the forest codes might have garnered K'iche' municipal elites, it was also in their class interest to protect the forests. Access to wood was crucial for the kind of urban production in which many K'iche' political elites were engaged. Masons and carpenters relied on timber for construction, and wood was needed to stoke the fires in the kilns, forges, and furnaces of tanners, smiths, shoemakers, quarrymen, and other artisans. And as only four of the sixty founders of El Adelanto were engaged to a significant extent in animal husbandry and most owned more than enough land for subsistence production, there was little incentive to turn forest land into pasture or agricultural land.

The following incident provides a good example of how K'iche's used the new forest codes not only to maintain their authority over other Indians but also to secure their political power in relation to local Ladinos. On 31 July 1894, Santiago Coyoy petitioned the municipality for a leave of absence from his public responsibilities to travel to the capital to attend to personal business.[72] In Guatemala City, he and the other indigenous regidores, along with a "very respectable number of Indians," met with President Reina Barrios to express their concern about the rapid deforestation of municipal lands.[73] They complained that many individuals, aside from their legitimate personal needs, were showing up with mules and wagons to extract wood illegally for profit, turning the forest into a "*filón* (gold vein, or source of wealth) that is exploited to the detriment of all." They asked the president for help in protecting the woodlands. Manuel Estrada Cabrera, the minister of government who would soon become Guatemala's first twentieth-century dictator, wrote to Quetzaltenango's jefe político, Manuel Solórzano, ordering him to be more vigilant in protecting the city's forests and to build fences and ditches around municipal land.[74] Meanwhile, the jefe político and the alcalde, Mariano Molina, convened a special emergency session to discuss the matter and to "find out the truth and punish those responsible" for the complaint, which, they claimed, was greatly "exaggerated." By going "directly to the government, as if there was no authority here," Molina charged, Coyoy compromised the good name of the municipality.

The exchange between Coyoy and the local Ladino authorities, recorded in script in the municipal minutes, is revealing and warrants extensive presentation. It captures nuances of power that move from the most mundane—that of the common racism of local Ladinos who use their power to silence Indians while at the same time claiming to give them voice—to the highest reaches of national power—that of a consolidating state attempting to check the regional aspirations of local elites.

Molina: I don't understand what reason they had to pass over the municipality and the *jefatura* when here there is full administration of justice. If not, can the indigenous councilmen tell us how many times they came to the municipality or the jefatura with complaints that were not heard and dealt with?

Coyoy: It was not a complaint against the municipality, or the jefatura, that we presented in Guatemala. It was a request that they give us help in conserving the forest, which is for the good of all. It is not a complaint. It is true that when we informed the mayor of some abuses, he gave us orders to correct them; the same happened with the jefe político. It is not a complaint that we made but a request for help in protecting the forests.

Solórzano: I now see that there is a contradiction in what you say and the note sent by the ministro de gobernación.

Daniel Meza [4th regidor]: Tell us who are the ones abusing the forest, because the note from the minister implies that it is a municipal officer. Tell us who are using mules and wagons.

Solórzano: By any chance, does it occur to the Señor concejal [Coyoy] that the wood from the commons are for the fires of all ... the tailor, the blacksmith, the cook, the machinist, the schools, etc.? It is not just for exclusive use but for everyone. Does it occur to you that there are different kinds of work ... that some look for their means of subsistence in agriculture, others as artisans, and others as wood sellers? The forest needs to be exploited in the thousand ways that meet the needs of the people; for this there is no other option and today it needs to be accepted.

Coyoy: We do not say that wood should not be used but that only dry wood should be cut. Small trees should not be cut because this damages the forest. We had presented a motion to the municipality, but it was not addressed, maybe because we are Indians (*tal vez por ser indios*).

Alejandro Montes [6th regidor]: The indigenous councilmen presented a motion, but it referred to the prevention of pasturing in the woodland, and not to abuses committed by individuals.

Molina: As Señor Meza well said, the note implied that the municipality is abusing the forests, or that some councilman is, or that the Indians' complaints have not been attended to. As nothing of the sort has happened, it is important to establish the truth in order to demonstrate the injustice of the complaint: How many motions have the concejales Indígenas presented that have not been addressed because they are Indians?

Solórzano: To that I want to add that you (Coyoy) came to inform me that some individual was trying to take a part of the ejidos, and I ordered you to make a deep ditch so as to mark the municipal land. But the note from the minister recommends that I establish markers, surely because you did not tell him that I already gave such orders.

Julián Aguilara [syndic]: There is no truth to the complaint; it is an attack on the municipality and the jefatura, an abuse that should be punished so that it does not happen again. It is clear that the intention of the Indians is that they want to be the only ones to use the forest. They want to be the only ones to sell wood, and because we have not permitted it, they went to complain. I ask that you punish them.

Coyoy: The conservation of the forest is not only for Indians but for all. It is the general good that we want. As I already said, it was not a complaint that we presented. As I am a merchant, I asked for leave to go to the capital. There I met with other merchants and we decided to present the request.

Jefe Político: By what has been said it is clear that you [pointing to Coyoy] asked for permission to go to Guatemala on personal business and there you joined with other merchants and presented a request that the municipality help you in conserving the forests. As there was no lack of support, as you yourself say ... then there was no reason for the request. It should be declared unjust and improper and a reprimand be issued so that puerile matters are not presented to the government.

Molina: I am in agreement ... but I insist that Coyoy tell us how many requests or complaints of abuses he made that were not attended to. Until now, he has not given a categorical answer about these abuses or the people committing them.

Montes: The way I see it, the question comes down to two points. First, find out who are the ones abusing the forest so as to prove once and for all the veracity of the complaint. Many times Coyoy has been asked who these people are and he has not answered. Second, establish if the municipality has complied with the forest codes.

Molina: The secretary informs us that the only motion [made by the indigenous regidores] was in reference to the pasturing of livestock in the forests.

José María de León [2nd alcalde]: When the Indígenas reported to me that some were taking wood, I told them to order the forest sentries to make these people replant the trees they had cut.

Coyoy: That order was carried out.

Solórzano: The discussion indicates that the authorities fulfilled their obligation and there is no merit to the complaint.

Antonio Porres [2nd regidor]: I believe that we should vote on a motion of censure so that complaints such as these do not again compromise the good name of the municipality.

The municipality, by majority vote, resolved that the discussion proved that it was living up to its responsibilities, that the complaint was unjust, and that the authors of the complaint be censured. The jefe político closed the proceedings by exhorting the indigenous councilmen to work in harmony with the rest of the municipality, "because all represent the interests of the citizens. There is no justification for the antagonism which has existed between the indigenous and Spanish race, and even less so now under the current regime in which all enjoy the same rights and equality as demonstrated by the fact that *el indio* holds public offices in the same manner as do Ladinos."

Note that we have come a long way from 1826, when the K'iche' authorities were thrown in jail for three days and fined fifty pesos for refusing to cooperate with the Ladinos on land reform. If prison is one of the state's last recourses for those who refuse to submit to its hegemony, then censure, perhaps, is only effective for those who are bound by it. The privatization of land brought with it the dissolution of the colonial compact that supposedly guaranteed access to subsistence production to all. Through this compact, indigenous principales, throughout Guatemala, could defend the community's interest based on the expected entitlement of enough land to survive. In the past, principales defended this land from the advances of other communities and non-Indians or from unsanctioned use by members of their own community. If population growth stretched production thin, they could petition the Crown or state for more land. But with this entitlement removed, K'iche' elites came to rely on new ideologies surrounding land relations—including new forest codes—to regulate land use. In turn, K'iche's used these laws and ideologies to check the power of local Ladinos. They appealed to national elites so as to consolidate their authority as protectors of the municipal forests and to limit the degree of Ladino exploitation of city woodlands. The following year, as noted earlier, K'iche's were put in charge of overseeing the forests. But as K'iche's deftly learned to play within the new rules laid out for them, they, in turn, quickly became bound by them. Municipal forest land was now, K'iche's admitted, for the "common good of all Quetzaltecos."[75] Hence censure, a weaker measure than jail time but one that actually presupposes greater political power, was the only punishment meted out.

The exchange between Coyoy and the Ladinos cited above suggests how racism structured political relations on a daily level. While Ladino officials felt free to chime in as they wished, the rest of the indigenous authorities—four others attended the session—did not defend Coyoy, perhaps silenced by their inexperience in using Spanish in public debate. Coyoy, well versed in the use of Spanish in political deliberations, after facing a barrage of accusations, was reduced to short affirmative responses. The jefe político's closing cant on the equality of the races and the role of Indians as public officials effectively ended all discussion. And despite Ladino claims to the contrary, the municipality did not take up the motion presented by the indigenous officers until after they received the rebuke from the ministro de gobernación.[76]

Principales repeatedly spoke directly to national elites "as if there was no [local] authority"—a practice that was particularly irksome to the Ladino municipal authorities. This of course was not a new strategy, but it proved particularly effective during the presidency of Reina Barrios, whose policy of strengthening indigenous authority in Quetzaltenango and elsewhere weakened the power of his local rivals.[77] Time after time—most notably with the complaint regarding forest use, the establishment of the sociedad, the construction of the monument, and the demand for greater representation in the municipality—K'iche' elites skillfully played national elites off against local elites.[78] Whereas Carrera had cultivated Indian dissatisfaction to end Guatemala's most successful separatist movement, Reina Barrios, while perhaps not seeking active Indian support, benefited from indigenous indifference in his suppression of what was to be the last serious regional threat to the centralization of state power.

In 1897, highland Ladinos disaffected because of Reina Barrios's economic policies declared themselves in revolt against Guatemala City.[79] The rebellion did not spread throughout the country as the rebels had hoped. After three weeks of laying siege to the insurgent occupied city, the national army entered Quetzaltenango's plaza and the revolution ended.

Again, as during Carrera's time, highland ethnic relations were crucial in the centralization and maintenance of state power. Little information exists regarding the role of the K'iche' elite during the rebels' occupation of the city, but it is clear that surrounding indigenous communities did not support the revolution. A number of key pueblos that provided crucial support to Carrera's 1840 punitive expedition, such as San Sebastián, San Andrés Xecul, and San Cristóbal Totonicapán, immediately declared themselves loyal to Reina Barrios.[80] It was indicative of highland ethnic relations that Ladinos proved incapable of forging sustained military alliances with indigenous communities. Over one hundred Ladino soldiers from San Carlos Sija, for example, arrived in Buenabaj, a hamlet of Momostenango, and killed, looted, and raped members of the community, while in Zunil, Ladino revolutionary leaders arrived, put guns to the chests of the indigenous authorities, and demanded a contribution of 1,500 pesos.[81] Events such as these, opined one rebel leader, were certain to earn indigenous support for government troops.[82] Again, as with Carrera's 1840 incursion, it seems that city Indians hedged their bets and waited for the outcome. Many ran to the woods to wait out events.[83] And while K'iche' municipal officers, including Santiago Coyoy, signed the act in favor of the revolt, those arrested claimed that the first alcalde, once again Mariano Molina, "tricked" and "forced" them to do so.[84]

The ability of Quetzalteco K'iche' elites to play off national and local elites against one another in pursuit of their political and cultural interests strengthened the state and furthered its formation. The historic strategy of appealing to a more distant authority for protection from local elites became nationalized. Moreover, at the same time as they were using the rhetoric of nationalism and liberalism to check local Ladinos, K'iche's were developing an alternative vision of progress and the nation that allowed them to make sense of far-reaching social transformations. In doing so, they helped broker the local creation of the liberal state, limiting regionalist aspirations and translating liberal political economy into ethnic terms.

As Quetzalteco K'iche' principales have demonstrated, subordinate classes and groups can develop alternative conceptions of the nation. Within the process of nation build-ing, these competing visions are in a constant state of contestation and negotiation, a process through which a certain body of ideas becomes linked to an emerging dominant class.

For the K'iche's, their receptivity to new ideological possibilities, as well as their ability to re-articulate them, stemmed from their ambiguous ethnic and class iden-tities and was delimited by their particular historical and political moment. Partha Chatterjee, cited in Mallon, identifies three "moments" within the hegemonic process that are useful in understanding nation building.[85] The first moment—the "moment of departure"—is an open conjuncture where "different possible projects or discourses emerged to compete for influence in the emerging balance of power."[86] It is in this moment that we can best locate alternative indigenous understandings of race and nation. But these alternative visions neither sprung full-blown from K'iche' heads nor suddenly emerged from some buried, autonomous popular tradition. Indian elites drew on their long-standing practice of borrowing from the dominant political discourse to fashion an ideology that could justify their continued cultural authority in the face of rapid and dramatic political and economic changes.

It is in Chatterjee's second moment—a "moment of manoeuvre" when new elites forge a ruling alliance through the "mobilization of the popular elements"—that we can place the K'iche's' attempt to deploy this new ideology in their dealings with Ladinos.[87] Here we can abandon the "simplified" state versus Indian dichotomy that has plagued Guatemalan historiography and move on to a more subtle interpretation. The liberal state, from Barrios to Ubico, was extremely adept at allying itself with certain "popular" sectors to further its aims. In some communities, for example, the promise of liberalism for poorer Indians meant access to municipal land previously deemed off-limits by community elites.[88] In other communities, indigenous princi-pales formed alliances with the new liberal state in order to shore up their authority. In Quetzaltenango, both of these phenomena occurred. These alliances, however, consisted of more than just the dominant emerging class "mobilizing" popular forces for its own ends. In Quetzaltenango, it was the K'iche's who took advantage of local Ladino dependence on them to secure their power in relation to both poorer Indians and local Ladinos.

But at the same time that K'iche's were attempting to articulate this vision, Ladinos, at least partially and superficially, managed to present their project as *the* national project. According to Chatterjee, this is the very nature of hegemony during the third moment—the "moment of arrival": A political discourse emerges that attempts to speak in a "single, consistent, unambiguous voice ... glossing over all earlier contradictions, divergences and differences."[89] Nonetheless, as we shall see in chapter 7, this dominant discourse never entirely silences alternative voices; rather, it seeks to ignore or reinterpret them.

The question of course remains: Did Coyoy really mean it when he protested to the jefe político that "it is the general good that we want," or was he just playing out an expected performance? Although this is a fair question, it could likewise be asked of the mayor and the jefe político. Did Solórzano, for example, really believe that the new regime had brought about the equality of the races? Did Molina really believe indigenous concerns were addressed with the same attention as those of Ladinos? If Coyoy's options at this point were restrained by fear and power, then the performances of the Ladino officials were similarly conditioned both by their reliance on the indigenous authorities to help administer the city and the restraints imposed by the national state. The initial call to punishment, therefore, devolved into a mild rebuke.

Derek Sayer writes that the rituals that structure hegemony do not entail belief or acceptance but rather the "knowledge of everyone involved that they are living a lie."[90] It is coercion, not acquiescence, that compel individuals to participate. But for Sayer, it is a complex coercion that not only represses but also "powers and enables."[91] With this power, "spaces [are] opened."[92] Whether they believed that liberalism and progress would bring about equality between the races or not, K'iche' elites took advantage of these opened spaces to push forward an alternative vision of the nation and an expanded conception of indigenous identity.

NOTES

1. Marshall Berman, *All That Is Solid Melts into Air: The Experience of Modernity* (New York: Penguin, 1982), p. 16.
2. See AGQ, El común de indígenas de esta ciudad sobre que los ex-gobernadores rindan cuentas, 1871.
3. In 1882, during a conflict between the Municipalidad de Indígenas and a city priest over who was to keep the fees charged to ring church bells for the dead, Barrios again sided with the K'iche' authorities. He ordered the priest to turn over the funds. See AGCA, B 28691 439.
4. See AGCA, B 28670 299.
5. See AGCA, B 28670 292.
6. For the single treasurer, see AHQ, caja 1882. For the municipal sessions and commissions, see AHQ, Actas, 1886–94. Although Barillas, now president, officially abolished the K'iche' cabildo in 1887, it continued to function until 1894. For ignored decrees abolishing the indigenous municipalidad, see AGCA, B 28710 1489, and AHQ, caja 1887; for the real end of the municipality, see AHQ, caja 1894, and below.
7. See AGCA, B 2826 373.
8. See AGQ, 1873.
9. See AGCA-LP, J. Domingo Andrade, 12 June 1882.

10. See AHQ, Tomás Pac y Pioquinto Guzmán presentan sus títulos, 1895.
11. See AGQ, Denuncia de la Municipalidad de Indígenas contra Gregorio Morales, 1879, and AHQ, Elección verificada el 11 de diciembre de 1881, 1881.
12. Ibid.
13. See Grandin, "La Mancha Negra," for this situation in nearby Cantel.
14. See AGQ, El común de indígenas de esta ciudad sobre que los ex-gobernadores rindan cuentas, 1871.
15. As they did, for example, in 1879, when then protested a new market tax on "la más pobre y mas infeliz." See AHQ, caja 1879.
16. See AHQ, Estado de ingresos y egresos, 1875 and 1876.
17. See AHQ, Actas, 2 January 1895.
18. Ibid.
19. See AHQ, caja 1899.
20. See AHQ, caja 1910.
21. See AHQ, José María Pac, Serapio García, y José María Orozco, guardabosques ... declaran no tener ningún derecho de propiedad en los terrenos que la municipalidad les ha permitido sembrar, 1903.
22. See AHQ, Libro de entregas y de inventarios de las cofradías de esta ciudad, 1928, and Libro de inventarios, 1928–49.
23. In 1895, for example, repair of the road to the coast was done by a work gang of two hundred men, all from the rural cantones of Xecaracoj, Pie de Volcán, Chicalajá, and Pacajá, and all recruited by the K'iche' alcalde; see AHQ, caja 1895.
24. Throughout the 1890s, public work gangs were brought in from the nearby Mam towns to work on city projects; see, for example, AHQ, correspondencia, 1896.
25. See AHQ, partes de tercer alcalde, 1912.
26. See AHQ, Escritura publica en que don Agatón y don Enrique Boj y don Felix del mismo apellido, se comprometen a construir la nueva fachada del teatro municipal, 1906; Agatón Boj encargado de la construcción de la fachada del teatro, 1907; and AHQ, Agatón Boj pide en nombre de Manuel Estrada Cabrera se le venda veinticinco varas cuadradas de terreno en el cementerio, 1907.
27. See AHQ, Actas, 24 November 1905. There was also the case of the construction contractor David Coyoy, who in the twentieth century was a prominent member of Sociedad El Adelanto (see below) and held a number of municipal offices, including third alcalde in 1924. He won a number of lucrative city and national contracts, including work on the Ferrocarril Nacional de los Altos in the 1920s and the construction of an underground aqueduct in 1950. See *El Correo de Occidente*, 4 July 1950. See *El Correo de Occidente*, 22 November 1950, for protests of his firing of a number of the project's workers.
28. See AHQ, Los regidores indígenas sobre que se críen varios funcionarios de su clase, 1894.
29. See AGCA, B 28868 1009. From 1895, a fixed number of K'iche' councilmen served in the city government. This endurance of Indian power was not unique to Quetzaltenango. In other "pueblos de indios" that also contained large numbers of non-Indians, such as Chichicastenango, Totonicapán, and Sololá, various working arrangements allowed for differing levels of indigenous autonomy. Likewise, Reina Barrios issued a number of decrees that guaranteed indigenous representation in selected municipalities. See Skinner-Klée, ed. *Legislación indigenista*, pp. 46–68.
30. Starting in the middle decades of the last century, national historians increasingly began accounts of Guatemala's long march toward the present with a description of preconquest society and history, and the 1820 uprising in Totonicapán was heralded as a precursor to independence. See, for example, Antonio Batres Jáuregui's *Los indios: Su historia y su civilización* (Guatemala City: Tipográfico La Unión, 1894), and *La América Central ante la historia*, vols. 1 and 2 (Guatemala City: Marroquín Hermanos "Casa Colorada," 1915); Jesús Carranza, *Un pueblo de los altos: Apuntamientos para su historia, Totonicapán* (Quetzaltenango: Tipografía Popular, 1897); Francisco de Paula García Peláez, *Memorias para la historia del antiguo Reyno de Guatemala*, vol. 1 (Guatemala City: Tipográfico de L. Luna, 1951); and Juan Gavarrete Escobar, *Anales para la historia de Guatemala: 1491–1811* (Guatemala

City: Editorial José de Pineda Ibarra, 1980). One of José María Reina Barrios's first acts as president in 1892 was to sponsor a national essay contest whose topic was the best system to "civilize Indians"; Batres Jáuregui's essay, subsequently published as *Los indios*, was the winner. During his six years as president Reina Barrios founded and funded a number of Escuelas de Indígenas in various parts of the country and passed numerous pieces of legislation that were supposed to protect the rights of Indians qua Indians. This liberal indigenista nationalism would continue into the twentieth century in the works of Adrián Recinos, *Memorial de Solola, Anales de los Cakchiqueles* (Mexico: Fondo de Cultura Económica, 1950); Virgilio Rodríguez Beteta, *Ideologías de la Independencia* (Paris: Editorial París-America, 1926); José Antonio Villacorta Calderón, *Memorial de Tecpán-Atitlán* (Guatemala City: Tipografía Nacional, 1934), and *Prehistoria e historia antigua de Guatemala* (Guatemala City: Tipografía Nacional, 1938).

31. See, for example, Francisco Antonio Fuentes y Guzmán, *Recordación florida* (Guatemala: Ministerio de Educación Pública, 1951).

32. There is little scholarship on Reina Barrios's very important transitional period of Guatemalan liberalism. Palmer, "A Liberal Discipline," pp. 189–97, offers the best discussion to date.

33. As McCreery points out, the end of the mandamiento did not necessarily mean the end of the mandamiento. The same decree that abolished the corveé expanded forced public work obligations. And under Reina Barrios and his successor, Manuel Estrada Cabrera, the state repeatedly made exceptions and allowed for labor drafts. Further, the state, until 1944, vigorously enforced peonage and vagrancy laws. See McCreery, *Rural Guatemala*, pp. 189–94.

34. See, for examples, the debate in *Diario de Centro América*, 10 and 14 April, and 5 October 1893, and *La Nueva Era*, 14 and 21 April 1893.

35. Batres Jáuregui, *La América Central*, p. 448.

36. Ibid. It must be said, however, that Batres was less sanguine about the possibilities the future offered. For other examples of the liberal belief in the disappearance of the Indians, see Rodríguez Beteta, *Ideologías de la Independencia*, and Villacorta Calderón's *Memorial de Tecpán-Atitlán* and *Prehistoria e historia antigua de Guatemala*, especially p. 180.

37. A good example of this diversity of opinion could be found at the First Central American Pedagogical Congress, which took place in Guatemala in 1893. One delegate called for the creation of indigenous protected areas where instruction would be provided in native languages so as to gradually incorporate Indians into the national life; see Juan Fernández Ferraz, *Estudio acerca las nueve tesis del programa del primer congreso pedagógico Centroamericano* (San José, Costa Rica: Tipografía Nacional, 1893), pp. 9–14. See also Nicolás Aguilar, *Discurso pronunciado por el Doctor D. Nicolás Aguilar, delegado de El Salvador ...* (Guatemala City: Tipografía La Unión, 1893), and José María Vela Irisarri, Angel María Bocanegra, and Lucas T. Cojulún, *Informe presentado al primer congreso pedagógico Centro-América sobre el tema VIII* (Guatemala City: Sánchez y De Guise, 1893), for the conference. See Francisco Lainfiesta, *A vista de pájaros (cuento fantástico)* (Guatemala: El Progreso, 1879) for a particularly upbeat view of the Indian in the future nation; then see Francisco Lainfiesta, "La esclavitud del indio," *La República*, 27 June 1893, written after his optimism turned sour; also see Palmer, "A Liberal Discipline," pp. 194–195. The logic of Guatemala's political economy was of course often at odds with these more imaginative programs; see David McCreery, "Coffee and Class: The Structure of Development in Liberal Guatemala," *Hispanic American Historical Review* 56, no. 3 (1976): 452.

38. Batres Jáuregui, *Los indios*. Later, during the Mexican Revolution, *Regeneración* would be the name of the Magón brothers' influential anarchist newspaper.

39. See Batres Jáuregui's *La América Central*, p. 448, and *Los indios*, pt. 3 and chaps. 3 and 4. Batres, the archetypal indigenista nationalist, wrote scores of books on *lo Americana*, which, aside from his work on history and indigenous culture, include topics on creole colloquialisms and literature.

40. Batres Jáuregui, *Los indios*, pp. 177–78. These views were not new to the later part of the nineteenth century, although they did become more pronounced. See José Luis Reyes M., *Apuntes para una monografía de la Sociedad Económica de Amigos del País* (Guatemala City: Editorial José de Pineda Ibarra, 1964), and Manuel Rubio Sánchez, *Historia de la Sociedad Económica de Amigos del*

País (Guatemala City: Editorial Académica Centroamericana, 1981), for the work of the Sociedad Económica, which Batres served as president for a period.

41.   From a series of interviews I conducted in July 1997 with older members of the Sociedad El Adelanto (which will be discussed below), it is clear that this antiassimilationist, racialist view of indigenous ethnicity still resonates among Quetzalteco K'iche's. For these men, ethnicity was defined by blood rather than cultural or class traits. "We have the blood of Tecún, they [the Ladinos] have the blood of Pedro de Alvarado," replied one interviewee to the question: "What is the difference between Indians and Ladinos?" Genovevo Bautista Coyoy, interview by author, Quetzaltenango, 9 July 1997.

42.   See AHQ, caja 1892.

43.   See "Pobre Raza," in *La Lechuza*, 11 October 1896, and *El Comercio*, 5 October 1899.

44.   See AHQ, caja 1894.

45.   Sociedad El Adelanto, *Estatuto de la Sociedad El Adelanto* (Quetzaltenango: Tipográfico "La Unión Liberal," 1894), found in AHQ, Sobre la fundación de la sociedad "El Adelanto," 1894.

46.   Another intriguing aspect of the establishment of the Sociedad El Adelanto is its apparent connection with the Masonic movement in Quetzaltenango. Although no member today can explain why, El Adelanto's first standard bore the Masonic symbol of a compass and ruler. Late-nineteenth-century Guatemalan liberals were strongly influenced by Freemasonry and its promotion of enlightened rationalism. By 1901, there existed fifteen thousand masons and twenty-one lodges in Central America. Quetzaltenango's lodge was under the jurisdiction of Mexican masons. See Unknown (H. P. F.), *Resumen de las conferencias dadas en la resp. log. Alianza no. 24* (Guatemala City: Tipografía de Síguere y Cía, 1903). With its use of artisan symbols and rhetoric, there was perhaps a natural affiliation with the workers societies being established throughout Guatemala. See also the newspaper *El Fénix*, published in 1895 by Quetzaltenango's Masonic lodge, and *El Ron-Ron*, an early promoter of Freemasonry in Quetzaltenango.

47.   The society's president told me in 1994 that "El Adelanto was founded one hundred years ago; before that we were the Municipalidad de Indígenas."

48.   Sociedad El Adelanto, *Estatuto*, lists fifty-nine founding members, while Sociedad El Adelanto, *100 años de vida social y educativa, 1894–1994* (Quetzaltenango: Sociedad El Adelanto, 1994), only lists thirty. Not all the names on the two lists correspond. The names in Grandin, "Blood," Appendix 8, are taken from the former, with the exception of Lorenzo Aguilar.

49.   See Grandin, "Blood," Appendix 8.

50.   E. P. Thompson, *The Making of the English Working Class* (New York: Vintage, 1963), chap. 8. In Quetzaltenango, in the decades that followed the establishment of the Sociedad El Adelanto, artisans and Indians founded a number of similar societies and guilds, which provided important welfare services. See chap. 7.

51.   Thompson, *The Making of the English Working Class*, p. 244.

52.   The information on cofradía charges is incomplete, covering only a few years. The information also only lists those who filled the two most important positions—that of alcalde and mayordomo—and ignores those who occupied lesser positions. For this reason, it is difficult to assess the relevance of the city's cofradía system at any given point. See Grandin, "Blood," Appendix 8.

53.   See AHQ, Sobre la fundación de la sociedad "El Adelanto," 1894.

54.   Ibid.

55.   Ibid.

56.   For the president's approval, see AGCA, Libro de Acuerdos y Decretos de Gobernación, folio 125, 1894.

57.   See Joseph and Nugent, eds., *Everyday Forms of State Formation*.

58.   Stuart Hall, "The Problem of Ideology: Marxism without Guarantees," in *Stuart Hall: Critical Dialogues in Cultural Studies*, ed. David Morley and Kuan-Hsing Chen (New York: Routledge, 1996), p. 41.

59.   Hall, "The Problem of Ideology," p. 41.

60.   For "field of force," a metaphor first used by E. P. Thompson, see Rose-berry, "Hegemony and the Language of Contention," and Hall, "The Problem of Ideology," pp. 41–42. For how the concept of

"liberalism" came to hold diverse meanings for competing groups in prerevolutionary Nicaragua, see Gould, *To Lead as Equals*.

61. See AGCA, Libro de acuerdos de gobernación, B 32880.

62. The linking of hegemony to political formation owes much to a return to Gramsci's original work on the concept; see Hall, "The Problem of Ideology," and Roseberry, "Hegemony and the Language of Contention."

63. See AHQ, La sociedad "El Adelanto" compuesta de indígenas de esta cabecera, 1894.

64. See AHQ, caja 1879.

65. See AHQ, Tomás Pac quejándose de la comisión que fue a medir su terreno, 1892, and Tomás Pac y Pioquinto Guzmán presentan sus títulos, 1895.

66. See AGQ, La Municipalidad de San Mateo solicita del Supremo Gobierno les conceda el terreno denominado "Las Barrancas," 1887.

67. Both are in AHQ, cajas 1891 and 1892.

68. See AHQ, caja 1891.

69. See AHQ, cajas 1895 and 1896.

70. See AHQ, Tomás Pac y Pioquinto Guzmán piden que en la comisión que debe informar sobre la remedida de sus terrenos asiste un miembro imparcial, 1896.

71. Ibid.

72. See AHQ, caja 1894.

73. The account of the following encounter is taken from AHQ, Actas, 25 August 1894.

74. A copy of the letter is in AHQ, caja 1894.

75. See AGQ, Letter from the K'iche' juez de ejidos to jefe político, 1897.

76. The K'iche's presented the motion in May, and by July it had still not been addressed. On 10 July 1894, three weeks before Coyoy requested his leave, he once again urged the municipality to attend to the issue, claiming that a good part of the forest was being destroyed by sheep; AHQ, La Municipalidad de Indígenas de esta ciudad con el más profundo respeto pasamos a exponer que hace más de dos meses que presentamos una moción, 1894.

77. In 1892, Reina Barrios also institutionalized the power of indigenous authorities in nearby Totonicapán when he ordered that the municipality's third mayor, second syndic, and six of thirteen regidores be indigenous. In 1893, he ordered that separate elections be held for Indians and Ladinos, and in 1894, he decreed that two more indigenous regidores be added to the municipal corporation, from the "*parcialidad de principales*." See Skinner-Klée, ed. *Legislación indigenista*, pp. 48, 50–51, and 68.

78. An example of a more mundane petition is the request by Lorenzo Aguilar, an original founder of El Adelanto, that President Manuel Estrada Cabrera compensate him for land he lost owing to an expansion of the city's graveyard. Estrada Cabrera personally ordered that Aguilar be given land in another part of town. See AGCA, Libro de Acuerdos, 32916, 12 February 1910.

79. For the causes of this revolt, see Todd Little-Siebold, "Guatemala y el anhelo de modernización: Estrada Cabrera y el desarrollo del estado, 1898–1920," *Anuario de Estudios Centroamericanos* 20, no. 1 (1994): 25–41; J. Lizardo Díaz O, *De la democracia a la dictadura* (Guatemala City: Imprenta Hispana, 1946); Un Patriota, *La verdad de los hechos* (Guatemala City: 1899), located in Biblioteca César Brañas, call no. 18697; Dolores de Aparicio, *Acusación contra el coronel y diputado Roque Morales presentada a la Asamblea Legislativa* (Guatemala City: Tipografía A. Síguere & Cía, 1898). See also Salvador Meza, *Manuel M. Reyna, justas aclaraciones* (Cobán: Tipografía El Porvenir, 1898); the opposition paper started in Quetzaltenango in early 1897, *El Sufragio*, which opposed Reina Barrios; *La Guillotina*, which supported him; and *Los Ecos de la Revolución*.

80. Díaz O, *De la democracia*, pp. 24–25.

81. See AGQ, Letter from Manuel de León to Prospero Morales, 1897; see also AGQ, La Municipalidad de Zunil solicita exhonerarse de 1,500 pesos que hurtaron los reveldes, 1897.

82. See AGQ, Letter from Manuel de León to Prospero Morales, 1897, and *Los Ecos de la Revolución*, 30 September 1897.

83. *Los Ecos de la Revolución*, 17 September 1897.

84. Díaz O, *De la democracia*, pp. 84–88. There is circumstantial evidence suggesting that some indigenous authorities may have aided the revolutionaries. Sinforoso Aguilar, a prominent liberal and mason who actively supported and perhaps influenced the Sociedad El Adelanto's educational initiatives, was one of the opposition leaders killed by government officials. Personal allegiances may have led some of the indigenous authorities to support the rebellion.

85. See Partha Chatterjee, *Nationalist Thought and the Colonial World: A Derivative Discourse?* (Delhi: Oxford University Press, 1986), pp. 50–52, for the following "moments."

86. Cited in Mallon, *Peasant and Nation*, p. 13.

87. Chatterjee, *Nationalist Thought*, p. 51.

88. This is what happened in nearby Cantel, where poor Indians allied themselves with the state to push through privatization. See Grandin, "La Mancha Negra."

89. Chatterjee, *Nationalist Thought*, p. 52.

90. Derek Sayer, "Everyday Forms of State Formation: Some Dissident Remarks on 'Hegemony,'" in Joseph and Nugent, eds., *Everyday Forms of State Formation*, p. 374.

91. Sayer, "Some Dissident Remarks," p. 376.

92. Ibid.

WORKS CITED

Archives
Quetzaltenango
Archivo de Gobernación de Quetzaltenango (AGQ)
Archivo Histórico de Quetzaltenango (AHQ)
Holdings of the Sociedad El Adelanto, which I have called the Archivo de la Sociedad El Adelanto (ASA)
(Neither the AGQ nor the AHQ are ordered in any way except by year. Documents from the AHQ are kept in boxes (*caja*) by year, and that is how I have identified their location, unless another reference was available. I have cited material used from the AGQ by year only. For these two collections, where possible I also noted the type or title of document.)

Guatemala City
Archivo General de Centro América (agca)

Newspapers and Magazines
Guatemala City
Diario de Centro-América
La Lechuza
La Nueva Era

Quetzaltenango
El Comercio
El Correo de Occidente
El Fénix
El Ron-Ron

Published Primary Sources
Aguilar, Nicolás. *Discurso pronunciado por el Doctor D. Nicolás Aguilar, delegado de El Salvador....* Guatemala City: Tipográfico La Unión, 1893.

Fuentes y Guzmán, Francisco Antonio. *Recordación florida*. Guatemala City: Ministerio de Educación Pública, 1951.

García Peláez, Francisco de Paula. *Memorias para la historia del antiguo Reyno de Guatemala*. Vol. 1. Guatemala City: Tipográfico de L. Luna, 1951.

Gavarrete Escobar, Juan. *Anales para la historia de Guatemala: 1491–1811*. Guatemala City: Editorial José de Pineda Ibarra, 1980.

Sociedad El Adelanto. *Estatuto de la Sociedad El Adelanto*. Quetzaltenango: Tipografico "La Unión Liberal," 1894.

———. *Estatutos de la Sociedad El Adelanto*. Quetzaltenango: Tipografía "La Industria," 1915.

———. *100 años de vida social y educativa, 1894–1994*. Quetzaltenango: Sociedad El Adelanto, 1994.

Unknown (H. P. F.). *Resumen de las conferencias dadas en la resp. log. Alianza no. 24*. Guatemala City: Tipografía de Síguere y Cía, 1903.

Published Legislation

Skinner-Klée, Jorge, ed. *Legislación indigenista de Guatemala*. 2d ed. Mexico: Instituto Indigenista Interamericano, 1995.

Guatemalan Nationalist and Indigenista Writing
(History, Economics, Literature, and Pedagogy)

Batres Jáuregui, Antonio. *Los indios: Su historia y su civilización*. Guatemala City: Tipográfico La Unión, 1894.

———. *La América Central ante la historia*. Vols. 1 and 2. Guatemala City: Casa Colorada, 1915.

Carranza, Jesús. *Un pueblo de los altos: Apuntamientos para su historia, Totonicapán*. Quetzaltenango: Tipografía Popular, 1897.

Fernández Ferraz, Juan. *Estudio acerca las nueve tesis del programa del primer congreso pedagógico Centroamericano*. San José, Costa Rica: Tipografía Nacional, 1893.

Recinos, Adrián. *Memorial de Sololá, Anales de los Cakchiqueles*. Mexico: Fondo de Cultura Económica, 1950.

Reyes M., José Luis. *Apuntes para una monografía de la Sociedad Económica de Amigos del País*. Guatemala City: Editorial José de Pineda Ibarra, 1964.

Rubio Sánchez, Manuel. *Historia de la Sociedad Económica de Amigos del País*. Guatemala City: Editorial Académica Centroamericana, 1981.

Villacorta Calderón, José Antonio. *Memorial de Tecpán-Atitlán*. Guatemala City: Tipografía Nacional, 1934.

———. *Prehistoria e historia antigua de Guatemala*. Guatemala City: Tipografía Nacional, 1938.

Unpublished Manuscripts and Dissertations

Grandin, Greg. "The Blood of Guatemala: The Making of Race and Nation, 1750–1954." Ph.D. diss., Yale, 1999.

Palmer, Steven. "A Liberal Discipline: Inventing Nations in Guatemala and Costa Rica, 1870–1900." Ph.D. diss., Columbia University, 1990.

Secondary Sources

Berman, Marshall. *All That Is Solid Melts into Air: The Experience of Modernity*. New York: Penguin, 1982.

Chatterjee, Partha. *Nationalist Thought and the Colonial World: A Derivative Discourse?* Delhi: Oxford University Press, 1986.

Díaz O, J. Lizardo. *De la democracia a la dictadura*. Guatemala City: Imprenta Hispana, 1946.

Gould, Jeffrey L. *To Lead as Equals: Rural Protest and Political Consciousness in Chinandega, Nicaragua, 1912–1979*. Chapel Hill: University of North Carolina Press, 1990.

Grandin, Greg. "The Strange Case of 'La Mancha Negra': Maya-State Relations in Nineteenth-Century Guatemala." *Hispanic American Historical Review* 77, no. 2 (1997): 211–43.

Hall, Stuart. "The Problem of Ideology: Marxism without Guarantees." In *Stuart Hall: Critical Dialogues in Cultural Studies*. Edited by David Morley and Kuan-Hsing Chen. New York: Routledge, 1996.

Joseph, Gilbert M., and Daniel Nugent, eds. *Everyday Forms of State Formation: Revolution and the Negotiation of Rule in Modern Mexico*. Durham: Duke University Press, 1994.

Little-Siebold, Todd. "Guatemala y el anhelo de modernización: Estrada Cabrera y el desarrollo del estado, 1898–1920." *Anuario de Estudios Centroamericanos* 20, no. 1 (1994): 25–41.

Mallon, Florencia E. *Peasant and Nation: The Making of Postcolonial Mexico and Peru*. Berkeley: University of California Press, 1995.

McCreery, David. "Coffee and Class: The Structure of Development in Liberal Guatemala." *Hispanic American Historical Review* 56, no. 3 (1976): 438–60.

_____. *Rural Guatemala, 1760–1940*. Stanford, Calif.: Stanford University Press, 1994.

Roseberry, William. "Hegemony and the Language of Contention." In *Everyday Forms of State Formation: Revolution and the Negotiation of Rule in Modern Mexico*. Edited by Gilbert M. Joseph and Daniel Nugent. Durham: Duke University Press, 1994.

Sayer, Derek. "Everyday Forms of State Formation: Some Dissident Remarks on 'Hegemony.'" In *Everyday Forms of State Formation: Revolution and the Negotiation of Rule in Modern Mexico*. Edited by Gilbert M. Joseph and Daniel Nugent. Durham: Duke University Press, 1994.

Thompson, E. P. *The Making of the English Working Class*. New York: Vintage, 1963.

Black Politics in Latin America

An Analysis of National and Transnational Politics

Ollie A. Johnson III

INTRODUCTION

In the last 25 years, scholars have made significant contributions to our understanding of race and ethnicity and, more specifically, of Black populations in Latin America. Most of these books and articles have come from historians (Andrews 2004; Appelbaum, Macpherson, and Rosemblatt 2003; Davis 1995a), anthropologists (Wade 1993, 1997; Whitten and Torres 1998; Yelvington 2001), and sociologists (Hasenbalg 1986; Twine 1998; Winant 2001). As a result, we have a better sense of the central roles that Africans and their descendants have played in shaping Latin America. Contemporary Latin American religion, cuisine, music, style, language, and social relations all bear the marks of African influence. However, in the area of government and politics, intellectuals have paid far too little attention to Afro-Latin American movements, organizations, and struggles for justice, equality, and democracy.[1]

For example, in *Utopia Unarmed: The Latin American Left after the Cold War* (1993), Mexican political scientist Jorge G. Castañeda argues that the post–cold war period represented a great opportunity for the Latin American Left to influence the direction of social and political change. He maintains that the economic crises and processes of democratization opened political space throughout the region for leftist policies that could promote economic growth and reduce inequality. Like most progressives, Castañeda identifies poverty and social inequality as the key problems to be overcome. Unfortunately, he fails to examine how these fundamental problems are directly related to race and ethnicity.

Castañeda is hardly the only political scientist to ignore Afro-Latin American political activity. Centrist, conservative, and other leftist political scientists who study Latin America have also neglected this area of inquiry. Scholars must investigate Blacks in Latin America as political actors to increase our understanding of Latin American politics. A few political scientists such as Hanchard (1994), Nobles (2000), and Thorne (2003) are beginning to join historians, anthropologists, and sociologists in highlighting the roles of Blacks in Latin America. These scholars are following the initiatives of Afro-Latin American intellectuals and activists (Fontaine 1980; Moore 1989; Mosquera 2000; Nascimento 1978; 1982) who have been condemning pervasive racial inequality and discrimination and documenting Black political action for decades. In this tradition, this chapter examines Black political participation in several Latin American countries and discusses the development of Black transnational advocacy networks in the Americas. I conclude by highlighting ongoing Black political activity in the Americas.

In the last two decades, Black Latin Americans have made progress in publicizing their political agendas. Black groups have become more politically active. This progress has highlighted several challenges for Black political struggle that vary by country and often within countries. First, after Blacks gain government recognition and formal support for specific public policies, the crucial question becomes how to implement those policies, laws, and programs. Frequently, policy implementation does not follow policy formulation. Second, Blacks are divided by various political, economic, social and cultural cleavages. One of the most important is the ideological debate over autonomy. Should Blacks work primarily within their own communities to build strong organizations, movements, and identities? Or should Blacks struggle primarily in alliance with sympathetic White, Mestizo, and Indigenous groups to improve their socioeconomic and political conditions? Generally, Afro-Latin Americans have pursued both strategies. Third, political context greatly shapes Black political activity in Latin America. Socialist revolution in Cuba and civil war in Colombia are two clear examples of major events and processes impacting the evolution of Black politics.

WHERE ARE BLACKS IN LATIN AMERICA? QUESTIONS OF IDENTITY AND VISIBILITY

People of African ancestry represent approximately 30 percent of the more than 500 million Latin Americans (Minority Rights Group 1995; *Race Report* 2003, 1–2; Rout 1976). Most Latin American governments have not attempted to count the number of Blacks or African descendants as part of their regular censuses. This failure has created a situation of official invisibility for Blacks in many government reports, studies, and policies. Some argue that Latin American population groups have mixed so much over the years that categorizing them by race or ethnicity would be impossible or extremely difficult to do accurately. Other scholars have argued that race and ethnicity are of limited relevance in Latin America because these group identities are weak and rarely politically relevant. In contrast, Black Latin American leaders generally state that race does matter, that there is a sense of Black or Afrodescendant group identity, and that Blacks are victims of discrimination and neglect in education, employment, housing, health care, and other sectors of social life (*Alianza Estrategica*; Cowater International Inc. 1999; Hasenbalg 1986).

Blacks live in all Latin American nations, though they tend to be most visible in the Caribbean and coastal areas of Central and South America. Haiti, the Dominican Republic, Cuba, Brazil, Colombia, Panama, Venezuela, and Puerto Rico have the largest and most visible Black populations. Ecuador, Peru, Mexico, and the other Central American countries have smaller African descendant communities. Uruguay, Argentina, Chile, Paraguay, and Bolivia generally have the smallest Black populations in Latin America (Cowater International Inc. et al 1996; Minority Rights Group 1995; *Race Report* 2003).

In *Shades of Citizenship: Race and the Census in Modern Politics* (2000), political scientist Melissa Nobles has argued persuasively that racial censuses are not neutral and objective instruments of scientific study. Rather, they are fundamentally political means by which the state classifies and categorizes its population. Although most Latin American countries have not regularly conducted racial, ethnic, or color censuses, Black activists have been encouraged by recent political developments in Brazil, Colombia, and Ecuador.

Afro-Brazilian intellectuals and organizations have advocated for inclusion and worked with the census bureau, scholars, and other groups to influence the process of census taking. Brazil stands out in Latin America in that most of its censuses since 1872 have nominally included a color question. The census currently allows individuals to identify as *Branca* (White), *Preta* (Black), *Parda* (Brown), *Amarela* (Yellow), and *Indigena* (Indigenous) or not to identify. Black Brazilian leaders consider it a victory that Afro-descendants are counted. But they generally do not endorse the division between Blacks and Browns. Most Black leaders and groups use terms like *Negros* (Blacks) and *Afro-Brasileiros* (Afro-Brazilians) to refer to Blacks and Browns or people of African ancestry.

The Colombian national government has been inconsistent and ineffective in conducting a racial census. Government and private sector estimates of the Black population vary widely. Black groups are working with the census bureau, DANE (*Departamento Administrativo Nacional de Estadistica* [National Administrative Statistics Department]) to ensure an accurate count of Afro-Colombians in the next census. This author attended public meetings in Cartagena and Bogota, Colombia, in 2003 and 2004, in which Black leaders expressed their fear that if DANE conducts the census without outside participation it will undercount Afro-Colombians. Dr. Cesar Augusto Caballero Reinoso, DANE director, acknowledged these concerns. Nevertheless, many Afro-Colombian leaders remained skeptical that DANE would discover the true Afro-descendant percentage of the Colombian population (Thorne 2003, 315).

Although the Colombian constitution of 1991 defines the nation as pluri-ethnic and multicultural, Colombia's many Black elected officials and activists have been protesting the Black population's exploitation and neglect by the state. These leaders have also been working to guarantee implementation of Law 70, which recognizes the Afro-Colombian population as an ethnic group with certain territorial, economic, political, and cultural rights. Black activists also question the effectiveness of the Office of Black Community Affairs (*Direccion de Asuntos para las Comunidades Negras*) formed in 1994 within the Interior Ministry to develop public policies to assist Black communities in attaining their full constitutional rights (DACN 1997).

The Ecuadorian constitution of 1998 defines the country as pluri-cultural and multiethnic among other characteristics. There is also specific reference to "*los pueblos negros o afroecuatorianos*" (Black peoples or Afro-Ecuadorians) having collective rights (*Constitución Política* 2002). Although the Indigenous movements in Colombia and Ecuador have led the campaigns for officially recognizing racial and ethnic diversity, Black groups in both countries and throughout the region have used these constitutions to call attention to their cultural uniqueness.

Throughout Latin America, Black politicians and social movement leaders often invoke historical struggles against racial oppression to give a positive connotation to Black racial identity. This strategy attempts to counter the negative image of Blackness as intrinsically related to poverty and backwardness and the alleged political irrelevance of Blackness in societies dominated by notions of miscegenation, *mestizaje*, and racial democracy. To increase their potential constituency, Afro-Latin American leaders have tended to adopt a broad and flexible view of Black identity. These leaders have demanded that national censuses include race or color questions to determine the national racial composition. Moreover, Black leaders have supported efforts to define their countries as multicultural, multiethnic, and pluri-national. In addition, these leaders and activists have developed ties with Blacks in other countries as a way of strengthening a transnational Black identity. Together these efforts are consolidating a subnational Black identity, a national identity that includes people of African ancestry, as well as a Pan-African identity in the international sphere (*Alianza Estrategica*; Cowater International Inc. 1999; de la Torre 2002; Nascimento and Nascimento 1994; Moore et al 1995).

BLACK NATIONAL POLITICS IN LATIN AMERICA

The most intractable problem for both the state and society in the matter of Afro-Latin Americans is how, for the first time in their collective history, to incorporate demands of nondominant groups into the system of governance. (Dzidzienyo 1995, 346)

The literature on race and politics has recently begun to address the causes and consequences of Black political struggles in Latin America. Black Latin Americans have organized themselves, allied with other political groups and politicians, and demanded recognition as political actors, as well as the implementation of government initiatives to improve their living conditions. The confluence of Black political activism, democratization, and alliances with major politicians has led to a series of racially explicit state agencies and policies that are unprecedented in postslavery Latin American politics (Andrews 1991; Conniff and Davis 1994; Guimarães 1995).

Throughout Latin America, democratization over the last two decades has brought about a change in the political opportunity structure for groups traditionally marginalized from power. In the 1960s and 1970s, most countries experienced some type of authoritarian rule. Military dictatorships routinely violated the rights and liberties of the people and often cancelled and manipulated elections. Since the 1990s, most countries have made the transition to civilian rule, and this process has increased opportunities for partisan electoral competition and popular participation.

In this more democratic environment, Black political organizations and social movements have been more successful in calling attention to the political existence of Black Latin Americans as citizens (Hanchard 1994; Wade 1997, 95–110; Walker 2001, 284–347). This is no small achievement. Activists have changed the political debate in Latin American societies in three main ways. First, they have hammered at the point that racism and racial discrimination exist. This view contradicts the popular perspective that racism does not exist in Latin America and instead is a problem unique to societies that experienced rigid racial segregation, such as the United States and South Africa. Black activists have also emphasized that Afro-Latin Americans tend to trail White Latin Americans in practically every country on the standard indicators of socioeconomic status, such as income, education, and health. Second, they have argued that because racism and racial inequality exist, it is the government's responsibility to improve the situation through institutional measures, policies, and programs. Third, Black leaders and groups have been most responsible for challenging negative scholarly and public opinion about Blacks and Blackness in Latin America (Bello and Rangel 2002; Cowater International Inc. 1999; Minority Rights Group 1995).

Blacks have been elected to executive and legislative offices throughout Latin America, but at rates well below their proportion of the population. Given this political underrepresentation and the economic marginalization of their communities, Afro-Latin American politicians and activists often support race-specific public policies. They argue that these policies are necessary to combat racial discrimination, Black subordination, and racial inequality. The public policies vary considerably by country. A brief review of several countries demonstrates this diversity.

Brazil

Brazil is the most populous country in Latin America with more than 180 million people. Forty-five percent of the population is of African ancestry. In the 1970s, Afro-Brazilian activists founded the Unified Black Movement (MNU [*Movimento Negro Unificado*]), the Black Cultures Research Institute (IPCN [*Instituto de Pesquisas das Culturas Negras*]), and other groups to protest against racial discrimination, police violence, and poverty. Blacks also participated actively in the leading labor union, community, and student groups fighting against the Brazilian military dictatorship (1964–1985). Over the last thirty-five years, many Black activists and intellectuals have formed organizations to mobilize Blacks to improve all areas of Black life. One of the most significant developments is the emergence of Black women's groups, such as the Black Women's Institute (Geledes–*Instituto da Mulher Negra*) and the Black Women's House of Culture (*Casa de Cultura da Mulher Negra*). These groups work to reduce sexism and domestic violence and advocate for human rights (Fontaine 1985a, b; Gonzalez 1985; Hanchard 1994; Reichmann 1999). Although all these groups and others continue to fight against Brazilian racism, much of the literature emphasizes their organizational and ideological weaknesses (Burdick 1995; Marx 1998; Twine 1998).

Leading Black politicians and activists, including Abdias do Nascimento, Lelia Gonzalez, Helio Santos, and Benedita da Silva, worked consistently to convince their political parties and party leaders to recognize the ongoing negative influence of racism within the country. Eventually, Nascimento and da Silva became the strongest and most visible Afro-Brazilian advocates in the Brazilian Congress. During the 1980s and 1990s, they criticized the "myth of racial democracy" within the national Chamber of Deputies and Federal Senate, and da Silva attempted to organize fellow Black elected officials and educate the nation about the specific difficulties still facing Afro-Brazilians (da Silva et al. 1997; Nascimento and Nascimento 1994). One of the problems Nascimento and da Silva faced was the underrepresentation of Blacks in Congress. In a country in which Afro-Brazilians (Blacks and Browns) make up almost 50 percent of the population, they comprise less than 5 percent of congressional representatives (Johnson 1998; Valente 1986). Continuing the efforts of Nascimento and da Silva, Deputy Luiz Alberto from Bahia and Senator Paulo Paim from Rio Grande do Sul are working with other politicians and Black movement activists to pressure political parties and the state to address more effectively the issue of race.

In the Latin American context, Black Brazilian leaders have been successful in getting government officials to acknowledge their concerns. At the state and local levels in São Paulo, Rio de Janeiro, Minas Gerais, and Rio Grande do Sul, such government agencies as the Council for Participation and Development of the Black Community (*Conselho de Participação e Desenvolvimento da Comunidade Negra*) and the Special Office for Afro-Brazilian Affairs (*Secretaria pela Promoção e Defesa Afro-Brasileira*) were created to incorporate Blacks into the policymaking process. Nationally, the Brazilian government in 1988 created the Palmares Foundation (*Fundação Cultural Palmares*), whose purpose is to work with educational, governmental, and private institutions and the public to increase awareness of Afro-Brazilian contributions to Brazilian society and culture. The foundation publishes materials by and about Afro-Brazilians and sponsors educational forums. More recently, the foundation has become involved in assisting traditional rural Black communities in gaining legal title and ownership of their communal lands. Moreover, the Fernando Henrique Cardoso presidential administration (1995–2003) created the Interministerial Working Group with representatives from all cabinet ministries to develop public policies to improve the situation of Blacks (Santos 1999). By the end of the Cardoso administration, the national government and some state governments began passing affirmative action legislation. The most controversial is the affirmative action policy in education. The state government of Rio de Janeiro and several others have adopted fixed percentages or quotas for Black public university admissions (Heringer 2002; Htun 2004).

The administration of President Luiz Inácio Lula da Silva (2003–present) has also been formally responsive to the demands of the Workers Party's Black activists and elected officials. The Lula government created the Special Office for the Promotion of Racial Equality (SEPPIR [*Secretaria Especial de Politicas de Promoção da Igualdade Racial*]) on March 21, 2003. This unit was designed to advocate for racial equality throughout all policy areas. The head of the Special Office is Matilde Ribeiro, a Black activist from São Paulo who has been given cabinet minister status to recognize the government's commitment to pursuing pro-racial equality policies. Minister Matilde Ribeiro has had to struggle for resources to staff and structure her office. She sees her mission as one of building support within the government and the public for affirmative action and other public policies that will reduce racial inequality and improve the socioeconomic situation of Afro-Brazilians. In an interview with this author in November 2003, Minister Ribeiro stated that she has already been successful in working with the ministries of Education, Health, and Culture. A lack of resources to fully implement its agenda represents the main challenge for Minister Ribeiro's Special Office.

In an unprecedented move, President Lula appointed three additional Afro-Brazilians, Marina Silva (Environment), Gilberto Gil (Culture), and Benedita da Silva (Social Welfare), to cabinet minister positions. Despite her close relations with President Lula, da Silva was forced to resign early in Lula's administration because of her questionable use of public funds for personal travel. It is unclear whether other cabinet ministers, agency heads, and thousands of government workers fully embraced the government's policies of reducing racial inequality and Black poverty while giving Blacks more educational and employment opportunities. To what degree did government officials support, resist, or ignore Minister Ribeiro's efforts? New research is necessary to answer this question.

Ecuador

Ecuador is politically unstable and economically vulnerable. A large percentage of its population of 13 million is poor and lacks access to quality education and employment. At 5 percent of the national population, Afro-Ecuadorians are virtually absent from the country's political and economic elite. For many years, leftist Jaime Hurtado was the most visible Afro-Ecuadorian politician. Hurtado was assassinated on February 17, 1999, in Quito near the national Congress building. Hurtado's political party, the Democratic Popular Movement (MPD [*Movimiento Popular Democratico*]), a leftist party that doesn't prioritize racism generally has been successful in the majority Black province of Esmeraldas. Rafael Erazo, an outspoken leader of Hurtado's party from Esmeraldas, is a first-term member and the only Black deputy in Congress.

In Ecuador, there has been less governmental attention paid to the concerns of Black political groups than in Brazil and Colombia. However, the powerful Indigenous social movement has forced the Ecuadorian government to create a range of policies and agencies for that population. PRODEPINE (*Programa de Desarrollo de los Pueblos Indigenas y Negros del Ecuador*) is a foundation that has distributed government funds to Indigenous and Black communities for diverse development projects. The Afro-Ecuadorian Development Corporation, a government agency, has recently begun operation. It has a mandate to develop policies and programs to improve the living conditions of Blacks. Moreover, there have been specific government initiatives in the cities of Esmeraldas and Quito directed toward the Black population (de la Torre 2002).

Cuba

Cuba is a crucial case for examining the role of Blacks in Latin American politics. The Cuban Revolution of 1959 brought Fidel Castro and his brother Raul Castro to power, where they remain almost 50 years later. This Caribbean socialist revolution transformed social relations, political institutions, and culture. The revolutionaries created a more egalitarian society with an emphasis on free education and health care, and a comprehensive social welfare state. On its own terms, the revolution endures despite the counter-revolutionary activities of the U.S. government and the Cuban exile community concentrated in southern Florida. As the poorest segment of the country, Blacks have benefited from the revolutionary government's policies (De la Fuente 2001; McGarrity and Cardenas 1995; Perez Sarduy and Stubbs 1993, 2000).

The demise of the Eastern European socialist regimes and the Soviet Union devastated the Cuban economy. Cuban trade with and aid from these governments declined dramatically in the 1990s and forced President Castro to declare a "Special Period" of sacrifice. In response, the Cuban government opened the country to foreign investment, promoted tourism, and allowed Cubans to open small businesses. Despite tremendous pain and suffering resulting from the economic crisis and decreased governmental support in the areas of health and social services, the government survived when some commentators thought it would not (Centeno and Font 1997; Oppenheimer 1992). However, Afro-Cubans experienced a new level of racism as they were discriminated against in the revitalized tourist industry. They also had fewer relatives abroad to send them cash remittances (De la Fuente 1998, 2001). This reality created new tensions in race relations and necessitates a review of the Cuban Revolution's impact on Blacks, despite the assertions of the government and its supporters of its positive characteristics.

This author spoke with various Cuban diplomats from the Cuban Interests Section in Washington, DC, during the 1990s and with Cuban government and Communist party officials in Havana, Cuba, in January 2000. These representatives highlighted the brutality of the old Batista regime and the social progress of the revolution. For example, Felix Wilson, Afro-Cuban diplomat and then First Secretary of the Cuban Interests Section in Washington, DC, lectured at the University of Maryland, College Park, in September 1997, emphasizing the improvement in literacy and life expectancy and the decline in infant mortality and racial and gender discrimination between 1959 and 1997. He also pointed out that in 1997 there were five Black government ministers and several Black ambassadors and that Afro-Cubans were one-third of the parliament. In the face of ongoing hostility from the most powerful government in the world, Wilson offered a strong defense of the revolution in terms of human development and Black progress.

Not all Afro-Cubans have such a positive evaluation. Carlos Moore, a prominent ethnographer, has offered the most sustained critique of the Cuban Revolution from an Afro-Cuban perspective. Moore, an initial supporter of the Revolution, had an early falling out with the new government and has since conceptualized Fidel Castro and the Revolution as perpetuators of White supremacy. He argues that Castro, his brother Raul Castro, and most political leaders are White and have refused to allow an open national discussion of race in Cuba. Moore acknowledges that the government's commitment to national integration appealed to all Cubans, especially Black Cubans, but maintains that the government's closing of all independent organizations and its failure to allow organized dissent prohibits Blacks from fully protesting racial discrimination and creating groups to promote their collective cultural and political interests (Moore 1989, 1995, 199–239).

Few have studied the evolution of Cuba's racial question in the depth and nuance of Cuban scholar Alejandro de la Fuente (2001). One of his main points is that too many scholars have examined Cuban and Latin American race relations through North American eyes. De la Fuente argues that this has led to misunderstandings of Latin American racial discourse and dynamics. He calls for renewed attention to the concept of racial democracy. He argues that White Cubans have tended to accept this idea as descriptive and have used it to prevent a full debate on Cuba's racial reality. On the other hand, Afro-Cubans have more often embraced racial democracy as an ideal or goal to be achieved. These divergent interpretations have led to Cubans generally embracing independence hero José Martí's formulation of Cuban identity as "more than mulatto, black, or white" but differing substantially over the meaning of that identity.

De la Fuente has argued that Cubans have often worked together across racial and class lines in the army, political parties, labor movements, and other areas. His defense of the Cuban myth of racial democracy and other "Latin American paradigms of racially mixed, integrated nations" highlights the positive characteristics of these ideologies in restraining racist elite behavior, providing an inclusive and participatory vision of the nation, and criticizing the brutal segregationist and White supremacist patterns of race relations in the United States. Moreover, these ideologies provided a stronger basis for Black social mobility and political leadership in Latin America than is found in the United States. De la Fuente maintains that scholars, especially those using the North American model, have assumed incorrectly "that blacks should mobilize separately and that racially based political mobilization is the legitimate—perhaps even only—way to fight racism effectively" (2001, 9). He concludes by noting that, because formal racial segregation was not the norm in postslavery Latin America, Afro-Latin American political participation and social action usually assumed nonracial forms.

De la Fuente's analysis tends to minimize the negative aspects of Latin American myths of racial democracy. These myths often serve to cover up and defend manifestations of racism. The 1912 massacre of Afro-Cubans in the name of defending the nation against racist Blacks is an important case in point (Helg 1995). The fact that Brazilian, Venezuelan, Cuban, and other Latin American officials have condemned acts of racial discrimination and their governments have passed laws banning such discrimination means little if political leaders then fail to actively fight against racial prejudice and enforce antidiscrimination laws. Finally, myths of racial democracy are usually actively hostile to independent Black political organization. Black Latin American activists and intellectuals, such as Brazilian Abdias do Nascimento, Venezuelan Jesús "Chucho" García, Colombian Juan de Dios Mosquera, and Cuban Carlos Moore, have consistently made this point.

Summary of Black National Politics in Latin America

Major obstacles remain to the development of Black politics in Latin America and public policies that address specific Black concerns. Despite the formal transition to democracy in most Latin American countries, political instability, violence, and poverty have led to ongoing human rights violations and limited opportunities for Blacks and other groups to participate in politics. For example, Colombia continues to suffer from civil war, and Ecuador has experienced major government instability in recent years. As Latin America's largest country, Brazil has achieved political and economic stability, but at a tremendous cost. Socioeconomic and racial inequality, crime, and violence are widespread in Brazil's urban centers and rural areas. In addition, there remains the widespread political and social belief that Latin Americans have transcended race. This idea delegitimizes race-specific initiatives to overcome Black poverty and racial inequality.

Black political activists continue to overcome obstacles in their struggle to improve Afro-Latin American living conditions. They work in political parties, labor unions, community groups, professional associations, and their own Black movement organizations. Slowly, they are gaining more visibility in public debates and the mass media. Some Afro-Latin American activists have drawn on earlier Pan-African experiences and recent Indigenous campaigns to internationalize their struggle by establishing relationships with each other across borders and taking their concerns to major international financial and government institutions.

BLACK TRANSNATIONAL POLITICS

Afro-Latin American Conferences and Meetings

> Perhaps the most important contemporary phenomenon in the African world is the emergence and re-assertion of the African people of South and Central America within the context of Pan-Africanism. (Nascimento 1980, 1)

During the last thirty years, leading Afro-Latin American activists and intellectuals have organized across national borders and worked continuously to unify their forces and overcome various obstacles. These leaders have succeeded in meeting regularly, exchanging information, outlining common problems, and proposing solutions. However, they have not been able to implement many of their proposals. Still, the totality of their efforts has created a transnational advocacy network committed to working to improve the situation of Blacks in the Americas.

The network began in the 1970s and has gone through several phases. The key events in the creation of this network were the four Congresses of Black Culture in the Americas. They were held in Cali, Colombia (August 1977); Panama City, Panama (March 1980); São Paulo, Brazil (August 1982); and Quito, Ecuador (1984). The outstanding achievement of the Congresses was the recognition that Blacks had to unite across national boundaries to affirm their culture and identity as people of African ancestry. Scholars and activists presented papers and offered analyses on diverse aspects of Black life in the Americas. Hundreds of Blacks from many countries in the Americas and several representatives from African countries participated in each Congress along with non-Black activists and scholars. The lead organizer of each Congress was a citizen of the host country. The first three host leaders were Colombian Manuel Zapata Olivella, Panamanian Gerardo Maloney, and Brazilian Abdias do Nascimento (*AfroDiaspora* no. 1, 3, 4, 1983–1984; Davis 1995b; Nascimento 1980; *Primer Congreso* 1988).

The Congresses evolved over time in substance and form, maintaining the organizational structure of dividing into working groups and having all delegates approve resolutions and recommendations in the concluding sessions. Although the working groups varied, together they debated the central cultural, socioeconomic, and political issues facing Blacks in the Americas. The Congresses approved resolutions condemning racism, racial discrimination, and White supremacy. More important, they asked individual participants and their organizations to do everything possible to improve the Black condition.

Congress leaders considered each gathering to be successful and created an organizational structure to continue the work, which nonetheless was not maintained for various reasons. First, the leadership of the host government was supposed to assume primary responsibility for the meeting arrangements. In Brazil, Don Rojas of Grenada agreed to host the fourth Congress. However, before it could be held, the Grenadian Revolutionary Government of Maurice Bishop was overthrown and the U.S. government invaded and occupied the country. This U.S. intervention interrupted activities of the Congress and required that it be moved to a new location, Ecuador. The main problem leading to the demise of the Congress was an inability to raise sufficient funds from Black individuals and groups, thereby creating a dependency on outside governmental and civic institutions, such as the Organization of American States. Abdias do Nascimento described in depth his difficulties in getting financial support for the 3rd Congress in Brazil (*Afrodiaspora* 1983, 42, 71–82).

Nevertheless, the Congresses of Black Culture in the Americas represented a tremendous achievement. For the first time Black leaders from throughout the Americas united to discuss problems and propose solutions to the serious challenges facing Blacks in the hemisphere. Congress participants were usually already activists and leaders in their respective countries, but the debates, discussions, and activities helped them educate each other about their collective reality. Many participants continued their work in their home countries, realizing the importance of maintaining ties with their brothers and sisters throughout the Americas.

After the last Congress was held, numerous meetings and gatherings throughout the Americas have emphasized various aspects of Black life. Perhaps most important was the First Seminar on Racism and Xenophobia held in Montevideo, Uruguay, on December 8–10, 1994. This meeting was hosted by *Mundo Afro*, a prominent Afro-Uruguayan organization. Participants divided themselves into five major commissions and agreed that a permanent network of organizations and activists would be necessary to maximize their effectiveness. Although *Mundo Afro* would maintain a coordinating role, the network was divided into geopolitical regions: North America, the Caribbean and Central America, and South America (*Alianza estrategica*; Davis 1995b, 364–69).

Black legislators from Latin America organized three unprecedented meetings that laid the foundation for a new Black transnational network. On November 21–23, 2003, in Brasília, Brazil, on May 19–21, 2004 in Bogota, Colombia, and on August 28–31, 2005 in San José, Costa Rica, Black elected officials from the Caribbean and Latin America met to examine the situation of Afro-descendants in the Americas. The deputies, representatives, and senators agreed that Black people in different countries often face similar hardships. They decided to continue meeting and discussing how they as elected officials can best work to improve the living conditions of their people. They summarized and distributed their views in two documents: *Carta de Brasília* and *Carta de Bogota*.

Afro-Brazilian–African American Network

A key component of the internationalization of Afro-Latin American politics involved U.S.-based institutions. Over the past twenty-five years, African Americans have made numerous efforts to improve their relationship with Afro-Brazilians, working through the U.S. government, nongovernmental organizations, political organizations, and individual contacts. As a result, there is currently an informal network of African Americans who travel regularly to Brazil; host Black Brazilians when they visit the United States; teach African Brazilian history, culture, and politics at the university and community levels; and in general advocate strengthening pan-African ties between the two largest groups of the African diaspora. Other Americans interested in racial issues have also contributed to and are part of this network in key ways.

This section illuminates the immediate history, recent development, and current status of this network by focusing on key events, organizations, individuals, and activities in the 1970s, 1980s, and 1990s. Clearly, there has been much controversy, conflict, and relationship-building over the years. However, as a result of numerous factors, African Americans and African Brazilian leaders have not yet been able to build the formal and lasting organizational ties that they desire.

The 1970s

In the early 1970s, Afro-Brazilians were suffering with the rest of the country under the most repressive period (1968–1973) of the twenty-one years of military authoritarian rule (1964–1985). Leading Black political activists like Abdias do Nascimento were severely constrained in their work, and some radical Black leaders such as Joel Rufino were tortured. Nascimento eventually went into exile, and Rufino and others spent time in prison. In general, publicly discussing racism in Brazil, attempting to organize Blacks for political action, and drawing inspiration from the racial struggles of Blacks around the world were considered subversive activities (Hanchard 1994; Nascimento and Nascimento 1994).

In contrast to the Nixon administration's support of the brutal Médici administration, some U.S.-based institutions working in Brazil were not supportive of authoritarian rule. Two in particular played important roles in assisting Brazilian Blacks. The Ford Foundation and the Inter-American Foundation (IAF) established a presence in Brazil in the early 1960s and early 1970s, respectively, and since then have made numerous grants to Afro-Brazilian political organizations and individuals. The IAF was created in 1969 as an independent agency of the U.S. government to provide development assistance to organizations active in Latin America and the Caribbean. The Ford Foundation is a private philanthropic foundation created in 1936 and has had a worldwide mission to improve human welfare.

Although the IAF had been funding diverse groups throughout Brazil since the early 1970s, it made a grant on February 4, 1977, that would have serious consequences. On that day, the IAF gave $82,000 to the Research Institute of Black Cultures (IPCN [*Instituto de Pesquisas das Culturas Negras*]) to buy office space and support various community outreach programs. IPCN was a leading Black political organization founded in 1975 to raise Black consciousness and organize and mobilize Blacks against racial discrimination. In an interview with this author on September 15, 1997, Carlos Medeiros revealed that IPCN founders emphasized academic and cultural concerns to prevent drawing unwanted attention from the military government and its repressive intelligence agencies to their political activities. Nonetheless, the government did take notice of the grant and protested to the IAF. The IAF refused to rescind the award and was asked by the Brazilian government to leave the country. In 1978, the IAF did so and suspended its operations in Brazil for five years, until 1983.

The conflict between the IAF and the Brazilian government coincided with President Jimmy Carter's criticism of military dictatorships in Latin America and their long record of human rights violations. The Brazilian military president, Ernesto Geisel, did not appreciate Carter's blunt remarks and considered them attacks on Brazilian sovereignty. Diplomatic relations improved enough for the IAF to return only after Ronald Reagan came to power in the United States and General João Figueiredo became Brazil's president. On its return, the IAF initially made fewer grants to Black political groups in Brazil.

As a result of the IAF grant, IPCN was able to purchase a building in the Lapa neighborhood near downtown Rio de Janeiro. IPCN remains one of the few Black Brazilian groups to own its meeting space. The organization developed an extensive program of activities related to the racial question in Brazil. IPCN held numerous meetings, educational classes, lectures, and cultural events and was a hub of Black movement activities in the late 1970s and throughout the 1980s. In addition, the IPCN office became an obligatory stop for African Americans with an interest in race and politics. In the author's interview with Carlos Medeiros, he noted that some of the personal and political relationships between Black Brazilians and Black Americans developed through IPCN in the 1970s and 1980s still continue today.

The 1980s

The Ford Foundation opened its Brazil office in Rio de Janeiro in 1961 and has maintained an uninterrupted presence in the country since then (Brooke and Witoshynsky 2002). As did the IAF, the Ford Foundation awarded money to various Black intellectuals and activists in the 1970s, 1980s, and 1990s. In the last few years, Ford has given millions of dollars to Afro-Brazilian groups, including the Black Women's Institute (Geledes–*Instituto da Mulher Negra*) for its innovative and respected legal and educational programs. The Casa Dandara National Association received $30,000 for an international conference on African Brazilian rights and citizenship. Geledes and Casa Dandara are led by African Brazilians Sueli Carneiro and Diva Moreira, respectively. These Black women have visited various cities in the United States and met with African American intellectuals and activists, such as Professor Ronald Walters and Gisele Mills.

The Ford Foundation's generous funding of Afro-Brazilian scholarship and community activism can be traced to its generally liberal and racially tolerant mission and to two important Black American program officers in Rio de Janeiro, Michael J. Turner and Patricia Sellers, in the early 1980s (Brooke and Witoshynsky 2002, 426). Before joining the Ford Foundation, Turner was a scholar on Brazil and professor of African and Latin American history from New York, and Sellers was a criminal defense lawyer and activist from Philadelphia. Turner and Sellers recommended the generous funding of Afro-Brazilian scholarship and community activism. The foundation provided significant grants to one of the leading Brazilian academic units on race relations and the situation of Blacks, the Center of Afro-Asian Studies (*Centro de Estudos Afro-Asiáticos*), based at Candido Mendes University in Rio de Janeiro. During the tenure of Turner and Sellers, the Ford Foundation also funded numerous community and economic development programs in shantytowns and other low-income areas.

While working as Ford program officers, Turner and Sellers developed an extensive range of Afro-Brazilian contacts. In numerous formal and informal settings, these African Americans described and discussed the situation of Blacks in the United States with Afro-Brazilian leaders, students, and professionals. A tremendous cross-fertilization and exchange of ideas, experiences, and future plans occurred. African Brazilians became connected indirectly to the Black U.S. experience. Afro-Brazilians who wanted to visit the United States often received advice and contacts from Turner and Sellers. Similarly, the two were visited in Brazil by their family and friends from the United States, who would then be introduced to African Brazilians.[2]

In the 1980s, political events occurred in the United States that had repercussions in Afro-Brazil. In 1984 and 1988, the Reverend Jesse Jackson campaigned for the Democratic Party's nomination for president. In his campaigns, Rev. Jackson questioned the elitist and Eurocentric aspects of U.S. foreign policy. He called for more attention to Africa and the Caribbean, better relations with Fidel Castro's Cuba, and more Black participation in international affairs (Stanford 1997). Jackson's rescue missions to the Middle East and other regions, as well as his dramatic campaign and speaking style, caught the attention of African Brazilian leaders. Jackson's strong campaigns for one of the most important political positions in the world inspired several Black Brazilians to greater political activism (da Silva et al, 1997, 134–36).

Brazilian military rule ended in 1985. One of the important results of this transition has been the election of more Black members to the national Congress. Several of these politicians have an interest in learning from the Black American political experience and developing ties between African Brazilians and African Americans. Abdias do Nascimento is a key figure for understanding relations between Blacks in Brazil and the United States. Nascimento lived part of his exile in the United States, where he met with a broad spectrum of the African American community: artists, professionals, Black Panthers, intellectuals, members of Congress, and students. Nascimento always respected and admired the level of organization and political activity in the U.S. Black community. At the same time, he found that African Americans had little knowledge of, but great interest in, the situation of Blacks in Brazil. Consequently, he has consistently devoted significant time to educating African Americans on the racial situation in Brazil. In 1980 and 1983, Nascimento spoke to members of the Congressional Black Caucus. In his speeches, he shocked American audiences by describing the reality of Afro-Brazilians as more oppressive than that of American Blacks. He invited U.S. Blacks to visit Brazil and witness this racial oppression for themselves (Nascimento and Nascimento 1994, 49–53, 56–57).

The 1990s

Several times during the decade, politician Benedita da Silva and a group of Black Brazilian leaders visited the United States and met with Congressional Black Caucus members and other Black leaders. Appalled by their lack of knowledge about Brazil in general and Afro-Brazil in particular, the Brazilians commissioned an English-language video on Blacks in Brazil for U.S. audiences. This excellent documentary, *Images of the Heart*, was made by Afro-Brazilian filmmaker Joel Zito Araújo in 1995. Furthermore, these Afro-Brazilian leaders created *VisBrasil* (*Centro AfroBrasileiro de Informação, Cooperação, e Capacitação* [Afro-Brazilian Center for Information, Cooperation and Training]). Based in Rio de Janeiro, this organization was formed to increase the visibility of Brazilian Blacks who were notoriously underrepresented in Brazilian mass media and usually stereotyped when they were presented.

VisBrasil illustrates well the dilemma of many Black groups. Regina Domingues and Judith Rosario, Afro-Brazilian researchers and activists, were chosen to run the Rio de Janeiro office along with a very small support staff. Domingues and Rosario were in the process of establishing the office and collecting demographic data on the Afro-Brazilian population when they faced serious financial difficulties. They both worked other full-time jobs and were unable to secure sufficient funds from the sponsoring individuals and groups or to raise adequate funds from other sources. Although *VisBrasil* had the backing of da Silva, João Jorge (leader of *Olodum*, a popular Black cultural group in Bahia), and many notable Black political and cultural figures, it folded after less than two years because of a lack of financial resources and a clear plan of action.

In the 1990s, three national African American figures visited Brazil and met with top African Brazilians. Lee Brown, drug czar of the first Clinton administration, traveled to Brazil to discuss the country's increasing use as a shipment point for drugs on their way to the U.S. market. Commerce Secretary Ron Brown also visited Brazil in an official capacity to discuss commercial relations between the two countries. He also visited a *favela* (shantytown) and met with Black Brazilian political figures. Finally, in an interview with this author, former member of Congress Adalberto Camargo explained that Jesse Jackson visited Brazil and met with a broad range of Black politicians and activists, primarily to engage in dialogue about problems shared with African Americans.

African American Political Exiles in Cuba

For the last forty years, prominent Black progressives, radicals and revolutionaries from the United States have visited or moved to Cuba. Some have gone out of curiosity. Others have gone out of solidarity. Still others have gone out of necessity. Fidel Castro and his government have consistently encouraged African Americans to visit (Reitan 2001; Tyson 1999; Brock and Castañeda Fuertes 1998). Some African Americans, and Americans in general, continue to visit Cuba despite the recent measures to restrict travel and limit relations between the American and Cuban peoples.

The Cuban Revolution triumphed at a critical time in American history. Formal, explicit White supremacist segregation in the United States had been declared illegal by the Supreme Court's *Brown v. Board of Education* decision in 1954. However, because many White Americans in the South disagreed with this decision, widespread segregation and brutal racial oppression still existed in the late 1950s and throughout the 1960s. Robert Williams was one of the most dynamic grassroots leaders fighting against White racism. Forced from his leadership position in the NAACP because of his outspoken activism and embrace of armed self-defense in Monroe, North Carolina, Williams argued vigorously that Blacks should defend themselves against White terrorism and violence. He had expressed early interest in the Cuban Revolution, visited Cuba, and met Fidel Castro. Williams was impressed with Castro's denunciation of racial discrimination. Williams also perceived that Afro-Cubans were supportive of the revolution (Tyson 1999, 220–43).

In the United States, Williams continued to denounce racism and segregation as illegal and un-American. He traveled throughout the country speaking and organizing against White terrorism. Williams, believing that segregationists in Monroe would unite with White racists in the state and national government to kill him and his family, left the country through Canada and eventually settled in Havana in October 1961. Castro and the Cuban government treated him as a fellow revolutionary fighting for freedom. Initially, the Cuban government assisted Williams in producing "Radio Free Dixie," a progressive radio program broadcast to the United States. Radio Free Dixie combined music and commentary to criticize American racism and encourage Black Americans to fight against it (Tyson 1999, 287–92).

After four years in Cuba, Williams and his family left Cuba for China in 1965 for two main reasons. First, never one to engage in self-censorship, Williams had spoken out publicly on the lack of racial diversity among Cuban leadership. This commentary was unwelcome. As Carlos Moore has noted, the revolutionary Cuban government has never allowed a full, open, and democratic debate on the role of Blacks in Cuban society and government. Second, after the U.S.-government-sponsored Bay of Pigs invasion in 1961, the Cuban government was becoming increasingly concerned about its national security. More violent intervention was a definite possibility. Cuban leaders felt that allowing Williams to continue to antagonize its big neighbor to the north might hasten more violent intervention. Consequently, Williams's ability to speak his mind about what was happening in the United States and Cuba became increasingly limited (Reitan 2001; Tyson 1999, 292–94).

After the departure of Williams, other Black American leaders received political asylum in Cuba. Black Panther leader Eldridge Cleaver arrived in Cuba in December 1968, hoping to train Black American militants in guerrilla warfare in preparation for waging revolution in the United States. However, by that time, the Cuban situation had become even more restrictive. Airplane hijackers from the United States had forced the Cuban government to become extremely cautious because it was uncertain whether the hijackers were legitimate revolutionaries or U.S. government spies. Cleaver also left Cuba unsatisfied (Reitan 2001, 172–73).

William Lee Brent, a former Black Panther, hijacked an American plane to Cuba in June 1969. After spending almost two years in a Cuban jail, Brent was granted political asylum and remains in Cuba today (Brent 1996). Brent was one of the first African American activists who fled to Cuba beginning in the late 1960s to avoid legal charges related to their political activism in the United States. He was followed by Black Panther Party cofounder Huey P. Newton, who lived in exile in Cuba from 1974 to 1977. Former Black Panther and Black Liberation Army soldier Assata Shakur arrived in Cuba in 1986. Nehanda Abiodun, a grassroots Black nationalist from New York, also fled the U.S. and lives in exile in Cuba. These activists have been supported by the Cuban government. Some like Huey P. Newton returned to face their charges. Others like Brent, Shakur, and Abiodun have refused to return to the United States and have experienced the triumphs and tragedies of Cuban socialism (Brent 1996; http://www.afrocubaweb.com).

CONCLUSION: BLACK POLITICS IN THE AMERICAS

Despite their significant presence throughout Latin America, Blacks have not had much power and influence on government policies. However, since the 1970s, Afro-Latin Americans have renewed their historic struggle for political inclusion and social justice. Their efforts have been partially successful. Latin American leaders and the general public are more aware that Blacks exist as political actors and that racial discrimination and inequality are problems that cannot be reduced to poverty and social inequality. Throughout the region, governments have passed and begun to implement race-specific policies and initiatives that respond to Afro-Latin American demands.

Afro-Latin American leaders, activists, and intellectuals have protested continuing racial discrimination, pervasive poverty and hardship, and the lack of governmental attention to their specific problems. These activities have contributed to projects that illustrate both the successes and the challenges facing Blacks. In 2000, international development agencies and private groups (largely based in the United States) founded the Inter-Agency Consultation on Race in Latin America (IAC). The IAC is an effort to coordinate the activities of important institutions in addressing the concerns of Afro-Latin American groups. The first director of the IAC and the Inter-American Dialogue (IAD) Race Program was Afro-Brazilian scholar and activist, Luiz Claudio Barcelos. For four years, Barcelos was based in IAD's office in Washington, DC, working with representatives from international governmental organizations, Latin American governments, the U.S. government, Black activist groups, and scholars (*Race Report* 2003). Barcelos helped organize the meetings of Black elected officials in Brazil in 2003 and Colombia in 2004. He also worked with Afro-Costa Rican leader Epsy Campbell in her capacity as an elected official and as a leader of the Afro-Caribbean and Afro-Latin American Women's Network (*La Red de Mujeres Afrocaribeñas y Afrolatinoamericanas*). The Network has given Black women a forum to organize against racism and sexism (Campbell Barr and Careaga 2002).

Judith Morrison became the new executive director of the IAC in 2004. An African American scholar, activist, and management/foundation executive, Morrison has continued and expanded the IAC's work. She has traveled throughout the United States and Latin America lecturing on the situation of Afro-Latin Americans, organizing visits and exchanges among Black leaders, and encouraging governments and other institutions to do more to reduce poverty, racial discrimination, and racial inequality.

The activities of Judith Morrison and the IAC, Epsy Campbell and the Black women's network, and Black politicians from Latin America are among the many initiatives that demonstrate the urgent need for political scientists to document and analyze contemporary Black politics in Latin America. At the local, national, and international levels, Afro-Latin Americans are continuing their struggle against racial oppression. One aspect of that struggle is convincing non-Blacks that formal and informal racial discrimination is wrong. Finally, there is the unfinished task of building strong political, cultural, financial, and social organizations and institutions to defend Black interests. Mapping the main trends of Afro-Latin American political activity and researching the most important Black political leaders and organizations are jobs that have only just begun.

NOTES

1. I would like to thank Lori S. Robinson for extensive comments and Kelli Morgan for research assistance. The Race and Democracy in the Americas research group within the National Conference of Black Political Scientists (NCOBPS) provided and continues to offer stimulating debate on the issues discussed in this chapter. Some of the ideas and formulations in this chapter were presented at Arizona State University at the Consortium on Qualitative Research Methods (CQRM) in January 2003 and received constructive criticism from several participants. The anonymous reviewers for Temple University Press also offered important suggestions for revisions.
2. In addition to research on the Ford Foundation at the Library of Congress in Washington, DC, the author lived in Rio de Janeiro, Brazil for extended periods in the 1980s and 1990s, and observed and participated in various activities organized by Turner and Sellers.

REFERENCES

Afrodiaspora 1, no. 1 (January–April 1983).

Afrodiaspora 2, no. 3 (October 1983–January 1984).

Afrodiaspora 2, no. 4 (1984).

Alianza estrategica Afrolatinoamerica y Caribena 1a and 2a Etapa. Montevideo, Uruguay: Organizaciones Mundo Afro.

Aliança estrategica Afrolatinoamericanos e Caribenhos 2000–2002. Montevideo, Uruguay: Organizaciones Mundo Afro. [Portuguese version of *1a Etapa*]

Andrews, George Reid. 1991. *Blacks and whites in São Paulo, Brazil, 1888–1988*. Madison: University of Wisconsin Press.

_____. 2004. *Afro-Latin America, 1800–2000*. New York: Oxford University Press.

Appelbaum, Nancy P., Anne S. Macpherson, and Karin Alejandra Rosenblatt, eds. 2003. *Race and nation in modern Latin America*. Chapel Hill: University of North Carolina Press.

Bello, Alvaro, and Marta Rangel. 2002. La equidad y la exclusión de los pueblos indígenas y afrodescendientes en America Latina y el Caribe, *Revista de la CEPAL* 76 (April): 39–54.

Brent, William Lee. 1996. *Long time gone: A Black Panther's true-life story of his hijacking and twenty-five years in Cuba*. New York: Times.

Brock, Lisa, and Digna Castañeda Fuertes. 1998. *Between race and empire: African Americans and Cubans before the Cuban Revolution*. Philadelphia: Temple University Press.

Brooke, Nigel, and Mary Witoshynsky, eds. 2002. Os 40 anos da Fundação Ford no Brasil: Uma parceria para a mudança social. In *The Ford Foundation's 40 years in Brazil: A partnership for social change*. São Paulo: Editora da Universidade de São Paulo.

Burdick, John. 1995. Brazil's black consciousness movement. In *Fighting for the soul of Brazil*, by John Burdick, 174–83. New York: Monthly Review Press.

Campbell Barr, Epsy, and Gloria Careaga, eds. 2002. *Poderes cuestionados: Sexismo y racismo en América Latina*. San José: Diseno Editorial.

Castañeda, Jorge G. 1993. *Utopia unarmed: The Latin American left after the cold war.* New York: Alfred A. Knopf.

Centeno, Miguel Angel, and Mauricio Font. 1997. *Toward a new Cuba? Legacies of a revolution.* Boulder, CO: Lynne Rienner.

Conniff, Michael L., and Thomas J. Davis. 1994. *Africans in the Americas: A history of the black Diaspora.* New York: St. Martin's.

Constitución política de la República del Ecuador: Comentarios, legislación conexa, concordancias, Índice Temático. 2002. Quito: Corporacion de Estudios y Publicaciones.

Cowater International, Inc., ed. 1999. *Forum proceedings on poverty alleviation for minority communities in Latin America: Communities of African ancestry.* Washington, DC: Inter-American Development Bank.

Cowater International, Inc., Margarita Sanchez, and Michael J. Franklin. 1996. *Communities of African ancestry in Costa Rica, Honduras, Nicaragua, Argentina, Colombia, Ecuador, Peru, Uruguay, Venezuela.* Washington, DC: Inter-American Development Bank.

da Silva, Benedita, Medea Benjamín, and Maisa Mendonca. 1997. *Benedita da Silva: An Afro-Brazilian woman's story of politics and love.* Oakland, CA: Institute for Food and Development Policy.

Davis, Darien J., ed. 1995a. *Slavery and beyond: The African impact on Latin America and the Caribbean.* Wilmington, DE: Scholarly Resources.

———. 1995b. Postscript to *No longer invisible: Afro-Latin Americans today.* London: Minority Rights Publications.

De la Fuente, Alejandro. 1998. *Recreating racism: Race and discrimination in Cuba's "Special Period."* Georgetown University: Cuba Briefing Paper series, no. 18, July.

———. 2001. *A nation for all: Race, inequality, and politics in twentieth-century Cuba.* Chapel Hill: University of North Carolina Press.

De la Torre Espinosa, Carlos. 2002. *Afroquiteños: Ciudadanía y racismo.* Quito: Centro Andino de Acción Popular.

Dirección de Asuntos para las Comunidades Negras (DACN). 1997. *Visión, gestión y proyección de la Dirección de Asuntos para las Comunidades Negras–DACN.* Santa Fe de Bogotá: Oficina Asesora de Publicaciones–Ministerio del Interior.

Dzidzienyo, Anani. 1995. Conclusion to *No longer invisible: Afro-Latin Americans today.* London: Minority Rights Publications.

Fontaine, Pierre-Michel. 1980. Research in the political economy of Afro-Latin America. *Latin American Research Review* 15, no. 2:111–41.

———, ed. 1985a. *Race, class, and power in Brazil.* Los Angeles: Center for Afro-American Studies.

———. 1985b. Blacks and the search for power in Brazil. In *Race, class and power in Brazil*, ed. Pierre Michel Fontaine, 56–72. Los Angeles: Center for Afro-American Studies.

Gonzalez, Lélia. 1985. The Unified Black Movement: A new stage in black political mobilization. In *Race, class and power in Brazil*, ed. Pierre Michel Fontaine, 120–34. Los Angeles: Center for Afro-American Studies.

Guimarães, Antonio Sergio Alfredo. 1995. Raça, racismo e grupos de cor no Brasil. *Estudos Afro-Asiáticos* 27 (April): 45–63.

Hanchard, Michael George. 1994. *Orpheus and power: The Movimento Negro of Rio de Janeiro and São Paulo, Brazil, 1945–1988.* Princeton, NJ: Princeton University Press.

Hasenbalg, Carlos. 1986. Racial inequalities in Brazil and throughout Latin America: Timid responses to disguised racism. In *Constructing democracy: Human rights, citizenship, and society in Latin America*, ed. Elizabeth Jelin and Eric Hershberg, 161–75. Boulder, CO: Westview.

Helg, Aline. 1995. *Our rightful share: The Afro-Cuban struggle for equality, 1886–1912.* Chapel Hill: University of North Carolina Press.

Heringer, Rosana. 2002. Ação afirmativa, estrategias pos-Durban. In *Observatorio da Cidadania.* Rio de Janeiro: Ibase.

Htun, Mala. 2004. From "racial democracy" to affirmative action: Changing state policy on race in Brazil. *Latin American Research Review* 39, no. 1:60–89.

Johnson, Ollie A., III. 1998. Racial representation and Brazilian politics: Black members of the National Congress, 1983–1999. *Journal of Interamerican Studies and World Affairs* 40, no. 4 (Winter): 97–118.

Marx, Anthony. 1998. *Making race and nation: A comparison of the United States, South Africa, and Brazil.* New York: Cambridge University Press.

McGarrity, Gayle, and Osvaldo Cardenas. 1995. Cuba. In *No longer invisible: Afro-Latin Americans today.* London: Minority Rights Publications.

Minority Rights Group, ed. 1995. *No longer invisible: Afro-Latin Americans today.* London: Minority Rights Publications.

Moore, Carlos. 1989. *Castro, the blacks and Africa.* Los Angeles: Center for African American Studies, University of California Los Angeles.

———. 1995. Afro-Cubans and the communist revolution. In *African presence in the Americas.* Trenton, NJ: Africa World Press.

Moore, Carlos, Tanya R. Sanders, and Shawna Moore, eds. 1995. *African presence in the Americas.* Trenton, NJ: Africa World Press.

Mosquera, Juan de Dios. 2000. *Las comunidades negras de Colombia hacia el siglo XXI: Historia, realidad y organizacion.* Bogota: Docentes Editores.

Nascimento, Abdias do, ed. 1982. *O negro revoltado.* Rio de Janeiro: Editora Nova Fronteira.

———. 1978. *O genocídio do negro brasileiro: Processo de um racismo mascarado.* Rio de Janeiro: Paz e Terra.

Nascimento, Abdias do, and Elisa Nascimento. 1994. *Africans in Brazil.* Trenton, NJ: Africa World Press.

Nascimento, Elisa Larkin. 1980. *Pan-Africanism and South America: Emergence of a black rebellion.* Buffalo, NY: Afrodiaspora.

Nobles, Melissa. 2000. *Shades of citizenship: Race and the census in modern politics.* Stanford, CA: Stanford University Press.

Oppenheimer, Andres. 1992. *Castro's final hour: The secret story behind the coming downfall of communist Cuba.* New York: Touchstone.

Perez Sarduy, Pedro, and Jean Stubbs, eds. 1993. *Afrocuba: An anthology of Cuban writing on race, politics and culture.* Melbourne, Australia: Ocean.

———. 2000. *Afro-Cuban voices: On race and identity in contemporary Cuba.* Gainesville: University Press of Florida.

Primer Congreso de la Cultura Negra de las Americas. 1988. Bogotá: UNESCO–Fundación colombiana de investigaciones folclóricas.

Race Report. January 2003. Washington, DC: Inter-American Dialogue.

Reichmann, Rebecca, ed. 1999. *Race in contemporary Brazil: From indifference to inequality.* University Park: Pennsylvania State University Press.

Reitan, Ruth. 2001. Cuba, the Black Panther Party, and the U.S. black movement in the 1960s: Issues of security. In *Liberation, imagination, and the Black Panther Party: A new look at the Panthers and their legacy.* New York: Routledge.

Rout Jr., Leslie B. 1976. *The African experience in Spanish America: 1502 to the present day.* Cam-bridge: Cambridge University Press.

Santos, Helio. 1999. Políticas públicas para a população negra no Brasil In *Observatorio da cidadania, no. 3.* Rio de Janeiro: Ibase.

Stanford, Karin L. 1997. *Beyond the boundaries: Reverend Jesse Jackson in international affairs.* Albany: State University of New York Press.

Thorne, Eva. 2003. Ethnic and racial political organization in Latin America. In *Social inclusion and economic development in Latin America*, ed. Mayra Buvinic, Jacqueline Mazza, and Ruthanne Deutsch. Washington, DC: Inter-American Development Bank.

Twine, France Winddance. 1998. *Racism in a racial democracy: The maintenance of white supremacy in Brazil.* New Brunswick, NJ: Rutgers University Press.

Tyson, Timothy B. 1999. *Radio Free Dixie: Robert F. Williams and the roots of black power.* Chapel Hill: University of North Carolina Press.

Valente, Ana Lucia E. F. 1986. *Política e relações raciais: Os negros e as eleições paulistas de 1982*. São Paulo: Faculdade de Filosofia, Letras e Ciências Humanas, University of São Paulo.

Wade, Peter. 1993. *Blackness and race mixture: The dynamics of racial identity in Colombia*. Baltimore: Johns Hopkins University Press.

———. 1997. *Race and ethnicity in Latin America*. London: Pluto.

Walker, Sheila, ed. 2001. *African roots/American cultures: Africa in the creation of the Americas*. Lanham, MD: Rowman & Littlefield.

Whitten, Norman E., Jr., and Arlene Torres, eds. 1998. *Blackness in Latin America and the Caribbean: Social dynamics and cultural transformations*. Bloomington: Indiana University Press.

Winant, Howard. 2001. *The world is a ghetto: Race and democracy since World War II*. New York: Basic Books.

Yelvington, Kevin A. 2001. Patterns of race, ethnicity, class, and nationalism. In *Understanding contemporary Latin America*, 2nd ed., ed. Richard S. Hillman, 209–36. Boulder, CO: Lynne Rienner.

Indigenous Mexico

Globalization and Resistance

Thomas D. Hall, James V. Fenelon, and Glen David Kuecker

INDIGENOUS PEOPLES IN Mexico have had continuous relationships with Euro-Americans for half a millennium. The southwestern United States was, in many ways, the northern limit of Latin America until the nineteenth century.

Mexico is the northernmost state of Latin America and home to "Indians" who occupy social positions that are, in most cases, the product of more than 500 years of colonization of indigenous peoples in the Western Hemisphere. Today their struggles for survival are against the spread of global capitalism as it manifests in Mexico—whether such struggle be intentional and overt, or neither. Mexico is often characterized by its difference from the United States, described with such labels as "semiperipheral state," "part of the third world," or a "global south." Given such nominal distinctions, it is not surprising that depictions of indigenous struggles in Mexico have also differed in many ways from those struggles in the neighboring United States. We use our examination of indigenous struggles in Mexico and in other parts of Latin America to develop an encompassing concept of indigeneity[1] and to underscore how different trajectories for states and regions in a changing world-system mutually influence each other.

Mexico is home to one of the most renowned of recent indigenous rebellions: the Zapatista movement centered in Chiapas and widely known as the EZLN (Ejército Zapatista de Liberación Nacional, or the Zapatista Army of National Liberation). However, the EZLN is only one of many indigenous movements in Mexico and throughout Latin America. Although these movements are certainly unique in their own ways, they also share several characteristics that are important to our analysis within a global context. First, according to some social analysts, indigeneity may be viewed as embedded in the ethnic/racial hierarchy of *Indio* and *mestizo,* and historically of *ladino* or contemporary *criollos* (Indian, mixed, Hispanic) permeating Latin America. In contrast, however, many indigenous peoples see themselves as culturally and historically separate, even while they live within the state and global systems. Second, some of these movements are examples of "transnational social movements" or "new social movements."[2] Yet, many indigenous scholars see their struggles as a continuation of resistance and revitalization efforts that address new contexts and often use new techniques to pursue these centuries-old goals, and not as some form of modern social movements (Hall and Fenelon 2008; Valandra 2006). Their struggles derive from centuries of interaction with and struggle against an expanding world-system that originated in Western Europe. These two different perceptions of indigeneity in Latin America—specifically in Mexico—also produce different worldviews, histories, and ideas about political participation and stratification, which we need to address by framing our discussion in particular places and times.

At the outset we underscore a profound difference in understandings of indigeneity, of struggles against forces of change, and of survival between indigenous peoples and mainstream social analyses. Often some social analysts (e.g., Barrett and Kurzman 2004; McAdam, Tarrow, and Tilly 2001; Tilly 2004; Kousis and Tilly 2005[3]) see these movements as "new" when in fact they are as old as first European contact. Indigenous peoples and many other analysts, including ourselves, do not see indigenous movements as a subcategory of some larger set of movements. Rather, they are much older and more complex, though they are related, especially to the new social movements, in important ways. Nonetheless, the historical roots and localized struggles are central features of indigenous movements and peoples. Understanding these different perspectives is critical. We discuss each of these perspectives briefly before discussing the Zapatistas and the EZLN, along with other indigenous movements, in detail. One of our goals is to connect these two perspectives while respecting their differences.

INDIGENEITY AND RACIALIZATION IN LATIN AMERICA

In the region that became Mexico there were several states and empires as well as many smaller groups before the arrival of Hernan Cortez and the *conquista* (Foster and Gorenstein 2000; Blanton, Kowalewski, Feinman, and Finsten 1993; Carmack, Gasco, and Gossen 1996). Among these pre-Cortez organizational structures was the Mayan Empire, whose classic period lasted from 300 C.E. to approximately 900 C.E., leaving many bureaucratic and ceremonial centers in the region located on what is now the Mexican state of Chiapas (there are others in the Yucatan and in Guatemala). Nearly a thousand years later the descendants of early Mayans initiated the Zapatista uprising. In southwestern Mexico, around the state of Oaxaca, the Zapotecs, descendants of another empire, developed after the Mayans but before the widely known Aztec empire. The Aztecs had conquered and incorporated many states and peoples left from cities such as Teotihuacán (see Plate 1.3.1). At the time of Cortez's invasion,

Tenochtitlán (present-day Mexico City) was one of the largest cities in the world. It had on the order of half a million residents and was the administrative center of an empire that included millions of people, roughly equivalent to the population of Texas or Afghanistan today, or England in the late nineteenth century.

Cortez and a small force of conquistadors, supplemented with local allies, managed to take the city, destroy Aztec control, and forever change what would later become Mexico. The conquest led to the deaths of many indigenous peoples, primarily from European diseases (Crosby 1972), and the subordination of those who survived. This, in turn, became a major context for the indigenous peoples who survived until the formation of the Mexican state in the early nineteenth century. Some indigenous peoples were incorporated into the Mexican state and apparently disappeared or melded into modern political structures. Postconquest Mexico developed a culture based in Spain and adopted Spanish as the national language, but with significant contributions from its indigenous peoples. An important point is that many residents of Mexico are descendants of one or more indigenous states and other indigenous peoples. There is a wide variation, from much to little, of their traditions that persist in some form or another in Mexico today. Many residents are of some sort of mixed ancestry, again with a great deal of variation. The net result is that there is a much higher proportion of "Indian-ness" in Mexico than in the United States or Canada, albeit often in forms quite different from what they were before the arrival of Europeans. The poorest *Indios* live closest to traditional culture, and the experiences of relocated peoples contrast sharply with those of indigenous peoples—throughout North America—who maintained languages, cultures, and traditional relationships to the land. Similar processes occurred elsewhere in Latin America, but with a great deal of country, regional, and local variations (for examples, see accounts in Guy and Sheridan 1998). Murals painted in the barrio Santo Domingo (in Mexico City), in an indigenous cultural center called La Escuelita, demonstrate a detailed knowledge of these relationships, and historical processes, even among more "urbanized" peoples (see Plate 1.3.2).

Indigenous struggles have often been over local autonomy, land tenure, community relations, and socioeconomic "development." These struggles usually involve decolonization "resistance" strategies, none more poignantly than Mexico: "The last five hundred years [in the history of Mexico] is the story of permanent confrontation between those attempting to direct the country toward the path of Western

PLATE 1.3.1 Teotihuacán ancient city capital ruins, outside Mexico City. (Photo courtesy of James V. Fenelon)

PLATE 1.3.2 Mural of 500 years of history at Escuelita community center, Santo Domingo, Mexico City. (Photo courtesy of James V. Fenelon)

civilization and those, rooted in Mesoamerican ways of life, who resist" (Bonfil Batalla 1996, xv).

During this half millennium of struggle, indigeneity became a critical factor in the foundation of many Latin American states built over preceding indigenous groups. Guillermo Bonfil Batalla sees a "historical process through which populations that originally possessed a particular and distinctive identity, based on their own cultures, are forced to renounce that identity, with all the consequent changes in their social organization and culture" (1996, 17). This cultural destruction of individual "Indian" or indigenous communities, nations, cultures, or collectivities[4] was done to promote domination built on deeply racialized concepts of "the Indian." This is a label that characterizes her or him as a generic primitive or "savage." These issues, and similar labels, are quite common for indigenous peoples globally.

In order to explicate what we mean by *racialized*, it is helpful to review some general issues. We begin by noting the general idea in social analysis that "race" is socially constructed, that is, something that is collectively, if unconsciously, decided by humans, as opposed to something that is natural or objective.[5] Such social construction is always embedded in specific flows of history in specific places; hence it is useful to review some general background on this issue.

In recent decades Mexico and much of Latin America have been far less rigid in the way they construct race and ethnicity than the United States has been. Racial categories are seen to be much more permeable and flexible than they are perceived to be in the United States. Indeed, individuals raised in the United States are often quite surprised to learn that "race" is a much more important social factor in the Americas than elsewhere in the world, and that in the Americas the United States is the most rigid in this regard (Russell 1994). Thus, an individual is often able to change his/her "race marker" by changing behaviors of speech, clothing, participation in variations of local cultures, and so on. Furthermore, many Latin American states see themselves as some sort of amalgam of various "races": Spanish, Indian, and occasionally African.

The history of racial distinctions in former colonies of Spain is quite complicated. In the early centuries there was a very elaborate system of *castas*, which might be glossed approximately as "caste" but is not the same as the term typically is used in South Asia (Mörner 1967, 1973, 1983). Some scholars see a conventional trinity of *Indio, mestizo,* and *ladino*[6] that historically approximated a racialized stratification system of lower, middle, and upper classes, but not perfectly, and with many variations throughout Latin America. However, systems in Mexico, and typically throughout Latin America, were in racial formation.

Major populations and colonial stratification in Mexico were changing over time. First there were the classical *conquistadores, ladinos,* and *Indios,* though ladino has fallen out use. Various attempts at bringing black slaves to the Spanishheld lands never really took hold, and thus many *Indios* were exploited for labor, indentured servants, and sometimes enslaved giving rise to caste-like divisions via the *encomienda* system. During this time there were generalized changes to the *peninsulares* (full-blooded Spaniards), *criollos* (Spanish blood born in the Americas), *meztisos* (mixed blood, typically indigenous mother and Spanish father), and the *Indios*, at the bottom of the social stratification. Gradually, the elite and well-educated were more likely to be descendants of the *criollos* and *peninsulares* or associated with more recent immigrants from Europe, all lighter skinned, as the meztiso population surged into the working (urban) and farming (*eijido*) classes (with some converging into a burgeoning middle class). The rural *Indios* population remained at the bottom, increasingly defined culturally and in terms of an origin place (thereby less racially).

Indios are, as the label suggests, Indians or indigenous persons. In many places they are peasants or former peasants, though in parts of Brazil, Mexico, Venezuela, and many other Latin American countries they often follow traditional customs. Typically they do not speak Spanish as a primary language, but rather as a second language. Often they wear forms of clothing different from those of the dominant Hispanic population. They may practice non-Christian religions or overlay their Christianity with pre-Christian practices. Economically they are among the poorest people.

Mestizos, or mixed-race people, are seen as a product of two races, Indian and Spaniard. Typically they speak Spanish, are Catholic Christian, and wear conventional Western clothing. They are clearly part of the national culture and can be part of a regional, if not national, middle class, as well as the backbone of the working class. This is the broadest, and vaguest, of the major categories.

Criollos/ladinos were historically of "pure" Spanish heritage and thus were seen as European. They seldom spoke languages other than Spanish and English, unless they learned them in school to facilitate commerce or education. Most *criollos* were part of the middle class, often the upper middle class. Nearly all of the current elites are drawn from this group or the *peninsulares.*

In popular conception, *Indios* are phenotypically distinctive, as were *ladinos,* while *mestizos* exhibit mixed phenotypical characteristics. However, in practice, they are often not easily distinguishable to an outsider. To be called "Indian" is usually degrading. These labels have, to some extent, migrated to the United States, but they often take different connotations.[7] These differences vary considerably across Latin America, from country to country, and within countries and regions. Often there are different local names for broad categories, and not infrequently there are more distinctions than these.

At one time Mexican intellectuals took this tendency further than in most other Latin American countries. Some argued that Mexico was made up of a new "cosmic race" forged of Indian and Spaniard and that the two were no longer distinct (Russell 1994; MacLachlan and Rodriguez 1980; Ortiz 1985). This conceptualization, referred to as *indigenismo,* was the official doctrine or ideology of the Partido Revolucionario Institucional (Institutionalized Revolutionary Party, or PRI). It originated during the Mexican Revolution, especially in response to the way the political elite subdued rebellious indigenous peoples through cooptation—drastically emphasizing the Spanish heritage over an indigenous one steeped in the reductionism of *mestizo* imagery. *Indigenismo* (according to Bonfil Batalla 1996) constitutes cultural control and is a tool of internal colonialism. Its central feature was paternalism, in which *mestizo*, Westernized Mexico recognizes an intrinsic beauty of the indigenous world but retains a modernizing agenda of de-Indianizing them. *Indigenismo* respected the Indians but sought to "help" them by making them "modern."

Bonfil Batalla (1996) advanced the concept of *Mexico Profundo,* which sought to expose the ills of *indigenismo.* His basic argument is that Mexico is *not* a *mestizo* nation; he rejects the "cosmic race" proposition advanced during the Mexican Revolution. He calls this erroneous conception "imaginary Mexico." It is *not* a rejection of the facticity of biological mixing but rather of the construction of that mixing as a new "race." Bonfil Batalla argues that the construction of the *mestizaje* (mixed-bloodedness) equates to a denial of the Indian portion of the *mestizo* and a privileging of the European portion. A *mestizo* nation is a colonial nation, or really an internal colonial nation, which, in the time of crisis of the early 1980s, needed to be rejected. Bonfil Batalla sought to replace it with the concept of *Mexico Profundo.*

He argued:

> We are not able to construct an imaginary country and it would be insane to insist on doing so. Mexico is what it is, with this population and this history. We cannot persist in the attempt to replace it with something it is not. The task is simpler: to make it better from within, not from without. We must stop denying what it is and, to the contrary, take it for something that can be transformed and developed starting from its own potentialities. We must recognize the Mexico Profundo, once and for all, because without it there is no worthwhile solution. (Bonfil Batalla 1996, 158)

One of the most important aspects of his argument is the proposition that *Mexico Profundo* is not exclusive to indigenous peoples. Instead, it incorporates Mexico's "de-Indianized" people, who may not think of themselves as being Indian, as well as *Indios.* These are mainly Mexico's *campesinos* or peasants. He also includes Mexico's urban poor, a social group that was becoming a major group during the 1970s and 1980s. Effectively, Bonfil Batalla takes Mexico's marginalized people, a huge proportion of the population (40–50 percent), from the "cosmic race"/*mestizo* grouping and incorporates them into the indigenous population. He argues that the marginalized people have retained the cultural trappings of Mesoamerican civilization and that they are more indigenous than those who descend from European immigrants. This argument is, however, problematic, in that it too significantly reconstructs the concept of indigenous peoples in ways that would not be congruent with the ways in which indigenous peoples think of themselves elsewhere in the world. Still, his ideas have had a great impact on Mexican thinking about indigenous peoples, but they are tightly embedded in debates within Mexico over the revolution and the domination of the PRI in Mexican politics.

While the concept of the "cosmic race" might have been useful for building a national identity, it flies in the face of the facts. But these facts, for Mexico, are notoriously difficult to ascertain with precision. Indeed, this ideology led the government to avoid collecting information on "Indians," although it did collect information on language use. More recently the government has begun collecting statistics relating to identity, but there is nothing like the deep historical records found in Canada and the United States. Nevertheless, there are separate groups, *Pueblos Indígenas* (indigenous communities in Mexico), especially in areas where Spanish remains a secondary language. "*La comunalidad Indígena*" is how many indigenous scholars refer to these communities (Maldonaldo 2002). Thus indigeneity for many Mexican *Pueblos Indígenas* stands opposed to historical and current cultural representations of who indigenous peoples are and will be.

With such a long history of labeling and domination and conceptual shifts, it is not surprising that the terminology shifts over time, typically with a great deal of contestation. These layers of domination illustrate Bonfil Batalla's indigenous "Indian" foundation, despite oppression in every aspect of life—cultural, political, economic, and social. This is why *indigenous* represents both the foundation of society itself and an "enemy" to be overtaken and destroyed, or at the least subordinated within lower strata of society. We need to address how indigenous peoples understand their history, in contrast to how it has been presented by dominant groups (see Plate 1.3.2).

Not surprisingly, many indigenous groups live in areas that straddle twenty-first-century national and provincial borders. This often generates conflicts as such individuals and groups try to ignore these lines, while states and provinces try to enforce them. This is one source of local opposition to the state. Whatever the reason for opposition, any group that opposes the state—whether for land, labor, increased representation, or increased regional autonomy—is often seen as, and labeled as, "revolutionary." During the Cold War (approximately 1945 to 1991) such opposition was often labeled "communist" or "socialist." The two terms seldom carried the same degree of opprobrium that they did, and often still do, in the United States. Since September 11, 2001, such opposition sometimes has been labeled as "terrorist" in a clear attempt to delegitimize and demonize it. Less often, such opposition is recognized as an ethnic movement by indigenous peoples.[8] In recent decades many movements have become more explicitly indigenous.

The Zapotec peoples in Oaxaca and other states of Mexico are an excellent example of indigenous diversity within contemporary Mexico. The Zapotecs arose after the apex of Mayan civilization, but before the rise of the Aztecs. Certainly there were cultural influences going in both directions. The ruins at Monte Alban are very instructive of the many accomplishments of the Zapotec civilization, with large pyramid-like temples constructed at this major ceremonial site located on a butte with views in four directions (Feinman and Nicholas 1991a, 1991b). Although primary institutional social life was in decay by the time of the rise of the Aztec empires, Zapotec communities kept much of their traditional knowledge alive until the strong destructive forces of the conquistador armies arrived. As the central valley became violently incorporated into the new Mexican society, communities and whole regions retained their language and customs, often in distinct ways. Highland communities were especially likely to retain a strong sense of traditional life and indigenous identity, sometimes rising up against the Mexican-imposed *hacienda* system of stratification, although nineteenth-century Sierra de Juárez communities advocated for liberalism, that opposed the elite versions of liberalism that did advocate the hacienda system (McNamara 2007). These insurrections took many forms, resisting any social reorganization that enriched incoming elites and *mestizo* middle classes, and attempted to seize land in addition to imposing their own political, economic, and justice systems.

The Mexican Revolution that began the twentieth century occasionally emphasized this sense of community in opposition to the dominant Mexican society. It also disrupted the colonial *modus vivendi* between indigenous communities and the colonizers that had been more or less stable for several centuries. In many more cases the communities were seeking a restoration of communal rights that had been secured during the colonial period and had been removed by the elite liberal project. Mexico had become part of an increasingly global system that sought deeper exploitation of labor and natural resources. Many of the highland Zapotec communities had thrown out European and Mexican managers and owners during the nineteenth century and had taken limited control of their own resources, sometimes under the *ejido* land tenure systems of Mexico, while others had formed a "popular" liberalism (Mallon 1997).

Thus, the historical memory of these Zapotec communities combined with contemporary resistance struggles, over systems of justice, the economy, local leadership, land tenure, and sociopolitical control. Therefore, when other movements, such as the Zapatistas, arose in recent years, some Zapotec communities were in a position to both resist and to revitalize their indigenous systems in opposition to local elites, regional control centers such as Oaxaca City, the Mexican dominance, and even against growing globalization.[9]

Plate 1.3.3, a photograph of a banner in Oaxaca City, illustrates these interactive systems. There are indigenous peoples who are still considered or treated solely as "minority" groups within states, and are the most vulnerable, yet they often form resistance movements such as Communidades Indígenas in Oaxaca (Maldonado 2002).

In these examples, we observe how indigenous movements have redefined themselves, renaming themselves in resistance to the imposed dominant typologies and as a form of revitalization that also constitutes decolonization. For instance, the Mexican government refers to people and individuals as *Indios,* used as a degrading term. However, many scholars and some activists referred to these peoples as *Pueblos Indios,* which has more of a sense of community or township. The government recently returned to the term *Pueblos Indígenas,* which may seem to be more respectful but also seems to imply they are peasants. *Communidades Iníigenas* is the preferred term by many indigenous movements such as those in Oaxaca. The movement groups are also unafraid to use the term *Resistance and Rebellion,* an outgrowth of the recent struggles in Chiapas and the highland Zapotecs.

Zapotec *Pueblos Indios,* mostly in the state of Oaxaca, Mexico, have used a variety of strategies or tactical approaches toward the incorporating process of the state and its economies, ranging from outright assimilation to relatively direct secessionist autonomy. Yavesia, a Zapotec community in the Sierra Juarez highlands, has formally organized its economy

SEE PRINTED BOOK FOR ORIGINAL ART

PLATE 1.3.3 Indigenous communities resistance banner at Oaxaca City, Zocalo, Mexico. (Photo courtesy of James V. Fenelon)

to resist the deforestation that nearby communities have experienced, developed a natural water bottling operation and formalized women's cooperatives, maintains a fishery, and employs computer programs including GIS mapping for its young students to learn about the land and history of their people. Additionally, Yavesia formally receives delegations from other indigenous communities throughout Mexico, and it studies like-minded social movements such as the Zapatistas for applications to its own situation. All decisions are taken in community meetings that include everyone, and they employ *cargo* systems that can demand people return from work in the United States, centering authority in the community, with local and global concerns (Maldonado 2002).

Not all Zapotec communities have been so proactive, especially with respect to globalization. One might expect that deforestation would be a bane for all indigenous peoples. As timber companies have coerced communities into short-term profits from lumber, they became more dependent on outside monies. When their forests were depleted, the result was a weakened social structure, less internal production, and greater dependency. Additionally, the new growth was more vulnerable to fires, flooding, and other natural disasters. Yavesia and some other communities, acknowledging their ancient symbiotic relationships with the land and the forests, banned timbering unless undertaken by community leadership as a whole, for the common good. This is simultaneously resistance and revitalization along ethnic, gender, and class lines (Stephen 2002, 2005).

The focus of the Zapotecs, similar and some would say precedent to the Tzotzil case (Rubin 1997), is representative of large numbers of Mayan-descent peoples in the states near the border with Guatemala. Five centuries of resistance to Euro-American systems of domination have produced constant uprisings, adaptation, assimilation, and cultural regeneration processes interspersed between long periods of quiet yet powerful suppression by elites from the colonial system and emerging states (Campbell

1994). Essentially, descendents of ancient civilizations such as the Zapotecan, Aztec, and Mayan were and continue to be "second-class" citizens in their own lands.

The Tzotzil people, among others, in the even more remote southern state of Chiapas were in a more vulnerable position, with direct suppression of *Pueblos Indios* in the highland areas and clear discrimination in the capital, San Cristobal. These indigenous peoples have retained their languages, customs, and identity from their roots as tributary groups under the Mayan civilization. With each incoming system, they have adapted to new circumstances. However, modern systems have attempted to break up their traditional culture and orientation to the land, including attempts to reduce them to peasant townships whose land could be appropriated for timbering, tourism, and natural resource extraction, under increasing globalization. Formal resistance was less common in the highlands and in the Lacandón jungle region, where relative remoteness and a qualified adaptation to Catholicism insulated the people. After more than a thousand years of living in subordination as a whole people, under Mayan, Aztecan, and Mexican state domination, their survival was threatened by capitalist intrusion and exploitation. They were finally ready to pursue more formal resistance.

The Tzotzil, and every other *Communidades Indígenas* in the highland and Lacandón areas of Chiapas, found their traditional collective orientation to the land, leadership, property distribution system, and often the community itself under duress and targeted for breakup by an increasing police and military function protecting new capital interests. Subsistence itself was in question as they were being forced into peasant labor systems. Resistance groups formed, with some external forces operating in the region as well. Early organization of the Zapatistas began to take place for the decade preceding 1994 (Muñoz Ramírez 2003). Interestingly, many communities had embraced Catholicism so deeply that they maintained a pacifist Christian orientation toward resistance and revitalization. These communities tended to support the Zapatistas philosophically, experiencing the injustice of the civil-military groups operating out of San Cristobal, Tuxtla Gutierrez, and Mexico proper, but were reluctant to take up arms. When EZLN forces mounted an armed rebellion, Tzotzil communities at places such as Nuevo Yibeljoj and Acteal found themselves making an age-old Faustian set of choices—whether to support traditional autonomous relations or give in to neocolonial military dominance. This is yet another example of the interaction of state globalism with indigeneity. When paramilitaries were supported by the Mexican government, these communities were defenseless. A terrible slaughter occurred at Acteal, supported by the local police (Álvarez Fabela 2000).[10] Similar threats of violence leading to death and rape caused the entire Nuevo Yibeljoj community to leave and spend over two years in refugee camps, barely surviving until its members could relocate to a hillside and start the rebuilding process once again.

Forces of globalization are even more extreme, indifferent to indigenous survival, and use old systems of domination and oppression from the states that in turn were borrowed from earlier colonial practices. Of course, these have led to new forms of resistance, newer adaptations, and even new movements to revitalize and reestablish community. Plate 1.3.4 shows the San Pedro Polho indigenous community sign just outside Oventik, near the Zapatista regional headquarters. This sign stresses autonomy, *Municipio Autónomo Rebelde Zapatista San Pedro Polho,* subordinating government leaders to the "people," or pueblo. This autonomous rebel community prohibits illegal drugs and its corruption, prohibits selling and buying stolen vehicles, and prohibits trafficking in alcohol. More important, it has revitalized traditional forms of social organization, making leaders respond to and be directed by the peoples themselves, evidenced in the phrase "*Aquí el pueblo manda y el gobierno obedece*" (here the people demand and the government obeys).

SEE PRINTED BOOK FOR ORIGINAL ART

PLATE 1.3.4   Community sign at San Pedro Polho, Chiapas, noting it as a "municipal autonomous rebel" for the Zapatistas. "Here the people demand and the government obeys." (Photo courtesy of James V. Fenelon)

ZAPATISTAS: SOCIAL MOVEMENT OF INDIGENOUS PEOPLES

The Zapatista movement is part of a continuous history of indigenous resistance to the colonialism of the Western world (Farris 1984). This resistance movement originated in the early 1960s and had two central features (Harvey 1998; Collier 1999; Womack 1999). First, it was a product of community organizing peasant groups independent of Mexico's dominant political party, the PRI, which had created peasant unions as a controlling mechanism in its patron-client system. Second, and corresponding to the first, was the important role of liberation theology. Under the guidance of Bishop Samuel Ruíz, a radicalized Catholic Church engaged in the formation of Christian Base Communities with the goal of empowering indigenous people to be full citizens (Meyer 2000; Womack 1999; Krauze 2002). Liberation theology created a new generation of community leaders and set the foundations for "*basta ya*" (enough already) thinking among the indigenous people of Chiapas. These two foundations provided the lived experiences necessary for consciousness formation and radicalization characteristic of new social movements and were precursors to the open rebellion of January 1, 1994 (Kuecker 2004; Harvey 1998; Nash 2001). The state was keenly aware of what was happening in Chiapas, and it used carrot-and-stick tactics of violent repression mixed with rewards for cooperation with PRI domination. One attempt at co-optation was the 1974 Indigenous Congress organized by Bishop Ruíz at the invitation of the PRI. The PRI thought it could "spin" events and the movement toward its favor. Instead, it became a collective radicalization as otherwise divided communities met together for the first time, sharing their stories of injustice and the nature of their struggles.[11]

On October 2, 1968, the Mexican military had killed several hundred citizens protesting in Mexico City's Plaza de Tres Culturas (Plaza of Three Cultures)—to be afterward known as the Tlatelolco Massacre (Poniatowska 1998; Preston and Dillon 2004, 63–93). Later, Marcos was a radical university professor in Mexico City who decided that the only way to change Mexico was by violent revolution.[12] In 1984 he went to Chiapas with the intent of implementing a revolution in which a vanguard of educated middle-class urbanites go to the rural areas to organize a peasant army that is used to take state power.[13] When Marcos and two others arrived in the jungles of Chiapas, they founded the revolutionary army, Ejército Zapatista de Liberación Nacional (Zapatista Army of National Liberation, the EZLN). Quickly, however, they encountered great difficulty and hardship, both in adjusting to the lifestyle of the guerrilla and in working with the indigenous communities. Their Marxist message failed to resonate with indigenous communities that had already begun organizing themselves in the early 1960s. Facing failure, the early members of the EZLN went through a process of critical reflection that led to a readjustment of their strategy and underlying philosophy (Guillermoprieto 2002; Henck 2007).

This ability and effort to reflect critically and to adjust to circumstances became one of the most significant features of the Zapatista movement. This led to a new style of "revolution," defined by the slogan "*mandar obediciendo*" (govern by obeying). In this style, decisions were to be made by the communities and given to the EZLN command for implementation. This invests power in the communities, not the vanguard elite. Marcos spent much of the 1980s reeducating himself, learning some degree of indigenous languages, as well as the "*normas y costumbres*" (norms and customs) of the communities. He also learned how to become a spokesperson for the indigenous peoples and to serve as a translator between the indigenous world and the Western world—but to do so in a fashion that allowed indigenous people to control the discourse and representation of their growing movement, effectively revitalizing under force of arms (Gossen 1995).

Three important national events took place during the 1980s that set the stage for the Zapatistas to evolve from a movement to open rebellion in 1994. First, Mexico experienced a severe economic crisis, which led to its defaulting on debt payments in 1982. The default opened the door to the imposition of neoliberal economic reforms, a process that eventually led to the North American Free Trade Agreement (NAFTA) in 1994. Implementation of these neoliberal reforms undermined the PRI's credibility among the popular classes. Second, the PRI lost further legitimacy due to its pathetic response to the catastrophic 1985 earthquake. This failure led citizens to build a revitalized civil society.[14] These changes proved crucial to the Zapatistas in the 1990s because they allowed them to tap into a mobilized civil society with grievances against the PRI. Third, in 1988 the opposition ran on an explicitly antineoliberal platform. The PRI nearly lost the presidential election, but for electoral subterfuge. This, in turn undermined the legitimacy of the new president, Carlos Salinas. These three events created a national context favorable for a rebellion (Preston and Dillon 2004).

The January 1, 1994, rebellion was deliberately planned to coincide with the date that NAFTA went into effect. The initial spark occurred in 1992 when President Salinas reformed Article 27 of the Constitution of 1917. Article 27 had allowed the revolutionary state (which became the PRI) to restore communal property through a process of land reform. NAFTA required a standardized land tenure system between Canada, the United States, and Mexico, and Article 27 was a barrier. The 1992 reform allowed for the transfer of communal lands back into private property (De Janvry, Gordillo, and Sadoulet 1997).

The indigenous people in Chiapas clearly saw this as an assault upon their "*normas y costumbres*" since communal land tenure was a key feature of their traditional practices. As we have seen, communal ownership of land is quite common among indigenous peoples throughout the world. It is this clear focus on communal land ownership that makes the Zapatista movement so salient to discussions of indigenous resistance to globalization. According to the Zapatistas, NAFTA was their "death sentence" (El Comité Clandestino Revolucionario Indígena-Comandancia General del EZLN 1994). The 1992 reform coincided with the quincentennial celebrations of the "discovery" of the New World by Christopher Columbus. These celebrations engendered interconnected protests by indigenous groups throughout the hemisphere. Indigenous people in Chiapas were keenly aware of and influenced by the movements in other parts of Latin America, especially Ecuador and Bolivia. Rebellion was the Zapatista response to the neoliberal assault on communal land tenure.

On January 1, 1994, the 3,000 armed soldiers of the EZLN struck violently. They caught the Mexican military by surprise and were able to take control of six towns in the three main geographic areas: *Los Altos* (the highlands), *Las Canedas* (canyon lands), and *La Selva Lacandón* (the Lacandon jungle). They even captured briefly the provincial capital and tourist center of San Cristóbal de Las Casas. President Salinas ordered the Mexican military to counterattack. The army's response lasted ten days, killed at least 145 indigenous people, and touched off national protests against what was seen to be a legitimate indigenous uprising. The Zapatistas used the Internet to gain the attention of international civil society. National mobilization, international protests, and an impending review of NAFTA by the United States Congress made the state's war against the Zapatistas impossible to sustain. President Salinas declared a cease-fire on January 12. A prolonged process of negotiation and stalemate set in.

Negotiations started in February 1994 and reached their apex in February 1996 when both parties signed the San Andreas Accords. The negotiations were sponsored by two mediating bodies. The first, CONAI (National Commission for Intermediation), was organized and directed by Bishop Ruíz, and was perceived by the government as being biased toward the Zapatistas. The second, COCOPA (Legislative Commission of Conciliation and Dignified Peace in Chiapas), was composed of Mexico's leading political figures and was commissioned by the federal congress as part of legislation for finding a just peace in Chiapas. The process was defined by sophisticated political maneuvering, which replaced military conflict with a "war of words and symbols" over the place of indigenous peoples in Mexican society. The Zapatistas used the crisis of legitimacy to outposition and outsmart the Mexican government and to gain the high moral ground in the debates (Couch 2001, 246–248; Bruhn 1999).

For the Mexican ruling class 1994 was a nightmare (Fuentes 1997; Preston and Dillon 2004, 229–256). The Zapatista rebellion merged with an ever-moreaggressive civil society to force latent contradictions within the ruling PRI to the surface. Political violence and assassinations marred electoral politics. Ultimately Ernesto Zedillo took office in December 1994. Within weeks the peso devalued 60 percent, which caused a run on foreign investment and the prospect of total economic collapse. The Clinton administration bailed Mexico out with a $60 billion loan secured by Mexico's future oil revenues. Attached to the bailout were very direct instructions, including a memo from Chase Manhattan Bank for Zedillo to end the Zapatista uprising (Weinberg 2000, 146).[15] Thus, while Zedillo was negotiating with the Zapatistas he was also implementing a military strategy to defeat them. Although the political crisis subsided, these events signified the demise of the PRI's domination of Mexican politics. In July 2000, a conservative opposition party leader, Vicente Fox, won the presidency.

Prolonged, multifaceted negotiations led to the San Andreas Accords. The accord only reached agreement on one of the negotiating points. It formally recognized the cultural rights of indigenous people in Mexico and would constitutionally make Mexico a plural-ethnic state, one where indigenous people would have autonomy to practice their "*normas y costumbres*" within their communities. This would explicitly include recognition of indigenous practices toward land and the use of natural resources, including oil, water, forests, and minerals. Autonomy meant that indigenous peoples had the right to decide how such resources would be utilized (Díaz-Polanco 1997; Navarro and Hererra 1998; Nash 2001; Esteva 1999). This would, in effect, have given Mexican indigenous peoples rights analogous to those held by treaty in the United States—despite Mexico's lack of a tradition of treaties.

The San Andreas Accords was a stunning victory for the Zapatistas: the state had agreed to their demands. Indigenous autonomy, however, was in clear contradiction to Mexico's commitment to neoliberalism, especially the provisions of NAFTA. The San Andreas Accords put President Zedillo in an impossible position. Under pressure from the United States and multinational corporations, he was compelled to betray the agreement his government had signed by subsequent revisions to which he knew the Zapatistas would never agree. This betrayal came in December 1996. It led to a stalemate. The Zapatistas refused to negotiate further until the government implemented the agreement.

During this process the Zapatistas manifested remarkable political ingenuity. First, they built upon the support of national and international civil society in a series of *encuentros* (gatherings or encounters similar to conventions) and plebiscites. The *encuentros* were designed to foster democratic participation in their movement and to highlight the undemocratic nature of the Mexican political system. These were highly successful events that kept the Zapatistas in the headlines and sustained their high moral ground. Second, the Zapatistas also moved to consolidate control over territory gained during the initial 1994 rebellion through the formation of thirty-eight formally autonomous communities independent of the Mexican state. These communities formed five municipal centers called *Aguascalientes* after a town where Mexicans rewrote their constitution during the Mexican Revolution (1910–1920). Third, they continued to utilize the Internet to manipulate media coverage in a propaganda war that kept the Mexican political elite off balance and greatly entertained civil society (Cleaver 1998; Froehling 1997; Hellman 1999; Arquilla and Ronfeldt 2000; Swett 1995).

The Mexican state responded with a strategy of low intensity conflict (LIC). An LIC is a war of attrition designed to demoralize and divide the enemy. Tactics include disrupting community economic production; psychological operations aimed at terrorizing a population into inaction through rumors of invasion, misinformation, and death threats; the use of military maneuvers to harass and intimidate the base of support; economic rewards such as food, health clinics, and new schools for those who turn against the enemy; and the use of paramilitary squads to carry out political violence such as targeted assassinations[16] (Pineda 1996; Marin 1998; Global Exchange 2000).

All told, Zedillo positioned 60,000 troops in Chiapas. These forces were one-third of Mexico's armed forces. They remain in Chiapas today. Between 1998 and 2000 the army expelled at least 150 international observers. This paramilitary violence exploded in December 1997 in the Acteal Massacre, when death squads affiliated with PRI murdered forty-five indigenous people. Despite its sophistication, the LIC strategy failed to defeat the Zapatistas (Centro de Derechos Humanos Fray Bartolomé de Las Casas A.C. 2005).

The election of Vicente Fox from the conservative PAN (National Action Party) in July 2000 followed the PRI loss of the governorship of Chiapas in August of that year, which undermined the local mechanisms of domination and control that had been in existence since the Mexican Revolution. During the presidential campaign Fox boasted that he could solve the Chiapas situation in fifteen minutes. The Zapatistas accepted Fox's offer when he took office in December. They asked for three indications of goodwill to resume negotiations: removal of all military checkpoints, release of all Zapatista political prisoners, and forwarding the San Andreas Accords to Congress. Fox responded by implementing all three—but only partially. Fox's main strategy was to continue the LIC strategy of attrition and to avoid any major event that would give the Zapatistas the political upper hand that they enjoyed with the Zedillo administration.

The Zapatistas' response to Fox's forwarding of the San Andreas Accords to Congress was remarkable. They organized a three-month-long caravan through Mexico's southern, most indigenous states, which climaxed on March 12, 2001, in a rally in the Zocalo, the central plaza in Mexico City, the most politically symbolic place in all of Mexico. The caravan was designed to mobilize civil society in support of making the San Andreas Accords into an indigenous law, which would require amending the constitution of 1917. The caravan met with unprecedented support, especially with *Pueblos Indios* in Oaxaca and many other states. The Zapatistas overshadowed Fox in the national attention. Fox was outfoxed. The Zapatista "leadership" participated in every moment of the caravan, making speeches and enjoying their contact with civil society outside of Chiapas.

They arrived in Mexico City as an armed revolutionary movement seeking to transform Mexico without taking state power. The moment symbolized all that was new and different about the Zapatistas. Their arrival met with no repression because of the immense popular support they enjoyed. The climax came when the Zapatistas were permitted to address Congress. Symbolic of the movement, they selected the lowest person in Mexico's race, class, and gender hierarchy of power, an indigenous woman, Commandante Ramona, to make the speech. Photographs of members of Congress revealed facial expressions of intense disapproval.

The Mexican Congress passed the indigenous law in April 2001, but without the provisions extending autonomy to indigenous peoples. Mexico's indigenous peoples organized in opposition and made a major effort to block the law from becoming part of the constitution. They failed. After the constitution was amended, indigenous peoples attempted multiple court challenges, which the Mexican Supreme Court refused to hear.

The Zapatista response to this defeat took nearly two years to formulate. It came as the Juntas de Buen Gobierno (Good Government Committees) in August 2003. Each of the five *Aguascalientes,* now renamed *Caracoles* (seashells), has a junta. Each member community has a junta member. The junta rotates positions every ten days in order to distribute representation and power. The juntas serve as a municipal administration and act as a conflict-resolution mechanism. The juntas approve or reject all initiatives undertaken within an autonomous community. In essence, they implement the San Andreas Accords within territory controlled by the Zapatistas. The juntas, however, were also a response to the demands of ten years of open rebellion, especially the problem of reproducing resistance in the face of LICs. The Zapatistas were losing members, as some individuals were tempted to accept government handouts, something not allowed within the movement (Stahler-Sholk 2005).

Making the juntas was one way the Zapatistas faced the problem of fence sitting, as some communities were not fully committed to the struggle, yet were clearly benefiting from the Zapastistas' revolution. A major component of solidifying their base also involved the movement's relationship with nongovernmental organizations (NGOs), domestic and international. NGOs have their own agendas, which do not always correspond to those of the Zapatistas despite intent of solidarity. Furthermore, many NGOs have little to no mechanism for accountability, a situation at odds with the fundamentals of autonomy. With formation of the juntas, the Zapatistas redefined the working rules with NGOs by placing each NGO in a position subordinate to the juntas. For many NGOs, this consolidation of power and reworking of the rules of engaging the Zapatistas was a rude awakening.

The juntas enjoy considerable legitimacy. Non-Zapatista communities, for example, often go to them for conflict resolution instead of the Mexican state, because they know the Zapatistas are honest, and they follow indigenous *"normas y costumbres"* in the conflict-resolution process. (Plate 1.3.5 shows the "Junta de Buen Gobierno" at Oventik, the *Caracole* for *Los Altos* and the "Heart of the Zapatistas and the World" that also respects the Tzotzil language spoken in the community as shown in the picture.) The juntas, in sum, serve as the mechanism for the Zapatistas to endure the stalemate, to reproduce their revolution, and to continue to survive as indigenous people within the ravages of neoliberalism (Stahler-Sholk 2005).

Many observers recognize that the juntas are a risky strategy. If they garner too much power they could, in effect, become a governing vanguard party. Even though their goal is "power to" rather than "power over," if they become too effective they severely undermine the credibility of the Mexican state. They could become an insufferable challenge to the state and bring down its wrath in a "hot war" replacing LIC. At this writing, it is far too early to tell. Whatever the result, they have set a model for how to institutionalize indigenous practices (*normas y costumbres*). In this they are roughly similar to Navajo Peacemaker Courts (see Chapter 1, note 15). In the larger global arena, they demonstrate that there indeed are alternatives to neoliberal globalizations—alternatives that promote democracy and the maintenance of autonomy and a continual evolution of indigenous values and practices. Furthermore, one clear lesson from the Zapatistas is that pursuit of such goals requires autonomous, serious efforts by and in collaboration with local indigenous populations. The Zapatistas are not a boilerplate model for how to resist globalization. Rather, they model one kind of process for resisting it. There are other processes, in different situations throughout Latin America and internationally, as we have seen in other chapters (also see Stahler-Sholk, et al. 2005).

PLATE 1.3.5   Junta de Buen Gobierno (good government) at Oventik, Chiapas. (Photo courtesy of James V. Fenelon)

INDIGENEITY IN LATIN AMERICA: EXAMPLES FROM CENTRAL AND SOUTH AMERICA

Perhaps the most important observation among the preceding examples is to see how social justice issues are developed and defined by indigenous leaders and peoples when confronting dominant societies and their systems of suppression arising from a colonial past. The Zapatista indigenous resistance and revitalization movement has at times been revolutionary, and it has always been about change that supports autonomous communities. It is one attempt to fuse traditional indigenous social justice with responsive and reflexive forms of "governance." This is also an important example of resistance to neoliberalism and attempts at revitalization of communities for other indigenous struggles.

Zapatista-led communities began to organize in new ways that attempted to respect traditional culture, simultaneously sowing new patterns as well, including equality and involvement for women, direct challenges to local and state authorities, and community self-defense. Conflicts took various forms, forcing struggles with paramilitaries, government officials, military forts, restive localities, peasant organizations, and a depressed economy. The social changes made by the Zapatistas in developing the "Junta del Buen Gobierno" (Muñoz Ramírez 2003) were similar to the restorative justice systems of North American Indian Nations such as the Lakota, which were written into treaties in the nineteenth century (Fenelon 1998, 2002). These exemplify mediating social structures that place community relations as the highest value for indigenous peoples interacting with dominant societies and their states.

Mexico City meetings of scholars and indigenous leaders from throughout the Americas found that "government, based on its monopoly of violence ... was a hierarchical power structure." They identified an indigenous equivalent of authority (*autoridad*) where "communal authority is the whole community in its assembly," including elders and others sharing with decision making: "The central idea is to maintain harmony within the community" (América Profunda 2003). The governance panel at the América Profunda meeting concluded that at the grassroots level a "consensus of the peoples" was in formation (América Profunda initial findings 2003).[17]

Indigenous peoples make up significant population percentages of many Latin American countries, and in some cases, when grouped together, constitute a majority. This is the case in Bolivia, where the Indian movement Pachacuti (led by Felipe Quispe Huanca, an Aymara) initiated protests in Bolivia, connecting with unions and other protest groups, leading to the downfall of a sitting president.

> We believe in the reconstruction of the *Kollasuyu,* our own ancestral laws ... our own philosophy. ... We have ... our political heritage [that] can be successful in removing and destroying neoliberalism, capitalism and imperialism.
>
> It is community-based socialism ... that is what the brothers of our communities hold as a model. ... In the Aymara and Quechua areas, primarily in La Paz, we have been working since 1984 on fostering awareness of community-based ideologies.
> (Felipe Quispe Huanca, *Washington Times,* March 3, 2004)

Quispe Huanca speaks of movements arising throughout "Indian" Latin America, shared struggles that are based on a diversity of indigenous peoples and states. While each is reconstructing traditions unique to its own culture, and often relative to the specific lands they inhabit, they are also finding commonalities across many fronts, notably in opposition to cultural domination and corporate expansion over their lands. Even as the essence of a community, economic cooperatives, shared decision making, and land tenure relations vary, indigenous peoples rely on these foundations to resist in their individual situations, and increasingly within global networks (Muñoz Ramírez 2003).

Miskito people in Nicaragua are an example that shows many of these contentions in reverse. Here a socialist revolutionary government tried to impose conditions, boundaries, and forced removal on an indigenous people. The Sandinistas were, no doubt, responding partly to hegemonic forces that attempted to employ Miskito in Honduras to support the Contras and U.S. interests (Harff and Gurr 2004; Hale 1994). However, the central indigenous concerns were against incursions over a limited but existing sovereignty, for Miskito "autonomy" over their lands and sociopolitical life. Although the majority of indigenous struggle is against neoliberal and state politics, heavily involved with capitalist exploitation and inside increasingly globalized systems, pressures to suppress resistance occur in noncapitalist states as well. There is speculation that these are less explicitly invasive and not as likely to be culturicidal. Nonetheless, these can rise to the level of genocide, and they have done so in the twentieth century.

The Miskito conflict erupted when Sandinista military forces attempted to suppress their Moravian-based religious practices that included their traditional culture and language. Miskito had resisted incorporation into the Nicaraguan and colonial systems preceding the U.S.-backed dictator Somoza, mostly in a live-and-let-live relationship that resembled conditions in Chiapas. Additionally, there had been significant inter-marriage with slave-descent African people, interjecting some race and racism into their relations with the dominant *mestizo* groups. When the Sandinistas had successfully led a socialist rebellion, Miskito leaders viewed them as another dominant group in patterns worked out over the past 400 years. Initially, schooling was bilingual and cross-culturally conscious, as were the local politics, and many thought a socialist orientation toward land and property would work out well. However, when political leaders attempted ideological indoctrination combined with party leadership, friction developed. When their traditional culture was suppressed, along with lack of respect for their councils and collective systems, they became more open to forming resistance groups. The Sandinistas, under Cuban and Soviet influence, attempted to relocate villages near the Rio Coco basin bordering with Honduras, and they went into open armed rebellion (Ortiz 1984).

Miskito forces operated in ways similar to the Lakota resistance in the nineteenth century, forming small groups with mobile bases and significant support from the rural villages (Reyes and Wilson 1992). These forces demanded autonomy for their peoples, insisting on traditional land tenure and justice systems. After two years of internecine warfare, the Sandinistas agreed to the Zelaya Norte Autonomous Zone for the Miskito, as long as their military operated small bases to observe Contra activity.

When Daniel Ortega and the FMLN (Farabundo Martí National Liberation Front) lost the elections in 1990, this autonomous region again became heavily marginalized, within an economy moving into an economic depression without American support, at least partly because of the breakup of the Soviet Union and containment of the Cuban influences. This demonstrates that globalization can have just as powerfully a negative effect over indigenous peoples involved in struggle with anticapitalist states.

Ecuador is an outstanding example, with recent protests and insurrection rising to levels of revolutionary activity, some of it in concert with mainstream military forces, leading to the Quito accords and ultimately a broken alliance. Indigenous peoples are often in the middle of social unrest and rebellion, especially when there are high numbers and they are well organized. Unfortunately, all too often they are left out of resolutions and agreements arising out of the conflict. This marginalization has been a distinctive feature of indigenous social movements, and when accompanied with cultural suppression and oppression has caused revitalization movements to arise. Usually the dominant society reacts with military pacification reminiscent of the *conquista* hundreds of years ago. Leon Zamosc (1994) finds that in Ecuador, as the Quechuan-speaking peoples made greater alliances, their demands "to redefine citizenship" to recognize Indian rights to cultural and political autonomy were seen "at odds with both the model of liberal democracy being enjoined by political elites and the dominant perceptions of national identity in Latin America" (p. 39).

As Quispe Huanca described earlier and Evo Morales speaks to as the elected head of Bolivia, and as traditionalists throughout the history and the current reality of the United States and Canada's indigenous nations have struggled with, it is the essence of community, economic cooperatives, traditional decision making, and land tenure relations that may sometimes lead to violent uprising or perhaps a more localized economic reorganization. Yet indigenous peoples rely on these foundations to resist in their individual situations and within global networks (Muñoz Ramírez 2003; Sklair 2002). These new movements have collective orientation toward communities that are transparently antiglobalization, and specifically target neoliberalism as modern "evil" for the poor, indigenous, marginalized peasants making up their constituency. Examples such as coca leaf growing in Bolivia—disconnected from U.S. cocaine markets—as indigenous horticultural practices, challenge regional dominance and hegemony operated by corporate economic practices.

As noted earlier (Bonfil Batalla 1996, 88), one of the basic relationships of indigenous peoples is having a relationship to the land. This relationship is often sacred, rarely has direct economic value, and is usually held collectively rather than by individual ownership. Mayan-descent peoples in Guatemala and in the states of Chiapas and Oaxaca, Mexico, are moving away from Liberation Theology to new indigenous "Liberation Philosophy," which is partly based on traditional understandings of culture, land, and community.[18] These are epistemological movements that reject not only the hierarchy of European social orders but also the very nature of their social organization. This orientation to the land is in direct opposition to how modern, capitalistic society approaches land, with direct economic values and individual title: "The larger problem for the Indians was the struggle against breaking up the communal lands. The Liberals made private property sacred. ... The communal ownership of land in Indian communities became an obstacle to be removed (Bonfil Batalla 1996, p. 100).

Invasive systems want to take over the land, stratify the economy to build a power elite, centralize political systems into hierarchies they control, and relate all social issues to ever-larger urban areas that dominate in all arenas the surrounding communities. Because indigenous peoples utilize alternative systems of social organization and do not dissolve relationships, they are seen as obstacles, and if they resist, they are seen as "enemy."

In seeing the "Indian as enemy," Bonfil Batalla observes (1996, 103–104) "the radical denial of the imaginary Mexico. The struggle over land involved one side, which wanted free trade and individual property, while the other side protested the land was communal and inalienable." With this we see how the historically developed concepts of the "hostile" against the U.S. conquest or domination are fully realized in many twenty-first-century Latin American conflicts. We also observe how important such racist icons and symbology are in American society, why they are fought over in many universities and social institutions by dominant groups, and how they connect with hegemonic histories and struggles over racialized imagery. Eric Langer (2003, xiii) finds that a "racist ideology" placing indigenous peoples at the bottom of Latin American societies, and by government policy, was accompanied by a greater push to dominate indigenous groups for the consolidation of territory by states. Autonomy movements such as the Zapatistas in southern Mexico and Aymara in Bolivia have become typified as "socialist" or even as "terrorist" in nature, even though they actually represent over 500 years of indigenous struggle in the Americas.

In describing the modern constructs of empire, George Steinmetz describes the early steps in the process: "colonialism entails the seizure of sovereignty from locals and the formation of a separate colonial state apparatus" (2005, 344). But countering that, recently elected Bolivian president Evo Morales (an Aymara "Indian") has stated, "With the unity of the people, we're going to end the colonial state and the neoliberal model." Morales went on to speak for indigenous peoples throughout the Americas: "The time has come to change this terrible history of looting our natural resources, of discrimination, of humiliation, of hate" (Associated Press 2006).[19]

CONCLUSIONS, REDEFINITIONS, SPECULATIONS, AND QUESTIONS

Whereas the United States had formal treaties with indigenous peoples until 1871, when they were replaced with agreements, Mexico seldom used either device.

Although the U.S. government usually abrogated and degraded treaties and pressured Native Americans to assimilate, treaty rights and sovereignty remained as tools for pursuing collective rights, conditional, of course, on sociopolitical survival. The San Andreas Accords, though derailed, were an attempt to negotiate similar rights to the Zapatistas. It is interesting that the accord would have formalized the right to retain cultural practices, *normas y costumbres,* obviating attempts at forced assimilation and the right to collective land ownership. Thus "self-determination" in the United States and "autonomy" in Mexico are the most recent forms of the continuing struggle to maintain separate political and cultural communities, even while participating in the larger state system. (Plate 1.3.6, taken outside Toluca not far from Mexico City, shows government leaders being blessed in a local indigenous ceremony, before an important conference on civil rights.) In pursuing this goal, indigenous peoples are pressuring states to become explicitly multiethnic. This is a fundamental assault on the concept of the need for a nation-state and nation-building. With the strong emphasis on collective ownership of land and maintenance of traditions, this is also a reaction to and an assault on the cultural aspects of globalization, what Sklair (2002) has called the "culture-ideology of consumerism."

SEE PRINTED BOOK FOR ORIGINAL ART

PLATE 1.3.6 Government leaders blessed by indigenous leaders at a congreso outside Toluca, Mexico. (Photo courtesy of James V. Fenelon)

Comparison of the Latin American cases with those from the United States further underscores the role of treaties and sovereignty in state-indigenous relations. These examples from Mexico further show the importance of widely divergent colonial histories in the shaping of identities and in engendering different forms of resistance. What begins to emerge is that the immense variety of forms of indigenous activism and resistance to colonization and assimilation is the consequence of complex interactions between the history of colonial relations and the specific forms of local social organization. The underlying unity is a continuous effort by indigenous peoples to maintain some level of autonomy and, where possible, legal sovereignty to manage their own affairs. Their sovereignty is becoming increasingly problematic, not only for indigenous peoples but also for all states in dealing with an increasingly globalized and transnational capitalism (Sklair 2002).

Another obvious and very interesting aspect of these examples is how, in the case of the Zapatistas, armed rebellion against the state has turned both nonviolent and into an effort to implement local control by providing much-needed culturally sensitive mediating services. It remains to be seen whether these efforts will be seen by the state and civil society as attempts at taking responsibility or as attempts to erode the power of the state. Movements have risen and receded over the past 500 years, some successful, others less so, with mixed results. Those indigenous peoples who have survived these conflicts have adapted to changing systems of domination, have resisted in key cultural areas, and usually have attempted to revitalize their sense of indigeneity. These have nearly always included cultural constructs around land tenure, collective distribution, traditional group leadership, and a strong focus on the community. Increasingly this has also meant claims for autonomy of one sort or another, especially in the area of resisting many neoliberal economic forces attempting to penetrate their region, in forms of corporatism and labor consumerism that disrupt the traditions and lifestyles that have sustained them for half a millennium of resistance and revitalization.

We have seen how the Zapatistas have energized indigenous resistance and formation in Mexico and elsewhere in Latin America, comparing that with short discussions of how other *Pueblos Indios* have fared, and some movements have formed. Increasingly, local leadership is making alliances within their states and in regional interactions, as we have identified with Bolivia and Ecuador. The example of Miskitos in Nicaragua indicates that it is not solely capitalism that is at issue, but also modernity per se. In many ways this is the legacy of the Enlightenment and its hubris that European states are somehow the best form of human society—a proposition that indigenous peoples have always rejected. The same example, however, does indicate that governmental forms that are not tightly harnessed to neoliberal globalization may be less adamant in their attempts to transform indigenous peoples.

Last, but far from least, the cases we have presented here underscore how theories of racialization, the social construction of race and ethnicity in general, and indigeneity specifically are severely distorted when they rely solely on the study of processes in the United States. The converse also applies. Theories of social construction of race, ethnicity, and indigeneity based solely on Latin American cases are also distorted. Again we see complex interactions among states, historical processes, and aboriginal indigenous social organizations in the ways these concepts and practices are socially constructed and transformed over time. And again, we see that these differences give rise to different forms of resistance and revitalization. Finally, the underlying unity in all this variation is the continuing struggle for survival and some degree of autonomy on the part of indigenous peoples. The election of Evo Morales on a unity platform explicitly to support indigenous groups in Bolivia is one indication of how these movements have adapted to political realities and changing circumstances in their countries, and are alienated by and struggling against neoliberalism with its notions of private property and corporatization.

With these discussions in mind, we now turn to reexploration of the situations of indigenous peoples in the United States.

NOTES

1. The term *indigeneity* has emerged in addition to, and as a replacement of, other similar terms such as indigenousness, indigenous identities, and indigenous cultures.
2. The use of the term "X social movements," whether X is replaced by "transnational" or "new," is fraught with intellectual land mines. We stated our position in Hall and Fenelon 2008 and in subsequent paragraphs. Glen Kuecker (2004) argues that the expression "new social movements" refers to the changed contexts of contemporary struggles that use new tactics and strategies of resistance. The collection edited by Stahler-Sholk, Vanden, and Kuecker 2008 provides many insightful discussions of movements in Latin America.
3. Tilly often does study much older movements, but not indigenous movements.
4. Described as "culturicide" in Fenelon 1998.
5. Briefly, "race" is in the eye of the beholder, not an objective fact. Cavalli-Sforza and Cavalli-Sforza 1995 via detailed exhaustive biological examination demonstrate that there are no sharp lines between the so-called races, and that each blends into the other through gradual and virtually imperceptible increments. Thus, the demarcation of "races" is socially determined. This, however, does not mean that they are arbitrary or capricious. There is a loose coupling to phenotypical manifestation, but it is both very loose and quite variable through time and space. For further discussion, see Smedley 1999, Omi and Winant 1994, Nagel 1996, and Hall 2004.
6. Scholars argue as to the exact origin and contemporary usage of the term *ladino,* though most see at least passing reference to the collusion of *La Malinche* with Cortez and the ensuing "mixed-blood" midlevel bureaucrats and administrators who ran the country. Over time, the term came to refer to Europeans, that is, putatively lighter-skinned and Spanish-speaking persons. Most observers do not find it in use today.
7. In New Mexico, in particular, the racialization of Hispanic identity has a long and complex history that is at considerable variance with usage elsewhere in the United States. On New Mexico, see Nostrand (1980, 1984, 1992, 2003); for parallel changes in Texas, see Montejano (1981, 1987); for California see Pitt 1966; Acuña 1988; and Barrera 1979 compares and contrasts all three.
8. See Stahler-Sholk et al. 2008, especially part 4 (pp. 147–211), for further discussions of the roles of race and ethnicity in Latin American social movements.
9. Uprisings in Oaxaca City in the last decade of the twentieth century and first decade of the twenty-first century, and their violent suppression, are near-perfect representations of these ongoing struggles that entail traditionalist indigenous groups, urbanized poor and working class, and social change agents, all challenging an entrenched elite who answer to Mexico City rather than its citizens; see http://www.ccha-assoc.org/oaxaca07/narrative.htm for more details, accessed December 11, 2008.
10. Álvarez Fabela was a university student who went on a civil society caravan to deliver material aid in the highlands. His group arrived a couple of days before the massacre. His book is *the* definitive account of what happened before, during, and after. It carefully documents the events through eyewitness accounts.
11. Two important caveats need to be made here. First is that Bishop Ruíz worked more for indigenous peoples than the government and paid a heavy cost for that, both with the PRI and later the Catholic Church. Also, eventually liberation theology itself underwent a strong reorientation, which local leaders in Chiapas have referred to as "liberation philosophy" (stated in San Cristobal meetings with author Fenelon, December 2003).
12. Marcos started university in 1977 and finished his philosophy degree in 1980. He started teaching at UAM (Universidad Autonoma Metropolitana) in 1979 and left for Chiapas in 1984. The Post Tlatelolco setting was when the left in Mexico went underground and turned to armed revolutionary movements and guerrilla warfare because the path of democratic change was completely shut down in 1968. Marcos gained his political education in this radicalized setting and was heavily influenced by the theoretical developments of poststructuralism as it pertained to the strategy and tactic of

revolutionary change (Henck 2007). Marcos said, "I'm definitely post-'68, but not the core of '68 ... I was a little kid. But, I do come from everything that followed" (Henck 2007, 14).

13. This is often called the Guevarrista model after Argentine revolutionary Ché Guevarra (Childs 1995; Johnston 2000). Chirot (1977, 1986) argues that the most radical socialist revolutions in the twentieth century grew out of an alliance between what he calls "westernized intellectuals" (local people either educated in Western universities or their outposts in the West) and rural peasants. This is a common world-systems explanation for such revolutions and in part accounts for the popularity of the Guevarrista model.

14. *Civil society* is a term referring to a situation in which citizens act politically but independent of state or party structures. For a fuller discussion, see http://pages.britishlibrary.net/blwww3/3way/civilsoc.htm, accessed December 11, 2008.

15. The text of this memo is as follows:

"It is difficult to imagine that the current environment will yield a peaceful solution. Moreover, to the degree that the monetary crisis limits the resources available to the government for social and economic reforms, it may be difficult to win popular support for the Zedillo administration's plans for Chiapas. More relevant, Marcos and his supporters may decide to embarrass the government with an increase in local violence and force the administration to cede to Zapatista demands and accept an embarrassing political defeat. The alternative is a military offensive to defeat the insurgency which would create an international outcry over the use of violence and the suppression of indigenous rights. ... While Chiapas, in our opinion, does not pose a fundamental threat to Mexican political stability, it is perceived to be so by many in the investment community. The government will need to eliminate the Zapatistas to demonstrate their effective control of the national territory and of security policy" (Weinberg 2000, 146).

16. The Chiapas LIC was implemented by large numbers of Mexican special forces who had trained at the School of the Americas at Fort Benning, Georgia, after January 1, 1994, paid for with the money of U.S. taxpayers (Weinberg 2000, 172–174).

17. "Consensus of the Peoples" (América Profunda 2003) includes the headings Radical Pluralism, Personal Dignity, Autonomy, New Political Regime, Subordinate the Economy, Radical Democracy, Conviviality, Communality, Create a New World, Autonomy in Exchange, Socialization, and Service and Reciprocity (defined in document).

18. This was reported to author Fenelon in 2003 meetings in San Cristobal, Chiapas, by an anonymous representative of the local leaders in support of social change and struggle by the Zapatistas.

19. Also in Forero and Rohter 2006.

RECOMMENDED READINGS

Barrera, Mario. 1979. *Race and Class in the Southwest: A Theory of Racial Inequality.* Notre Dame, IN: University of Notre Dame Press.

> A classical treatment of the legacies of colonial Hispanic concepts of race and ethnicity as manifested in the southwestern United States.

Farris, Nancy M. 1984. *Maya Society Under Colonial Rule: The Collective Enterprise of Survival.* Princeton, NJ: Princeton University Press.

> This is a detailed account of how Mayans have resisted and survived through centuries of colonial rule.

Guy, Donna J., and Thomas E. Sheridan, eds. 1998. *Contested Ground: Comparative Frontiers on the Northern and Southern Edges of the Spanish Empire.* Tucson: University of Arizona Press.

> This edited collection compares and contrasts colonial processes under Spanish, and some Portuguese, colonization between New Spain and the "southern cone" of South America, that is, what is now Argentina and Chile, and parts of neighboring countries.

Hale, Charles. 1994. *Resistance and Contradiction: Miskitu Indians and the Nicaraguan State, 1894–1987.* Stanford, CA: Stanford University Press.
> This is one of the most thorough and authoritative histories of the Miskito Indians.

Henck, Nick. 2007. *Subcommander Marcos: The Man and the Mask.* Durham, NC: Duke University Press.
> A recent, excellent biography of Marcos.

Muñoz Ramírez, Gloria. 2008. *The Fire and the Word: A History of the Zapatista Movement.* San Francisco: City Lights.
> Reports the struggles of the Zapatistas in Chiapas from their own perspective, a revised version of the Ramírez 2003 cited in the text.

Web Resources

Global Exchange: The San Andrés Accords, http://www.globalexchange.org/countries/americas/mexico/SanAndres.html (accessed December 11, 2008).

Zapatista Network, http://www.zapatistas.org/ (accessed December 11, 2008).

BIBLIOGRAPHY

Álvarez Fabela, Martin. 2000. *Acteal de los mártires: Infamia para no olvidar.* Mexico City, Mexico: Plaza y Valdés.

América Profunda. 2003. América Profunda colloquium, December, Mexico City, Mexico.

Arquilla, John, and David Ronfeldt. 2000. *Swarming and the Future of Conflict.* Santa Monica, CA: Rand Corporation.

Associated Press. 2008. "Congress May Apologize to American Indians." Diverse: Issues in Higher Education, February 22, http://www.diverseeducation.com (accessed October 9, 2008).

Blanton, Richard, Stephen A. Kowalewski, Gary Feinman, and Laura M. Finsten. 1993. *Ancient Mesoamerica: A Comparison of Change in Three Regions,* 2nd ed. New York: Cambridge University Press.

Bonfil Batalla, Guillermo. 1996. *Mexico Profundo: Reclaiming a Civilization.* Translated by Phillip A. Dennis. Austin: University of Texas Press.

Bruhn, Kathleen. 1999. "Antonio Gramsci and the Palabra Verdadera: The Political Discourse of Mexico's Guerrilla Forces." *Journal of Interamerican Studies and World Affairs* 41, 2: 29–55.

Campbell, Howard. 1994. *Zapotec Renaissance: Ethnic Politics and Cultural Revivalism in Southern Mexico.* Albuquerque: University of New Mexico Press.

Carmack, Robert M., Janine Gasco, and Gary H. Gossen. 1996. *The Legacy of Mesoamerica: History and Culture of a Native American Civilization.* Upper Saddle River, NJ: Prentice Hall.

Centro de Derechos Humanos Fray Bartolomé de Las Casas A. C. 2005. *La política genocida en el conflicto armado en Chiapas.* http://www.laneta.apc.org/cdhbcasas/genocidio/genocidio.htm.

Cleaver, Harry. 1998. "The Zapatista Effect: The Internet and the Rise of an Alternative Political Fabric." *Journal of International Affairs* 51, 2 (Spring): 621–640.

Collier, George A., with Elizabeth Lowery Quaratiello. 1999. *Basta! Land and the Zapatista Rebellion in Chiapas.* Oakland, CA: Food First Books.

Couch, Jen. 2001. "Imagining Zapatismo: The Anti-Globalization Movement and the Zapatistas." *Communal/Plural* 9, 2: 243–260.

Crosby, Alfred W., Jr. 1972. *The Columbian Exchange: Biological and Cultural Consequences of 1492.* Westport, CT: Greenwood Press.

De Janvry, Alain, Gustavo Gordillo, and Elisabeth Sadoulet. 1997. *Mexico's Second Agrarian Reform: Household and Community Responses.* La Jolla, CA: Center for U.S.-Mexican Studies, University of California, San Diego.

Díaz-Polanco, Héctor. 1997. *La rebelión Zapatista y la autonomía.* Mexico City, Mexico: Siglo Veintiuno Editores.

El Comité Clandestino Revolucionario Indígena-Comandancia General del EZLN. 1994. "Pliego de demandas." In *EZLN: Documentos y comunicados, 1 de enero/8 de agosto de 1994*. Mexico City, Mexico: Ediciones Era.

Esteva, Gustavo. 1999. "The Zapatistas and People's Power." *Capital and Class* 68: 153–182.

Farris, Nancy M. 1984. *Maya Society Under Colonial Rule: The Collective Enterprise of Survival*. Princeton, NJ: Princeton University Press.

Feinman, Gary M., and Linda M. Nicholas. 1991a. "The Monte Albán State: A Diachronic Perspective on an Ancient Core and Its Periphery." Pp. 240–276 in *Core/Periphery Relations in Precapitalist Worlds*, edited by Christopher Chase-Dunn and Thomas D. Hall. Boulder, CO: Westview Press.

——. 1991b. "New Perspectives on Prehispanic Highland Mesoamerica: A Macroregional Approach." *Comparative Civilizations Review* 24 (Spring): 13–33.

——. 1998. *Culturicide, Resistance, and Survival of the Lakota (Sioux Nation)*. New York: Garland Publishing.

——. 2002. "Dual Sovereignty of Native Nations, the United States, and Traditionalists." *Humboldt Journal of Social Relations* 27, 1: 106–145.

Foster, Michael S., and Shirley Gorenstein, eds. 2000. *Greater Mesoamerica: The Archaeology of West and Northwest Mexico*. Salt Lake City: University of Utah Press.

Froehling, Oliver. 1997. "The Cyberspace of 'War of Ink and Internet' in Chiapas." *Geographical Review* 87, 2 (April) 291–307.

Fuentes, Carlos. 1997 [1994]. *A New Time for Mexico*. Translated by Marina Gutman Castañeda. Berkeley: University of California Press.

Global Exchange. 2000. *Always Near, Always Far: The Armed Forces in Mexico*. San Francisco: Global Exchange.

Guillermoprieto, Alma. 2002. *Looking for History: Dispatches from Latin America*. New York: Pantheon Books.

Guy, Donna J., and Thomas E. Sheridan, eds. 1998. *Contested Ground: Comparative Frontiers on the Northern and Southern Edges of the Spanish Empire*. Tucson: University of Arizona Press.

Hale, Charles. 1994. *Resistance and Contradiction: Miskitu Indians and the Nicaraguan State, 1894–1987*. Stanford, CA: Stanford University Press.

Hall, Thomas D., and James V. Fenelon.2008. "Indigenous Movements and Globalization: What Is Different? What Is the Same?" *Globalizations* 4, 3 (September): 1–11.

Harff, Barbara, and Ted Robert Gurr. 2004. *Ethnic Conflict in World Politics*, 2nd ed. Boulder, CO: Westview Press.

Harvey, Neil. 1998. *The Chiapas Rebellion: The Struggle for Land and Democracy*. Durham, NC: Duke University Press.

Hellman, Judith Adler. 1999. "Real and Virtual Chiapas: Magic Realism and the Left." Pp. 161–186 in *Necessary and Unnecessary Utopias: Socialist Register 2000*, edited by Leo Pan-itch, and Colin Leys. New York: Merlin Press/Fernwood Press/Monthly Review Press.

Henck, Nick. 2007. *Subcommander Marcos: The Man and the Mask*. Durham: Duke University Press.

Krauze, Enrique. 2002. "Chiapas: The Indians' Prophet." Pp. 395–417 in *The Zapatista Reader*, edited by Tom Hayden. New York: Thunder's Mouth Press/Nation Books.

Kuecker, Glen. 2004. "Latin American Resistance Movements in the Time of the Posts." *History Compass* 2: 1–126.

Langer, Eric, ed. 2003. *Contemporary Indigenous Movements in Latin America*. Wilmington, DE: Scholarly Resources.

MacLachlan, Colin M., and Jaime E. Rodriguez. 1980. *Forging the Cosmic Race: A Reinterpretation of Colonial Mexico*. Berkeley: University of California Press.

Maldonado Alvarado, Benjamin. 2002. *Autonomia y Communalidad India, enfoques y propuestas desdeOaxaca*. INAH, Secretaria de Asuntos Indigenas, Oaxaca, Mexico: CEDI.

Mallon, Florencia. 1997. *Peasant and Nation: The Making of Postcolonial Mexico and Peru*. Berkeley: University of California Press.

Marin, C. 1998. "Plan del ejercito en Chiapas desde 1994." *Proceso* (January 4): 6–11.

McAdam, Doug, Sidney Tarrow, and Charles Tilly. 2001. *Dynamics of Contention*. Cambridge: Cambridge University Press.

McNamara, Patrick J. 2007. *Sons of the Sierra: Juárez, Díaz, and the People of Ixtlán, Oaxaca, 1855–1920*. Chapel Hill: University of North Carolina Press.

Meyer, Jean. 2000. *Samuel Ruiz en San Cristóbal*. Mexico: Tusquets.

Mörner, Magnus. 1967. *Race Mixture in the History of Latin America*. New York: Little, Brown.

_____. 1973. "The Spanish American Hacienda: A Survey of Recent Research and Debate." *Hispanic American Historical Review* 53, 2 (May): 183–216.

_____. 1983. "Economic Factors and Stratification in Colonial Spanish America with Special Regard to Elites." *Hispanic American Historical Review* 63, 2 (May): 335–369.

Muñoz Ramírez, Gloria. 2003. *EZLN: 20 y 10, el fuego y la palabra*. Mexico, DF: La Jornada Ediciones [rev. ed.: Muñoz Ramírez, Gloria. 2008. *The Fire and the Word: A History of the Zapatista Movement*. San Francisco: City Lights].

Nash, June. 2001. *Mayan Visions: The Quest for Autonomy in an Age of Globalization*. New York: Routledge.

Navarro, Luis Hernández, and Ramón Vera Herrera, eds. 1998. *Acuerdos de San Andrés*. Mexico: Ediciones Era.

Ortiz, Roxanne Dunbar. 1984. *Indians of the Americas: Human Rights and Self-determination*. New York: Praeger.

_____. 1985. "The Fourth World and Indigenism: Politics of Isolation and Alternatives." *Journal of Ethnic Studies* 12 (Spring): 79–105, 2: 113–120.

Pineda, F. 1996. "*La guerra de baja intensidad*." Pp. 173–196 in *Chiapas 2,* edited by Andres Barreda et al. Mexico: Instituto de Investigaciones Economicas.

Poniatowska, Elena. 1998. *La noche de Tlatelolco: Testimonios de historia oral*. Mexico: Ediciones Era.

Preston, Julia, and Sam Dillon. 2004. *Opening Mexico: The Making of a Democracy*. New York: Farrar, Straus, and Giroux.

Reyes, Reynaldo, and F. J. K. Wilson. 1992. *Rafaga: The Life Story of a Nicaraguan Miskito Comandante*. Norman: University of Oklahoma Press.

Rubin, Jeffrey W. 1997. *Decentering the Regime: Ethnicity, Radicalism, and Democracy in Juchitán, Mexico*. Durham, NC: Duke University Press.

Russell, James. W. 1994. *After the Fifth Sun: Class and Race in North America*. Englewood Cliffs, NJ: Prentice-Hall.

Sklair, Lelsie. 2002. *Globalization: Capitalism, and Its Alternatives,* 3rd ed. Oxford, UK: Oxford University Press.

Stahler-Sholk, Richard. 2005. "Time of the Snails: Autonomy and Resistance in Chiapas." *NACLA: Report on the Americas* 38, 5 (March–April): 34–40.

Steinmetz, George, ed. 2005. *The Politics of Method in the Human Sciences: Positivism and Its Epistemological Others*. Durham, NC: Duke University Press.

Stephen, Lynn. 2002. *Zapata Lives! Histories and Cultural Politics in Southern Mexico*. Berkeley: University of California Press.

_____. 2005. *Zapotec Women: Gender, Class, and Ethnicity in Globalized Oaxaca*. Durham, NC, and London: Duke University Press.

Swett, Charles. 1995. *Strategic Assessment: The Internet*. Office of the Assistant Secretary of Defense for Special Operations and Low-Intensity Conflict (Policy Planning), http://www.fas.org/cp/swett.html (accessed July 14, 2008).

Valandra, Edward Charles. 2006. *Not Without Our Consent: Lakota Resistance to Termination, 1950–59*. Champaign-Urbana: University of Illinois Press.

Weinberg, Bill. 2000. *Homage to Chiapas: The New Indigenous Struggles in Mexico*. New York: Verso.

Womack, John. 1999. "Chiapas, the Bishop of San Cristóbal, and the Zapatista Revolt." Pp. 3–59 in *Rebellion in Chiapas: An Historical Reader,* edited by John Womack. New York: New Press.

Zamosc, Leon. 1994. "Agrarian Protest and the Indian Movement in the Ecuadorian Highlands. *Latin American Research Review* 29, 3: 37–68.

The Myth of Racial Democracy in Brazil

Constructing New Ethnic Spaces for Afro-Brazilians

Emily Jullié

INTRODUCTION

Popular belief suggests that Brazil is a multiracial country without prejudice, equally founded by Portuguese, African and Indigenous people. Often described as "The Myth of Racial Democracy", this social construction is not necessarily based on legitimacy. Accordingly, this paper intends to explore the myth's origins as part of Brazil's national reconstruction and present it as an invented tradition designed to incorporate Afro-Brazilians into white public space. Currently, the myth has undergone attack as it is said to have masked the prevalence of racism in legislation and education. However, deconstructing the myth is not a simple black and white issue, as other social factors play a role in the disenfranchisement of any given racial or ethnic group.

This paper begins by describing how Brazil was founded as a racial hierarchy, not a racial democracy and looks at several early viewpoints regarding miscegenation. Next, it explains how the myth adopted African cultural symbols in the construction of a national Brazilian identity, and served to disguise an underlying racism present in Brazilian society. Then, it discusses current affirmative action politics in public universities and suggests that reform begin at the primary school level instead, providing examples of social programs aimed at educating marginalized youths. Finally, it examines how deconstructing the myth recognizes African cultural contribution to the formation of Brazilian identity yet acknowledges the on-going presence of racial disparities and stresses the need for equitable social opportunities.

RACIAL HIERARCHY NOT RACIAL DEMOCRACY

Brazil was founded on the precept of racial hierarchy, as a white hegemony that profited from its domination over other ethnic groups. To illustrate, Portuguese colonizers subjugated the indigenous people and brought over African slaves to work the land. In fact, long before the Portuguese arrived in Brazil, discriminatory legislation had already been established in Portugal against Jews, moors and blacks; and when the Portuguese arrived, only widened those forms of prejudice.[1] Hence, slavery ruled the new world economy until an international debate forced people to reevaluate its morality. With its abolishment in Brazil in 1888 by the Golden Law *(Lei Áurea)*, a new ethnic space opened up, creating the following dilemma: What role would Afro-Brazilians play in the new national identity?

Scientific racism sought to answer this question, led by French aristocrat, Count Joseph Arthur de Gobineau. In his essay, *The Inequality of Human Races,* he argued that all races did not share the same origin, nor have similar physical or intellectual capabilities. Thus, he created a taxonomic system in order to classify the world's races into three categories: whites, yellows and blacks. Additionally, he attributed a country's downfall to racial mixing, or miscegenation, and felt that "civilization" did not necessarily create a civilized nation. He cited the Greek and Roman empires as prime examples of this cultural degeneration and believed that the larger a civilization became, the more tainted its blood and ambiguous its essence. *"Their mixture, while it ennobles the baser, deteriorates the nobler; a new race springs up, inferior to the one, while superior to the other".*[2]

Consequently, Gobineau's work in the mid 1800's shaped the thoughts of Brazilian authors, Silvio Romero and Nina Rodrigues, who witnessed the end of slavery and the emergence of a new national identity. In the minds of the elite, racial diversity represented a threat and a great obstacle in the construction of a nation that though itself to be white.[3] On the one hand, Romero believed that Brazil could still become a white nation and encouraged *branqueamento,* or the whitening society through racial mixing. Unfortunately for this theory, German and Italian immigrants failed to participate in *branqueamento* and intermarried amongst themselves, forming European colonies in southern Brazil. On the other hand, Rodrigues completely denounced miscegenation and felt that such a forced and imposed adaptation would provoke imbalances and disturbances in the national psyche.[4] Instead of uplifting society, it would denigrate it, bringing about perpetual impurity through genetic atavism. Moreover, Rodrigues

---

1   Roberto da Matta, p. 46.

2   Joseph Arthur de Gobineau, p. 160. This book may be found in English under two titles: *The Inequality of Human Races* or *The Moral and Intellectual Diversity of the Races*. This quote is taken from the latter.

3   Kabengele Munanga, p.54.

4   Raimundo Nina Rodrigues, p. 90.

pushed for legal reform that would designate unequal penal responsibilities due to the supposed differentiated moral consciousness and mental faculty amongst the races. Like Gobineau, he also proposed a racial classification system, listing whites at the top, blacks at the bottom and mulattos in the middle.

Although Gobineau's philosophies may have inspired earlier writers, nowadays these theories are thought to be positively antediluvian. Brazilian anthropologist, Roberto da Matta, has named Gobineau the father and true genitor of racial prejudice of any hierarchical society. He identifies his problem as not the existence of different races, only that these "races" obviously keep in their place and naturally not mix. *"Seu problema, conforme estou revelando, não era a existência de raças diferentes, desde que essas "raças" obviamente ficassem no seu lugar e naturalmente não se misturassem. Gobineau, como se vê, foi o pai, ou melhor, o verdadeiro genitor de um dos valores mais earns ao preconceito racial de qualquer sociedade hierarquizada* [5] Thus, adopting a triangular model of social hierarchy, the perfect society for Gobineau, is one where *"cada um sabe muito bem o seu lugar"*.[6]

MIXED HERITAGE: *A MESTIÇAGEM*

However, "knowing one's place" in a multiracial country like Brazil is not easy, due to the fact that skin colors range the color spectrum and races have intermingled for centuries. Ever since Portuguese arrival over five hundred years ago, the meaning of mestizo has suggested various possibilities. It could mean **caboclo** (indigenous and white), **mameluco** (indigenous or *caboclo* and white), **mulato** (black and white), **cafuzo** (black and indigenous), **cabrocha** (mulato and indigenous) or **pardo** (brown). Clearly, there are many possible combinations when examining the roots of Brazil.

As Sérgio Buarque de Holanda pointed out in his 1936 book *Raizes do Brasil,* even the Portuguese were of mixed blood given that they had previously established a custom of intermingling with the natives in Africa. He showed how the adulterated Portuguese bloodline earned them a poor reputation as a hybrid race, one with the highest concentration of black blood. The indigenous people of West Africa considered the Portuguese as almost their equals and they respected them much less than the other civilized people, thus making the distinction between Europeans and Portuguese.[7] Thus when they came to Brazil, Portuguese men mixed freely with the indigenous women and miscegenation was not condemned. Instead, it was governmentally supported in *Alvará de 4 de abril de 1755,* which conceded privileges to those who married native Brazilians. It stated that interracial couples would not receive any

---

5   Roberto da Matta, p. 39.

6   Ibid., p. 47.

7   Dr. Hans Günther, p. 82; cited in Sergio Buarque de Holanda, p. 52.

infamy due to their situation, neither for their children or their descendants, and were eligible for work preference, honor and dignity.[8]

Hence began the long tradition of racial mixing in Brazil, yet it was not until the 20th century that the mestizo was freed from stigmatization and celebrated in literature. Published in 1933, Gilberto Freyre's novel *Casa Grande e Senzala* unmasked *mestiçagem* and broke with tradition by forcing society to reevaluate racial roles. An instant success, it portrayed miscegenation as the true source of Brazilian culture and helped identify the mestizo as a powerful new breed, full of cultural vitality and tropical fertility. It illustrated how racial mixing played a decisive role in Portuguese expansion by allowing them to compensate for their small population in large-scale colonization over a vast territory.[9] Freyre speculated that long-term contact with Muslim culture in Africa had left its mark on Portuguese men by eroticizing the dark skinned image of the *mulher morena* and by glorifying the beauty of Afro-Brazil. As a result, the mestizo stopped being a social evil and instead became an attractive symbol of national progress.

CONSTRUCTING THE MYTH

Both literary works, *Raizes do Brasil* and *Casa Grande e Senzala,* represented a movement for social change that helped create a new national identity known as *brasilidade*. It not only included African culture, but reinvented it as a marketable product and symbol of Brazilian heritage, popularized though samba and *carnaval* parades. Presently considered the Brazilian music *par excellence,* samba is a relatively new rhythm to Brazil of foreign origin. Thought to have derived from the Kimbundo language spoken in northern Angola, the word *semba* means belly button and may come from a traditional folk dance where *"two dancers, leaving the circle, advance trippingly toward each other, and, when near enough, simultaneously thrust forward their stomachs so that they touch.*[10]

In his book, *Hello, Hello Brazil* Bryan McCann details the history of Brazilian samba, when urbanization in the early twentieth century brought migratory flux from the northern state of Bahia to Rio de Janeiro. With it, came Afro-Brazilian music and culture, and in 1932, the city's samba schools held their first parade. Originally a commercial venture sponsored by the newspaper, *Mundo Sportivo,* the parade was a way to sell papers outside soccer season.[11] As fervor for the festival caught on, by 1934 the Rio de Janeiro City Council decided to endorse it and enforced a new set of rules.

---

8   Ségio Buarque de Holanda, p. 58.

9   Gilberto Freyre, p. 84.

10   Heli Chatelain, cited in Luis da Camara Cascudo, p. 136.

11   Bryan McCann, p. 59.

Partly due to the national debate about *brasilidade,* government sponsorship sought to define samba's Brazilian identity and banned wind instruments, giving samba a predominantly percussion sound. Similarly, Bahian women dressed in traditional white dresses danced to patriotic themes in order to give the parade a truly "Brazilian" feel.

Thus, samba and *carnaval* parades promoted a positive image of Afro-Brazil and allowed black and mestizo musicians to participate democratically in the music industry despite then-social marginalization. *Sambistas* from Brazil's low income hillside neighborhoods were coveted for their unique melodies, which were generally sung by other artists on the air. According to McCann, these songwriters *"played crucial roles in shaping new cultural expressions, gaining cultural influence over the nation that stood in marked contrast to their continued marginalization in the economic and formal political spheres".*[12] Resultantly, their participation in the music industry only reinforced the rhetoric of racial democracy since their contributions served to mask discrimination.

BRAZILIAN RACISM: *RAÇISMO À BRASILIERA*

Adopting Afro-Brazilian symbols was one way for the dominating white elite to hide racial discrimination while maintaining the status quo. *Raçismo à brasileira* slapped on a politically-correct carnival mask, exalted Afro-Brazilian culture and welcomed samba and *carnaval* as national symbols. Embracing these new customs was a way of reinforcing social harmony by encouraging interracial identity. However, it also made prejudice a social taboo, which was difficult to identify and complicated to denounce.

In comparison to other countries like the United States and South Africa, Brazilian racism was a subtle manifestation. In the U.S., for example, the post-slavery era immediately created overt laws and systems intended to keep the colored man in his place. Jim Crow laws were in effect from 1876–1965 and officially enforced segregation politics by creating separate schools, eating establishments and seats on public transportation. Sharecropping, although not governmentally backed, was a form of economic prejudice in which wealthy plantation owners indentured former slaves to the land. Similarly in South Africa, whites dominated the social structure and implemented *apartheid* from 1948–1994. This racist system established separate rules for Indians, Coloreds and Blacks, who were forced to carry documentation at all times and suffered travel restrictions, work limitations and medical and educational inequalities. Mixed marriages were forbidden and interracial sex, a crime. Black South Africans were relegated to "homelands", where the majority of the population lived on the minority of the land. Clearly, such marked social injustice brought South African racism to an international focus. The practices in both countries were explicit and direct ways of

---

12   Ibid., p. 11.

maintaining racial hierarchy and produced world renowned leaders in the fight for human rights, Martin Luther King, Jr. and Nelson Mandela, respectively.

In contrast, Brazilian racism was a covert operation and functioned as an underlying discrimination. In 1963 in the United States, Martin Luther King, Jr. publicly held his famous his "I Have a Dream" speech. However, in 1964 in Brazil, freedom of expression was halted due to the military *coup d'etat* and subsequent dictatorship until 1985. During those dark years, it was forbidden to speak out against the government and people who did were killed, tortured or exiled. When black leader Abdias do Nascimento of the Pan African Movement spoke out against inequality, he was accused of importing problems from the U.S. to Brazil and was forced into exile in 1968 for his opposition to the authorities.[13] Thus, Brazilian racism was quietly swept under the rug, as more pertinent issues, like terrorism and security were brought to the national forefront.

Consequently, Abdias do Nascimento, Afro-Brazilian scholar and Professor Emeritus at the University of Buffalo in New York, was exiled abroad until 1981. During that time, he continued his investigation on the subject of race and in an essay entitled, "The Myth of Racial Democracy" he asks: *"Are the descendants of African slaves really free? Where do Brazilian blacks really stand in relation to citizens of other racial origins, at all levels of national life?"*[14] He criticizes Brazilian society and accuses it of creating "a *fabric of slogans about equality and racial democracy that has served to assuage the bad national conscience. Abroad, it presents our country as a model of racial coexistence; internally, the myth is used to keep blacks tricked and docile".*[15] Nascimento later returned to serve in the Brazilian Senate and was nominated for a Nobel Peace Prize in 2004. He recently passed away on May 23, 2011, at the age of 97.

THE POLITICS OF QUOTAS

In modern times, debates over social inequality have resurfaced as Afro-descendants and indigenous groups were given new rights in Brazil's 1988 Federal Constitution. Legislative reform recognized ethnic and cultural diversity, and the government's duty to protect the previously disenfranchised and incorporate them into national identity.[16] As retribution for prior exclusion, the constitution granted special scholarships and university quotas to Afro-Brazilian students. Comparative to affirmative action in the United States, quotas guaranteed a certain amount of college slots based solely on race.

---

13   Felipe Arocena, p. 4.

14   Abdias do Nascimento, p. 379.

15   Ibid, p. 380

16   Feipe Arocena, p. 6.

In 2004, the University of Brasilia was the first to implement quotas and reserved 20% of the slots for "black" students, as a way to privilege those who had suffered a historical injustice.[17] A panel of judges was established, whose function was to evaluate photos and determine if a student possessed black features, like full lips, curly hair or a flat nose. Some students with Afro-Brazilian grandparents were judged as not meeting the criteria and in a famous case between two twins, one was considered black while the other white. Not surprisingly, the process was highly subject to criticism as judges' decisions were based on looks alone, resulting in racial discrimination.

Determining race, however, is a subjective assessment as no scientific method accurately verifies it. Unlike the "one-drop rule" in United States, which considers a person to be African-American if they have just one drop of African blood, defining what "black" is in Brazil becomes harder to define due to *mestiçagem*. Approximately 87% of Brazilian "whites" have at least 10% of African ancestry.[18] The Brazilian Institute of Geography and Statistics (IBGE) divides race into five categories: blacks, whites, browns *(pardos)*, yellows[19] *(amarelos)* and indigenous. Current 2010 results list whites as the dominant group with 91,298,042 members; browns next with 65,318,092; blacks at 10,554,336; yellows, 761,583; and finally indigenous with 734,127.[20]

Nevertheless, census surveys generally use self-classification in order to decide group association. This choice is often based on ethnic identity rather than racial heritage and in 1976, the IBGE commissioned a study in response to complaints that they had received regarding the five limited categories mentioned above. The results yielded 134 different categories, which included categories such as: blue, green, orange, purplish, reddish, strawberry blonde, bronze, cinnamon and copper, just to name a few; *azul, verde, laranja, roxa, vermelha, ruiva, bronze, canela, cobre,* respectively.[21]

As such, critics like Ali Kamel, journalist and social scientist, have denounced the politics of quotas for dividing the issue into one of black and white, forcing students to choose a racial identity not necessarily representative of their ethnic heritage. Blacks and browns were combined in order to manipulate statistics for social gain and the figures presented in favor of quotas were thus the following. Among the 56.8 million poor, "blacks" composed 65.8%; yet upon closer inspection, they were only 7.1%, while *pardos* represented 58.7% of Brazil's impoverished.[22] Thus, the majority of the population disappeared, adopting a new racial identity in order to qualify for economic benefits.

---

17 Marcos Cho Maio & Ricardo Ventura Santos, p. 1.

18 Ali Kamel, p. 46.

19 People of Asian descent.

20 IBGE, 2010 Census.

21 IBGE, p. 386–390.

22 Ibid, p. 11.

Affirmative action, also referred to as positive discrimination, favors one ethnic group over another and denies opportunities to other economically disadvantaged students on the basis of race. What about the remaining 34.2% of the poor who also lack educational possibilities? Rather than propagate a new system of racial exclusion, a better solution would be to include all ethnic categories in a single disenfranchised group due to class. This way, the nation would not be torn between two races, and would acknowledge the rights of all ethnicities who have been forgotten in this national debate of black and white.

ELEMENTARY EDUCATIONAL REFORM FOR SOCIAL EQUALITY

The politics of quotas espouses the idea that Affo-Brazilians are racially discriminated against and for that reason, deserve a university advantage. However, the problem with guaranteeing college seats based on race, is that under-educated students will bring down the quality of education in national universities. Professors will be required to teach basic concepts to weaker students, while holding back knowledge from the advanced ones. As such, equal educational opportunities should be given long before college age and offered to all disadvantaged students based on need rather than race.

One solution is to focus on primary education, and in 1996 basic scholastic guidelines were reassessed in Law n 9.394, which has defined education as the obligation of family and state and dictates equal conditions, pluralism of ideas, respect to liberty, appreciation of tolerance and cultural diversity in the classroom.[23] It is noteworthy that the law encourages parental participation, taking into account that family may be detrimental to their children's progress. Despite the fact that the law mandates free elementary instruction, many children do not go to school because their parents may lack money for additional costs or even interest in schooling. Hence, educational disadvantage is often linked to financial limitation and social class, not just race. Unfortunately, intermediate education is not legally required in Brazil, and many low income families send their children off to work, resulting in increased drop-out rates and reduced graduation numbers. *"About half of Brazil's labor force either has no formal schooling or did not complete primary school, and only 37% of the population aged 16–18 is enrolled in secondary schools ".*[24]

Notwithstanding, this study recognizes racial disparities in education. A study by Psacharopoulous and Patrinhos revealed that Brazilian whites complete approximately 7.9 years of schooling, while students of mixed heritage (*pardos*) complete 5.4 and blacks, only 5.1.[25] Additionally, a recent survey by the IBGE concluded that public

---

23   Fernando Henrique Cardoso, I & II.

24   Aumary de Souza, p. 65.

25   Psacharopoulos and Patrinos, p. 12.

opinion indicates that color or race negatively influences the quality life. A total of 63.7% of Brazilians notice racial prejudice, with the highest concentration occurring in the federal district of Brasilia at 77%, felt particularly in the area of education. Throughout Brazil, women (66.8%) perceived it more than men (60.2%) and Brazilian youths between the ages of 25–39 (67.8%) and 15–24 (60.2%), felt the brunt of this discrimination. Areas in which it was most felt was in the workforce (71%), the justice and legal system (68.3%), in social spheres (65%) and in education (59%). These figures representing public perception of racial disparities clearly point out social inequity among the different groups.[26]

In order to close this educational gap, poor communities deserve the same privileges as rich ones and government programs have a responsibility to provide resources that could otherwise not be afforded. For example, *Bolsa Escola, Acessa São Paulo* and *ProJovem Urbano* create educational opportunities for underprivileged youths. In conjunction with UNICEF, Bolsa Escola gives a monthly cash stipend to low-income families on the condition that all of their school-age children attend class regularly. It has resulted in improved class performance and lower dropout rates, in addition to stimulating the local economy and improving health conditions.[27] State programs also contribute to underprivileged communities, like *Acessa São Paulo*, a digital inclusion project which has brought technology to poor neighborhoods by providing free use of computers in community centers. Additionally, it has encouraged an intellectual movement among disadvantaged area youths and emphasized the importance of community.[28] Finally, ProJovem Urbano promotes the social inclusion of Brazilians aged 18–29 who did not finish elementary education. It reinserts them in schools and the workforce, providing them with opportunities for human development and effective citizenship.

Therefore, until the issue of equality in primary education is addressed, the true disadvantage to students will continue to be ignorance rather than race. This is the case not only in Brazil, but internationally and explains why the United Nations aims to achieve universal primary education in Millennium Development Goal 2, second only to eradicating extreme poverty and hunger. Its target is to *"ensure that, by 2015, children everywhere, boys and girls alike, will be able to complete a full course of primary schooling"*.[29] Goal 3 aims to eliminate gender disparity in primary and secondary education, proving that educational disenfranchisement goes beyond race and socio-economics, even affecting gender.

---

26   Globo.com, 22/07/2011

27   Cristovam Buarque, p. 1.

28   Paloma Cotes, p. 1.

29   MDG Report 2010, p. 16.

EXAMINING THE MYTH

Popularly conceived as a retribution for past wrongs, racial democracy was not an intentional campaign launched on the Brazilian public. Instead, it functioned as an urban myth in the late 1920's, gained momentum through national symbols and was accepted due to its progressive optimism. Society readily accepted an idea that encouraged national pride in multicultural heritage and grouped all races together under *brasilidade*. Worthy of being incorporated into the country's belief system, a new tradition was invented.

In this way, myths do not describe realties, but serve to make sense of them. As such, the myth of racial democracy was society's reaction to historical injustice. According to Hobsbawm and Ranger in *The Invention of Tradition,* when cultures reinvent themselves, it represents a collective change in attitude and incompatibility with an old system, which in the case of slavery, was rigid, resistant to change, and incapable of modernization. According to this model, the myth of racial democracy legitimized minority status, established social cohesion and proposed new ideas, value systems and behaviors.[30] As such, myth does not signify untruth, but hope for a modern, multiracial identity and the end of discrimination. Therefore, if the myth of racial democracy serves as a direction in which to head, why deconstruct it?

Considering that it is not a historical truth, critics denounce the myth as a misrepresentation of reality. Professor Jessé Souza says it has not left its mark on those institutions responsible for the socialization, production and distribution of wealth and power, and that all political and economic institutions have been established by Iberian people.[31] Even ex-president Fernando Henrique Cardoso, who publicly boasts his Afro-Brazilian roots, dismisses the myth as being founded on "romantic visions" and encourages dismantling the structures, institutions and mentalities strengthened over centuries of social exclusion.[32] For that reason, if Brazil has always been a white racial hierarchy, racial democracy propagates fiction and confuses the public with mythical fantasies.

RECOGNITION AND IDENTITY

As people identify with each other through shared experiences, they build common manners of societal relations. Therefore, it is necessary to recognize cultural groups, giving dignity to their people and validating them among other members of society. Although elevating cultural symbols does show recognition, it does so only

---

30   Eric Hobsbawm & Terence Ranger, p. 17.

31   Jessé Souza, p. 137–144.

32   Fernando Henrique Cardoso, p. 15.

superficially since this does not alter political infrastructure nor foment political equality. Instead, it supports an untruth by ignoring the existence of racial disparities. Individual differences thus allowed, racial democracy would mean that all groups had equal rights, privileges and recognition.

Charles Taylor in *The Politics of Recognition* states that public acknowledgement is not a courtesy but a vital necessity. Whereas open prejudice hurts ethnic minorities, ignoring them is also detrimental, given that identity is formed by recognition or the absence of it. Furthermore, *"nonrecognition or misrecognition can inflict harm, can be a form of oppression, imprisoning someone in a false, distorted, and reduced mode of being."*[33] As such, minority groups still need representation in public spheres, like education and politics. Hence, the International Day for the Elimination of Racial Discrimination on March 21st helps foment social consciousness, along with the many Afro-Brazilian organizations that give voice to the movement and broach issues of social taboo.

CONCLUSION

Brazil reinvented itself in the 1920's with hopes of changing white hegemony. In the construction of a new national identity, the country adopted multicultural traditions and created ethnic spaces for Affo-Brazilians. Bom out of the desire for a better society, racial democracy aimed to change social stratification and contributed to the optimistic construction of a progressive new nation. Presently, however, attacks on racial democracy denounce the myth and taint its image with racism, ignoring the fact that the tradition was created to counteract it.

Although Brazil is not a racial utopia, its citizens have lived under the myth for most of the 20th century. Deconstructing it creates new ethic wounds, as in the case of quotas. Afro-descendants feel slighted for wrongs caused centuries ago, and students of mixed heritage change racial group in order to qualify for economic benefits. Other races are ignored, while divisions increase between blacks and whites. As a result, quotas offer educational opportunities based on race rather than economics and discriminate against non-black, underprivileged students.

Therefore, separate laws prioritizing students at university level are neither the answer to past social injustices nor the solution to the problem. Instead, equality at the primary school level is a better way to close the gap in educational disparities. All marginalized students, regardless of race, ethnicity or income deserve encouragement to attend and exceed at school.

In sum, ignorance is the enemy, not the myth of racial democracy. The myth represents a country of multiracial heritage and diverse ethnic backgrounds.

---

33   Charles Taylor, p. 25.

Deconstructing it destroys the idea of a singular Brazilian identity and creates new prejudice, by making race the leading factor of social disadvantage, when poverty, education and even gender play a part. Nevertheless, deconstructing it lays the groundwork for a more racially aware and socially progressive Brazil, by celebrating cultural groups' contributions to the national identity, as new ethnic spaces are created, pushing the previous boundaries of Brazilian identity.

WORKS CITED

Arocena, Felipe. "Multiculturalism in Brazil, Bolivia and Peru". *Institute of Race Relations, Vol. 49 (4) 1–21. Race & Class*. Los Angeles: Sage, 2008.

Buarque, Cristovam. *Bolsa Escola: Bridging Two Worlds*. World Bank: 2005.

Cardoso, Fernando Henrique. LEI N 9.394: Lei de Diretrizes e Bases. Brasilia: December 20, 1996.

Cardoso, Fernando Henrique. *"Mensagem do presidente da República por ocasiäo do Dia Internacional pela Eliminaçäo da Discriminaçäo Racial",* 21 mar, 2001. Cited in: Maggie, Yvonne. MAGGIE, Yvonne. "Mário de Andrade ainda vive? O ideário modernista em questäo". *Rev. bras. Ci. Soc.* [online]. 2005, vol.20, n.58 [cited 2011-04-30], pp. 5–25.

Chatelain, Heli. *Folk-Tales of Angola*. New York: Negro Universités Press, 1969. Cited in Cascudo, Luís da Câmara. *Made in Africa*. São Paulo: Global, 2002.

Cotes, Paloma. *Tabuleiropopular*. São Paulo: Época, December 13, 2004.

Freyre, Gilberto. *Casa Grande e Senzala*. Caracas: Biblioteca Ayachucho, 1977,

Globo.com. "Para 63,7% dos brasileiros, cor ou raça, influencia na vida, aponía IBGE", 2011.

Gobineau, Joseph Arthur de. *The Moral and Intellectual Diversity of the Races*. Philadelphia: J.B. Lippincott &Co., 1856.

Günther, Hans. *Rassekunde Europas*. Munich, 1926. Cited in Holanda, Sérgio Buarque de. *Raízes do Brasil*. 3 ed. Rio de Janeiro: Livraria José Olympio Editôra, 1956.

Hobsbawm, Eric & Ranger, Terence. *A invençäo das tradições*. Rio de Janeiro: Paz e Terra, 1984.

Holanda, Sérgio Buarque de. *Raízes do Brasil*. 3 ed. Rio de Janeiro: Livraria José Olympio Editôra, 1956.

Instituto Brasileiro de Geografía e Estadística. "What Color Are You?", 1976.

Instituto Brasileiro de Geografía e Estadística. *Sinopse do Censo Demográfico*, 2010.

Kamel, Ali. *Näo Somos Racistas: Urna reaçäo aos que querem nos transformar numa naçäo bicolor*. Rio de Janeiro: Nova Frontera, 2006.

Maio, Marcos Chor & Santos, Ricardo Ventura. "Política de cotas raciais, os "olhos da sociedade" e os usos da antropologia: o caso do vestibular da Universidade de Brasilia (UnB)". *Horizontes Antropológicos*. Porto Alegre, v. 11, n. 23, June 2005

Matta, Roberto da. *O que faz o brasil, Brasil?* 10 ed. Rio de Jainero: Rocco, 1999.

McCann, Bryan. *Hello, Hello Brazil: popular music in the making of modern Brazil*. Durham: Duke University Press, 2004.

Munanga, Kabengele. *Rediscutindo a mestiçagem no Brasil: identidade nacional versus identidade negra*. 2 ed. Belo Horizonte: Autêntica, 2006.

Nascimento, Abdias do. "The Myth of Racial Democracy", 1968. Published in: Levine, Robert M. and Crocitti, John J. *The Brazil Reader*. Duke University Press, 1999.

Psacharopoulous, G, Patrinos, H. A. *"Indigenous people and poverty in Latin America: an empricial analysis"*. Washington, DC: The World Bank, 1994. Cited in: Patrinos, Harry Anthony. "77ze *Cost of Discrimina-tioin in Latin America "*. *Studies in Comparative International Development,* 2000.

Rodrigues, Raimundo Nina. *As raças humanas e a responsabilidadepenal no Brasil*. Salvador: Livraria Progresso Editora, 1957.

Souza, Amaury de. *"Redressing Inequalities: Brazil's Social Agenda at Century's End"*. Published in: Kaufman Purcell, Susan & Roett, Riordan. *Brazil under Cardoso.* Boulder: Lynne Rienner Publishers, 1997.

Souza, Jessé. (1997). *Multiculturalismo e racism: uma comparação Brasil-Estados Unidos.* Brasília: Paralelo 15, (137–144)

Taylor, Charles. "The Politics of Recognition". *Multiculturalism.* Princeton: Princeton University Press, 1994.

United Nations. *Millennium Development Goals Report.* 2010.

Ethnicity and Racialism

POSTREADING QUESTIONS

1. Outline the actions that *K'iche principales* undertook to retain Ladino cultural authority.
2. Explain the Latin American racial democracy myth. Provide examples of the effects that this perspective had on Afro Latinos.
3. What did Bonfil Batalla mean by Mexico *profundo*?
4. Outline the main national events that set the stage for the Zapatistas to become a national rebellious movement in 1994.

SUGGESTED ADDITIONAL READINGS

Bonfil Batalla, G. (1996). *Mexico Profundo: Reclaiming a civilization.* Translations from Latin America Series. Austin, TX: University of Texas Press.

Law, I., & S. Tate (2015). *Caribbean racisms: Connections and complexities in the racialization of the Caribbean region.* Mapping Global Racisms Series. London, UK: Palgrave Macmillan.

Telles, E. (2014). *Pigmentocracies: Ethnicity, race, and color in Latin America.* Chapel Hill, NC: The University of North Carolina Press

Vinson, B., & M. Restall. (2009). *Black Mexico: Race and society from Colonial to modern times.* Series Dialogues. Albuquerque, NM: University of New Mexico Press.

Wade, P. (2010). *Race and ethnicity in Latin America. Anthropology, culture, and society.* 2nd Edition. London, UK: Pluto Press.

Drugs: History, Production, and Trade in Latin America

IN PREHISTORIC TIMES, plants native to Latin America such as ayahuasca, coca leaves, peyote, and psilocybin mushrooms were considered sacred with multiple religious and medicinal uses. The hallucinogenic properties of these plants were significant to the performance of rituals, divination, and healing sessions. Access to these hallucinogenic drugs was mostly limited to priests and shamans. In the 15th century, the arrival of European Christianity changed the perception of these plants and led to the disregarding of their ritual function and healing properties—instead transforming them into illegal substances associated with demonic rites. Nonetheless, European colonizers incorporated these hallucinogenic plants into their repertoire of recreational drugs along with Old World drugs such as cannabis and opium novel to the New World. In 1860, Albert Neiman first isolated cocaine, the main psychoactive alkaloid, from coca leaves. Though initially used as a medical local anesthetic, cocaine's recreational popularity changed it into a global commodity by the 20th century (Conzelman et al., 2008, pp. 182–186). Cocaine, cannabis, opiates, opioids, and amphetamine-type stimulants have become global commodities in the international market of illicit substances. Today, Latin America and the Caribbean are considered major illicit drug producers and drug-transit regions in the world (International Narcotics Control Strategy Report, 2018, p. 5).

The readings in Section II provide a holistic understanding of the history, environmental impact, biases inherent, and ensuing sociocultural impact of the production and trade of illicit drugs in Latin America and the Caribbean. Conzelman et al. (2008) briefly discuss the history of the coca leaf and its transformation from a traditional symbol of indigenous heritage to an illegal drug and global commodity in Bolivia. Diaz-Cotto (2005) examines how gender, ethnic, and racial biases inherent to the criminal justice system are directly contributing to the increasing number of Latinas' drug-related arrests and incarceration in Latin America and the United States. The negative environmental impact of illicit drugs production and the "War on Drugs" military strategies aimed to deter it are the subject of Smith, Hooks, and Lengefeld's (2014) reading. Finally, Tekin's (2015) article provides an overview of the Merida Initiative, a Mexico–United States counterdrug policy designed to curtail the drug-related violence and instability in Mexico and Central America.

REFERENCES

Bureau for International Narcotics and Law Enforcement Affairs. (2018). *International Narcotics Control Strategy Report*. Volume 1. Washington DC: United States Department of State.

Conzelman, C. S., Youngers, C. A., Shultz, J., Esch, C., Olivera, L., & Farthing, L. (2008). Coca: The leaf at the center of the War on Drugs. In J. Schultz & M. C. Draper (eds.), *Dignity and defiance: Stories from Bolivia's challenge to globalization*, pp. 181–210. Berkeley: University of California Press.

KEYWORDS

Aymara, Bolivia, bright value, cartels, climate change, coca leaf, cocaine, Colombia, commodification, corruption, counterdrug policy, courier, dark value, drug offenses, drug trafficking organizations, ecological damage, ethnicity, Europe, financing of violence, gender, global drug market, herbicides, heroin, insecurity, *Latinas*, mandatory sentencing laws, military initiative, marihuana, Merida Initiative, methamphetamine, Mexico, *Plan Colombia*, racism, risk-transfer militarism, smuggling routes, transnational crime, treadmill of destruction, *trueque*, United States, War on Drugs, water pollution.

Coca

The Leaf at the Center of the War on Drugs

Caroline S. Conzelman, Coletta A. Youngers, Jim Shultz, Caitlin Esch, Leny Olivera, and Linda Farthing

NO ISSUE HAS dominated Bolivia's recent struggle with powers from abroad more than coca. This small green leaf embodies the clash between Bolivian tradition and identity and the international policies that call for its eradication. It is a leaf that has been used in ceremonies, consumed as a medicine, and traded as a valuable commodity by Andean civilizations for over four thousand years. But the leaf is also the raw ingredient to manufacture cocaine, a drug that plagues communities and feeds violence on the streets of Brazil, Europe, and the United States.

Here, a series of writers lay out the many aspects of the controversial and complex coca issue. The chapter begins with a historical description of coca's place in Andean culture and society and how it became an object of interest to Spanish conquistadors and an international commodity. It goes on to examine how outside forces continue to play a role in Bolivia with the imposition of the "war on drugs," an international effort initiated by the United States to eradicate coca due to its connection to cocaine. Following that are the stories from Bolivians who have been intimately affected by that war—an innocent mother punished by the country's antidrug law and the families who depend on coca cultivation for their monthly income. The chapter ends with an analysis of the alternatives to coca production and considers the viability of alternative crops as well as alternative uses of coca.

ANCIENT SYMBOL, TRADITION, AND COMMODITY

CAROLINE S. CONZELMAN

When Doña Corina harvests her coca bushes, each leaf makes a soft *snap*, indicating that she has picked it off whole, not torn or crushed. With all the women working together in her field, the air is filled with these snaps, a rhythm that

Caroline S. Conzelman, et al., "Coca: The Leaf at the Center of the War on Drugs," *Dignity and Defiance: Stories from Bolivia's Challenge to Globalization*, ed. Jim Shultz and Melissa Crane Draper, pp. 181–210, 325–329. Copyright © 2008 by University of California Press. Reprinted with permission.

decorates the women's conversation like the sequins embroidered on their festival skirts at home. At the end of the day they will have accumulated a large cloth bag of the leaves that Corina can carry on her back along the winding paths to her adobe home. There she has a slate patio called a *kachi*, where she will spread out the leaves the next morning in the sun to dry. This is all the processing that coca needs before it is put into bags to sell at the legal market or stored for her family to use for tea, medicine, and ceremonies.

The leaf is regularly chewed by people in her community because of its many beneficial properties and because it is a potent symbol of their indigenous heritage. "Coca is our life," said Doña Corina, quite literally, for coca sustains her community's health, economy, and spirituality. However, for centuries coca has been despised, misunderstood, and controlled by colonial and elite powers, or maligned for its notorious derivative, cocaine. Its popular image has veered from one extreme to the other, perceived as either the sacred leaf or the devil's leaf. All the while, indigenous people in Bolivia have considered coca a fundamental aspect of their livelihoods, politics, and traditions.

If you travel over the mountain pass from the city of La Paz and the altiplano highlands down into the steep eastern slope of the Bolivian Andes—where you can simultaneously see the snowy peaks of the Cordillera to the south and the rivers deep in their valleys flowing north toward the Amazon—you arrive at the legendary coca fields of the Yungas region. The Yungas is one of two major coca-growing regions in Bolivia and is recognized as the main traditional coca-growing zone. The Chapare, in central Bolivia, is another important coca-growing area that gained notoriety beginning in the 1960s due to the influx of migrants who moved in from the highland regions and began growing coca, much of which, in the 1980s, became destined for the burgeoning cocaine market abroad.

The telltale signature of a Yungas coca field, or *cocal*, is the row upon row of low earthen terraces stacked up in vertical columns until they cover the hillside, radiating a brilliant emerald green. The old Inca stone terraces are even still visible in some places. Because coca leaf has been grown here for many centuries by Aymara and Quechua people, its cultivation is legal in the Yungas for domestic markets. The sweet coca grown here is preferred over the leaf grown at lower altitudes, like that found in the Chapare, and is thus sold around the country for chewing and making herbal tea, its most common and ancient uses.

Coca leaf is used this way as a mild stimulant—comparable to how people in other parts of the world use coffee and tea—and offers significant nutritional value for daily life in the fields, mines, meeting halls, and markets. Compared with fifty other native plants consumed in Latin America—including a variety of nuts, vegetables, cereals, and fruits—coca ranks higher than average in protein, carbohydrate, calcium, iron, and vitamins A and E.[1] Coca is an important source of nourishment for rural and urban indigenous laborers who often have only limited means to sustain a balanced diet.

The leaf is also a remedy for a variety of physiological ailments, including altitude sickness, gastrointestinal inflammation, and hypoglycemia.[2]

It makes sense that coca cultivation evolved together with potatoes in the Andes because chewing the leaf after a meal helps regulate the blood sugar produced by potato starch. Local communities also benefit from the leaf's high calcium content.[3] Coca can be used as a healing agent for minor wounds and as a mild topical anesthetic owing to the presence of the leaf's fourteen alkaloids, one of which is the cocaine alkaloid. The minute amount of the cocaine alkaloid ingested by chewing the leaf or drinking coca tea is not in any way similar to the effect of consuming the drug cocaine. Nor is coca leaf addictive, as pure cocaine can be.[4]

It is not difficult to understand why coca has been a sacred and central component of life in the Andes and parts of the Amazon for more than four thousand years.[5] One Aymara myth says that coca leaf was a gift from Pachamama (Mother Earth) long ago when her people needed sustenance during a food crisis in the Yungas.[6] She guided them to a simple shrub that was able to survive under these conditions and told the people to suck on the small flat leaves. Thus the Aymara began to discover the nutritional and medicinal properties of coca. They continue to offer coca leaves in their ceremonies to honor their connection to the land and the divine realm of the spirits, especially Pachamama.

Coca is a hardy crop. It can grow in acidic or rocky soil and remain productive for thirty years. The Aymara developed a method of terracing, which they still use today, to take advantage of the extreme topography and mild climate of the high-altitude, subtropical forests. The hard work of building these terraces, primarily the men's work, is punctuated by breaks to chew coca. Coca is also shared by the sisters, daughters, aunts, and other women who spend their days picking coca surrounded by swirling mist, warm sunshine, and stunning mountain vistas.

In the Yungas, coca is the principal export crop within a diversified subsistence agriculture system, with each coca field harvested three to four times a year. The labor involved is a shared enterprise, in which extended families and neighbors join together to plant and to harvest. This practice of reciprocity, which has a long history in the Andes, is called *ayni* in Aymara.

The principle of *ayni* is at the heart of the ancient Aymara political economic system called the *ayllu,* created to take advantage of the tremendous ecological diversity of the region. Each of the three primary climate zones produces certain goods that are essential to people's survival—potatoes, quinoa, and llamas from the altiplano; root vegetables, maize, medicinal herbs, and coca from the lowlands; fish and salt from the Pacific coast. All families of an *ayllu* took turns holding positions of authority, overseeing the distribution of resources, like food and land, for the benefit of the entire *ayllu.*[7] The philosophy and practices of *ayllu* live on in many Bolivian communities, where coca leaf continues to be shared at social and political gatherings to represent their essential bonds of reciprocity.

Coca as Commodity

Tata José (*tata* is an Aymara term of respect for an older man) has many stories to tell about the *nayra pacha,* the old times of the Aymara culture, which he learned from the oral history passed down through generations of his indigenous ancestors in the Yungas. He explains that long ago, coca leaf was the most valuable product the Andean people had, next to their fine wool textiles, so it was often used to trade for other goods or to compensate someone for labor.[8] This use of coca was only one component of a comprehensive system of barter exchange called *trueque,* in which products and labor, not money, were the basis of trade. This type of bartering and exchange remains common today in Bolivia among people who live outside the formal cash economy.

When the conquistadors destroyed the Inca Empire in the 1500s and replaced it with a Spanish Catholic empire, they viewed the sacred leaf as the devil's leaf. The Spaniards were appalled at the pervasive practice among the indigenous people of chewing coca leaf, and they called for its elimination. Their perception was that coca "was used extensively in heathen rites, and was almost worshipped for its magical power as a stimulant. It formed a bond among the natives and was an important obstacle to the spread of Christianity. Because of this, coca was condemned and attacked with passion [by Catholic priests, who] declared that 'Coca is a plant that the devil invented for the total destruction of the natives.'"[9]

It did not take long, however, for the Spanish to realize how coca could be useful to them. Obsessed with acquiring wealth by any means, the Spanish had established a repressive feudal system of estates called haciendas that gave enormous tracts of land—along with the indigenous inhabitants—to the conquistadors and their descendents. They realized that coca could support the indigenous field workers and silver miners to work longer and harder.[10] They took control of the production and commercialization of coca throughout the Andean region.[11] Aymara and Quechua miners were able to endure the interminable shifts that lasted for weeks deep inside the mountain of Potosí by chewing the leaf. Coca staved off hunger, thirst, and fatigue and also signified protection by the god of the underground, called Tío.[12]

Coca also became an important symbol for the Aymara and their strength in resisting Spanish control. During the rebellion of 1780–81, led by Tupac Katari and his wife, Bartolina Sisa, La Paz was cut off by the Aymara rebels for seven months. Chewing coca and carrying out rituals with coca was the way the indigenous men and women surrounding the capital endured the rain and harsh temperatures. Coca, a Bolivian historian wrote, "raised their spirits, and gave them strength and bravery in combat."[13] The rebellion was eventually defeated, and Katari was brutally killed by Spanish forces. According to legend his last words were, "You kill me now, but I will return, and then I will be millions."[14]

After Bolivia gained its independence from Spain in 1825, the ruling elite continued its control over coca, using it to sustain the exploited workforces in the mines that were key to increasing their profitable mineral exports. Tata José explained what it was like to pick coca as an indigenous *peón* before the Revolution of 1952 brought agrarian reform: "Aymara children did not go to school, or even learn to speak Spanish, but worked in the *cocales* with their parents. That was our education, learning how to pick coca."

Coca and Cocaine

In 1860, a German chemist was the first to isolate coca leaf's cocaine alkaloid and concentrate it into a white crystalline powder. Cocaine soon became a popular bourgeois recreational drug in Europe and the United States and was also considered a medical panacea, endorsed by figures such as the Pope, Sigmund Freud, and Ulysses Grant.[15] Coca-Cola was created in the 1880s as an elixir of cocaine and caffeine and became an international sensation. By the early 1900s, however, cocaine's deleterious effects were becoming clear. In 1914, the United States passed the Harrison Narcotics Act, which prohibited the possession and use of cocaine. In 1929, Coca-Cola eliminated cocaine from its popular soda but retained the unique flavoring of the leaf in its recipe.[16]

Records from the 1920s show that 87 percent of Yungas coca was consumed in Bolivia—primarily in the mines—and of the 13 percent exported, most supplied laborers in Argentina and Chile, while the rest was sent to Europe to be used in pharmaceuticals.[17] Yungas hacienda owners fiercely defended their right to grow the leaf as a mainstay of the national economy and a crucial source of public tax revenue. They also stressed that coca did not pose health risks.[18] These voices were initially honored in international agreements, but coca leaf was becoming increasingly confused with the drug cocaine. As one researcher described it, "A mild stimulant that had been used with no evidence of toxicity for at least two thousand years before Europeans discovered cocaine came to be viewed as an addictive drug."[19]

The link between coca and cocaine became the basis for international law in 1961 with the approval of the United Nations Single Convention on Narcotic Drugs, which classified coca leaf as a narcotic, alongside heroin and cocaine.[20] The accord prohibits Bolivia from exporting coca leaf or other products such as tea that are made from it. It also set into motion a plan to eradicate all illicit coca cultivation in Bolivia and Peru within twenty-five years and to eliminate the practice of coca chewing altogether within that same time period. Backers of the plan argued that coca was a root cause of underdevelopment and poverty in the region.[21]

In the two decades following the passage of the UN convention, the fear that Bolivia's coca leaf would become broadly used for cocaine production persisted. In the mid-1980s, however, two phenomena would lead to a surge in coca cultivation in

Bolivia that would turn that fear into a reality. At the international level, the cocaine boom in the United States and Europe spiked demand for the coca leaf. In Bolivia, economic crisis and radical changes in national economic policy left thirty thousand people without jobs practically overnight. Scrambling to find a new income, these Bolivians turned to their best option: to become coca farmers in the Chapare. Ironically, the Chapare was precisely where government programs were encouraging the newly unemployed to migrate. Soon after, the United States and its international partners would launch the massive initiative that came to be known as the "war on drugs" in the Andes.

BOX 2.1.1 COCA AND COCAINE: WHAT IS THE DIFFERENCE?

Coca leaf is to cocaine what grapes are to wine—it is a raw material that must be altered significantly in order to turn it into a drug. Coca leaf contains a small concentration of the cocaine alkaloid, which is what is extracted to make pure cocaine. Chewing coca leaf is the traditional way of consuming coca in the Andean culture and produces none of the euphoria or paranoia that occur with cocaine use, because the alkaloid is ingested as a component of the whole leaf and is absorbed slowly by the body through the digestive system.[1] The World Health Organization (WHO) reported in 1995 that even long-term users of coca leaf experience no detrimental health effects and do not suffer from addiction.[2]

Turning coca leaf into cocaine requires an elaborate process involving a set of specific chemicals. First, the dried coca leaf is turned into coca paste using sodium carbonate and kerosene.[3] Coca paste is then elaborated into cocaine through an even more sophisticated process using special equipment and more noxious chemicals. It takes about 390 pounds of coca leaf to make one pound of cocaine.[4] Although the numbers are highly contested, the director of Bolivia's antinarcotic force, FELCN, claimed in early 2007 that as much as 50 percent of coca leaf produced in Bolivia eventually goes to making cocaine.[5]

1. Andrew Weil, "Letter from the Andes: The New Politics of Coca," *New Yorker,* May 15, 1995, 77.
2. Roberto Laserna, *Veinte juicios y prejuicios sobre coca-cocaína* (Twenty judgments and prejudices about coca-cocaine) (La Paz: Edición Clave, 1996), 14.
3. "Coca Cultivation and Cocaine Processing: An Overview," Drug Enforcement Administration, Intelligence Division, September 2003, www.druglibrary.org/Schaffer/GovPubs/cocccp.htm (accessed March 30, 2007).
4. Kevin Riley, "Snow Job? The Efficacy of Source Country Cocaine Policies," Rand Graduate School Dissertation series, RGSD-102, 1993, 78.
5. "EEUU exige 'resultados' en reducción de coca" (The U.S. demands "results" on coca eradication), *Los Tiempos* (Cochabamba), March 30, 2007.

A BRIEF HISTORY OF THE U.S. "WAR ON DRUGS" IN BOLIVIA

COLETTA A. YOUNGERS

In September 2006, Bolivian president Evo Morales stood before the United Nations General Assembly and held up a small coca leaf. The nation's first indigenous president declared: "This is the green coca leaf; it is not white like cocaine. It represents Andean culture." A leader of the Bolivian coca growers, Morales had been denied a U.S. visa to attend a UN Special Session on Drug Policy a decade earlier. As president, he has had access to an international platform to defend the historic, religious, and cultural uses of the coca leaf and to distinguish it from the illicit substance cocaine with which it had become indelibly linked. He also has had a historic opportunity to put an end to the U.S. "war on drugs" in Bolivia.

Bolivians have paid a high price waging Washington's war. U.S.-backed coca eradication efforts have long been characterized by human rights violations in the Chapare coca-growing region. Although abuses have not reached the level of the executions and disappearances carried out by some of Bolivia's military dictators in past years, a disturbing pattern of killings, mistreatment, and abuse of the local population has prevailed. The primary victims are not drug traffickers but poor farmers who support their families through the production of coca and other agricultural products. Coca crop eradication has plunged communities and families deeper into poverty, generating social unrest, violence, and political instability. That discontent ultimately led to the creation of the political party MAS (Movement toward Socialism), that later elected the country's most visible coca grower leader to its highest office.

Garnering 54 percent of the vote in the December 2005 elections, Morales earned an unprecedented mandate for change. Well aware of the negative consequences and failures of past policy, his government adopted a radically different approach to the drug issue, best characterized by its slogan "coca yes, cocaine no." Other coca grower leaders began directing the government agencies responsible for carrying out the new policy, giving it greater credibility and legitimacy in Bolivia. The new strategy offered the possibility for the long-term success in limiting coca production that had eluded past governments by promoting economic development in poor rural areas and cooperative coca crop reduction.

The U.S. "War on Drugs"

The explosion of the crack cocaine epidemic in the United States in the mid-1980s led the U.S. Congress to pass increasingly draconian legislation intended to thwart both illicit drug abuse and the violence and other social problems associated with the drug trade at home. U.S. officials placed blame on the foreign countries where illicit drugs were produced—primarily the Andean region of South America and Mexico. Policies were developed to decrease the supply of illicit drugs by eradicating the production of coca, curbing cocaine production in overseas laboratories, and seizing shipments en route.

For the past two decades, approximately two-thirds of federal funding for drug control programs has gone to programs to limit supply, with only one-third designated for treatment and education to reduce demand. The premise for the policy was that limiting supply would drive up the price of illicit substances and lead to decreased consumption. Both the premise and the policy would prove to be a failure.

The U.S. appetite for drugs was also cast in national security terms. In 1986, President Reagan first declared illicit drugs a national security threat. In 1989, President George H. W. Bush launched the Andean Initiative, which led to a dramatic increase in U.S. involvement in the socalled source countries of Bolivia, Colombia, and Peru, where coca is grown. At the same time, the U.S. Congress designated the Defense Department as the single lead agency for the detection and monitoring of illicit drugs. Latin American militaries and police forces were provided with U.S. economic assistance, training, and intelligence and logistical support to carry out counterdrug initiatives.

The expanded role of the United States and Latin American security forces in domestic counterdrug efforts is commonly referred to as the militarization of U.S. drug policy. Since September 11, 2001, coca grower leaders have been included on U.S. terrorist lists, targeted as "narco-terrorists." Within this policy framework, economic development and democratic institution building were usually minimized.

Governments in the Andean region initially resisted the forced eradication at the heart of the U.S. approach—particularly the nascent civilian government in Bolivia, where the military had only recently returned to the barracks after decades of violent dictatorships. (Bolivia has notoriously suffered 182 military coups since gaining independence in 1825—a regional record.) While U.S. officials considered coca farmers to be the first link in the chain leading to drug abuse in the United States, Bolivian and other Andean officials saw poor farmers who were trying to eke out a subsistence-level living. Forced coca eradication pitted government forces against one of the most vulnerable segments of the population; conflict and violence resulted.

Despite this initial resistance, Washington used its political muscle to ensure compliance. In 1986, the U.S. Congress passed legislation mandating the president to annually "certify" that major drug-producing and transit countries were cooperating fully with U.S. antidrug programs. Countries that were not certified faced a range of sanctions, including a cutoff in U.S. financial assistance, *no* votes on loans from multilateral development banks, and discretionary trade sanctions.[22] In Bolivia's case, annual coca eradication targets had to be met to receive U.S. certification.

Bolivia is particularly susceptible to such pressure. As one of the most impoverished countries in Latin America, it is heavily dependent on U.S. foreign aid and on aid from international lending institutions closely tied to the U.S. government. As a result, Bolivia has long followed Washington's marching orders on drug control policies. U.S.

lawyers reportedly drafted the Bolivian "Law to Regulate Coca and Controlled Substances," commonly referred to as Law 1008, while the U.S. Embassy lobbied heavily for its approval by the Bolivian Congress in 1988. Ultimately, the U.S. government made approval of the law a condition for releasing U.S. aid.[23]

Until the election of President Morales, Law 1008 provided the legal framework for repressive coca eradication efforts. The draconian statute, among other features, set up a special U.S.-funded team of antidrug prosecutors and required that all Bolivians accused of a drug offense be held in jail, with no option for bail or release, until the process of trial was completed. Given that these trials often took years to complete, the effect was that those arrested were treated as guilty until proven innocent.

In May 1990, the Bolivian government also capitulated to U.S. pressure and signed a secret agreement that formalized a role for the Bolivian armed forces, including the army, in counterdrug operations. As it was a wildly unpopular move, the Paz Zamora government repeatedly denied the existence of the agreement. Despite the public outcry after news of the accord finally leaked out, the Bolivian armed forces had already gained a growing foothold in the drug war, with little if any oversight by civilian officials.

The Bolivian military and police forces dedicated to counterdrug efforts have been funded almost solely by Washington, creating even greater dependency and further skewing bilateral relations. The U.S. government has provided antidrug forces with everything from uniforms to weapons and the cost of feeding the arrested, as well as the special U.S. bonuses paid directly to Law 1008 prosecutors. Critics have complained that the country's judiciary has become directly subservient to the United States and that prosecutors have jailed innocent people by the thousands to satisfy U.S. officials. Because the U.S. government has held the purse strings and accounting has been far from transparent, the Bolivian government has been unable to calculate the budget for its counterdrug program. "We don't even know the cost of a basic antidrug operation," complained one former Bolivian official, "as it is all paid for by the U.S. Embassy."[24]

Throughout the 1990s, the Chapare coca-growing region experienced cyclical patterns of dialogue and conflict. Wanting to avoid social unrest among the powerful coca grower movement, successive governments offered economic compensation in exchange for voluntary eradication, even while forced coca eradication continued. However, such promises were rarely fulfilled, and minimum eradication goals had to be met to keep the U.S. aid spigot open. Inevitably, as the annual deadline neared, periods of relative calm were followed by conflict and violence.

Plan Dignidad and the High Cost of Eradication

The cycle was interrupted by the election of former dictator Hugo Banzer Suárez to the presidency in 1997, which eliminated dialogue and made conflict the norm.

Banzer declared that Bolivia would achieve "zero coca" in five years and launched a massive eradication offensive as part of Plan Dignidad, or "Plan Dignity." Coca in the Chapare was the primary target of this initiative; the traditional growing zone of the Yungas was not. The armed forces were used for on-the-ground operations, and approximately five thousand troops were moved into the Chapare, greatly increasing tensions. Young military conscripts guarded by antidrug police made their way across the region, pulling out coca plants as distraught families watched their primary source of cash income going up in fire and smoke.

Initially, the program produced impressive gains in decreasing coca production. By 2000, the government said it had almost met its goal of zero coca. The gains, however, proved to be short-lived. By 2001, coca production was on the rise and had increased by 23 percent in 2002.[25] The reason that the policy was not sustainable in the long run was simple: eradication far outpaced the provision of economic alternatives. "Alternative Development," which was intended to offer coca growers other cash crops, was one of Plan Dignidad's primary pillars and showed little success. Poor peasants had no choice but to replant coca—which they did at a rapid rate.

The economic, social, and political costs of the U.S.-backed "war on drugs" in Bolivia, and Plan Dignidad in particular, were extremely high. Forced eradication efforts led to human rights violations including executions, illegal detentions, and torture. Massive sweeps of the coca-growing region led to hundreds of arbitrary detentions where those arrested were presumed guilty until proved innocent. Though ultimately released, most detainees were never presented before judicial authorities or allowed to notify family members of their arrest. Reports of mistreatment and even the torture of detainees became disturbingly common.

As coca production plummeted, so did the incomes and hence the health and nutrition standards of local residents. As income levels fell, families had less to spend on health needs and children were taken out of school so they could work in order to supplement the household income. Though hard data are not available, local health care and education officials repeatedly complained of a surge in malnutrition-related illnesses and declining school attendance.[26] Social discontent resulted in violent confrontations and blockades of highways that shut down regions of the country for months at a time. During these protests, food supplies rotted on trucks and commerce ceased, with a significant negative impact on the Bolivian economy.

Many lives were lost during these years. Dozens of coca growers were killed during eradication campaigns or during protests that turned violent. Police and military officials were also killed. In some cases, circumstances were murky; however, even clear-cut murders have not been investigated or sanctioned.

The killing of coca grower Casimiro Huanca presents a particularly disturbing case. It began in December 2001, when a small protest took place in the town of Chimoré.[27] Coca growers had stacked boxes of fruit on the side of the road to protest lack of markets for alternative crops. At one point, soldiers followed coca growers, including

Huanca, as they headed toward a union office. According to those present, Huanca was shot twice at close range. He bled to death from the wounds. His killer was identified as Juan Eladio Bora, a member of the Expeditionary Task Force (ETF), a paramilitary antidrug force funded by the U.S. government. The Bolivian military tribunal determined that Bora acted in self-defense, despite the evidence indicating that neither Huanca nor any of his colleagues threatened him or other ETF members at any time.[28]

As in other cases, the U.S. Embassy defended the military's action. In a 2002 interview with U.S. Embassy officials, the "human rights" officer said that the shooting of Huanca could not be considered a human rights violation, because he was shot in the groin. He even went so far as to accuse local human rights activists of his death, saying they did not get him adequate medical attention. However, the health facilities necessary to treat him did not exist in the region.[29]

Angry farmers, sometimes armed with machetes, have also posed a threat to the police and soldiers called out to quash protests. Between 1997 and 2004, 35 coca growers and 27 police and military personnel were killed; nearly 600 coca growers and 140 military and police were injured.[30] Impunity became the norm for human rights violations attributed to members of the Bolivian security forces, as well as for farmers accused of killing soldiers or police.

Eventually Bolivians' patience with outspoken U.S. ambassadors and repeated U.S. meddling in domestic politics wore thin. During the 2002 presidential elections, U.S. ambassador Manuel Rocha spoke out directly against Morales, who was a candidate, warning that Bolivia would lose U.S. economic support and become an international pariah if the electorate "played footsie with coca growers."[31] Morales shot up in the polls and lost by only 1.5 percent of the vote. Morales's stunning presidential victory in 2005 was in part due to Washington's relentless—and ultimately unsuccessful—antidrug crusade. The conflict, violence, and economic hardship caused by coca eradication policies, among other issues, helped propel Morales into the national spotlight and generated popular support for his anti-U.S. rhetoric.

Coca Yes, Cocaine No

As a coca grower himself, President Morales has had an unprecedented opportunity to put into place an antidrug strategy that could win broad Bolivian support.[32] The new government's goal was to limit coca production that fuels the cocaine market but avoid the conflict and violence that have characterized previous policy. Morales also made clear his intention to continue combating the illicit drug business, stating in his inaugural address, "We are convinced that drug trafficking is a disease afflicting humanity."[33]

The basis of Morales's plan was to carry out cooperative coca reduction and extend it into other coca-producing areas previously unaffected by forced eradication. Based on an agreement signed in October 2004 by the then president Carlos Mesa, the

Morales government continued to allow each coca-growing family to maintain one *cato* of coca (1,600 square meters, or a little more than one-third of an acre). The agreement required that any coca grown beyond that be subject to eradication. In addition, coca farmers accepted eradication in the two major national parks in the region. Initially with a one-year mandate, the October 2004 agreement put an end to forced eradication. If cooperative coca eradication is going to have long-term success, it will require that effective monitoring systems be put in place.[34]

In the Chapare, the strategy to limit coca production appears to be working, and the lack of conflict and violence has contributed to an environment that is conducive to economic development. According to local journalist Juan Alanoca, "In economic terms, the situation has improved. People are now assured that they will have some money from coca."[35] This allows them greater flexibility to experiment with other agricultural products and seek out other income-generating opportunities—key elements of a long-term coca reduction strategy (discussed in more detail later in this chapter). In both its first and second years in office the Morales government met its goal of eliminating 5,000 hectares (12,350 acres) of coca but without the violence characteristic of previous administrations.

"Popular participation and cooperation has increased with this government," says Col. Miguel Vásquez, former director of the country's antidrug police.[36] With that participation comes cooperative regulation that is far more effective than the heavy hand of unilateral forced eradication and interdiction. However, the continued use of the Bolivian military in coca reduction efforts and U.S. pressure to meet eradication targets have led to violence in other coca-growing regions. In September 2006, two coca growers were killed in a confrontation with members of a joint military-police eradication force in the Vandiola Yungas. The tragedy illustrates the difficulties the government faces in implementing its coca strategy in areas where coca has traditionally been grown and where farmers are largely dependent on the cultivation of coca as their principal crop.

Challenges for the Future

Despite skepticism and resistance to some aspects of the new Bolivian government's approach, the U.S. government has continued its antidrug programs in Bolivia and collaborates closely on drug interdiction efforts in particular. While tensions often run high and the uneasy truce could easily dissipate, both governments point out that a rupture in bilateral relations would not benefit either country.

The key to the potential success of the new government's approach on eradication will be its ability to prevent the replanting of destroyed crops, a problem that has thwarted long-term success in the past. To date, initial results are promising. In 2006 and 2007, government efforts to work collaboratively with coca grower federations and individual communities to reduce cultivation met with success. At the time of this

BOX 2.1.2. WHO'S WHO IN BOLIVIA'S "WAR ON DRUGS"

Some of the key players in the drug war include:[*]

Coca grower unions: Local grassroots organizations in the coca-growing regions that have been the basis for resistance for coca farmers against "war on drugs" initiatives.

The Expeditionary Task Force (ETF): A paramilitary antidrug force funded by the U.S. government, which was disbanded after repeated accusations of serious human rights violations in the Chapare.

The Joint Task Force (JTF): A combined military and police unit in charge of eradication until 2006 and then voluntary coca eradication under the Morales government.

The Bolivian Special Antinarcotic Police (FELCN): A special branch of the national police that oversees interdiction of illicit drugs and precursor chemicals used to make drugs.

The U.S. State Department's Bureau of International Narcotics and Law Enforcement Affairs (INL): Through its Narcotic Affairs Section (NAS) and Air Wing, the INL supports and assists all interdiction and eradication forces.

The Narcotic Affairs Section (NAS): A section of the U.S. State Department that oversees drug war policy on the ground.

The Mobile Rural Patrol Unit (UMOPAR): The rural arm of the FELCN, whose members have special training in antinarcotics intervention.

The U.S. Embassy, La Paz: Meets routinely with Bolivian government officials to coordinate policy and implement programs and operations.

The U.S. Agency for International Development (USAID): Represents the largest of all international donors in efforts of alternative development.

---

[*] U.S. Department of State, International Narcotics Control Strategy Report 2007, Bolivia section: www.state.gov/p/inl/rls/nrcrpt/2007/

writing, violence and conflict have, for the most part, been avoided, creating a climate more propitious for rural economic growth.

The future challenge, however, will be to provide economic opportunities to improve overall quality of life for those traditionally dependent on coca cultivation. To the extent that drug crop eradication efforts have succeeded, it has been in Asia—most notably Thailand—where the government put into place comprehensive development programs to increase both the income levels and the standards of living of local farmers, which were then weaned from opium poppy production. Eradication efforts were carried out in collaboration with the local community and within a framework of respect for the rule of law and human rights. Development and law enforcement efforts were kept separate in order to ensure the continued support of the local population. In adopting a similar approach, the Bolivian government could be the first Latin American country to repeat this Asian success story.

PORTRAITS FROM THE BOLIVIAN DRUG WAR

Beyond the debate over the public policies involved in Bolivia's U.S.-backed "war on drugs" lie the stories of the people affected. The chief victims of that war are the thousands of innocent people sent to jail to beef up arrest statistics and the subsistence farmers trying to eke out a living by growing the small, green leaf.[37]

A Baby Turns One in Jail Courtesy of the "War on Drugs"

JIM SHULTZ

If it hadn't been her mother's birthday that day, Lourdes Mamani probably wouldn't have spent twenty-two months in a Cochabamba jail. Her son Marcos wouldn't have spent his first birthday, on the fourth of July, in that same jail with her, courtesy of the U.S. "war on drugs."

On June 23, 1999, Lourdes was in her mother's kitchen baking her a cake when a distant cousin, Eduardo, showed up at the front door. He said he had come to pick up two small sealed opaque plastic bags, which Lourdes's older brother had stored in their father's small tool room. The bags were filled with *q'owa*, he told her, a common plant burned like incense during the first-Friday-of-each-month rituals by the same name. She helped him carry the bags to a waiting taxi. He declined an invitation to join them for cake, and he left.

Two hours later there was another knock at the door. This time it was two uniformed officers from the FELCN, Bolivia's special antinarcotics police. Lourdes's cousin, they told her, had been arrested with two bags of marijuana and had given the police a false name. The officers had traced the cousin back to the house where he picked up the bags and demanded that Lourdes or her mother come with them to the jail to identify him.

With a promise that they would drive her to the jail and promptly return her to her mother's house, Lourdes swept her baby into her arms and got into the backseat of the officers' car. At the jail she gave them the identification of her cousin that they asked for, but instead of being driven home, Lourdes and Marcos were locked in a ten-by-fifteen-foot concrete cell with a dozen other women and their children and infants. "I've always accepted that I am poor, that I wear old clothes," she explained. "I never chose to do anything illegal to change that. Never in my life did I think I would be here."[38]

Law 1008 Claims a New Victim

Like all those accused of a drug-related crime in Bolivia, Lourdes was prosecuted under Bolivia's notorious Law 1008, the draconian statute under which all those accused are held in jail, with no option for bail or release. In 1999, the year Lourdes was jailed, more than 1,000 of the nearly 1,400 prisoners in Cochabamba had never been sentenced, never had the chance to defend themselves at a trial. The situation became so desperate that women prisoners went on hunger strikes—sewing their mouths shut with heavy needles and thread, or crucifying themselves to a jail balcony—in a desperate move to call public attention to their situation.

In 2001, a new penal code was passed with the intention of lessening the wait period for cases. While that may provide better treatment for some, it still makes little difference to those who can't afford an able lawyer. In 2007, Cochabamba's six prisons still confined 1,315 inmates, half of whom were sent to jail under Law 1008. In the San Sebastian women's prison, three-quarters of the 122 women were there as a result of the drug law.[39] Most of those women live in the prison with their young children.

The prosecutor who put Lourdes behind bars was one of those receiving a special salary bonus directly from the U.S. Embassy. A former member of the prosecution team explained at the time: "If I heard it once, I heard it a hundred times, 'we have to justify the bonuses.'"[40] What that meant was clear, ever-increasing arrest statistics that U.S. officials could use as evidence of success. In 1999, the year Lourdes was one of those statistics, the number of arrests boasted by the U.S. Embassy was 2,050. That also included the twenty-two-year-old taxi driver who had the misfortune of picking up Lourdes's cousin as a passenger that June day. For that turn of fate, he also spent twenty-two months locked in jail. By 2005, the number arrested had more than doubled, to 4,376.[41]

It is clear when you enter any of the Cochabamba jails that the people most often caught in the drug war's net are Bolivia's poor. Those with resources can often buy their way out, or at least hire a capable lawyer to argue their case. Those who can't, end up in the frustrating and frightening maze of the Bolivian drug courts.

In Cuffs in Front of Her Daughters

A month after her arrest, and after Marcos's first birthday, Lourdes was allowed to transfer from the special drug jail, where she and her cellmates slept on rotation for lack of floor space, to the San Sebastian jail for women. Set off a quiet plaza near the center of town, the decaying brick building was constructed to house a hundred prisoners. When Lourdes—for a two-hundred-dollar fee—was allowed to move there, more than two hundred women occupied the jail, plus their children.

Lourdes's trial could hardly have been more different from the stuff of a television drama. The process dribbled out in bits and pieces over nearly two years. Each piece—the reading of charges by the prosecutor, the response by the defendants, the offering of testimony—took place separately, often with months passing in between. Lourdes would wait nervously for each new hearing date to be set. Each trip to court meant hope that the case might slowly be inching forward to a conclusion. Each also meant the humiliation of being escorted into the courtroom in handcuffs before the downcast eyes of her four young daughters. On a number of occasions the lawyers, the witnesses, the families, and the cuffed defendants, all crowded anxiously into the hallway outside the courtroom, would just be sent away because the three-judge panel hearing the case hadn't managed to make it back from lunch.

During the course of her time in jail, Lourdes missed the birth of her first grandchild, had to send her baby son off to the doctor in the hands of her teenage daughters, and missed the high school graduation of her eldest daughter. The graduation ceremony, it turns out, was just across the street from the jail. As a family friend remembered, "I will never forget the silhouette of a girl in cap and gown making her way through the entrance of the jail to see her mother."

By the start of 2001, Lourdes had been in jail for eighteen months and, because her trial had still not delivered a verdict, she became eligible for provisional release. Four months later, after spending twenty-two months in jail, Lourdes walked out the doors of San Sebastian and went home with her children.

But Lourdes's name still had not been cleared. As her trial was ending, two of the judges sitting on the panel abruptly resigned and were replaced. The new panel pulled the names of each defendant out of a hat to decide who would rule on which case.[42] The judge who drew Lourdes's name had been on the court for only a few weeks, hadn't been present for any of the testimony by any of the witnesses, had never set eyes on Lourdes or her family. He found her guilty and sentenced her to five years in jail. Her conviction was sent for appeal to the Bolivian Supreme Court in Sucre, where it sits along with thousands of others, lost in a maze of paperwork that will probably never be looked at again. Every month, as she awaits a final verdict, Lourdes has to take a bus downtown to the courthouse in Cochabamba to sign a book verifying that she still lives in the city and hasn't fled.

Cocaleros: Stories from the Chapare

CAITLIN ESCH AND LENY OLIVERA ROJAS

A curvy mountain road connects the dry, high valley city of Cochabamba to the steamy jungle town of Villa Tunari. The air thickens and oppresses the lungs throughout the four-hour descent. The small town sits on the main highway that connects Cochabamba with Santa Cruz and serves as the political center of the Chapare, the coca-growing region most associated with export of the leaf for the drug market. The town's dirt roads are puddled from the region's frequent cloudbursts. Palm trees line the streets, and a handful of hotels and restaurants cater to the town's seasonal surge in tourism. Peasant farmers with wheelbarrows full of bananas, oranges, and tropical fruit sell their crops along the main road. Verdant mountains loom in the background.

The Transplanted Farmer

Forty minutes by car outside of Villa Tunari, the main road passes through a military drug checkpoint, then turns from pavement to cobblestone to dirt. Marina, a thirty-six-year old *cocalera,* lives deep in the green overgrowth, beyond the town of Eterazama. A few houses, elevated on stilts, peek out through the thick greenery. Women wash colorful clothing where the river crosses the road, while children splash and take cold baths.

A light rain sounds on the tin roof of the small structure that Marina uses as her kitchen. The dirt floor is freshly swept and the space is tidy. Marina sits on a stool, leaning over the three large stones and flaming kindling wood that serve as her stove. She is stirring a large pot of broth, talking to herself quietly in her native Quechua. Two long black braids twisted skillfully over her head are tied tightly with hair ornaments common in the region.

In 1982, at the age of twelve, Marina moved to the Chapare from Tarabuco, an arid region near the highland city of Sucre, where her family farmed.[43] She said that the droughts forced her family of ten to relocate. Marina spent the remainder of her childhood in the Chapare and eventually was able to rent a *chaco,* a small plot of land, on which to grow coca. Half of her crop went to the landlord and half she kept, either to sell or for personal use. By the time Marina was eighteen, she had saved up enough money to buy her own *chaco* with her husband. Today, Marina grows her crop on a little bit more than half an acre. "It isn't enough," she asserted. Abandoned nine years ago by her husband, Marina continues to work her land alone, "which," she said, "is extremely difficult." Living at a subsistence level, Marina supports herself, her two teenage daughters, and a grandchild on eight hundred bolivianos (about one hundred U.S. dollars) a month earned from the coca she grows and sells.[44]

The Miner's Daughter

Cintia, twenty-eight years old, is also a *cocalera* from the Chapare. But unlike Marina, Cintia has temporarily exchanged life in the Chapare for a life in the city of Cochabamba.[45] The daughter of a Cochabambino father, the dusty-eyed Cintia spent her early years in the mountain town of Potosí, where her father worked in the mines. Along the way her father contracted *mal de minas,* a colloquialism used to refer to the serious lung infection, silicosis, that commonly afflicts miners. No longer able to work in the mines, Cintia's father decided to pursue an agricultural life in the lowlands. While his family (his wife and eight children) stayed in Cochabamba, her father went to the Chapare in hopes of establishing himself as a *cocalero.* In 1990, after five years of renting land on which to grow his crop, Cintia's father was able to buy his own *chaco* deep in the jungle of Ivirgarzama—a half hour by car from the highway.

Cintia said her father chose to grow coca because it was the most lucrative crop available to him in 1985. He was eventually able to move Cintia and her siblings to live with him in the Chapare. Since 1990, the family *chaco* has grown, enabling the family to produce three hundred pounds of coca leaf every three months, which amounts to a little less than four hundred dollars in income.

Coca Growing as a Family Tradition

Juan, now forty-six, was born and raised in the Chapare into a family where the tradition of growing coca goes back generations.[46] In 1952, his grandparents were among the first coca growers to come from Yungas de Vandiola, a small pocket of traditional coca farms near the Chapare, to settle in Paracti, a town just a few miles outside of Villa Tunari.

"All my life I have been a *cocalero* like my grandparents." Juan said that he grows coca because "the plant has been cultivated in this zone for centuries and is the sustenance of my family. There used to be ancient trees [of coca] here that you could pick from. But these trees disappeared during the forced eradication." He described the ancestral techniques of coca cultivation, passed down through generations, but noted, "The miners who migrated here do not know of these practices." Juan, his wife, and the three children who still live with them (two of his sons have emigrated to Spain) cultivate the family's land. "We earn, more or less, 2,500 bolivianos ($300) every three months. This is our salary; this is our sustenance."

Facing the Drug War

Coca grower unions are an important part of life in the Chapare. Before the drug war, the unions assigned land, resolved disputes, and undertook community projects such as building schools or roads. After the U.S.-backed forced eradications began in the 1990s, the unions became the forefront of *cocalero* organizing to protect their crops. "Huge numbers of men would come in trucks. Hundreds of them," Marina recounted, "and they would beat me and my daughter." The eradication soldiers would smash cooking ware and steal leftover food so that Marina would have nothing left to feed her family. Then they would destroy her crops. She knows several women, she said, who were raped. It was in response to experiences like these that the *cocaleros* became one of the most radical and politicized forces among Bolivia's impoverished, a trajectory that would eventually make their leader, Evo Morales, the nation's president.

Both Marina and Cintia said that things are getting better for coca growers. When asked about the current MAS government, which took office in January 2006, Marina said she unequivocally supported President Morales. "Evo used to come to my *chaco* and we would dance. But now that he's president, he doesn't come anymore." For many coca growers, Morales is still a local personality, and it has taken time for them to adjust their vision of his new responsibilities as president of the country.

The challenges confronting *cocaleros* in the Chapare region are still significant. Single mothers, common in the Chapare, are faced with the task of raising children and maintaining *chacos* entirely on their own. "Who is going to help me on my *chaco*?" Marina asks rhetorically with an exasperated sigh. But Cintia, five months pregnant and engaged to a military official, looks forward to moving her immediate family back to the Chapare after having been in Cochabamba to study. Thanks to coca, she said, she was able to save enough money to go to college in Cochabamba in 1996. Now she wants to return to the Chapare and buy her own *chaco* and grow coca with her father and siblings. Despite the challenges of farming in this tropical region, Cintia, like many other coca farmers, chooses to make her life in the Chapare.

COCA AND THE SEARCH FOR ALTERNATIVES

LINDA FARTHING

"Coca substitution completely failed under past governments," Bolivia's vice minister in charge of drug control, Felipe Cáceres, told reporters in August 2006. "But our government's plan has an important innovation: the focus is on the struggle against poverty. We will work on health, education, roads, electrification and ... opening markets. ... The best way that countries can help us in the struggle against drugs is to open up their markets to us."[47]

Offering a viable alternative to coca cultivation has long been the Holy Grail to reducing production and ensuring that coca is not going into the drug trade. Throughout the long "war on drugs" in Bolivia, its architects have promised that alternative development is the best option for coca farmers to earn their income in other ways. Coca growers, however, have always questioned whether alternative development is a real strategy for crop replacement or merely a fig leaf to distract attention from harsh eradication measures. Evidence of alternative development's failure to deliver on its promises can be seen in the empty buildings—optimistically constructed over the last two decades to process crops such as palm hearts or milk products—that are now rapidly deteriorating in the hot and steamy Chapare lowlands.

Part of the problem is that coca is an almost perfect crop. It generates four harvests per year and weighs much less than alternatives such as fruit, important in regions where products have to be hand-carried partway to market. Despite sometimes sharp fluctuations in prices, coca has consistently provided a relatively stable income to farmers. What, then, can provide enough security to farmers to convince them to take the risk to switch to a new crop? This is a particularly difficult task given an economic environment that is more often than not in crisis, and in a country with one of the highest rates of rural poverty in the world.

Alternative Development and the Flawed U.S. Approach

Alternative development refers to a spectrum of development strategies that aim to provide income to farmers so that they no longer have to depend economically on the cultivation of coca. Since the Chapare region has long been pegged as the largest source of the country's illicit coca production, it has been the primary focus of such programs. Since 1982, the U.S. Agency for International Development (USAID) has relied on two basic approaches—first, try to stem migration into the Chapare, and second, promote direct crop replacement among the families already there and growing coca. Reliable figures on how much has been spent by the United States to pursue these objectives are extremely hard to come by, but estimates are approximately $300 million over the course of two decades.[48]

The USAID approach to crop substitution tried to entice coca growers into shifting to banana, pineapple, passion fruit, palm hearts, and black pepper. But all of the U.S. projects centered around alternative crops have failed for four basic reasons. First, alternative crops can rarely compete economically with coca. Second, alternative development was poorly planned and executed with the focus on reducing coca instead of reducing poverty. The United States promoted crops without serious market analysis and without adequate thought to transportation, infrastructure, and adequate technical support. Third, participation in these development programs was consistently conditioned on total eradication of coca, which is unrealistic considering that without coca, most farmers would have no income at all beyond the crops they grow for their own consumption. Finally, the United States refused any cooperation with existing coca-growing unions and municipal governments in implementing its projects.

When asked about her experience with alternative development, Chapare coca grower Marina scoffed softly: "It doesn't work."[49] "You can't make enough money growing palm hearts and pineapples when you only get forty centavos [$0.05] for a palm heart and three to four pineapples for one boliviano [$0.13]." Compared to the one thousand bolivianos ($125) reaped for one hundred pounds of coca, alternative development crops face stiff competition.

Juan explained that "the price of fruit is so low that it doesn't even cover the cost of renting a truck to transport it."[50] He noted that one hundred mandarin oranges in the Chapare can be sold by small-scale farmers for between three and six bolivianos ($0.40 and $0.80). Cintia concurred: "Growing fruit is difficult because it can only be harvested once a year and [in some cases] needs to be replanted after every harvest. It is time-consuming and expensive." Juan explained how he tried to grow pineapples, but since alternative development projects had promoted the crop widely, the fruit flooded the domestic market and prices dropped to $0.03 each. Juan made twenty-seven bolivianos (less than $4) on his crop. Farmers reported similar alternative development failures with crops such ginger root and palm hearts.

Coca grower frustration and distrust was only reinforced after visits to "model farms" in fancy agricultural stations, staffed by Bolivian professionals often earning in a month what farmers earn in a year. The presence of highly paid U.S. supervisors, racing back and forth in new jeeps from the Chapare to offices in one of Cochabamba's most luxurious office buildings, contributed to suspicions among farmers that the primary goal of the projects was to eradicate coca, not to create viable alternatives.

U.S. alternative development programs have been carried out against a backdrop of systematic and persistent harassment and repression of coca-growing families rather than being paired with regional initiatives that could help make alternative development successful. Police and military repression—not economic development—has consistently characterized U.S. policy. Coca growers on the ground have demanded just the opposite, wanting to trade in the international notoriety that coca has brought them for the kinds of resources that have never been available to Bolivia's rural indigenous poor. Teófilo Blanco expressed what coca growers have repeated for twenty years: "We have no potable water, health [services], or education systems. For us to give up coca, we have to have some of those things. We are demanding fair rights according to Bolivia's political constitution."[51]

Despite repeated promises for high levels of investment in basic infrastructure, few concrete results could be seen on the ground. Teófilo Blanco went on to explain: "They promised to build a bridge, but they haven't done it. I planted coffee but haven't been able to sell a single kilo. If you think I'm lying, I invite a high level commission to come to my farm to verify if there are any roads or development."[52] This frustration, combined with constant U.S.-financed militarized repression, created almost constant unrest throughout the 1990s in the Chapare, often disrupting the entire region.

Repeated failure was ensured by the United States' determination to condition assistance on coca eradication. This type of conditionality has long been perceived by U.S. officials as key to successful eradication programs.[53] Until the late 1990s, coca farmers were induced, usually through mounting repression, to give up coca in exchange for financial and technical assistance in switching to new crops. But often assistance arrived late or not at all or was insufficient when it did. With no work elsewhere in the country, and faced literally with concerns about survival, many growers went back to coca shortly after the eradicators left. Teófilo Blanco explained: "Many farmers have taken their kids out of school because they no longer have the economic means, and they're planting coca again."[54]

Alternative development programs have also historically been plagued by political considerations.[55] Until recently, USAID continually refused to see coca as anything other than a potential ingredient for cocaine and would not work with local peasant unions. From 1995 on, USAID also refused to work with the newly formed municipal governments, since they were dominated by the coca growers' political party, MAS. U.S. officials claimed that the poor peasant farmers—who make an estimated average one thousand dollars a year—were drug dealers. To override the existing local organizations, USAID created alternative structures, called "associations," which fomented suspicion and distrust. Some associations have existed on paper only, and many members kept a foot in both camps by retaining their union affiliation.

Coca grower Jorge Bautista explained: "I was one of the first producers in my zone to participate in alternative development programs. I formed the first association of my region and four other associations. But now I am poorer and almost lost my house. I know I have deceived many of my fellow coca growers with these associations and that only through the union can we effectively push our demands."[56]

A Different Path

In the mid-1990s, two initiatives not associated with the United States brought new direction to alternative development and ultimately planted the seeds for a new vision forward. In 1994, a decentralization measure known as the Law of Popular Participation mandated that 20 percent of national tax revenues go to newly formed municipalities, accompanied by community oversight of the funds. Coca growers quickly appropriated this new political opening and won control of Chapare municipalities, forming a base that later became the MAS party.[57] The second initiative began with the European Union's (EU) Chapare Alternative Development Program in 1998. The EU's approach reflects the recommendations made by hundreds of experts on alternative development: focus on economic development without conditions requiring eradication.[58] According to Felipe Cáceres, the vice minister who was previously a coca grower and Chapare mayor, the EU program "in eight years, with one fourth of the money, achieved ten times what USAID accomplished in twenty years."[59]

In early 2003, U.S. policy began a gradual shift. Although it maintained its emphasis on eradication and its discourse that coca growers are drug dealers, USAID began to work directly with Chapare municipalities for the first time. By 2005, it had put a new face on its program by renaming it "integrated alternative development." The United States boasts that the value of alternative development crops and products leaving the Chapare in 2005 increased by a third in just one year, to a total of $34.9 million, demonstrating a modest success after twenty years.[60] It was not to be long-lived however. In 2004–2005 U.S. funding for economic aid dropped while funds for law enforcement increased.[61]

In the Yungas, the region associated with coca grown for traditional use, the United States has pursued a different strategy. In 2002, USAID started working through local municipalities, providing training for municipal employees and support for projects including construction of potable water systems, college scholarships, tourism infrastructure, and improved specialty coffee production for export.

The MAS Vision and Its Challenges

The Morales government, in its policy of "*coca si, cocaína no*" (coca yes, cocaine no) has aimed to redefine eradication and alternative development. The key strategic premise of its policy is centered on three points: cooperative eradication rather than forced eradication; a focus on alternative uses of coca in addition to alternative crops; and the industrialization of coca into new products and finding dependable legal markets for these products. This new approach has valued not only the leaf but also the producers as active decision makers in their own economic development.

In October 2006, President Morales announced a half-million-dollar project financed by the Venezuelan government to set up a coca industrialization plant in the Chapare. The plant would produce coca wine and tea, medicines and sweets, all of which will be purchased by Venezuela.[62] Two coca industrialization plants in the Yungas, built and then abandoned by the United Nations' AgroYungas project in the 1980s, have been reactivated to manufacture coca flour and bagged coca tea. By providing more legal market alternatives for coca, the Morales administration has hoped to build a new national economy supportive of indigenous communities and divert the sale of coca from the drug trade.[63]

To be sure, the new administration's policy faces a number of difficult challenges. Internationally, in order to open up markets, Bolivia will need to win approval to remove the coca leaf from the UN list of controlled substances, where it has been since 1961. The 1995 World Health Organization study, which indicates that coca has no deleterious effects, will be critical for the Bolivian government's argument to win a decision that would allow it to market coca teas, foods, and medicines. The United States' suppression of the report indicates just how political that fight will be.[64]

After attending a Vienna meeting of the International Narcotics Control Board in March 2006, Vice Minister Felipe Cáceres returned to Bolivia less optimistic about a quick overturn of coca prohibition. In March 2007, the UN officials reiterated their opposition to an increase in the promotion of coca. The Morales government, however, pledged to continue its push to develop a plan for international decriminalization of the leaf. In February 2008, the UN went an extra step, asking Peru and Bolivia to ban all uses of coca, including chewing the leaf and drinking coca tea. UN representatives claimed that their job was to ensure compliance with the UN convention of 1961.

Another challenge will be to unify coca growers, whose interests differ from region to region. This will include winning acceptance among all coca growers, particularly those outside the Chapare, of the one-*cato*-per-family limit on coca cultivation. In November 2006, Chapare coca grower Vitalia Merida explained the new scenario to a visiting delegation, revealing that disagreements between Chapare growers and the Morales administration could lie ahead: "Having Evo as president has changed things a lot. We don't need the police or military anymore. Union leaders meet to figure out who has extra coca and then they take it out themselves. But the permitted amount is not enough to cover our needs, even though for now we respect the agreement on it."[65] In other areas, such as the formerly protected legal zone of the Yungas, coca growers have openly disagreed with the *cato* limit. Developing a common platform among coca growers is crucial to opening opportunities for industrialization and the decriminalization of the leaf abroad.

While the MAS victory led the United States to moderate its longstanding hard-line position, a new path for the "war on drugs" and alternative development will depend on just how patient the United States is with Bolivia. After Morales's election in December 2005, U.S. officials began distinguishing between coca and cocaine for the first time ever. They initially expressed a willingness to work with the new administration, although they largely suspended aid to the Chapare after the election and failed to release other promised funding.

Despite this uncertainty, hope exists that a more effective and humane policy can emerge. To date, however, the Morales government has failed to concretely develop and implement rural development plans or an economic assessment of the *cato* and industrialization initiatives.[66] How long the United States—and coca growers—will wait patiently for the MAS government to act remains to be seen. After twenty years of suffering and failed promises, coca growers expect substantial changes, and the Morales government understands this. As Felipe Cáceres explained: "If there are real alternatives, the Coca Grower Federations will welcome them. My whole life has been involved in this, and this awful situation has to change. I really want something else for my children."[67]

CONCLUSION: A TALE OF TWO PERSPECTIVES

Coca leaf has been part of Bolivia's indigenous culture for nearly four thousand years. It is a leaf that represents the gifts of Pachamama to her people and that provides income for families that barely have enough to feed their children. To U.S. antidrug officials and others, the coca represents an addictive drug that spreads crime and destroys communities. It is the raw ingredient for a white powder against which successive U.S. governments have declared open war. It has also become a leverage point by which foreign governments have maintained their influence in Bolivia over several decades. The gap between these views could not be any wider, and each side is clearly willing to fight to support what they believe in.

It is because of this conflict of views that, in Bolivia, coca has become a symbol of resistance. In the face of foreign policies demanding its eradication by force, under the heavy hands of special military units, coca became an emblem for how foreign powers impose their will on Bolivians from abroad. Fierce resentment against these policies pushed coca growers to organize. A culture of social resistance that was born five hundred years ago, and again in Bolivia's mines and haciendas from the 1930s on, was reborn in the coca fields of the Chapare in the 1980s and 1990s, often among the children and grandchildren of miners. Coca grower *sindicatos,* or unions, became the defense mechanisms for those who wanted to protect their right to their economic livelihood and those who seek to preserve their cultural sovereignty. Those unions, in turn, became both catalysts and teachers for other resistance movements that followed, including the battles against the privatization of water and the bargain-priced exportation of Bolivian gas.

If the architects of the "war on drugs" want to understand why their strategies continue to meet unyielding resistance in Bolivia, it is because that war has chosen as its target a way of life that is rooted in centuries of history and is also key to many families' economic survival. In reality, the conflict in perspectives between U.S. officials and Bolivian coca growers is based more on blindness that an actual conflict of interests. There is no reason *cocaleros* cannot simultaneously defend their cultural and economic right to grow coca while also recognizing the real damage that this plant can cause elsewhere if turned over to the drug market and transformed into cocaine. On the other hand, the United States can certainly pursue its interests in fighting drug addiction without destroying the cultural richness and the economic necessity of Bolivian coca cultivation.

If both sides can see this, then Bolivia has a real chance now to adopt practical solutions that can serve the interests of both. Coca growers have already shown a willingness to limit coca cultivation in excess of legal uses. Creative solutions that involve the participation of coca-growing communities, rather than the use of force, could bring economic alternatives to farmers while bolstering community vigilance against those who do supply coca to the drug trade. For new constructive solutions to work, however, U.S. and other drug officials must recognize coca's long-standing cultural and economic significance and, most important, Bolivia's sovereignty to make its own decisions.

The United States has had two decades to apply its approach, and its effects can be measured in numbers. The number of dead can be counted in the dozens. The number of innocent people jailed can be counted in the thousands. The number of U.S. tax dollars spent can be counted in the millions. Yet cocaine availability in the United States and abroad continues unabated. The moment has come for a different approach, and it is Bolivia's turn to take the lead.

NOTES

1.   Timothy Plowman, "Botanical Perspectives on Coca," *Journal of Psychedelic Drugs* 11, no. 1–2 (1979): 103–17; James A. Duke, David Aulik, and Timothy Plowman, "Nutritional Value of Coca," *Harvard University Botanical Museum Leaflets* 24, no. 6 (1975): 113–19; also in William Carter, ed., *Ensayos científicos sobre la coca* (Scientific essays about coca) (La Paz: Librería Editorial Juventud, 1996). This research shows that the normal amount of coca chewed by an indigenous worker in one day—about

one hundred grams—more than satisfies the U.S. recommended dietary allowance for these vitamins and minerals.

2. Roderick E. Burchard, "Una nueva perspectiva sobre la masticación de la coca" (A new perspective on chewing coca), *América Indígena* 38, no. 4 (1978): 809–35.

3. Wade Davis, *One River: Explorations and Discoveries in the Amazon Rainforest* (New York: Simon and Schuster, 1996), p. 419. For more on calcium of coca leaf, see Paul T. Baker and Richard B. Mazess, "Calcium: Unusual Sources in the Highland Peruvian Diet," *Science* 124 (1936): 1466–67; and Carter, *Ensayos científicos*, 67–70.

4. Fernando A. Montesinos, "Metabolism of Cocaine," *Bulletin on Narcotics* 17, no. 2 (1965): 11–17; see also Carter, *Ensayos científicos*, 99–111; Andrew Weil, "Letter from the Andes: The New Politics of Coca," *New Yorker*, May 15, 1995, pp. 70–80.

5. Enrique Mayer, "El uso social de la coca en el mundo andino: Contribución a un debate y toma de posición" (The social use of coca in the Andean world: A contribution and position taken in a debate), *América Indígena* 38, no. 4 (1978): 849–65.

6. Anthony Henman, *Mama coca: Un estudio completo de la coca* (Mother coca: A complete study of coca) (La Paz: Hisbol S.R.L., 1992 [1978]), p. 85.

7. Silvia Rivera Cusicanqui, "Liberal Democracy and *Ayllu* Democracy in Bolivia: The Case of Northern Potosí," *Journal of Development Studies* 26, no. 4 (1990): 97–121.

8. John V. Murra, "Introducción al estudio histórico del cultivo de la hoja de coca (*Erythroxylum coca*) en los Andes" (Introduction to the historic study of coca leaf cultivation), in *El mundo andino: Población, medio ambiente y economía* (The Andean world: Population, environment, and economy) (Lima: IEP Ediciones, 2002 [1992]), p. 360.

9. John Hemming, *The Conquest of the Incas* (London: Macmillan, 1970), p. 354.

10. James M. Malloy, *Bolivia: The Uncompleted Revolution* (Pittsburgh, PA: University of Pittsburgh Press, 1970), p. 17.

11. William E. Carter and Mauricio Mamani, *Coca en Bolivia* (Coca in Bolivia) (La Paz: Librería Editorial Juventud, 1986).

12. June Nash, *We Eat the Mines and the Mines Eat Us: Dependency and Exploitation in Bolivian Tin Mines* (New York: Columbia University Press, 1993 [1979]).

13. Gabriel Carranza Polo, *Inal Maman Sarta Wipa: El levantamiento de la madre coca* (Inal Maman Sarta Wipa: The rise of mother coca) (La Paz: 2001), p. 23. Translation by author.

14. Pablo Stefanoni and Hervé Do Alto, *Evo Morales, de la coca al palacio: Una oportunidad para la izquierda indígena* (Evo Morales, from coca to the palace: An opportunity for the indigenous left) (La Paz: Malatesta, 2006).

15. Davis, *One River*, p. 414.

16. Lynn Sikkink, "A History of Coca, Part 1: Andean Folk Medicine and Victorian Tonic," *South American Explorer* 72 (2003): 6–11; and "Coca, Part II: Casualty of the Drug Wars," *South American Explorer* 73 (2003): 6–11; Richard Davenport-Hines, *The Pursuit of Oblivion: A Global History of Narcotics* (New York: Norton, 2002); Dominic Streatfeild, *Cocaine: An Unauthorized Biography* (New York: St. Martin's Press, 2001); P. Gootenberg, ed., *Cocaine: Global Histories* (London: Routledge, 1999); Madeline B. Léons and Harry Sanabria, eds., *Coca, Cocaine, and the Bolivian Reality* (Albany: State University of New York Press, 1997); Roberto Laserna, *Veinte juicios y prejuicios sobre coca-cocaína* (Twenty judgements and prejudices about coca-cocaine) (La Paz: Edición Clave, 1996); Davis, *One River*; and Henman, *Mama Coca*. See also the Washington Office on Latin America, www.wola.org; and the Andean Information Network, www.ain-bolivia.org.

17. José Agustin Morales, *Monografía de las provincias de Nor y Sud Yungas (Departamento de La Paz)* (Monograph of the North and South Yungas Provinces—Department of La Paz), 157. (Ayacucho, Peru: Imp. Artística, 1929).

18. Ibid., p. 159; Paul Gootenberg, "Reluctance or Resistance? Constructing Cocaine (Prohibitions) in Peru, 1910–1950," in Gootenberg, *Cocaine: Global Histories*, p. 56.

19. Davis, *One River*, p. 417. Accepted estimates of traditional use of coca is closer to four thousand years.

20. For a comprehensive history of the legal control of coca leaf and cocaine, see "Coca Yes, Cocaine No?" Transnational Institute Drugs and Democracy Programme Debate Paper #13, June 2006, www.tni.org/drugs/index.htm.

21. Davis, *One River,* p. 418; Harold Osborne, *Bolivia: A Land Divided* (London: Oxford University Press, 1964), p. 116.

22. While Bolivia was never fully decertified, in 1994 and 1995 it was granted a national security waiver, which eliminated the sanctions to protect U.S. national security. The certification process was modified in 2002. See Coletta A. Youngers and Eileen Rosin, eds., *Drugs and Democracy in Latin America: The Impact of U.S. Policy* (Boulder, Colo.: Lynne Reinner Publishers, 2005), p. 372.

23. Kathryn Ledebur, "Bolivia: Clear Consequences," in Youngers and Rosin, *Drugs and Democracy,* p. 151; and Theo Roncken, "El enigma boliviana: Bilateralizar la agenda bilateral" (The Bolivian enigma: Bilateralize the bilateral agenda), in *Democracias bajo fuego: Drogas y poder en América Latina* (Democracies under fire: Drugs and power in Latin America), ed. Martin Jelsma and Theo Roncken (Montevideo, Uruguay: Ediciones de Brecha, no date), p. 305.

24. Washington Office on Latin America (WOLA) interview with former Bolivian government official, October 1, 2006.

25. U.S. Department of State, International Narcotics Control Strategy Report 2002, Bolivia section.

26. WOLA interview with Godofredo Reinicke, former Human Rights Ombudsman in the Chapare, August 11, 2005.

27. Kathryn Ledebur, *Coca and Conflict in the Chapare,* Washington Office on Latin America's Drug War Monitor series, July 2002, p. 13.

28. Ibid., pp. 164, 170.

29. Andean Information Network (AIN)/WOLA meeting at the U.S. Embassy in La Paz, November 2002.

30. Ledebur, *Coca and Conflict,* p. 164; and written communication from Kathryn Ledebur, August 11, 2005.

31. AIN/WOLA interview with Phil Chicola, U.S. State Department, July 15, 2002.

32. This section is based on Kathryn Ledebur and Coletta A. Youngers, *Crisis or Opportunity? Bolivian Drug Control Policy and the U.S. Response,* WOLA/AIN, June 2006.

33. "Morales reitera a EE.UU. necesidad de alianza" (Morales reiterates need for alliance to the U.S.), *El Diario,* January 23, 2006.

34. Carol Conzelman, "Yungas Coca Growers Seek Industrialization of Coca but Split on Its Legalization," AIN Report, February 8, 2007.

35. AIN/WOLA interview with Juan Alanoca, director of Radio Fides Chapare, September 28, 2006.

36. AIN/WOLA interview with Col. Miguel Vásquez Viscarra, October 4, 2006.

37. The names in this section have been changed to protect people's privacy and safety.

38. Personal interviews with the author, Cochabamba, June–July 1999.

39. Figures based on data from the Régimen Penitenciario del Departamento de Cochabamba (Prison Authority for the Department of Cochabamba), received upon written request February 2007.

40. Personal interview with the author, July 1999, Cochabamba.

41. U.S. State Department, International Narcotics Control Strategy Report, Volume 1: Drug and Chemical Control, March 2006, www.state.gov/p/inl/rls/nrcrpt/2006/vol1/html/62106.htm (accessed April 2, 2007).

42. This is based on the personal observation of the author, who was present at the trial.

43. Personal interview with the authors, November 4, 2006, Eterazama, Bolivia.

44. To date, there have been many fluctuations in the exchange rate between the boliviano and the U.S. dollar. Throughout this chapter, the exchange rate is based on the numbers from late 2006, approximately eight bolivianos to one U.S. dollar.

45. Personal interview with the authors, November 29, 2006, Cochabamba, Bolivia.

46. Personal interview with the authors, January 4, 2007, Parajti, Bolivia.

47. "Los precursores, el blanco del nuevo plan antidrogas" (The precursors, the target of the new anti-drug plan), *La Razón,* August 31, 2006. Translation by author.

48. Estimate based on data from C. Araníbar and A. Alarcón, *Desarrollo alternativo y erradicación de cultivos de coca* (Alternative development and coca crop eradication) (La Paz: Viceministerio de Desarrollo Alternativo, Ministerio de Agricultura, Ganadería y Desarrollo Rural, 2002); General Accounting Office, *Drug Control Efforts to Develop Alternatives to Cultivating Illicit Crops in Columbia Have Made Little Progress and Face Serious Obstacles* (Washington, D.C.: GAO, 2002; M. Lifsher, "In U.S. Drug War, Ally Bolivia Loses Ground to Coca Farmers," *Wall Street Journal,* May 13, 2003; and the U.S. Agency for International Development, "The USAID Assistance Program in Bolivia," http://bolivia.usaid.gov. Considerable variation exists in these numbers, with some estimates ranging as high as $700 million up to 2002 if PL 480 funds (U.S. food aid program) are taken into account. G. A. Potter, *Rhetoric vs. Reality: Alternative Development in the Andes: Final Report* (New York: Drug Policy Alliance, 2002).

49. Personal interview with the authors, November 4, 2006, Eterazama, Bolivia.

50. Personal interviews with the authors, January 4, 2007 (Juan), and November 29, 2006 (Cintia).

51. Andean Information Network, "Coca Grower Views on Alternative Development" (Cochabamba: AIN, 2002), 6.

52. Ibid.

53. United States Agency for International Development (USAID), "USAID Vision Statement on Conflict" (Washington, D.C.: USAID, 2004).

54. Ibid.

55. Linda Farthing and Benjamin Kohl, "'Conflicting Agendas': The Politics of Development Aid in Drug Producing Areas," *Development Policy Review* 23 (2005): 183–98.

56. AIN, "Coca Grower Views on Alternative Development."

57. Benjamin Kohl and Linda Farthing, *Impasse in Bolivia: Neoliberal Hegemony and Popular Resistance* (London: Zed Books. 2006).

58. German Enterprise for Technical Cooperation and the United Nations Drug Control Program, "The Role of Alternative Development in Drug and Development Co-operation" (2002).

59. Interview with Felipe Cáceres, July 31, 2003, Villa Tunari.

60. USAID/Bolivia, "Integrated Alternative Development Strategic Objective 2006," www.bolivia.usaid.gov/U.S./5ID.htm, (accessed February 28, 2007); USAID/Bolivia, "Licit Economy in Coca Growing and Associated Areas Increasingly Sustainable."

61. Ibid.

62. "En diciembre comienza industrialización de la coca y Venezuela comprará toda la producción" (Coca industrialization begins in December and Venezuela will buy the products), Agencia Boliviana de Información, October 8, 2006, www.cocasoberania.org/131020061.html.

63. Conzelman, "Yungas Coca Growers."

64. Susan Taylor Martin, "U.S. Policy Not Limited to Borders," *St. Petersburg Times,* July 29, 2001.

65. E-mail communication from Andean Information Network, November 16, 2006.

66. E-mail communication from Andean Information Network, October 20, 2006.

67. Interview with the author, July 2003.

Latinas and the War on Drugs in the United States, Latin America, and Europe[1]

Juanita Díaz-Cotto

THE IMPACT OF criminal justice policies on Latinas in the United States, Latin America, and Europe must be viewed within an international context wherein Latinas(os) are targeted for arrest and incarceration under the auspices of the U.S.-sponsored "war on drugs."[2] Whereas Latin American governments criminalize particular groups of people within their own countries, the United States criminalizes entire Latin American nations while pursuing the war on drugs. The United States highlights the role that Latinas(os) play in the production, processing, trafficking, and consumption of "illicit drugs" such as marijuana, heroin, and cocaine. At the same time, it masks the demand for such drugs in the United States and Europe[3] and the role played by U.S. government agencies,[4] law enforcement officers,[5] and private corporations[6] in the development of the drug industry.

Studies of the war on drugs in relation to the United States and Latin America have tended to focus on one region or the other. Likewise, few have analyzed the impact of such policies on Latinas or made a passing reference to them.[7] The aim of this chapter is to bring together diverse sources of information in order to compare the effects the war on drugs is having on Latinas in diverse geographic regions. Thus, we gain a deeper understanding of how the globalization of the war on drugs has affected Latina(o) communities.

LATINAS(OS) AND U.S. CRIMINAL JUSTICE POLICIES

On December 31, 2000, there were more than two million persons imprisoned in state, federal, and local facilities in the United States.[8] These numbers were complemented by prisoners held in private jails and prisons. As of December 2003, the United States had the highest incarceration rate in the world despite declining national crime rates during the 1990s.[9] Latina(o) overrepresentation within the prisoner population was evidenced by the fact that whereas in 1999, Latinas(os) were already 15.5 percent of those held in local jails,[10] in 2000 they composed only 12.5 percent of the U.S. population.[11] At year end 2000, they were 16.4 percent of sentenced prisoners under state and federal jurisdiction.[12] When analyzed separately, findings showed that, in 1999, Latinas were one in seven of women in state prisons and one in three of women in federal prisons.[13] States such as New York and California tended to have an even greater over-representation of Latinas(os) within their jail and prisoner population, sometimes composing one third of all those imprisoned.[14]

The increase in the prisoner population has been due primarily to the passage of mandatory sentencing and drug-related laws. By 1999, 57 percent of those in federal prisons[15] and 21 percent of those under state jurisdiction were sentenced for drug offenses. Latinas(os) have been particularly adversely affected by the war on drugs because of the overemphasis placed on drug crimes by criminal justice agencies,[16] the overrepresentation of Latinas(os) in drug arrests, and the fact that drug offenses are among the most harshly punished.[17]

Tougher parole board decisions and law enforcement practices have also colluded with state and federal drug-related and mandatory sentencing laws[18] to reduce defendants' ability to plea bargain, increase sentence length for some offenses, and make imprisonment mandatory for others. In New York and California, those most affected by such laws include African Americans and Latinas(os) and persons convicted for drug offenses (mainly possession) and nonviolent property crimes (e.g., theft and burglary).[19]

Elsewhere I have discussed additional factors that have contributed to the over-representation of Latinas(os) in rates of arrest, sentencing, and imprisonment in the United States.[20] Some of the contributing factors are that the Latina(o) population is a young population and that the young are the most likely to be arrested, criminal justice policies that target poor and working-class people for arrest and incarceration, inadequate legal representation and lack of knowledge of the inner workings of the criminal justice system, and language barriers throughout the criminal justice system. Added to these are excessive patrolling of poor and working-class neighborhoods by law enforcement personnel, discriminatory enforcement of criminal justice and immigration policies, and the fact that Latinas(os) are not as likely as whites and African Americans to be channeled into alternatives-to-incarceration programs. As a result of these facts, Latinos, but particularly Latinas, are disproportionately arrested, convicted, and imprisoned. Because of the lack of support services before, during, and after incarceration, they also have one of the highest recidivism rates.

LATINAS AND THE WAR ON DRUGS IN THE UNITED STATES

Men have always composed the overwhelming number of those arrested and incarcerated in the United States.[21] However, during the 1980s and 1990s, the number of women arrested for drug-related offenses increased alarmingly. By 1991, one in three women prisoners in the United States were serving sentences for drug offenses.[22] In states such as New York and California, among the most ardent supporters of drug-related and mandatory sentencing laws, women were more likely than men to be imprisoned for drug-related crimes. For example, in 1996, 32.5 percent of the men but 60.4 percent of the women in prison in New York were incarcerated for drug crimes.[23] In California, on December 31, 1999, 43 percent of the women but only 26.7 percent of the men were imprisoned for drug-related offenses.[24] Furthermore, women in federal prisons convicted for low-level drug offenses tended to receive sentences similar to those of men sentenced for serious drug-related crimes.[25]

Added to discrepancies based on gender were those based on race and ethnicity. Several studies have shown that racism plays a role in drug enforcement. For example, in New York and California, Latinas(os) and African Americans were more likely than whites to be imprisoned for drug offenses even when whites were more likely[26] or just as likely to use drugs as African Americans and Latinas(os).[27] The disproportionate impact of these combined factors is demonstrated by the fact that throughout the 1990s, Latinas in New York were more likely to be sentenced to prison for drug offenses than black but, particularly, white women. A 1990 study conducted by Coramae Richey Mann found that in New York, Latinas were 28.8 percent of women arrested for drug offenses but 41.2 percent of women imprisoned for such offenses.[28] By 1994, 82 percent of Latinas, 72 percent of black women, and 41 percent of white women imprisoned in New York were committed for drug offenses.[29]

Similarly, Mann found that whereas in California white women felons were arrested more often for drugs, theft, and burglary, they were less likely to be imprisoned for theft and drug offenses than Latina and black women.[30] Hence, Latinas made up only 18.7 percent of women arrested but 26.1 percent of women imprisoned for drug violations.[31] Latinas in California were also more likely to be imprisoned for felonies (23.8 percent) than white (16.8 percent) or black women (18.3 percent).[32]

As a result of the combination of gender and ethnic factors, Latinas in New York, for example, were more likely to be imprisoned for drug-related offenses than Latinos. Hence, 62.3 percent of Latinas but only 36 percent of Latinos were imprisoned for drug offenses on December 31, 1987.[33] By December 2001, 38.8 percent of Latinos but 61.5 percent of Latinas were imprisoned for drug-related offenses.[34] A number of additional factors could account for Latinas' overrepresentation in drug-related imprisonment rates compared with Latinos and whites. Latina drug use could have escalated significantly during the 1980s and 1990s. In fact, data compiled by the Bureau of Justice Statistics show that half of the women in state prisons on December 1999 had been using alcohol and/or other drugs while committing the offense for which they were arrested.[35]

Hence, Latina imprisonment rates could reflect their increasing drug use and subsequent arrests for drug-related crimes. Latina addicts and former addicts interviewed by the author in California seemed to think this was one possible explanation. However, they offered additional explanations for Latinas' increasing imprisonment. On the one hand, they argued that Latinos have become less willing than in the past to take full responsibility for joint drug offenses committed with Latinas. On the other hand, they felt that more Latinos now try to convince Latinas to take full responsibility for such crimes in order to avoid long prison sentences they may face because of mandatory and drug-related sentencing laws and their more extensive contacts with the criminal justice system.

Latinas were also affected by the fact that Latina and black women from Africa, South America, and the Caribbean were more likely than Latinos to be profiled as drug couriers[36] by criminal justice personnel and in the mass media. Hence, they were more likely to be stopped and searched for drugs than men or whites. This was so despite the fact that the typical drug courier was a male foreign national.[37] Moreover, Latinas were sometimes used as "decoys" on flights by drug dealers who wanted to divert attention from others on the same flight transporting larger quantities of drugs.[38]

Once arrested, Latinas did not generally have the same plea-bargaining power as Latinos. This was partly due to the fact that Latinas did not tend to play major roles in drug-trafficking networks. Thus, even when they were willing to cooperate with state authorities, Latinas seldom had the type of information most sought after by police and district attorneys.[39] When given the opportunity to plea bargain, even innocent Latinas frequently pled guilty hoping to get reduced sentences.[40] Others who could not afford to hire competent defense attorneys generally received long prison sentences when they chose trial over plea bargaining.[41] Although some Latinas who cooperated with criminal justice personnel might have been able to negotiate better sentencing terms, those who refused to become informants were frequently given harsher sentences in retaliation for their silence.[42] In all such instances, non–English-speaking Latinas were among the most vulnerable.[43]

Once imprisoned, many Latinas in New York and California, but particularly those who were Spanish monolingual, faced discriminatory treatment at the hands of the overwhelmingly white guard force. Such discrimination was compounded by overcrowded and unsanitary living conditions, economic exploitation by jail and prison administrators, and the lack of programs that would allow women to obtain adequate employment upon their release. Moreover, women prisoners had to contend with discrimination on the basis of sexual orientation; verbal, physical, and sexual abuse at the hands of jail and prison staff; and cleavages among prisoners based primarily on race, ethnicity, and sometimes class.[44]

The fact that many incarcerated women were single heads of households meant that once they were arrested, their families lost both their main caretaker and their breadwinner. The separation of children and mothers also led to the development of severe emotional and psychological problems as families tried to cope with the loss.[45] Often, the incarceration of parents, repressive criminal justice policies targeting poor youths and youth of color, and the lack of adequate social, educational, and financial support structures contributed to the eventual institutionalization and incarceration of prisoners' children.[46] Women in Latin America faced similar issues as a result of the exportation of the U.S. war on drugs to the South.

WOMEN IN LATIN AMERICA AND THE WAR ON DRUGS

The U.S. military was enlisted into domestic law enforcement efforts[47] in 1981, when President Ronald Reagan endorsed its use to assist civilian agencies in law enforcement operations along the 2,000 mile U.S.–Mexico border. The primary objectives were to end the illegal importation of drugs, contraband, and people into the United States[48] and quash revolutionary movements in Latin America.[49] Both drug trafficking and revolutionary movements were seen as major national and international security threats.[50]

The militarization of the U.S.–Mexico border has led to incarceration of large numbers of undocumented Latinas(os), primarily Mexicans, in the United States. Once arrested for drug-related crimes, foreign nationals can be held for extended periods of time in Immigration and Naturalization Service (INS) detention facilities and private prisons. From these they can be deported to their countries of origin or detained while awaiting trial. Various human rights organizations[51] have exposed the treatment women, men, and children receive in such facilities. It will, therefore, not be discussed here. Suffice it to say that such treatment includes exposure to severely overcrowded and unsanitary living conditions as well as physical and/or sexual abuse.

Women in Mexico

The militarization of the U.S.–Mexico border has taken place alongside the push from the United States for Latin American countries to militarize their war on drugs.[52] As in the United States, the militarization of the war on drugs in Latin America has been accompanied by the passage of drug-related and mandatory sentencing laws, a drastic increase in the number of persons arrested and imprisoned for drug crimes, and the construction of more jails and prisons. It has also promoted the involvement of both the U.S. and Latin American military in civilian law enforcement efforts. The result of these joint efforts has been the weakening of Latin American civilian governments and a surge in the number of human rights violations in the region.

The Mexican government initially objected both to the militarization of the U.S.–Mexico border and to U.S. incursions into Mexican soil to pursue suspected traffickers and undocumented workers.[53] However, in response to political and economic pressure from the United States, in 1988, Mexican President Carlos Salinas announced that drug-trafficking was a "national security issue,"[54] thus placing Mexican law enforcement priorities on par with those of the United States.

War on drugs policies have resulted in an increase in the number of Mexican women arrested for low-level trafficking on both sides of the border. In some cases, Mexicans trying to cross the border have been falsely accused of drug trafficking because they were unable or unwilling to pay the bribes Mexican police officers demanded for their release.[55] Those detained in Mexico for drug-related crimes are generally held in preventive detention prior to sentencing. Those who have the money to pay the frequently exorbitant bail have sometimes been able to obtain their release while awaiting adjudication. Others have been able to obtain their freedom only through the payment of bribes to criminal justice personnel.[56] While held in detention, many Mexican women have been subjected to sexual and other forms of physical abuse, including rape and torture. Law enforcement personnel have also coerced women into signing confessions by threatening to harm family members who have also been arrested.[57] In fact, children have been tortured to make women comply with the goals of law enforcement personnel. As in the case of Latinas and other women prisoners in the United States, once sentenced and imprisoned, many of the women continued to be sexually and physically abused.[58]

A study conducted by the Women's Studies Program of *El Colegio de Mexico* during 1993 and 1994 revealed that 50 to 64 percent of imprisoned women in Mexico were being held for *delitos contra la salud* (crimes against health), that is, crimes related to the consumption and trafficking of drugs.[59] Although a small number of Mexican, Colombian, and Bolivian women have become drug lords,[60] the sexism rampant in the industry has meant that the overwhelming number of women trafficking drugs are actually transporting small amounts of drugs across national and international borders.

Ironically, a significant number of women arrested in Mexico for drug trafficking, particularly those in the larger Mexican cities, have become addicted to illegal drugs while imprisoned. Once addicted, many support their drug habit through sex work.[61] Others resort to sex work in order to support the drug habit of male partners by whom they are intimidated. As in the United States, women addicts in Mexico experience frequent incarceration both for their addiction and for the actions they take to support their habit.

Also, like most Latina prisoners in the United States, women imprisoned in Mexico face overcrowded and unsanitary living conditions. Those who are able to work while imprisoned are generally restricted to unpaid traditional women's work such as sewing, cooking, cleaning, and washing clothes. Discriminatory penal policies allow male prisoners in both countries to have a greater access to educational, vocational, and work programs than women.

As in the case of Latina prisoners in the United States, women prisoners in Mexico tend to be poor and working-class, even when they are employed prior to their incarceration. Those working outside the home tend to be employed in the service sector.

Many have little or no formal education. Approximately 70 percent are between eighteen and thirty-five years old. They are overwhelmingly both mothers and single heads of households.[62]

Women in Bolivia

Indigenous peoples in the Andes have grown and consumed coca leaf safely for over three thousand years. It is used as medicine, tea, food, and in religious and social rituals.[63] Thus, initially, Bolivia, like Mexico, resisted expanding and militarizing the war on drugs.[64] However, in 1988, the Bolivian Congress, in response to economic and military threats from the United States,[65] passed Law 1008, or the Law to Regulate Coca and Controlled Substances. Although much coca production for domestic consumption remained legal, the law expanded the definition of trafficking to include areas of the country and activities not previously regulated.[66]

Law 1008 is enforced by several agencies, including the Fuerza Especial de Lucha Contra el Narcotráfico (FELCN), composed of members of the national police and the armed forces. The FELCN collaborates with the Bolivian Environmental Police[67] and several U.S. military and civilian agencies, including the Drug Enforcement Administration (DEA).[68] Thus, U.S. military forces trained and equipped Bolivian law enforcement agencies financed by the U.S. government,[69] and DEA agents have joined Bolivian officers in searches, confrontations, the destruction of coca fields and cocaine laboratories, and the bombing of roads, villages, and housing complexes. They have participated in arrests, kidnappings, detentions, and the interrogation and torture of civilians. They have helped set up houses of torture or "security houses." DEA agents have also threatened family members of detainees and, on occasion, physically abused relatives in order to force defendants to testify against themselves. Furthermore, DEA agents have elicited bribes in exchange for the release of prisoners.[70] Ironically, the DEA collaborated with local government forces, many of whom are themselves involved in drug trafficking.[71]

The sectors of the population that have openly objected to the eradication of coca, the forced evacuation of their homes and villages, and the treatment received from local and U.S. agents have been severely repressed.[72] Leaders of peasant organizations have been particularly targeted for repression and numerous murders and massacres of men, women, and children have taken place.

> Women have been violently attacked by UMOPAR troops who have tied them to trees, cots, and have put handkerchiefs in their mouths so they will not ask for help. There are complaints of sexual harassment and rape. ... They also pressure the children so that they will accuse their parents and they use them to make the parents come out of the woods.[73]

The number of women who have been threatened, arrested, beaten, raped, tortured, pressured to confess to illicit actions, and killed has risen alarmingly.[74] So has the number of children who have been subjected to physical abuse and/or killed.

The war on drugs in Bolivia has also led to an alarming increase in the number of men, women, and minors arrested and detained in Bolivian prisons as well as local detention centers.[75] By 1993, there were five thousand male and female prisoners held in Bolivian prisons.[76] The majority were incarcerated for violation of Law 1008. Minors (15- to 20-year-olds), who tend to be sentries or couriers, composed a significant percentage (16.5 percent) of those imprisoned for drug offenses.[77] Women were more likely to be imprisoned for drug-related crimes than men. Thus, in 1993, 40.5 percent of women in prison but only 23.3 percent of imprisoned men had been arrested for drug-related crimes.[78] By 1997, 16 percent of those imprisoned in Bolivia were women, an exorbitant number when compared with the United States, where women made up 6.6 percent of all prisoners under the jurisdiction of federal or state authorities at year end 2000.[79]

The involvement of Bolivian women in the drug trade has been primarily as intermediaries or as participants in lower-level activities. Some have assisted their families "in the production of coca paste by mashing the leaves and precursors with their feet."[80] Others have acted as drug couriers, transporting small amounts of coca paste or chemical precursors within national borders.[81] According to Gloria Rose M. de Achá, the majority of women imprisoned for drug trafficking in Bolivia were between the ages of twenty-five and thirty-five.[82] A significant number had little or no education. Most of them came from rural areas and spoke little or no Spanish. Like their sisters in the United States and Mexico, the majority had been victims of physical and sexual abuse prior to their arrest. Many were the sole caretaker for their children before and during imprisonment. As in the case of their counterparts in the United States, those with male partners on the outside tended to be abandoned by them when they were incarcerated.

Once people were arrested for drug crimes, Law 1008 "dangerously reduced both the evidence required to sentence the accused and the rights of the accused to a defense."[83] According to the Andean Information Network:

> The law violates principles universally recognized as fundamental rights of the accused: the presumption of innocence, the safeguards against self-incrimination, the right to a defense, the right to an impartial judge, the right to due process, the right to parole and the right to a speedy trial.[84]

Those arrested under Law 1008 were frequently detained on scant evidence provided by police and military officers who often secured confessions under duress and violence, including torture. Others were framed by the same officers. Although such procedures violated both local and international accords,[85] many pleaded guilty in order to avoid additional abuse.

In 1994, 65 percent of prisoners charged with violating Law 1008 were kept in "preventive detention" despite the fact that they were generally charged with low-level, nonviolent offenses and had not been tried by the courts.[86] Many of them claimed to be innocent of the charges. Most of those incarcerated had not been processed by the courts. A three-stage court process meant that detainees on drug-trafficking charges were generally held between one-and-a-half and three years prior to the adjudication of guilt or innocence.[87] Minimum sentencing requirements imposed sentences ranging from one to thirty years in prison.[88] To the sentences were added fines, the confiscation of property, and court costs. According to Human Rights Watch (HRW), all attempts to reform the law were initially blocked by the United States.[89]

Mandatory sentencing laws meant that once sentenced, women served long minimum sentences. The result was that all male and female prisons in Bolivia have experienced a rapid rate of overcrowding.[90] Moreover, with the financial assistance of the United States, some new prisons have been constructed.[91] Peasants in coca-growing areas who were not arrested during drug raids or those arrested and released from prison have lost everything they owned and found themselves displaced, unemployed, and forced to migrate to urban areas or other parts of the country. Sometimes they return to the illegal growing of coca leaf as a result of economic necessity.

During the 1980s and 1990s, coca-growing peasants joined other sectors of the Bolivian population to demand an end to oppression by government agencies, the redistribution of wealth, and the cessation of foreign intervention in domestic affairs.[92] Although some of these peasant communities have had a long history of activism, others have been politicized by the war on drugs. The women of the coca-growing region have become active participants in such struggles. To this end, they have confronted local police and military forces attempting to destroy their crops, demanded the release of imprisoned husbands, and held hunger strikes, marches, and demonstrations. Some have simultaneously demanded equality between the sexes and an end to the abuse of women by men inside and outside the home.

THE WAR ON DRUGS AND LATIN AMERICAN WOMEN IN EUROPE

According to a study conducted by María C. Dorado (1998) between 1996 and 1997, the largest number of women detained for drug trafficking in Britain and in cities such as Madrid and Frankfurt were Colombian.[93] In all three countries, imprisoned Colombian women interviewed by Dorado were predominantly single women between the ages of twenty-six and forty years who lived in urban areas in Colombia. Although most were poor, approximately 85 percent of them were financially responsible for their children and sometimes other relatives.[94] Few were illiterate, but they tended to have low educational levels.

As in the case of Latin American women couriers arrested in New York's JFK Airport, most Colombian women arrested in Europe transported drugs to support themselves and their families. Some had been tricked by friends, acquaintances, or male partners into transporting the drugs. Others had their lives or those of their children and other relatives threatened if they refused to traffic drugs. In a few cases, the children of Latinas arrested in Europe were murdered in retaliation for the women's failure to deliver the drugs.[95]

Once again, like Latina drug couriers arrested in New York, Colombian women frequently transported small quantities of drugs. Approximately 60 percent of Dorado's sample were imprisoned for transporting less than a kilo of cocaine.[96] Frequently, the women were unaware of the actual amount of drugs their were carrying, the types of drugs involved, or the value of the merchandise. Once arrested, Colombian women were subjected to long periods of questioning, isolation, and preventive detention. Those who had swallowed balloons were subjected to recurrent X-rays and physical examinations. Frequently, during this waiting period, they were given laxatives and were not allowed to eat much food, take showers, or change their clothes. Sometimes their hands and feet were shackled to their hospital beds even while sleeping.[97] As a result, they endured many days of physical pain and discomfort until they had expelled all the balloons from their bodies.

Although several international conventions (e.g., European Convention on Human Rights, Vienna Convention) stipulate that in cases involving drug trafficking, imprisonment should be used as a last resort and only for short periods of time and that sentences should be uniform across countries, Colombian and other Latin American women were arrested and quickly sentenced to various lengths of time depending on the country, the city, and the court jurisdiction involved.[98]

As in the United States, Spanish-monolingual women were provided with interpreters during some part of their criminal proceedings. Nonetheless, the lack of adequate legal representation, their unfamiliarity with the workings of the criminal justice system, and the legal restrictions imposed on their attorneys made the women unable to provide adequate defenses.[99] As a result, in countries such as England, they frequently received longer sentences than other women arrested for similar crimes.[100] Once imprisoned, they faced isolation as a result of language barriers and the fact that their families and friends were thousands of miles away. Many were unable to inform their relatives of their predicament. Others felt too ashamed to let anyone know. Even Latin American women in Spain faced cultural alienation.[101]

Like Latina couriers detained in the United States, Colombian women were first detained at the airport and questioned because, in one way or another, they fit some stereotype of a drug carrier. According to Dorado, they looked Latin, Asian, or hippie. They came from countries listed as "distributors" or "producers" of drugs. Sometimes they seemed nervous, made too many phone calls, wore certain clothes, had new luggage, carried too much cash on them, or simply walked too fast or too slow. Others carried dirty travel bags but traveled first class.[102] With few exceptions, being profiled as drug couriers was what led Latinas in Europe to be stopped for questioning in the first place.

CONCLUSION

The war on drugs spearheaded by the United States at the domestic and international levels has led to the increasing arrest and incarceration of Latinas in the United States, Latin America, and Europe for low-level, nonviolent, drug-related and/or economic crimes. For Latinas, such offenses are motivated by the need to support their addiction, themselves, and/or their families. Wide income disparities, ethnic and racial discrimination, and structural barriers have made it necessary for Latinas to search continuously for new ways to support themselves and their families. For many who live in coca-producing regions, the demand for cocaine from predominantly Anglo/European consumers in the United States and Europe has become an additional source of income. However, although involvement in drug-related activities has allowed some Latinas in both rural and urban areas to fare a bit better off financially than others in their countries, the minor roles they play in such enterprises have not allowed them to escape permanently the dire economic conditions under which most of them live.

Latina involvement in drug-related activities has also become one of the means by which they have become incorporated into the global market. Such incorporation, however, has placed them at the center of the international war on drugs. The globalization of the war on drugs has, in turn, led to the severe repression of entire Latina(o) communities and the incarceration of thousands of women, men, and minors throughout the United States, Latin America, and Europe. At the national and international levels the militarization of the war on drugs has led to the weakening of civil society as military authorities have encroached on areas previously reserved for civil authorities and law enforcement agencies. The militarization of the war on drugs has also been accompanied by an increase in human rights violations by law enforcement and military personnel; the growing incarceration of women, men, and minors; and the building of more jails and prisons.

During the period of time in which the war on drugs has been pursued, Latinas addicted to drugs have been repeatedly arrested and incarcerated by governments that deny them adequate access to drug rehabilitation programs and continuously interfere with Latinas' attempts to recover from alcohol and drug abuse. Ironically, the same elites who continuously arrest Latinas for low-level, nonviolent, drug-related crimes also allow drug kingpins and others working within local, state, and federal agencies to engage in illegal drug enterprises.

While governmental leaders have recognized that education and drug treatment are the most effective means of reducing the demand for illegal drugs[103] and some states have begun to carry out corrections and sentencing reforms,[104] state and federal elites continue to pursue policies that fundamentally emphasize repressive legislation and law enforcement practices as well as imprisonment. The repeal of drug-related and mandatory sentencing laws continues to be resisted by those who oppose diverting funds from law enforcement and military agencies into education and drug rehabilitation programs.

The ill-founded and intransigent nature of the U.S.-sponsored war on drugs and its total disregard for human rights abroad led to the expulsion of the United States from both the United Nations (UN) Human Rights Commission and the UN International Narcotics Control Board in May 2001,[105] a year before the U.S. invasion of Iraq. With the passage of the USA PATRIOT Act in October 2001[106] and its current use to pursue drug-related crimes, the war on drugs in the United States has reached a new level. Justice Department agents, under the guise of a terrorist threat, now frequently invoke intelligence powers to seize records and carry out surveillance of suspected drug traffickers and others involved in crimes not connected to terrorism.[107] Such actions only serve ultimately to weaken the civil rights of all.

REFERENCES

1. The term "Latinas" is used in this chapter to refer to women of Latin American ancestry, including women of Mexican ancestry in the United States who define themselves as Chicanas. Although "Latinos" is commonly used as a gender-neutral plural, the author prefers "Latinas(os)" when referring to both men and women. Latin America as used here refers to the nineteen Spanish-speaking countries located in South and Central America and the Spanish-speaking Caribbean.

2. Although this chapter focuses on Latinas, African Americans in the United States continue to be among the most severely affected by the war on drugs and constitute the majority of those imprisoned nationally. See chapters by Richie, Borhman and Murakawa, Gilmore, and Smith in this volume.

3. Peter Reuter, "Foreign Demand for Latin American Drugs: The USA and Europe," in E. Joyce and C. Malamud, *Latin America and the Multinational Drug Trade* (New York: St. Martin's, 1998); Adriana Rossi, *Narcotráfico y Amazonia Ecuatoriana* (Buenos Aires, Argentina: Kohen and Asociados International, 1996).

4. Bruce M. Bagley, ed., *Drug Trafficking in the Americas: An Annotated Bibliography* (Coral Gables, FL: North South Center, University of Miami, 1996); Centro de Documentación e Información-Bolivia, *DEA y Soberanía en Bolivia* (Cochabamba, Bolivia: CEDIB, 1994); Alexander Cockburn and Jeffrey St. Clair, *Whiteout* (New York: Verso, 1998).

5. Christopher Commission, Report of the Independent Commission on the Los Angeles Police Department (Los Angeles, 1991); James G. Kolts, The Los Angeles County Sheriffs' Department: A Report (Kolts Report) (Los Angeles: Board of Supervisors, 1992); Mollen Commission, Commission Report (New York City, 1994); U.S. House of Representatives, Committee on the Judiciary, Police Misconduct, Hearings before the Subcommittee on Criminal Justice, Serial No. 50, parts 1 and 2, 98th Congress, 1st Session (Washington, D.C., 1984).

6. *Federal News Service*, U.S. Congress, Senate Governmental Committee, Permanent Investigations Subcommittee Hearing, *Drug Money Laundering* (February 27, 1992); Anthony P. Maingot, "Offshore Banking in the Caribbean: The Panamanian Case," in Joyce and Malamud 1998, 149–171.

7. See Evelin Agreda, Norma Rodríguez, and Alex Contreras, *Mujeres Cocaleras* (Cochabamba, Bolivia: Comité Coordinador de las Cinco Federaciones del Trópico de Cochabamba, 1996); Amnesty

International, *Mexico, Overcoming Fear*, 1996; Elizabeth Azaola and Cristina J. Yucamán, *Las Mujeres Olvidadas* (México, D.F.: Centro Nacional de Derechos Humanos, Colegio de México, 1996); Barbara Bloom, "Triple Jeopardy: Race, Class, and Gender in Women's Imprisonment," Ph.D. diss., University of California, 1996; Correctional Association of New York (CANY), *Injustice Will Be Done* (1992); CANY, *Mandatory Injustice* (1999); Gloria R. M. de Achá, "Características de las Mujeres Encarceladas en Bolivia," in R. del Olmo, ed., *Criminalidad y Criminalización de la Mujer en la Región Andina* (Caracas, Venezuela: Nueva Sociedad, 1998); Gloria R.M. de Achá, *Violaciones a los Derechos Humanos Civiles Durante la Investigación Policial en Casos Detenidos Bajo la Ley 1008* (Cochabamba, Bolivia: Red Andina de Información, CEDIB, 1996); R. del Olmo, ed., *Criminalidad y Criminalización de la Mujer en la Región Andina* (Caracas, Venezuela: Nueva Sociedad, 1998); Juanita Díaz-Cotto, *Chicana Lives and Criminal Justice: In Their Own Words* (Austin: University of Texas, forthcoming 2006); J. Díaz-Cotto, "Latina Imprisonment and the War on Drugs," in M. Bosworth and J. Flavin, eds., *Race, Gender, and Punishment* (New Brunswick, NJ: Rutgers University Press, 2005); Human Rights Watch (HRW), *Bolivia: Human Rights Violations and the War on Drugs* (1995a); HRW, *Cruel and Usual: Disproportionate Sentences for New York Drug Offenders* 9 (2)(B), 1997a; Coramae R. Mann, "Women of Color and the Criminal Justice System," in B.R. Price and N.J. Sokoloff, eds., *The Criminal Justice System and Women* (New York: McGraw-Hill, 1995).

8.   Bureau of Justice Statistics (BJS), *Census of Jails, 1999* (Washington, D.C.: Department of Justice, 2001a); BJS, *Prisoners in 2000* (Washington. D.C.: Department of Justice, 2001b).

9.   Eric Lichtblau, "U.S. Crime Decrease Sets Record," *Press and Sun Bulletin* (May 8, 2000); The Sentencing Project, *New Inmate Population Figures Demonstrate Need for Policy Reform* (Washington, D.C., 2003). The combination of increasing imprisonment rates and decreasing crime rates and the manner in which private and public agencies profit from prison construction led prisoners rights advocates to speak of the "prison-industrial complex."

10. BJS 2001a: 3.

11. U.S. Census Bureau, Department of Commerce, *The Hispanic Population* (Washington, D.C.: Department of Commerce, May 2001), 1.

12. BJS 2001b: 11.

13. BJS, *Special Report: Women Offenders* (Washington, D.C.: Department of Justice, December 1999), 7.

14. California Department of Corrections, *CDC Facts: 4TH Quarter 2002* (Sacramento, 2002); California Department of Corrections, Administrative Service Division, *Historical Trends Institutions and Parole Population, 1977–1997* (Sacramento, June 1998); New York Department of Correctional Services (NYSDOCS), *The Hub System: Profile of Inmates under Custody in January 1, 1996* (Albany, 1996); U.S. Census Bureau, *The Hispanic Population: Census 2000 Brief* (Washington, D.C.: Department. of Commerce, May 2001): Table 2, p. 4.

15. BJS 2001b: 11–12.

16. Katherine Beckett and Theodore Sasson, *The Politics of Injustice* (Thousand Oaks, CA: Pine Forge, 2000).

17. CANY 1992, 1999; HRW 1997a.

18. Examples of drug-related and mandatory sentencing laws include New York's Rockefeller Drug Laws, Second Felony Offender Laws, Violent Felony Offender Laws, changes in Consecutive Sentence Provisions, California's Three Strikes Law, and Truth-in-Sentencing Laws. These laws were complemented by the 1994 Federal Crime Control Act. In 1991, there were over 100 federal crimes regulated by mandatory sentencing laws. By 1994, all fifty states had passed at least one such law (Beckett and Sasson 2000: 176). See also Barbara Bloom, Meda Chesney-Lind, and Barbara Owen, *Women in California Prisons* (San Francisco: Center on Juvenile and Criminal Justice, 1994); CANY 1992; HRW 1997a; NYSDOCS, Division of Program Planning, Research, and Evaluation, *Characteristics of Female Inmates Held under Custody, 1975–1985* (Albany, 1986a); Michael Tonry, *Sentencing Matters* (New York: Oxford University, 1996); U.S. Sentencing Commission, *Special Report to the Congress: Mandatory Minimum Penalties in the Federal Criminal Justice System* (Washington, D.C., 1991).

19. CANY, *Do They Belong in Prison?* New York, 1985; CANY 1992, 1999; Díaz-Cotto 2006; HRW 1997a; HRW, *Punishment and Prejudice: Racial Disparities in the War on Drugs* (New York, 2000).

20. See Juanita Díaz-Cotto, *Gender, Ethnicity, and the State: Latina and Latino Prison Politics* (Albany: SUNY-Press, 1996); Juanita Díaz-Cotto, "The Criminal Justice System and Its Impact on Latinas(os) in the United States," *The Justice Professional* 13 (1) (April 2000): 49–68; Díaz-Cotto, 2006.
21. U.S. Department of Justice, Federal Bureau of Investigations, *Uniform Crime Reports: Crime in the U.S.* (Washington, D.C., 1961–2002).
22. BJS, Special Report: Survey of State Prison Inmates, 1991: Women in Prison (Washington, D.C.: Department of Justice, 1994).
23. HRW 1997a: 13.
24. California Department of Corrections, Administrative Service Division, *California Prisoners and Parolees, 2000 Summary Statistics* (Sacramento, June 2000), Table 13.
25. Marc Mauer and Tracy Huling, *Young Black Americans and the Criminal Justice System: Five Years Later* (Washington, D.C.: The Sentencing Project, 1995).
26. Michael Isikoff, "Study: White Students More Likely to Use Drugs," *Washington Post*, February 25, 1991; Sam Meddis, "Whites, Not Blacks, at the Core of the Drug Crisis," *USA Today*, December 20, 1989.
27. Pettiway found that 31.2 percent of Latinas, 33.8 percent of white women, and 35 percent of black women reported heroin and opiate. Leon E. Pettiway, "Participation in Crime Partnerships by Female Drug Users," *Criminology* 25 (3) (1987): 746.
28. Mann 1995: 128.
29. HRW 1997a: 14.
30. Mann 1995: 128.
31. Mann 1995: 128. Black women were 30.5 percent of women arrested in California for drug offenses but 34.1 percent of those incarcerated for such offenses. White women were 48.5 percent of women arrested for drug violations but only 38.3 percent of those imprisoned for such offenses (Mann 1985: 128).
32. Mann 1995: 128.
33. NYSDOCS, Division of Program Planning, Research, and Evaluation. *Men and Women Under Custody: 1987–2001* (Albany, September 2002), 87.
34. Ibid.
35. BJS 1999: 8
36. CANY 1992; Penny Green, *Drug Couriers* (London: Quartet Books, 1996).
37. CANY 1992: 11. Men are also more likely to swallow "balloons" filled with drugs (CANY 12).
38. CANY 1992.
39. CANY 1999.
40. CANY 1992.
41. CANY 1992.
42. Díaz-Cotto 2006.
43. CANY 1992.
44. Díaz-Cotto 1996, 2006; HRW, Women's Rights Project, *All Too Familiar: Sexual Abuse of Women in U.S. State Prisons*, 1996; Barbara Owen, *In the Mix* (Albany: State University of New York, 1998); Katherine Watterson, *Women in Prison* (Boston: Northeastern University, 1996).
45. Zelma W. Henriques, *Imprisoned Mothers and Their Children* (Lanham: University Press of America, 1982).
46. Katherine Gabel and Denise Johnston, eds., *Children of Incarcerated Parents* (New York: Lexington Books, 1995).
47. Timothy Dunn, *The Militarization of the US-Mexico Border, 1978–1992* (Austin, TX: Center for Mexican American Studies, University of Texas, 1996).
48. Dunn 1996.
49. Carlos Alonso, *Guerra Antidrogas, Democracia, Derechos Humanos y Militarización en América Latina* (Ciudad de Guatemala, Guatemala: CEDIB, Transnational Institute, and Inforpress Centroaméricana, 1997).
50. Nicholas Dorn, J. Jepsen, and E. Savona, *European Drug Policies and Enforcement* (London: Macmillan, 1996); United Nations, *Single Convention on Narcotic Drugs* (New York: UN, 1977); UN Department

of Public Information, *UN Convention Against the Illicit Traffic of Narcotics* (New York: UN, 1991); U.S. Department of State, *International Narcotics Control Strategy* (Washington, D.C., 1991); Office of National Drug Control Policy, Executive Office of the President, *The National Drug Control Strategy, 1997* (Washington, D.C., 1997).

51.　Amnesty International, United States of America, Human Rights Concerns in the Border Region with Mexico (May 1998); HRW, Crossing the Line: Human Rights Abuses Along the U.S. Border with Mexico Persist Amid Climate of Impunity (1995b); HRW, Children's Rights Project, Slipping through the Crack: Unaccompanied Children Detained by the U.S. Immigration and Naturalization Service (1997b).

52.　Alonso 1997; Dunn 1996; M. Jelsma and T. Ronken, eds., *Democracias Bajo Fuego* (Uruguay: TNI, Ediciones Brecha, Acción Andina, 1998); Roberto Laserna, ed., *Economía Política de las Drogas* (Cochabamba, Bolivia: Centro de Estudios de la Realidad Económica y Social-Consejo Latinoamericano de Ciencias Sociales, 1993); Rossi 1996; U.S. Congress, House Committee on Armed Services, *The Andean Drug Strategy and the Role of the U.S. Military*, 101st Congress, 1st Session (Washington, D.C., January 1990).

53.　Hugo B. Margain, "The War on Drugs: A Mexican Perspective," *Voices of México* (October-December 1990): 3–8.

54.　Dunn 1996: 138.

55.　United Press International, "Mexican Border Police Abuse Illegal Immigrants, Report Says," February 24, 1992.

56.　Azaola and Yucamán 1996.

57.　Azaola and Yucamán 1996.

58.　Azaola and Yucamán 1996.

59.　Azaola and Yucamán 1996: 400. The second most important cause for imprisonment was property crimes, particularly theft and fraud.

60.　Mario Arango, *Impacto del Narcotráfico en Antioquia* (Medellín, Colombia: J.M. Arango, 1988); Michael Levine and Laura Kavanau-Levine, *The Big White Lie* (New York: Thunder's Mouth, 1993).

61.　Azaola and Yucamán 1996.

62.　Azaola and Yucamán 1996.

63.　Roberto Laserna, *Twenty (Mis)conceptions on Coca and Cocaine* (La Paz, Bolivia: Clave consultores, s.r.l., 1997); Rossi 1996.

64.　Andy Atkins, "The Economic and Political Impact of the Drug Trade and Drug Control Policies in Bolivia," in Joyce and Malamud 1998.

65.　Jelsma and Ronken 1998.

66.　Andean Information Network (AIN), *The Weight of Law 1008* (Cochabamba, Bolivia: AIN, 1996).

67.　Agreda et al., 1996.

68.　U.S. federal agencies involved in the war on drugs have included Department of Defense (DOD), DEA, INS, Central Intelligence Agency (CIA), Federal Bureau of Investigation (FBI), Customs Service, the Federal Aviation Administration, the Bureau of Alcohol, Tobacco, and Firearms, the Department of Justice, the Department of State, and the Treasury Department (Bagley 1996).

69.　HRW 1995a.

70.　See: AIN 1996; CEDIB 1994; de Achá 1996; HRW 1995a.

71.　Jelsma and Ronken 1998; Levine and Kavanau-Levine 1993.

72.　Agreda et al., 1996; de Achá 1996.

73.　Agreda et al., 1996: 19. Author's translation.

74.　de Achá 1996; AIN 1996.

75.　de Achá 1998: 132.

76.　AIN 1997: 9.

77.　Laserna 1997: 117–118.

78.　Ibid., 116.

79.　BJS 2001b: 1.

80.　AIN 1996: 90.

81.　de Achá 1998: 132.

82. de Achá 1998. For more on the conditions of women in Bolivian prisons see AIN 1997; Díaz-Cotto 2004b.
83. Atkins 1998: 108.
84. AIN 1996: i.
85. AIN 1996; AIN, *Children of Law 1008* (Cochabamba, Bolivia: AIN, 1997); United Nations Department of Public Information, *Body of Principles for the Protection of All Persons under Any Form of Detention or Imprisonment* (New York: UN, 1989).
86. Atkins 1998: 108–109.
87. Atkins 1998; AIN 1996, 1997; de Achá 1998.
88. Sentences varied depending on whether a person was convicted of planting, manufacturing, or trafficking drugs and whether the person was "found guilty of having sold drugs to someone who becomes intoxicated to the point of death" (Laserna 1997: 150).
89. HRW 1995a.
90. AIN 1997: 9–11.
91. Juan C. Pinto Quintanilla, *Cárceles y Familia* (Cochabamba, Bolivia: Terre des Hommes, 1999).
92. Agreda et al., 1996.
93. According to Dorado, in 1995, 75 percent (47) of Latin American women detained in Frankfurt were Colombian; another seven were Chilean. In 1996, all ten Latin American women detained in England were Colombian. In 1997, 71 percent of the 368 women imprisoned in Madrid were Colombian; another 4.6 percent were Venezuelan. See Maria C. Dorado, "Mujeres Latinoamericanas en Europe: el Caso de Colombia," in del Olmo 1998.
94. Dorado 1998: 80.
95. Dorado 1998: 82–84, 88.
96. Dorado 1998: 86.
97. Dorado 1998: 88–90.
98. K. Ambos, "A Comparison of Sentencing and Execution of Penalties," in CEP, ed. *European Conference on Drug Couriers* (Zurich: CEP, 1996), 25–27; Dorado 1998.
99. CANY 1992; Dorado 1998: 94–95.
100. Green 1996: 9.
101. Dorado 1998: 94–97.
102. Dorado 1998: 92–93.
103. The White House 1997.
104. Ryan S. King and Marc Mauer, *State Sentencing and Corrections Policy in an Era of Fiscal Restraint* (Washington, D.C.: The Sentencing Project, 2002).
105. *Australian Financial Review*, "U.S. Kicked off UN Drug Body" (May 9, 2001); Ian Williams, "U.S. Lost Seat on U.N. Human Rights Commission Follows Threat to Veto Mideast Resolutions," *Washington Report on Middle East Affairs* XX (5) (July 2001).
106. Richard C. Leone and Greg Anrig Jr., eds., *The War on Our Freedoms* (New York: Public Affairs, 2003).
107. Eric Lichtblau, "U.S. Uses Terror Law to Pursue Crimes from Drugs to Swindling," *New York Times* (September 28, 2003).

SELECTED BIBLIOGRAPHY

de Achá, Gloria R. M. *Violaciones a los Derechos Humanos Civiles Durante la Investigación Policial en Casos Detenidos Bajo la Ley 1008*. Cochabamba, Bolivia: Red Andina de Información, CEDIB, 1996.
_____. "Características de las Mujeres Encarceladas en Bolivia." In *Criminalidad y Criminalización de la Mujer en la Región Andina*, edited by R. del Olmo. Caracas, Venezuela: Nueva Sociedad, 1998.
Agreda, Evelin, Norma Rodríguez, and Alex Contreras. *Mujeres Cocaleras*. Cochabamba, Bolivia: Comité Coordinador de las Cinco Federaciones del Trópico de Cochabamba, 1996.

Alonso, Carlos. *Guerra Antidrogas, Democracia, Derechos Humanos y Militarización en América Latina.* Ciudad de Guatemala, Guatemala: CEDIB, Transnational Institute, and Inforpress Centroaméricana, 1997.

Ambos, K. "A Comparison of Sentencing and Execution of Penalties." In *European Conference on Drug Couriers,* edited by CEP. Zurich: CEP, 1996.

Amnesty International. *Mexico, Overcoming Fear.* New York, 1996.

————. *United States of America, Human Rights Concerns in the Border Region with Mexico.* May 1998.

Andean Information Network. *The Weight of Law 1008.* Cochabamba, Bolivia: AIN, 1996.

————. *Children of Law 1008.* Cochabamba, Bolivia: AIN, 1997.

Arango, Mario. *Impacto del Narcotráfico en Antioquia.* Medellín, Colombia: J.M. Arango, 1988.

Atkins, Andy. "The Economic and Political Impact of the Drug Trade and Drug Control Policies in Bolivia." In *Latin America and the Multinational Drug Trade,* edited by E. Joyce and C. Malamud. Basingstoke: Macmillan Press, 1998.

Azaola, Elena and Cristina José Yacamán, *Las Mujeres Olvidadas: Un Estudio Acerca de la Situación de las Cárceles Para Mujeres de la República Mexicana.* México: Programa Interdisciplinario de Estudios de la Mujer, El Colegio de México/Comisión Nacional de Derechos Humanos, 1996.

Bagley, Bruce M. (ed). *Drug Trafficking in the Americas: An Annotated Bibliography.* Coral Gables, FL: North South Center, University of Miami, 1996.

Beckett, Katherine and Theodore Sasson. *The Politics of Injustice.* Thousand Oaks, CA: Pine Forge, 2000.

Bloom, Barbara. "Triple Jeopardy: Race, Class, and Gender in Women's Imprisonment." Ph.D. dissertation, University of California, 1996.

————. *Special Report: Women Offenders.* Washington, DC: Department of Justice, December 1999.

————. *Prisoners in 2000.* Washington, DC: Department of Justice, 2001.

————. *Census of Jails, 1999.* Washington, DC: Department of Justice, 2001.

California Department of Corrections. *Historical Trends Institutions and Parole Population, 1977–1997.* Sacramento, June 1998.

————. *California Prisoners and Parolees, 2000 Summary Statistics.* Sacramento, June 2000.

————. *CDC Facts: 4TH Quarter 2002.* Sacramento, 2002.

Centro de Documentación e Información-Bolivia. *DEA y Soberanía en Bolivia.* Cochabamba, Bolivia: CEDIB, 1994.

Christopher Commission. *Report of the Independent Commission on the Los Angeles Police Department.* Los Angeles, 1991.

Cockburn, Alexander and Jeffrey St. Clair. *Whiteout.* New York: Verso, 1998.

Correctional Association of New York. *Do They Belong in Prison?* New York, 1985.

————. *Injustice Will Be Done.* New York, 1992.

————. *Mandatory Injustice.* New York, 1999.

Díaz-Cotto, Juanita. *Gender, Ethnicity and the State: Latina and Latino Prison Politics.* New York: State University of New York Press, 1996.

————. "The Criminal Justice System and Its Impact on Latinas(os) in the United States," *The Justice Professional* 13, 1 (April 2000).

————. *Chicana Lives and Criminal Justice: In Their Own Words.* Austin: University of Texas, forthcoming 2006.

————. "Latina Imprisonment and the War on Drugs." In *Race, Gender, and Punishment,* edited by M. Bosworth and S. Bush-Baskette. Boston: Northeastern University, forthcoming 2004.

Dorado, Maria C. "Mujeres Latinoamericanas en Europe: el Caso de Colombia." In *Criminalidad y Criminalización de la Mujer en la Región Andina,* edited by R. del Olmo. Caracas, Venezuela: Nueva Sociedad, 1998.

Dorn, Nicholas, Murji Karim, and Nigel South. *Traffickers. Drug Markets and Law Enforcement.* London and New York: Routledge, 1992.

Dunn, Timothy. *The Militarization of the US-Mexico Border, 1978–1992.* Austin, TX: Center for Mexican American Studies, University of Texas, 1996.

Gabel, Katherine and Denise Johnston (eds). *Children of Incarcerated Parents*. New York: Lexington Books, 1995.

Green, Judith. "Bailing Out Private Jails." *The American Prospect* 12, 6 (September 10, 2001).

Human Rights Watch. *Police Brutality in the United States*. New York, 1991.

_____. *Bolivia: Human Rights Violations and the War on Drugs*. New York, 1995.

_____. *Crossing the Line: Human Rights Abuses Along the U.S. Border with Mexico Persist Amid Climate of Impunity*. New York, 1995.

_____. *Slipping through the Crack: Unaccompanied Children Detained by the U.S. Immigration and Naturalization Service*. New York, 1997.

_____. *Cruel and Usual: Disproportionate Sentences for New York Drug Offenders* 9 (2)(B). New York: 1997.

_____. *Punishment and Prejudice: Racial Disparities in the War on Drugs*. New York, 2000.

Jelsma, M. and T. Ronken (eds). *Democracias Bajo Fuego*. Uruguay: TNI, Ediciones Brecha, Acción Andina, 1998.

King, Ryan S. and Marc Mauer. *State Sentencing and Corrections Policy in an Era of Fiscal Restraint*. Washington, DC: The Sentencing Project, 2002.

Kolts, James G. *The Los Angeles County Sheriffs' Department: A Report (Kolts Report)*. Los Angeles: Board of Supervisors, 1992.

Laserna, Roberto (ed). *Economía Política de las Drogas*. Cochabamba, Bolivia: Centro de Estudios de la Realidad Económica y Social-Consejo Latinoamericano de Ciencias Sociales, 1993.

_____. *Twenty (Mis)conceptions on Coca and Cocaine*. La Paz, Bolivia: Clave consultores, s.r.l., 1997.

Leone, Richard C. and Greg Anrig Jr. (eds) *The War on Our Freedoms*. New York: Public Affairs, 2003.

Levine, Michael and Laura Kavanau-Levine. *The Big White Lie*. New York: Thunder's Mouth, 1993.

Maingot, Anthony P. "Offshore Banking in the Caribbean: The Panamanian Case." In *Latin America and the Multinational Drug Trade*, edited by E. Joyce and C. Malamud. New York: St. Martin's, 1998.

Mann, Coramae R. "Women of Color and the Criminal Justice System." In *The Criminal Justice System and Women* edited by B. R. Price and N. J. Sokoloff. New York: McGraw-Hill, 1995.

Margain, Hugo B. "The War on Drugs: A Mexican Perspective," *Voices of México* (October–December 1990): 3–8.

Mauer, Marc and Tracy Huling. *Young Black Americans and the Criminal Justice System: Five Years Later*. Washington, DC: The Sentencing Project, 1995.

Mollen Commission. *Commission Report*. New York City, 1994.

New York Department of Correctional Services. *The Hub System: Profile of Inmates Under Custody in January 1, 1996*. Albany, 1996.

Office of National Drug Control Policy, Executive Office of the President. *The National Drug Control Strategy, 1997*. Washington, DC, 1997.

Pettiway, Leon E. "Participation in Crime Partnerships by Female Drug Users," *Criminology* 25, 3 (1987): 746.

Pinto Quintanilla, Juan C. *Cárceles y Familia*. Cochabamba, Bolivia: Terre des Hommes, 1999.

Reuter, Peter. "Foreign Demand for Latin American Drugs: The USA and Europe." In *Latin America and the Multinational Drug Trade*, edited by E. Joyce and C. Malamud. New York: St. Martin's, 1998.

Rossi, Adriana. *Narcotráfico y Amazonia Ecuatoriana*. Buenos Aires, Argentina: Kohen and Asociados International, 1996.

The Sentencing Project. *New Inmate Population Figures Demonstrate Need for Policy Reform*. Washington, DC, 2003.

UN Department of Public Information. *UN Convention Against the Illicit Traffic of Narcotics*. New York: UN 1991.

U.S. Census Bureau, Department of Commerce. *The Hispanic Population*. Washington, DC: Department of Commerce, May 2001.

U.S. Department of Justice. Federal Bureau of Investigations. *Uniform Crime Reports: Crime in the U.S.* Washington, DC, 1961–2002.

U.S. House of Representatives, Committee on the Judiciary. *Police Misconduct*, Hearings Before the Subcommittee on Criminal Justice, Serial No. 50, parts 1 and 2. 98th Congress, 1st Session. Washington, 1984.

The War on Drugs in Colombia

The Environment, the Treadmill of Destruction and Risk-Transfer Militarism

Chad L. Smith, Gregory Hooks, and Michael Lengefeld

In this article, we document the manner in which the militarized "war on drugs" waged by the United States contributes to environmental degradation in Colombia. The U.S. involvement includes military support and training, weaponry, fumigation of crops, and logistical and surveillance support. In addition to documenting the scope and magnitude of this militarized war on drugs in the Colombian Andes, we assess its impact on the environment, most notably with respect to deforestation and climate change. Our goals are two-fold: first, we pinpoint the spatial, historical, and social dimension of the treadmill of destruction in Colombia; second, we utilize the case of Colombia's war on drugs and its connections to the treadmill of destruction in order to contextualize several nascent developments, namely the emergence of risk-transfer militarism and the "new" wars of the 21st century.

"Catastrophic convergence" (Parenti 2011) is the collision of multiple social, economic and environmental catastrophes (poverty, violence, climate change) playing out in the tropics of the Global South. Parenti describes the changing climate not only as the backdrop for these social and economic problems, but highlights an additional concern: climate change will exacerbate these problems and, thereby, produce a feedback loop. Parenti (2011: 8) contends that "Cold War-era militarism and the economic pathologies of neoliberalism" paved the way for this catastrophic convergence. Failed states can offer little institutional resistance to and are further weakened and delegitimized by the emergence of illegal trading of guns and illicit drugs. We believe that this militarized war on drugs contributes to the convergence Parenti has identified. Although our focus is upon the environmental costs borne by Colombia, it is clear that states, worldwide, are undergoing a series of crises. Chase-Dunn

(2013) identifies the global scale of this crisis, and although we do not directly address all five of his "linked crises" we do think this case is reflective of this larger set of dynamics Chase-Dunn identifies.

In the pages that follow we situate the treadmill of destruction within the context of failed and struggling states with particular attention on the history of conflict in Colombia. We address the environmental and social effects that coca cultivation and the production of cocaine has in Colombia and, in turn, how efforts to curb its production, primarily through the U.S. policy of "Plan Colombia," are problematic. As the metaphor of a treadmill suggests, the intensification of militarized drug production and destruction has resulted in an escalation of the accompanying environmental devastation. Finally, our argument reframes the treadmill of destruction by emphasizing the role of risk-transfer militarism within the emergence of "new" wars as represented in the case of Colombia.

TREADMILLS, ENVIRONMENTAL DAMAGE, AND FAILED STATES

The treadmill of production (ToP) is driven by commercial demands, primarily growth, market shares and profitability (Gould, Pellow and Schnaiberg 2008; Schnaiberg 1980; Schnaiberg and Gould 1994). The treadmill of destruction (ToD) is driven by the distinctive demands of geopolitics, militarism and war making. To highlight the distinctive effects of the ToD we begin with a discussion of the commercially oriented ToP stemming from the lucrative and globalized commodification of cocaine.

The ToP points to capitalist economic production as the driving force behind environmental damage. The treadmill refers to the relentless quest for economic growth and the high (and growing) levels of social inequality that result from this quest. With respect to the environment, the ToP makes unsustainable demands on the environment in the form of extraction of raw materials used in the production and distribution goods and in the form of waste.

When first developing the concept, Schnaiberg (1980) was largely focused on the United States. However, the ToP framework has been extended to shed light on processes operating at a transnational and global scale (Gould, Pellow and Schnaiberg 2008). Consideration of global commodity chains and the resulting unequal environmental exchange provides valuable insights into the transnational implications of the treadmill of production. Hopkins and Wallerstein (1982:159) define global commodity chains as "a network of labor and production processes whose end result is a finished commodity" (see also, Ciccantell and Smith 2009). Global commodity chains introduce demands from distant and powerful actors, disrupting and distorting local economic and social relationships, resulting in "unequal environmental exchanges" that impose steep environmental costs on vulnerable people and places (Rice 2007).

Clelland (2014), adopting a metaphor from physics, distinguishes between "bright" value and "dark" value. Physicists estimate that dark energy and dark matter account for the preponderance of the universe (more than 90%). "By analogy, that invisible human and natural energy flows are converted into the dark value that forms part of the basic structure of the world-system" (Clelland 2014: 85). Dark value is added in the periphery—externalized to workers, communities, households and ecosystems. The United Nations' Office on Drugs and Crime (2010: 170) estimates that a markup of roughly 30 times between coca derivatives (in the Andean producer states) and cocaine wholesale prices in the United States, and even more, 60 times, in Europe. Only a small portion of the spectacular street value of cocaine (its "bright" value) is derived from the risk (street violence and incarceration) confronted by organized criminal organizations that distribute cocaine in the Global North. The many externalities—ecological degradation and the coerced and undercompensated labor by Andean growers (cocaine's "dark" value) form the basis of cocaine's value. Ribot (1998), in a study of the commodity chain impacting Senegalese forestry, offers a reminder that securing access can be far more important than formal ownership in determining who profits. In the Andean regions of Colombia and especially the remote Amazonian regions where coca cultivation has spread in recent decades, access is often more important than nominal property rights. Without a formal title, squatters, guerrilla/ paramilitary armies, and organized criminal networks take effective control of lands used for coca cultivation and coca processing. The prevalence of coercion in Colombian coca cultivation and processing contributes to the high rates of uncompensated negative externalities (unpaid labor by direct producers and ecological degradation), i.e., dark value.

The era of globalization—with the cheapening of transportation and communication—made possible the commodification of cocaine in the late-20th Century. The coca plant is indigenous and well adapted to the Andean region. As such, coca could be cultivated with few deleterious consequences for the environment. But the commodification of cocaine has set in motion powerful treadmill dynamics, sharply unequal environmental exchange, and widespread damage to the environment. Exacerbating this impact, a large number of ecological hotspots in the region have been severely damaged.

THE TREADMILL OF DESTRUCTION AND THE "NEW" WARS OF THE 21ST CENTURY

With a focus on the United States in the 20th Century, Hooks and Smith (2004, 2005) introduced the "treadmill of destruction" by detailing the environmental dangers posed by the military. In this initial formulation, the understanding of the treadmill drew attention to the environmental degradation and inequality sustained by the world's leading military powers and fully professionalized military organizations. A number of scholars have extended the treadmill of destruction framework to consider its global reach (Clark and Jorgenson 2012; Jorgenson 2005; Jorgenson and Clark 2009; Jorgenson, Clark and Kentor 2010; Lengefeld and Smith 2013; York 2008). But this focus did not fully consider the growing ability of powerful nations to intervene in and shift the risk of war to less privileged peoples and less powerful nations. Moreover, this focus does not allow full consideration of the wars (and attendant environmental degradation) attributable to less formal (and less powerful) military organizations.

Arms races and wars generate and are sustained by a treadmill dynamic that is distinct from that driven by commercial competition. In the context of "old" wars (involving professionalized armed forces under the state's control), acquiring and controlling territory loom large. Military forces routinely degrade the territory controlled by opposing forces, and battlefields remain toxic long after peace is declared. To cripple the war-making potential of adversaries, military forces degrade the industrial and agricultural assets controlled by opposing forces; this routinely entails widespread, significant, and deliberate environmental degradation (Hooks and Smith 2005). To understand the environmental footprint of the "new" wars of the 21st Century, the treadmill of destruction framework must be refined and updated. The world's most powerful nations are motivated to shift the risk of war to peoples and places of the Global South (Hooks and Smith 2012; Shaw 2002, 2005). At the same time, formal military organizations and the ability to sharply distinguish between combatants and noncombatants is less common in the "new" wars of the 21st Century. Instead, a wide range of armed organizations (e.g., guerrilla armies, temporary militias and organized criminal organizations of various size and capabilities, etc.) is playing a prominent role (Kaldor 1999). Finally, the control of territory is typically less important in "new" wars. Nonetheless, the environment is often degraded as these wars are pursued. To generate revenue to support privatized and less formal war making, military forces pursue unsustainable production and extractive efforts and maintain predatory relations with direct producers. These irresponsible practices are fueled by arms races and military competition; as the ferocity and stakes of military conflict accelerate so do the treadmill dynamics and the attendant impact on the environment.

War—defined broadly as organized violence by Kaldor (1999)—is and has been a social activity that builds on and reflects extant social relationships and structures. In the 19th and 20th Centuries, the world's leading military powers maintained professionalized standing armies and navies. As such, waging war was monopolized by states and soldiers were sharply demarcated from the civilian population: "war made the state, and the state made war" (Tilly 1975: 142). The state as war maker remains intact for the United States and other major powers concentrated in the Global North. However, Shaw (2005) contends that the nations of the Global North, especially military powers such as the United States, are pursuing risk-transfer militarism. For the Global North, the homeland and citizens are shielded from the horrors of war and militarization because wars are fought on the terrain of vulnerable nations. If soldiers from the Global North are deployed, they fight from a distance, taking advantage of qualitatively superior military technologies. But the state's monopoly over violence is not guaranteed. In the new wars of the 21st Century, especially those fought in the Global South, a wide range of armed groups wage war. Instead, these wars "are characterized by a multiplicity of types of fighting units both public and private, state and non-state, or some kind of mixture" (Kaldor 1999: 92) of these various combinations of combatant units. In turn, the environmental degradation and inequality resulting from war—the treadmill of destruction—varies with the manner in which military forces are organized, how they are financed and the manner in which battles are fought. Table 2.3.1 summarizes key features of the "new" wars of the 21st Century and the environmental implications.

The Colombian case brings into sharp relief the new forms of war and associated assaults on the environment. As will be discussed in greater detail below, there have been a wide range of *military forces* operating in Colombia, including the Colombian military, organized criminal organizations, paramilitary forces allied with the government, anti-government guerilla forces, and a variety of less formal and more transient (but still armed) fighting forces. The United States has participated directly and indirectly in this conflict, minimizing the risk to the United States' territory and personnel, while heightening the scale of violence in Colombia and surrounding countries. In Colombia, *patterns of violence* diverge markedly from those characteristics of "old" wars. Instead of pitched battles among formally organized and state-controlled military units, violence is widely dispersed, sustained battles have been rare, and the violence has often involved efforts to generate revenues from illegal activities (especially coca and cocaine) and efforts to suppress the drug trade. The *financing of this violence* is also distinctive relative to "old" wars. The Colombian military forces have been financed through taxation, but the United States has also played a prominent role by providing sizeable military aid and by directly participating in drug eradication and counterinsurgency efforts. Especially in drug-producing areas, income generated from illegal activities often surpasses revenues from legal businesses. In predatory fashion, the diverse fighting forces have fought to control and/or profit from these illegal activities (e.g., extraconstitutional taxation and a variety of protection rackets). The resulting environmental degradation—the *treadmill of destruction*—reflects the specific forms of warfare. The predation of armed forces leads to unsustainable coca cultivation and cocaine production processes. The widespread conflict (both in number of casualties and in the spatial dimensions) and the disproportionate harm imposed on noncombatants results in dislocation of those caught in the crossfire. This contributes to accelerated deforestation and rapid degradation of lands newly brought under cultivation. The United States, in calculated fashion, amplifies these dynamics. Most notably, the U.S. commitment to crop eradication and other forms of

TABLE 2.3.1   *New Wars and New Dynamics to the Treadmill of Destruction*

	"OLD" WARS[a]	"NEW" WARS GLOBAL NORTH[b]	GLOBAL SOUTH[a]
MILITARY FORCES	Professional (standing) army under the state's control	Professional forces under the state's control with use of mercenary forces to obscure culpability	State lacks monopoly on means of coercion. Diverse military forces operate.
PATTERNS OF VIOLENCE	Pitched battles, war and peace demarcated by formal treaties. Soldiers suffer highest casualty rates.	Risk-transfer militarism, military operations in Global South without formal declaration of war. Suffer very few casualties while relying on high-tech weaponry to inflict heavy losses on adversaries.	Violence deployed to achieve a variety of ends, including income generation, intimidation and genocide. Noncombatant casualties far exceed casualty rates among soldiers.
FINANCING VIOLENCE	State taxation; state plays prominent role in fiscal management of economy	State taxation supports interventions by nations of the Global North; aid provided to allied but failed states in the Global South.	Legitimate economy often collapses. Predation by armed forces on non-combatants: resource exploitation, kidnapping, extortion, and protection rackets.
SPREAD OF VIOLENCE	Battlefields where professionalized armies and navies encounter one another. In "total" war, industrial infrastructure and population centers become "legitimate" targets.	Global North intervenes indirectly or uses weapons that minimize risk to own troops. Rhetorical strategies deflect responsibility for violence and aftermath.	No clear spatial demarcation. Pockets of peace in violent regions; pockets of violence in peaceful areas. Armed forces extend zone of conflict; noncombatants relocate to more remote areas in search of safety.
TREADMILL OF DESTRUCTION	Highly toxified battlefields; weapons manufacture environmentally destructive. In total war: wide-spread destruction of major cities and degradation of infrastructure.	Wars and attendant environmental impacts shifted to Global South. Decisions to degrade environment and to deploy environmentally irresponsible weapons (e.g., uranium tipped projectiles) and tactics (e.g., aerial dispersion of herbicides).	Rapacious extraction of natural resources to finance military operations; toxification of ecosystem to deprive enemy of resources and sanctuary.

[a]Source: Mary Kaldor (1999). *New and Old Wars.*

[b]Source: Martin Shaw (2005). *The New Western Way of War.*

military aid escalates the scale of violence confronting noncombatants and amplifies the environmental degradation.

While our focus will center on environmental degradation, the human suffering is staggering. In the context of widespread, low-tech and disorganized skirmishes, the civilian population is often treated harshly, including rape, dismemberment, kidnapping, and coerced conscription. Between 1990–2012 over 10,000 Colombians were victimized by landmines in 31 of 32 departments, an issue further exacerbated by humanitarian displacement crisis that is second only to the Sudan (Ballvé 2013; United Nations Human Rights Council 2013). From 1945–2000, at the global level, roughly 41 million people died due to armed conflict (Leitenberg 2006); a disproportionate number of wars and casualties occurred in the nations of the Global South (Summerfield 1991). More alarming still, noncombatants bear the brunt of this violence. Civilian deaths comprised roughly 5% of all deaths in World War I, but by the end of the 20th Century, civilians suffered roughly 90% of all deaths in war (Summerfield 1991: 159). Thus, it appears that 21st Century warfare will exacerbate a host of social and environmental problems (crime, war on drugs, climate change), and the consequences for the civilian population will be disastrous.

THE TREADMILL OF DESTRUCTION IN COLOMBIA

The violence and conflict in Colombia has a long history, with much of it characteristic of "new" wars. As Guerrero Baron and Mond (2001:13) assert, "there is consensus that great social inequality and instability give rise to a dynamic that confers legitimacy on revolutionary projects and violent alternatives." The weak Colombian state lacked a firm monopoly on the means of violence long before the rise of guerilla armies, paramilitary groups and highly armed drug cartels (Holmes et al. 2008). The topography of Colombia and the longstanding history of regional and interdepartmental violence contributed to the Colombian state's weakness in the late 20th Century. Colombia has a poor land transportation and communication infrastructure, lacking both roads and railroads; river transportation continues to be of central importance (Holmes et al. 2008). The decentralized state, poor infrastructure, rugged topography, and geographic isolation of independent regional powers set the stage for intensified violence.

Beginning in the 1940's the Colombian people have endured political upheaval and civil war. Following the volatile years labeled as "la Violencia," rural lands became concentrated in the hands of Colombia's elite (known as the National Front agreement). In the 1960s, revolutionary peasant forces, such as the Revolutionary Armed Forces of Colombia (FARC), rejected the heightened inequality and challenged the state's legitimacy (Brittain 2010). In the context of the Cold War and in the shadow of the Cuban Revolution, the United States actively participated in counterinsurgency efforts. "Operation Marquetalia" (1964) was a joint US/Colombian operation that foreshadowed the weapons and tactics that would be featured in Vietnam, including the use of napalm; the effort cost roughly $3 billion (in inflation adjusted dollars) and though it was interpreted as a success by the Colombian government, this military action served as a rallying point for peasant forces (Brittain 2010). In subsequent decades (1970s-1980s) FARC increased its presence across the country, and by 1990 it had become a powerful force in and of itself. Wickham-Crowley (1992) emphasizes the expansion of modern capitalist agriculture—especially commercialized coffee production—to explain the growing peasant support for the FARC.

From these revolutionary origins, FARC moved in the direction of a "narco-guerrilla" organization. While the specificity of Colombia's history shaped this transformation, it is also characteristic of the "new" wars of recent decades (see Table 1). FARC and other left-leaning guerrilla forces taxed drug organizations in the regions under their control and used the funds to finance military and political activities (Peceny and Durnan 2006; Saab and Taylor 2009; Holmes et al. 2008; Stokes 2001, 2005). Even as FARC became directly involved in coca cultivation and cocaine manufacture, it attempted to preserve its political objectives "by manipulating the conventional coca industry in the hopes of strengthening sociopolitical and economic conditions for the marginalized" (Brittain 2010: 89).

Even though the U.S. war on drugs officially began under the Nixon administration in 1969, it genuinely began when the Posse Comitatas Act of 1878 was amended in 1981 to allow the Department of Defense (DoD) to mobilize the military in domestic legal threats, namely illicit drug trade (Ronderos 2003). With this legal backing, the Reagan Administration deemed the drug trade a national security threat and began employing military personnel and equipment to combat drug trafficking at the point of production (Bagley 1991). The militarization of the war on drugs is reflected in budgeting trends. In 1981, Congress allocated no funding to drug interdiction efforts, but by 1987 Congress allocated upwards of $379 million to such efforts (Bagley 1991; Mabry 1988). As the war on drugs became synonymous with military intervention, some influential leaders in the Pentagon voiced concerns (Mabry 1988; Zirnite 1997). In 1985 Secretary of Defense, Caspar Weinberger, argued that "reliance on military forces to accomplish civilian tasks is detrimental to both military readiness and the democratic process" (Zirnite 1997: 8). These reservations notwithstanding, a rapid militarization of the war on drugs ensued culminating in "Plan Colombia."

"Plan Colombia" originated with Colombian President Andres Pastrana in 1998 (Scott 2003). The Clinton and Bush Administrations used the claim that military training and engagement would improve Colombia's human rights climate to justify U.S. military involvement. Even though the human rights situation has seen little improvement since the initiation of this policy (Vaicius and Isacson 2003), Plan Colombia was supported, and at times expanded, by the George W. Bush administration and the Barack Obama administration. Between 2000–2010, under the auspices of Plan Colombia (and related programs), more than $7 billion in aid flowed to Colombia

(Congressional Research Service 2011); only Israel and Egypt received more military aid over this time period (Buxton 2006).

Pastrana's original plan included military components, but it placed considerable emphasis on development. Buxton (2006) argues that the U.S. government reworked the effort into a highly militarized "battle plan" and that Pastrana "bypassed or ignored" agencies charged with maintaining checks on presidential power and a number of elected officials had no opportunity to provide input as Plan Colombia was revised and implemented (Buxton 2006). The revised Plan Colombia expanded aerial spraying of defoliants and authorized U.S. support of interdiction efforts by the Colombian National Police. The Plan also included limited support for development programs and social justice reforms (Messina and Delamater 2006). But it must be borne in mind that roughly 80% of Plan Colombia outlays supported military operations. The sharp discrepancy between U.S. spending on coca eradication ($205 million) and economic development ($72 million) in Colombia for 2006 (Davalos, Bejarano, and Correa 2009) underscores the military emphasis in the policy. Thus, Plan Colombia was in large measure "a military offensive aimed at debilitating Colombia's powerful rebel groups and aerially fumigating the abundant coca and poppy crops" (Mugge 2004: 311).

Plan Colombia was adopted in 2000. In the following decade, the production of cocaine (and import into the United States) increased significantly. Furthermore, FARC and other left-leaning forces remained potent (relying on revenues generated through the drug trade to support military efforts). These failures were compounded by right wing paramilitary groups (promoted and/or condoned by the Colombian government to counter left-leaning insurgents) becoming major players in the drug industry. In short, the Colombian drug economy continued to expand and thrive (Scott 2003), thereby legitimizing FARC as a governing body and accepted taxation system throughout much of the coca producing region. FARC and its supporters would highlight that its involvement in coca cultivation and drug processing was more benign than alternatives (organized criminal organizations and rightwing paramilitary organizations). Regardless of which armed force was in control, the division between public and private and the distinction between military and civilian was obscured; coercion lay at or near the surface of coca cultivation and sale. In terms of treadmill of destruction dynamics, coca cultivation and drug manufacture became an indispensable source of revenue to support military operations, leading to widespread adoption of environmentally irresponsible practices.

The links between the drug trade and the financing of war insured far-reaching environmental degradation in Colombia. These treadmill dynamics were amplified by U.S. policies, especially those premised on risk-transfer militarism. To obscure its far-reaching interventions and complicity, the United States sought to distance itself from the ugly consequences of Plan Colombia and maintain good standing within the international community by utilizing "surrogacy" (Bonds 2013). Technically speaking,

U.S. policy only provides material support to the Colombian military by supplying helicopters, weapons, communications equipment and technology, infrastructure (i.e., building roads), and training (Mugge 2004). The Colombian government has allied itself (openly and covertly) with paramilitary forces. These paramilitary forces, at different times, have been both a legal and extra-legal means of confronting the left-leaning revolutionary force of FARC. The collusion of paramilitary factions with the Colombian military has convinced many analysts that these forces receive some share of the U.S.-sponsored equipment and training (Mugge 2004). It has been estimated that these paramilitary forces account for roughly 3,000 civilian casualties per year in Colombia (Mugge 2004; see also, Dube and Naidu 2010). Although the full range of U.S. involvement is cloaked in secrecy, the available evidence suggests that the United States is playing an active role. Priest (2013) reports that the Colombian military used Raytheon-produced smart bombs (weapons closely controlled by the U.S. Central Intelligence Agency) against FARC leader Raul Reyes inside Ecuadorian territory. This violation of Ecuadoran sovereignty sparked both a military and diplomatic crisis in 2008, leading to the deployment of Venezuelan and Ecuadorian troops on the Colombian frontiers. Ecuador filed lawsuits with the International Criminal Court and the Inter-American Commission on Human Rights against Colombia, claiming human rights violations related to violence and coca eradication efforts (both lawsuits were eventually dropped by Ecuador).

Colombia provides an unusually valuable lens in the tragic face of contemporary warfare. If we use Kaldor's (1999) definition of war—i.e., organized violence—Colombia has been enduring war for more than 50 years. In recent decades, this warfare has displayed the distinctive pathologies of the "new" wars. Internal to Colombia, powerful criminal organizations, left-leaning insurgent forces and rightwing paramilitary forces have tapped into the lucrative drug trade to finance war efforts (directly and indirectly) and to sustain a highly corrupt and coercive economy. In his context, the state's monopoly over the means of violence and its legitimacy is eroded. These dynamics are amplified by the direct and cynical involvement of the world's leading military power (Bejarano and Pizarro 2005; Hough 2011). The increased militarization of the Colombian government not only led to the degradation of Colombian democracy (Bejarano and Pizarro 2005), but it simultaneously motivated FARC and other guerilla armies to adopt more repressive treatment of the local population and, ultimately, to engage in "state like" activities such as war making, state making, extraction, and protection (Hough 2011). Although Plan Colombia was pursued under the apolitical banner of an anti-narcotics effort, it is clear that the United States actively supported the Colombian state's attempts to rid the country of left-leaning revolutionaries. As Buxton (2006: 186) points out: "Given the power and influence that the USA had over the Colombian government at the time, it is open to question how far the Colombian president would have been able to resist U.S. eradication plans and strategies." Colombian officials were not merely on the receiving end of arm-twisting. Colombia benefitted from this relationship and used resources flowing from Plan Colombia to weaken revolutionary challengers. The United States insulated its personnel and its homeland from the ravages of this prolonged war. The human costs were disproportionately borne by noncombatants, the environmental impacts were concentrated in some of Colombia's (and the world's) most ecologically diverse but vulnerable lands and resources.

THE ENVIRONMENTAL CONSEQUENCES AND HUMAN RISKS OF THE WAR ON DRUGS IN COLOMBIA

The "new" wars of the 21st Century continue and accelerate a disturbing trend: casualties among noncombatants far surpass those suffered by armed military forces. Casualties are inflicted—including a growing tolerance for casualties among noncombatants—where instrumental calculations point to strategies and tactics that achieve military objectives including a high casualty rate among noncombatants (even if inadvertent). The risk-transfer militarism adopted by leading military powers insures such outcomes. As is the case with other affluent nations of the Global North, the United States' overarching objective is to eliminate threats to the homeland and minimize casualties suffered by its own troops. Transferring risks and casualties to people (including noncombatants) and places in the Global South is inherent in this approach to warfare. Shaw (2005) points out that "small massacres" are inevitable and predictable in risk-transfer militarism. That is, when relying on high-tech weapons to fight from a distance, it is inevitable that errors in target selection and guidance systems will result in innocent people being hurt and killed. Because the overarching goal is to transfer risks, the United States accepts this trade-off between "small massacres" and remarkably low casualty rates among its soldiers.

The treadmill of destruction sheds light on the manner in which this extends to ecosystems and environmental systems. Just as the United States is willing to accept the loss of human life that occurs in "small massacres," it is also willing to accept the degradation of the environment to achieve national security objectives. Of course, this is in the context of risk-transfer militarism. By the same token, the predation of the various military forces operating in Colombia is not limited to acceptance of human suffering. Environmental resources and ecosystems are also squandered and sacrificed to support the war effort. This includes irresponsible and unsustainable cultivation techniques; it also includes the deliberate toxification of the environment to punish and constrain adversaries. Cocaine's "dark value" (Clelland 2014) includes both human and environmental casualties on a tragic scale.

ENVIRONMENTAL DEGRADATION AS A MILITARY TACTIC

The links between environmental degradation and the cocaine trade begins with cultivation practices and the processing of coca leaves. As Bunker (2005) reminds us, transportation and energy demands are integral to cultivation decisions and infrastructure. Coca leaves are bulky, requiring 250–500 kilograms of dried leaves to produce one kilogram of cocaine. Coca paste can and is consumed in the region. For cocaine manufacture, it is an intermediate product: 250–500 kilograms of dried leaves yields 2.5 kilograms of coca paste, depending on content of leaves and specifics of processing (Dombey-Moore, Resetar and Childress 1994). Transporting coca leaves, a bulky commodity, in the context of rugged topography and poor infrastructure would be quite costly. More to the point, coca leaves are also illegal and valuable. Transporting a large quantity of leaves over long distances risks detection by government officials and theft by armed forces operating in the area. For this reason, coca paste is typically fabricated near areas of cultivation, a process that is toxic for humans and damaging to ecosystems. The chemicals used include organic solvents (e.g., kerosene and diesel fuel), sulfuric acid, and potassium carbonate (Inter-American Drug Abuse Control Commission 2005). The fabrication process consumes and contaminates a great deal of water, resulting in pollution of streams in the area (Mejía and Posada 2008). Reflecting the treadmill of destruction dynamics, producers are driven to maximize harvests as soon as possible and anticipate that coca plants will be eradicated within years of initial planning. For these reasons, heavy and unregulated use of herbicides, fertilizers and insecticides is common. The runoff from these agricultural chemicals further degrades water resources and compounds the environmental harm.

Just as the military forces involved in coca cultivation and cocaine manufacture adopt calculated policies that lead to environmental degradation, so too do those attempting to suppress drug production. The War on Drugs in Colombia relies heavily on spraying herbicides. Neither the United States nor Colombia discloses the specific mixture being used, but most experts agree that some version of Monsanto's glyphosate (i.e., "Roundup") is the base herbicide, but it is mixed with a locally manufactured surfactant, Cosmo-Flux 411 (Mugge 2004; Messina and Delamater 2006). The practice of aerial eradication is a joint operation involving the Antinarcotics Directorate of the Colombian National Police (DIRAN) and the National Affairs Section (NAS) housed at the U.S. Embassy in Bogota (Mugge 2004).

The secrecy surrounding the eradication effort makes it impossible to determine the specific form of glyphosate being used. This is unfortunate because impacts vary with the concentration and specific chemical composition in use (Mugge 2004). In addition, the content of the surfactant is also unknown. All that is known about this chemical is that it is produced in Colombia, where fewer environmental regulations are in effect (Mugge 2004). Regardless of the specific chemicals being used, there is clear and compelling evidence that the use of these herbicides, as practiced in Colombia, would violate regulations in place in the United States (Mugge 2004). In Colombia, glyphosate is being delivered via aerial fumigation from a height of 15 meters (49 feet), but the Environmental Protection Agency requires that it be applied at a height of 3–10 meters (10–32 feet) away (Alvarez 2001b; Buxton 2006). Similarly, the recommended dosage of glyphosate is approximately 2.3 liters/hectare (0.60 gallons/hectare). In Colombia, it is being applied at five to ten times the recommended concentration (23.7 liters/hectare or 6.26 gallons/hectare) (Alvarez 2001b; Buxton 2006).

With few exceptions (Solomon 2007, 2009), a large body of research points to negative environmental impacts from these eradication efforts. These negative impacts include adverse effects for amphibians (Meza-Joy, Ramirez-Pinilla, and Fuentes-Lrenzo 2013; Relyea 2005a, 2005b, 2011; Solomon 2007, 2009), rats (de Liz Oliveira Cavalli et al. 2013) and mice (Jasper, Locatelli, Pilati, Locatelli 2012). Numerous on-the-ground reports point to the environmental damage attributable to these herbicides (Messina and Delameter 2006; Mugge 2004). While the evidence of environmental impacts is compelling, claims that the eradication program is having the desired effect of decreasing coca production are disputed. During the first ten years of Plan Colombia, there was little evidence that cocaine production suffered. Over the last several years, sharp reductions are in evidence. The Office of National Drug Policy (2012) reports that that cocaine production capacity in Colombia has declined 25% between 2010–2011. Likewise, the United Nations reports that the total area under coca cultivation in Colombia fell by one-quarter in 2011 (United Nations Office on Drugs and Crime 2012b). Although the recent evidence seems to indicate some decrease in coca production in Colombia, it is less clear that this is reducing the overall amount of cocaine available on world markets. It appears that coca cultivation and cocaine manufacture is shifting to other Andean nations, resulting in what is commonly referred to as the "balloon effect" (*The Economist* 2013; Hellin 2001).

The broader environmental consequences of these eradication policies include deforestation, contamination of water and water systems, eradication of non-coca crops and natural vegetation, and a generally negative impact on the biodiversity of the region (Alvarez 2002; Armenteras et al. 2006; Davalos et al. 2009; Davalos et al. 2011; Etter, et al. 2006; Fjeldsa et al. 2005; Messina and Delameter 2006; Mugge 2004).

HUMAN RISKS

Research indicates that glyphosate has negative consequences for human cells (Benachour and Seralini 2009) and human cell lines (Gasnier et al. 2009), that it induces insidious diseases in humans (Samsel and Saneff 2013) and promotes breast cancer growth in humans (Thongprakaisang et al. 2013). In the effected regions, villagers, farmers, and health care specialists have complained of skin illness, eye irritation, vomiting, diarrhea, and miscarriages (Mugge 2004; Transnational Institute 2001). The

United Nations, Office of the High Commissioner for Human Rights (2010) considers these reports to be "credible and trustworthy." Although millions of dollars are budgeted to pursue this militarized war on drugs, no funds have been committed to examine these persistent complaints. As is characteristic of the treadmill of destruction, still another risk is transferred to the Global South: to protect the U.S. population from "unsafe" drugs, the people of Colombia are being subjected to environmental dislocation and heightened health impairment. In previous research, Hooks and Smith (2004, 2012) focused on the environmental legacy of weapons (conventional and nuclear) used in the 20th Century's mass industrial wars and the ensuing Cold War. In the new face of militarism in the 21st Century, the most severe impacts on the environment and human health stem from chemical warfare waged on the people and places thought to be involved with coca cultivation.

Without providing details about specific chemicals, quantities and locations, the U.S. State Department acknowledges reliance on glyphosate; explanations of "defensive categorization" are used to justify its use (Bonds 2013). That is, the United States downplays adverse impacts of controversial (potentially illegitimate) military tactics by disputing and minimizing the harm they cause. Spraying in Colombia has been denounced by a wide range of critics in Colombia, throughout Latin America and around the world (Buxton 2006). The State Department describes Cosmo-Flux 411F as "essentially a soap that enhances the ability of the herbicide to penetrate the waxy cuticle of the leaf surface" (U.S Department of State 2002). Deflecting criticisms, the Department of State asserts that Cosmo-Flux 411F is *only* "lightly toxic." The State Department also claims that glyphosate is safe because it is "one of the most widely used agricultural herbicides in the world" (U.S Department of State 2002). In similar fashion, although failing to meet EPA guidelines in this regard, the State Department emphasizes the dilution of chemicals used for eradication to downplay reports of harm to human health:

> ... the irritation and toxicity potential of the individual ingredients are reduced when diluted during mixing (the final product is approximately 75 percent water) and the mixture is dispersed when sprayed. ... The symptoms of such exposure are likely to be short-term and reversible. (U.S. Department of State 2002)

The U.S. government does acknowledge widespread environmental degradation in coca-growing regions yet emphasizes the irresponsible environmental practices of peasants and military forces involved in coca cultivation and cocaine fabrication. "Over the past 20 years, coca cultivation in the Andean region has resulted in the destruction of at least 5.9 million acres of rainforest—an area larger than the states of Maryland and Massachusetts combined" (United States Department of State 2003). This report offers an extended discussion of the toxic chemicals and herbicides and reduction in biodiversity due to coca production; it goes on to discuss the implications for climate change. But, the Department of State makes no mention of its own emphasis on militarized eradication and how this amplifies the environmental impact of coca cultivation and cocaine manufacture. Relying on the rhetorical strategy of "defensive categorization" (Bonds 2013), the United States obscures its own role in the social and environmental disruption and shifts all responsibility to Colombians.

ENVIRONMENTAL AND ECOLOGICAL DAMAGE

Given that Colombia houses the largest number of bird species in the world and the second highest number of plant species in the world, the global implications of these developments are significant. Fjeldsa et al. (2005) find that biodiversity has decreased in the Andes (particularly in the Colombian Andes) due to the convergence of drug markets, decades of military conflict, and a paucity of economic alternatives for the rural poor in these regions (see also Alvarez 2002). In addition, crop eradication efforts are impacting water supplies and aquatic ecosystems. Monsanto acknowledges that glyphosate can have far-reaching impacts upon water quality and aquatic life. The assault on biodiversity extends to species that rely on water resources that are being compromised by coca cultivation and militarized eradication efforts (Mugge 2004). To date, neither the United States nor the Colombian government has undertaken a thorough study of the damage. Moreover, because neither government will provide detailed information on the extent and chemical composition of the herbicides deployed, independent researchers have been stymied as well.

The eradication of coca plants has had "the unintended consequence of defoliating not only coca but also contiguous and interspersed native forest and food crop parcels" (Messina and Delamater 2006: 127). Banana, corn, and yucca crops suffer when glyphosate is applied (Mugge 2004). This, in turn, has two consequences. In some cases, farmers return to growing coca to compensate for the loss of legal crops (banana, corn, yucca). Second, many farmers turn to forested lands to begin anew. Thus, the eradication program pushes farmers to increase the land under cultivation and, thereby, accelerates deforestation. As farmers are forced to continually move into forested lands—often remote, frequently part of forest reserves—for the purpose of crop production, whether that be for coca production or subsistence farming, there is both an increase in the release of carbon dioxide (cutting down the forest) and a subsequent loss of carbon sink (annual crops are a less effective carbon sink than forests).

Deforestation is on the rise and is threatening important aspects of biodiversity value (Armenteras et al. 2006; Etter et al. 2006). Drug eradication is not the only cause of deforestation. Deforestation has been linked to the presence of pasture and agricultural lands, distance to roads and cities (Armenteras, Rodriguez, and Retana 2013; Eraso, Armenteras-Pascual, Alumbreros 2012), colonization and population (Etter et al. 2006), and forestry export flows (Shandra, Leckband, and London 2009). Coca cultivation and eradication efforts intensify pressure on Colombia's forests. Coca cultivation is concentrated in the "coca belt" of southern Colombia (International Crisis Group 2005). This area is comprised of a low altitude humid forest wherein the cultivators of coca destroyed roughly 3.45 million acres of land between 1990 and 2000 (Buxton 2006). According to a report prepared by the Transnational Institute (2001), deforestation is a direct effect of the fumigation efforts sponsored by the U.S. military. Indiscriminate aerial herbicide spraying kills not only coca crops, but also food and alternative crops that are being promoted to reduce farmers' dependence on coca crops (Tenenbaum 2002). As coca crops are destroyed, the rural people migrate deeper into the rainforests or up the mountains to maintain their livelihood. Because "slash and burn" planting techniques provide the main method of farming in Colombia the result is increased rainforest destruction (Transnational Institute 2001; see also Achard et al. 2002; Nobre, Sellers, and Shukla 1991). Davalos et al. (2009: 382) concur, taking into consideration both the irresponsible practices used to cultivate and process coca and the damage caused by militarized eradication efforts, they conclude that "[c]oca is the single most important driver of deforestation in the country."

Alternative development initiatives meant to curb coca production have similarly exacerbated deforestation. Young (2004) observes that new road construction contributes to the spread of coca cultivation. Transportation improvements facilitate the acquisition of agricultural inputs, the purchase of chemicals for coca refinement, and shipment of coca leaves and coca paste. "Without exception, the current coca-growing areas are past tropical forest colonization projects ... this began in the 1960s and continued into the 1990s despite a near universal failure of these projects" (Young 2004: 365). Foreign assistance offered to drug "source" countries typically includes funding for alternative development initiatives and infrastructural enhancements. Road construction requires the bulldozing of tropical forest areas and typically includes the circumvention of environmental protection mandates. In turn, these new and improved roads facilitate illicit drug production by providing a more reliable and cheaper transportation and access to remote forest regions (Young 2004).[1]

While the social and environmental damage of Plan Colombia was immediate, the effects on coca suppression were mixed and slow to emerge. In the initial years

---

1 Two important topics are beyond the scope of this article. First, while we are focused on Colombia, the impact of this militarized war on drugs extends to other Latin American nations. In the 1990s, the US spent more than $500 billion attempting to immobilize the drug trade forcing illicit crops to the most ecologically fragile lands in Peru, Bolivia and Colombia: the Andean rainforest (Burke 2003; see also Count the Costs 2011). Second, it is essential to plan for remediation in the wake of this war. While challenging in many respects, removing economic incentives for growing crops (whether legal or illegal) would reduce the rates of deforestation and encourage farmers and citizens to invest in improvements in land already being cultivated (Alvarez 2002; Davalos et al. 2009; Davalos et al. 2011). For the sake of fairness and to promote durable social institutions, it will be essential to provide social and legal assistance to indigenous peoples (Young 2004) as they seek to recover from the adverse effects of this drug war.

of implementation, this militarized war on drugs may have contributed to expanded coca production in Colombia and other Andean nations After the adoption of Plan Colombia, the number of coca-growing provinces in Colombia increased from 12 to 23 (United Nations Office of the High Commissioner for Human Rights 2010). Further-more, roughly 42% of the land under coca cultivation between 2001–2011 is on land that was "formerly covered by forests" (United Nations Office on Drugs and Crime 2012a). The local and global environmental consequences of this are staggering as the local population relocates to more remote lands and releasing CO_2 as forests are sacrificed to coca cultivation.

CONCLUSION

Colombia faces formidable environmental challenges: deforestation, declining biodi-versity, and degraded land and water. Colombia's challenges extend to the political and social realm to include failed economic policies, chronic poverty and unemploy-ment, and overt and armed challenges to the Colombian government. The militarized war on drugs exacerbates these environmental, social and political crises. During its first ten years, Plan Colombia failed to stem the flow of illicit substances to the United States. Since 2010, it appears that coca cultivation and export of cocaine from Colom-bia has declined. Whether a final assessment concludes that Plan Colombia succeeded or failed to suppress cocaine exports to the United States, this militarized effort high-lights the workings of the treadmill of destruction in the 21st Century: diverse armed forces profit directly and indirectly from predatory relations with noncombatants and unsustainable environmental practices. These trends are amplified by the policies of global powers. The risks of militarism—social, political and environmental—are systematically transferred to and borne by the people, ecosystems and institutions of the Global South.

There are signs that Colombia's internal wars might recede. The Colombian govern-ment has met with FARC to negotiate an end to the war (Brodzinsky 2014). The nation's presidential election is becoming a referendum on these peace talks—to continue the incumbent's current negotiations or to embrace a more bellicose and punitive posture toward FARC (see BBC News 2013; International Crisis Group 2012; Maloney 2013). Even if we make optimistic assumptions (that the negotiations with FARC go well and that Colombia's role in coca and cocaine production recedes), Colombia's future and that of other Andean nations remains perilous. First, the "new" wars of the 21st Century are notable for their concentration in countries with a prior history of conflict, and this has not always been the case. As late as the 1960s, the majority of civil wars took place in countries with no prior history of civil war. From 2000 to 2010, however, ninety percent (90%) of all civil war onsets have occurred in nations with a prior conflict (Walter 2010). As is the case in Colombia, prolonged civil conflict undermine fragile social institutions, generate profound and long lasting grievances, and undermine the state's legitimacy. The people and places in greatest need for peace and development—the bottom billion (Collier 2008)—are likely to be in a war zone, recovering from a recent war and/or on the verge of another round of war. Second, suppressing coca cultivation and cocaine exports from Colombia does not guarantee an overall reduction in supply at the global level. Prior to 1980, Colombia trailed Peru and Bolivia in drug production (and by a wide margin). In what is referred to as the "balloon effect," as pressure was placed on drug production in these neighboring countries, Colombia's output increased many times over. As Colombian production has ebbed, Peru recently overtook Colombia and is now the largest producer and exporter of cocaine (Brodzinsky 2014). Further, using species better suited for lower altitude rainforests, coca cultivation now extends into the Amazon rainforest, including sites in Brazil (Duffy 2008). Even if one makes very optimistic assumptions about Colombia, the prospects that coca cultivation, cocaine manufacture, and militarized eradication efforts will continue to impose horrific suffering on the people and ecosystems in the region remain high.

In one important respect, Colombia is not a representative case of the "new" wars of the 21st Century. Ethnic tensions have not been pronounced; genocidal policies have not been pursued. These tensions and social cleavages are all too common in 21st Century wars (Kaldor 1999; Mann 2005; Wimmer 2013)—and they bring a very specific dynamics and challenges. However, in other respects, the Colombian case can be generalized. Specifically, Colombia's recent history provides a glimpse into dynamics where: (1) a state demonstrably lacks a monopoly over the means of coercion and has lost legitimacy in the eyes of many citizens, and (2) a wide array of non-state militarized groups establish predatory ties to a lucrative and illegal source of revenues, and (3) a prominent and affluent military power intervenes to amplify these dynamics while insulating its own troops and homeland from the human and environmental costs. In this context, the human suffering and human rights abuses are widespread and severe. With regard to environment damage, the consequences of the treadmill of destruction are alarming. Irresponsible production processes have been coupled with ecocidal eradication efforts to cause extensive damage to Colombia's water, soil and forests and has compromised entire ecosystems. In this way, Colombia exhibits several features of "catastrophic convergence" (Parenti 2011) and "linked crises" (Chase-Dunn 2013). Colombia faces years, perhaps decades, of environmental damage tied the cascade of multiple crises unfolding at once in a location where "new" war, illustrative of risk-transfer militarism, is commonplace. While this examination of Colombia's recent history offers preliminary insights, it will be important for researchers to continue studying war and its aftermath. And when doing so, it will be important to elucidate the distinctive drivers and dimensions of the treadmill of destruction.

REFERENCES

Achard, Federic, Hugh D. Eva, Hans-Jurgen Stibig, Philippe Mayaux, Javier Gallego, Timothy Richards and Jean-Paul Malingeau. 2002. "Determination of Deforestation Rates of the World's Humid Tropical Forests." *Science* 297(5583): 999–1002.

Alvarez, Maria D. 2001b. "Could Peace Be Worse than War for Colombia's Forests?" *The Environmentalist* 21: 305–315.

Alvarez, Maria D. 2002. "Illicit Crops and Bird Conservation Priorities in Colombia." *Conservation Biology* 16(4): 1086–1096.

Armenteras, Dolors, Guillermo Rudas, Nelly Rodriguez, Sonia Sua, Milton Romero. 2006. "Patterns and Causes of Deforestation in the Colombian Amazon." *Ecological Indicators* 6: 353–368.

Armenteras, Dolors, Nelly Rodriguez, and Javier Retana. 2013. "Landscape Dynamics in Northwestern Amazonia: An Assessment of Pastures, Fire and Illicit Crops as Drivers of Tropical Deforestation." *PLoS ONE* 8(1): e54310.

Bagley, Bruce Michael. 1991. "Myths of Militarization: The Role of the Military in the War on Drugs in the Americas." Pp. 1–37 in *Drug Trafficking in the Americas Series*. Miami: North-South Center, University of Miami.

Ballvé, Teo. 2013. "Grassroots Masquerades: Development, paramilitaries, and land laundering in Colombia." *Geoforum* 50:62–75.

BBC News. 2013. "Colombia Peace Talks Resume in Cuba." London: BBC News. Retrieved online July 11, 2013 (http://www.bbc.co.uk/news/world-latin-america-22853611).

Benachour, Nora and Gilles-Eric Seralini. 2009. "Glyphosate Formulations Induce Apoptosis and Necrosis in Human Umbilical, Embryonic, and Placental Cells." *Chemical Research in Toxicology* 22: 97–105.

Bejarano, Ana Maria and Eduardo Pizarro. 2005. "From 'Restricted' to 'Besieged': The Changing Nature of the Limits to Democracy in Colombia." Pp. 235–260 in *The Third Wave of Democratization in Latin America: Advances and Setbacks*, edited by F. Hagopian and Scott P. Mainwaring. Cambridge: Cambridge University Press.

Bonds, Eric. 2013. "Hegemony and Humanitarianism Norms: The US Legitimization of Toxic Violence." *Journal of World-Systems Research* 19(1): 82–106.

Brodzinsky, Sibylla. 2014. "FARC Peace Talks May Tip Balance in Tight Colombian Presidential Race. *The Guardian* (May 22, 2014).

Brittain, James. 2010. *Revolutionary Social Change in Colombia: The Origin and Direction of the FARC-EP.* New York: Pluto Press.

Bunker, Stephen. 2005. "How Ecologically Uneven Developments Put the Spin on the Treadmill of Production." *Organization Environment* 18: 38–54.

Burke, Tom. 2003. "Warning: Drugs Cost the Earth." *New Statesman* 132: 31.

Buxton, Julia. 2006. *The Political Economy of Narcotics: Production, Consumption and Global Markets.* London/New York: Zed Books.

Chase-Dunn, Christopher. 2013. "Five Linked Crises in the Contemporary World-System." *Journal of World-System Research* 19(2): 175–181.

Ciccantell, Paul and David A. Smith. 2009. "Rethinking Global Commodity Chains: Integrating Extraction, Transport, and Manufacturing." *International Journal of Comparative Sociology* 50: 361–384.

Clark, Brett and Andrew K. Jorgenson. 2012. "The Tread*mill of Destruction and the Environmental Impacts of Militaries." *Sociology Compass* 6/7: 557–569.

Clelland, Donald. 2014. "The Core of the Apple: Dark Value and Degrees of Monopoly in Global Commodity Chains." *Journal of World System Research* 20:82–111.

Collier, Paul. 2008. *The Bottom Billion: Why the Poorest Countries are Failing and What Can Be Done About It.* New York: Oxford University Press.

Congressional Research Service. 2011. "Latin America and the Caribbean: Illicit Drug Trafficking and U.S. Counterdrug Programs." Retrieved July 11, 2013 (http://publicintelligence.net/latin-america-and-the-caribbean-illicit-drug-trafficking-andu-s-counterdrug-programs/).

Count the Costs. 2011. "The War on Drugs: Causing Deforestation and Pollution." Count the Costs Environment Briefing. Retrieved January 4, 2012 (http://countthecosts.org/seven-costs/deforestation-and-pollution).

Davalos, Liliana M., Adriana C. Bejarano, and H. Leonardo Corea. 2009. "Disabusing Cocaine: Pervasive Myths and Enduring Realities of a Globalized Commodity." *International Journal of Drug Policy* 20: 381–386.

Davalos, Liliana M., Adriana Bejarano, Mark A. Hall, H. Leonardo Correa, Angelique Corthals, and Oscar J. Espejo. 2011. "Forests and Drugs: Coca-Driven Deforestation in Tropical Hotspots." *Environmental Science and Technology* 45: 1219–1227.

De Liz Oliveira Cavalli, Vera, Daiane Cattani, Carla Elise Heinz Rieg, Paula Pierozan, Leila Zanatta, Eduardo Benedetti Parisotto, Danilo Wilhelm Filho, Fatima Regina Mena Barreto Silva, Regina Pessoa-Pureur, and Ariane Zamoner. 2013. "Roundup Disrupts Male Reproductive Function by Triggering Calcium-Mediated Cell Death in Rat Testis and Sertoli Cells." *Free Radical Biology and Medicine* 65: 335–346.

Dombey-Moore, Bonnie, Susan Resetar, and Michael Childress. 1994. *A System Description of the Cocaine Trade*. Santa Monin, CA; Rand Corporation.

Dube, Oeindrila and Suresh Naidu. 2010. "Bases, Bullets, and Ballots: The Effect of U.S. Military Aid on Political Conflict in Colombia." Center for Global Development. Working Paper 197, Janurary 2010. Retrieved May 24, 2012 (http://www.cgdev.org/files/1423498_file_Dube_Naidu_Military_Aid_FINAL.pdf).

Duffy, Gary. 2008. "First Coca Find in Brazil Amazon." *BBC News*. Retrieved May 25, 2014 (http://news.bbc.co.uk/2/hi/7299964.stm).

The Economist. 2013. "Why is Less Cocaine Coming from Colombia?" *The Economist*. Retrieved March 5, 2014 (http://www.economist.com/blogs/economist-explains/2013/04/economist-explains-why-colombia-produces-less-cocaine).

Etter, Andres, Clive McAlpine, Kerrie Wilson, Stuart Phinn, Hugh Possingham. 2006. "Regional Patterns of Agricultural Land Use and Deforestation in Colombia." *Agriculture, Ecosystems and Environment* 114: 369–386.

Eraso, Nelly Rodriguez, Dolors Armenteras-Pascual, and Javier Retana Alumbreros. 2012. "Land Use and Land Cover Change in Colombian Andes: Dynamics and Future Scenarios." *Journal of Land Use Science* DOI: 10.1080: 1–21.

Fjeldsa, Jon, Maria D. Alvarez, Juan Mario Lazcano, and Blanca Leon. 2005. "Illicit Crops and Armed Conflict as Constraints on Biodiversity Conservation in the Andes Region." *Ambio* 34(3): 205–211.

Gasnier, Eline, Coraline Dumont, Nora Benachour, Emilie Clair, Marie-Christine Chagnon, and Gilles-Eric Seralini. 2009. "Glyphosate-base Herbicides are Toxic and Endocrine Disruptors in Human Cell Lines." *Toxicology* 262: 184–191.

Gould, Kenneth A., David N. Pellow, and Allan Schnaiberg. 2008. *The Treadmill of Production: Injustices and Unsustainability in the Global Economy*. Boulder, Colorado: Paradigm Publishers.

Guerrero Baron, Javier, and David Mond. 2001 "Is the War Ending? Premises and Hypotheses with Which to View the Conflict in Colombia." *Latin American Perspectives* 28(1): 12–30.

Hellin, Jon. 2001. "Coca Eradication in the Andes: Lessons from Bolivia." *Capitalism Nature Socialism* 12(2): 139–57.

Holmes, Jennifer S., Gutierrez De Pineres, Sheila Amin, and Kevin M. Curtain. *Guns, Drugs, and Development in Colombia*. Austin, Texas: University of Texas Press.

Hooks, Gregory, and Chad L. Smith. 2004. "The Treadmill of Destruction: National Sacrifice Areas and Native Americans." *American Sociological Review* 69:558–76.

_____. 2005. "Treadmills of Production and Destruction: Threats to the Environment Posed by Militarism." *Organizations and Environment* 18:19–37.

_____. 2012. "The Treadmill of Destruction Goes Global: Anticipating the Environmental Impact of Militarism in the 21st Century." Pp. 60–83 in *The Marketing of War in the Age of Neo-Militarism*, edited by Kostas Gouliamos and Christos Kassimeris. Routledge Press.

Hopkins, Terence and Wallerstein, Immanuel 1982. *World-Systems Analysis: Theory and Methodology.* Beverly Hills, CA: Sage.

Hough, Phillip. 2011. "Guerrilla Insurgency as Organized Crime: Explaining the So-Called 'Political Involution' of the Revolutionary Armed Forces of Colombia." *Politics & Society* 39: 379–414.

Inter-American Drug Abuse Control Commission (CICAD, OAS). 2005. *The Toxicology of Selected Chemicals Used in the Production and Refining of Cocaine and Heroin: A Tier-two Assessment* (D 2005–01). Washington, DC: Inter-American Drug Abuse Control Commission (CICAD), Organization of American States.

International Crisis Group. 2005. *War and Drugs in Colombia* (Latin America Report N°11). Brussels: International Crisis Group. Retrieved July 11, 2013 (http://www.crisisgroup.org/en/regions/latin-america-caribbean/andes/colombia/011-warand-drugs-in-colombia.aspx).

International Crisis Group. 2012. "Colombia: Peace at Last?" *Executive Summary and Recommendations.* Brussels: International Crisis Group. Retrieved July 11, 2013 (http://www.crisisgroup.org/en/regions/latin-america-caribbean/andes/colombia/045-colombia-peace-at-last.aspx).

Jasper, Raquel, Gabriel Olivo Locatelli, Celso Pilati, and Claudriana Locatelli. 2012. "Evaluation of Biochemical, Hematological and Oxidative Parameters in Mice Exposed to the Herbicide Glyphosate-Roundup®." *Interdisciplinary Toxicology* 5(3): 133–140.

Jorgenson, Andrew. 2005. "Unpacking International Power and the Ecological Footprints of Nations: A Quantitative Cross-National Study." *Sociological Perspectives* 48:383–402.

Jorgenson, Andrew and Brett Clark. 2009. "The Economy, Military, and Ecologically Unequal Relationships in Comparative Perspective: A Panel Study of the Ecological Footprints of Nations, 1975–2000." *Social Problems* 56:621–646.

Jorgenson, Andrew, Brett Clark, and Jeffrey Kentor. 2010. "Militarization and the Environment: A Panel Study of Carbon Dioxide Emissions and the Ecological Footprints of Nations, 1970–2000." *Global Environmental Politics* 10:7–29.

Kaldor, Mary. 1999. *New and Old Wars: Organized Violence in a Global Era.* Stanford, CA: Stanford University Press.

Leitenberg, Milton. 2006. "Deaths and Wars in Conflicts in the 20th Century." Ithaca, NY: Cornell University, Peace Studies Program. Retrieved May 22, 2012 (http://www.clingendael.nl/publications/2006/20060800_cdsp_occ_leitenberg.pdf).

Lengefeld, Michael and Chad L. Smith. 2013. "Nuclear Shadows: Weighing the Environmental Effects of Militarism, Capitalism, and Modernization in a Global Context, 2001–2007." *Human Ecology Review* 20(1): 11–25.

Mabry, Donald. 1988. "The US Military and the War on Drugs in Latin America." *Journal of Interamerican Studies and World Affairs* 30(2/3): 53–76.

Maloney, Anastasia. 2013. "Ten Things You Didn't Know about Colombia's Peace Talks." Thomas Reuters Foundation. Retrieved July 11, 2013 (http://www.trust.org/item/20130705105455-b396j).

Mann, Michael. 2005. *The Dark Side of Democracy: Explaining Ethnic Cleansing.* New York: Cambridge University Press.

Mejía, Daniel, and Carlos Posada. 2008. *Cocaine Production and Trafficking: What Do We Know?* (Policy Research Working Paper 4618). Washington, DC: World Bank.

Messina, J. P. and P.L. Delamater. 2006. "Defoliation and the War on Drugs in Putumayo, Colombia." *International Journal of Remote Sensing* 27(1): 121–128.

Meza-Joya, Fabio Leonardo, Martha Patricia Ramirez-Pinilla, and Jorge Luis Fuentes-Lorenzo. 2013. "Toxic, Cytoxic, and Genetoxic Effects of a Glyphosate Formulation (Roundup®SL-Cosmoflux®411F) in the Direct-Developing Frog *Eleutherodactylus johnstonei.*" Environmental and Molecular Mutagenesis 54: 362–373.

Mugge, Zachary. 2004. "Plan Colombia: The Environmental Effects and Social Costs of the United States' Failing War on Drugs." Colorado Journal of International Environmental Law and Policy 15(2): 309–340.

Nobre, Carlos, Piers J. Sellers, Jagadish Shukla. 1991. "Amazonian Deforestation and Regional Climate Change" *Journal of Climate* 4: 956–988.

Office of National Drug Control Policy. 2012. "Survey Shows Significant Drop in Cocaine Production in Colombia." Retrieved August 1, 2012 (http://www.whitehouse.gov/ondcp/news-releases-remarks/survey-shows-significantdrop-in-cocaine-production-in-colombia).

Parenti, Christian. 2011. *Tropic of Chaos: Climate Change and the New Geography of Violence*. New York: Nation Books.

Peceny, Mark and Michael Durnan. 2006. "The FARC's Best Friend: U.S. Antidrug Policies and the Deepening of Colombia's Civil War in the 1990s." *Latin American Politics and Society* 48(2): 95–116.

Priest, Dana. 2013. *Washington Post*. "Covert Action in Colombia." Retrieved January 1, 2013 (http://www.washingtonpost.com/sf/investigative/2013/12/21/covert-action-in-colombia/).

Relyea, Rick A. 2005a. "The Impact of Insecticides and Herbicides on the Biodiversity and Productivity of Aquatic Communities." *Ecological Applications* 15(2): 618–627.

Relyea, Rick A. 2005b. "The Lethal Impact of Roundup on Aquatic and Terrestrial Amphibians." *Ecological Applications* 15(4): 1118–1124.

Relyea, Rick A. 2011. "Amphibians Are Not Ready for Roundup®." Pp. 267–300 in *Wildlife Ecotoxicology: Forensic Approaches*, edited by J.E. Elliot, C.A. Bishop, and C. Morrisey. New York: Springer.

Ribot, Jesse. 1998. "Theorizing Access: Forest Profits along Senegal's Charcoal Commodity Chain." *Development and Change* 29: 307–41.

Rice, James. 2007. "Ecological Unequal Exchange: Consumption, Equity, and Unsustainable Structural Relationships within the Global Economy." *International Journal of Comparative Sociology* 48: 43–72.

Ronderos, Juan G. 2003. "The War on Drugs and the Military: The Case of Colombia." Pp. 207–236 in *Critical Reflections on Transnational Organized Crime, Money Laundering, and Corruption*, edited by Margaret E. Beare. Toronto: University of Toronto Press.

Saab, Bilal Y. and Alexandra W. Taylor. 2009. "Criminality and Armed Groups: A Comparative Study of FARC and Paramilitary Groups in Colombia." *Studies in Conflict & Terrorism* 32: 455–475.

Samsel, Anthony and Stephanie Seneff. 2013. "Glyphosate's Suppression of Cytochrome P450 Enzymes and Amino Acid Biosynthesis by the Gut Microbiome: Pathways to Modern Diseases." *Entropy* 15: 1416–1463.

Schnaiberg, Allan. 1980. *The Environment: From Surplus to Scarcity*. New York: Oxford University Press.

Schnaiberg, Allan and Kenneth A. Gould. 1994. *Environment and Society: The Enduring Conflict*. New York: St. Martin's Press.

Scott, Peter Dale. 2003. *Drugs, Oil and War: The United States in Afghanistan, Colombia, and Indochina*. Lanham, Maryland: Rowman and Littlefield.

Shandra, John M., Christopher Leckband and Bruce London. 2009. "Ecologically Unequal Exchange and Deforestation: A Cross-National Analysis of Forestry Export Flows." *Organization & Environment* 22(3): 293–310.

Shaw, Martin. 2002. "Risk-Transfer Militarism: Small Massacres and the Historic Legitimacy of War." *International Relations* 16:343–60.

———. 2005. *The New Western Way of War: Risk-Transfer War and Its Crisis in Iraq*. Cambridge, UK: Polity.

Solomon, Keith, Arturo Anadon, Gabriel Carrasquilla, Antonio L. Cerdeira, Jon Marchall, and Luz-Helena Sanin. 2007. "Coca and Poppy Eradication in Colombia: Environmental and Human Health Assessment of Aerially Applied Glyphosate." *Reviews of Environmental Contamination and Toxicology* 190: 43–125.

Solomon, Keith, E.J.P Marshall, and Gabriel Carrasquilla. 2009. "Human Health and Environmental Risks from the Use of Glyphosate Formulations to Control the Production of Coca in Colombia: Overview and Conclusions." *Journal of Toxicology and Environmental Health, Part A* 72: 914–920.

Stokes, Doug. 2001. "Better Lead than Bread? A Critical Analysis of the US's Plan Colombia." *Civil Wars* 4(2): 59–78.

Stokes, Doug. 2005. *America's Other War: Terrorizing Colombia*. New York: Zed Books.

Summerfield, Derek. 1991. "The Psychosocial Effects of Conflict in the Third World." *Development in Practice*. 1(3): 159–173.

Tenenbaum, David. 2002. "Coca-Killing Controversy." *Environmental Health Perspectives* 110(5): A236.

Thongprakaisang, Siriporn, Apinya Thiantanawat, Nuchanart Rangkadilok, Tawit Suriyo, and Jutamaad Satayavivad. 2013. "Glypohsate Induces Human Breast Cancer Cells Growth Via Estrogen Receptors." *Food and Chemical Toxicology* 59: 129–136.

Tilly, Charles. 1975. "Reflections on the History of European State-Making." Pp. 3–83 in *The Formation of National States in Western Europe*, edited by Charles Tilly. Princeton: Princeton University Press.

Transnational Institute. 2001. "Vicious Circle: The Chemical and Biological 'War on Drugs.'" Transnational Institute Report. Retrieved March 2, 2012 (http://www.tni.org/sites/www.tni.org/files/download/viciouscircle-e.pdf).

United Nations, Office of the High Commissioner for Human Rights. 2010. "Briefing 6: Human Rights and Drug Policy: Crop Eradication." New York: United Nations Retrieved May 25, 2012 (http://www2.ohchr.org/english/bodies/cescr/docs/ngos/IHRA_Colombia44.pdf).

United Nations, Office on Drugs and Crime. 2010. *World Drug Report 2010*. New York: United Nations. Retrieved March 5, 2014 (http://www.unodc.org/documents/wdr/WDR_2010/World_Drug_Report_2010_lores.pdf).

_____. 2012a. "Colombia Coca Cultivation Survey 2011." New York: United Nations. Retrieved August 1, 2012 (http://www.unodc.org/documents/crop-monitoring/Colombia/Colombia_Coca_cultivation_survey_2011.pdf).

_____. 2012b. "Colombia Grows Quarter Less Coca Crop, According to UNODC 2012 Survey." New York: United Nations. Retrieved March 5, 2014 (http://www.unodc.org/unodc/en/frontpage/2013/August/colombia-grows-quarter-lesscoca-crop-according-to-unodc-2012-survey.html).

United Nations, Human Rights Council. 2013. "Universal Periodic Review: National report submitted in accordance with paragraph 5 of the annex to Human Rights Council resolution 16/21." New York: United Nations. Retrieved January 13, 2013 (http://www.ohchr.org/Documents/HRBodies/HRCouncil/RegularSession/Session23/TF/A-HRC-RES-16-21_en.doc).

United States Department of State. 2002. "Chemicals Used for the Aerial Eradication of Illicit Coca in Colombia and Conditions of Application." Retrieved August 8, 2013 (http://www.state.gov/j/inl/rls/rpt/aeicc/13234.htm).

United States Department of State. 2003. "Environmental Consequences of the Illicit Coca Trade." Retrieved May 25, 2012 (http://2001-2009.state.gov/p/inl/rls/fs/3807.htm).

Vaicius, Ingrid and Adam Isacson. 2003. "The 'War on Drugs' meets the 'War on Terror:' The United States' Military Involvement in Colombia Climbs to the Next Level." International Policy Report. Retreived May 29, 2012 (http://www.ciponline.org/images/uploads/publications/0302ipr.pdf).

Walter, Barbara. 2010. *Conflict Relapse and the Sustainability of Post-Conflict Peace* (World Development Report 2011: Background Paper). Washington, D.C.: World Bank. Retrieved February 25, 2014 (https://openknowledge.worldbank.org/bitstream/handle/10986/9069/WDR2011_0008.pdf?sequence=1).

Wickham-Crowley, Timothy P. 1992. *Guerrillas & Revolution in Latin America: A Comparative Study of Insurgents and Regimes Since 1956*. Princeton, New Jersey: Princeton University Press.

Wimmer, Andreas. 2013. *Waves of War: Nationalism, State Formation, and Ethnic Exclusion in the Modern World*. New York: Cambridge University Press.

York, Richard. 2008. "De-carbonization in Former Soviet Republics, 1992–2000: The Ecological Consequences of De-modernization." *Social Problems* 55:370–390.

Young, Kenneth R. 2004 "A Geographical Perspective on Coca/Cocaine Impacts in South America." Pp. 363–367 in *WorldMinds: Geographical Perspectives on 100 Problems*, edited by Donald G. Janelle, Barney Warf, and Kathy Hansen. The Netherlands; Kluwer Academic Publishers. Retrieved April 22, 2012 (http://books.google.com/books?hl=en&lr=&id=0VxzNQj7feEC&oi=fnd&pg=PA363&dq=Threats+to+Biological+Diversity+Caused+by+Coca/Cocaine+Deforestation+in+Peru&ots=WCO2_beKXH&sig=Qw_lg-w0R4l_lwr-2HpE1KzB5Eg#v=onepage&q=Threats%20to%20Biological%20Diversity%20Caused%20by%20Coca%2FCocaine%20Deforestation%20in%20Peru&f=false).

Zirnite, Peter. 1997. "Reluctant Recruits: The US Military and the War on Drugs." Washington Office on Latin America (WOLA), Transnational Institute Report, Retrieved March 25, 2012(http://www.tni.org/sites/www.tni.org/files/download/Reluctant%20recruits%20report_0.pdf).

US and Mexican Cooperation

The Merida Initiative and Drug Trafficking

Yasemin Tekin

INTRODUCTION

In recent decades, Mexico has remained one of the world's key players in the global drug market. Mexico is the major supplier of heroin, methamphetamine, cocaine and marijuana in the Americas (Seelke et al. 2011). As a result, Mexico is one of the most problematic countries in the region regarding illegal drugs being exported into the US through the Central America-Mexico corridor. The illegal drug trade causes severe violence in the country and threatens US border security. According to the US National Drug Intelligence Center:

> Violent infighting among rival Mexican gangs, at least partially attributable to competition over control of lucrative crossing points along the Southwest Border, is occurring mainly on the Mexico side of the border. Criminal activity such as kidnappings and home invasion robberies directed against individuals involved in drug trafficking has been reported in some U.S. border communities (National Drug Treatment Assessment, 2011).

Although the violence in Mexico has generally declined since late 2011, analysts estimate that it may have claimed more than 70,000 lives between December 2006 and December 2013 (Seelke and Finklea, 2014). Thus, an increase in crime and violence among these groups over the control of drug smuggling routes along the US-Mexico border has made the drug trafficking problem even more serious and requires a permanent solution. According to Seelke (2010), drug trafficking is viewed as a major problem that poses a serious threat to the security of citizens and the US interests in Latin America. Since the production and trafficking of popular illicit drugs generates billions of dollars in black market profits, Mexican criminal organizations have engaged in illegal drug trafficking and threatened US national security. According to a report by the Congressional Research Service (2011), Mexican drug trafficking organizations control of illicit drug markets in the US and cooperation with US gangs is the main reason for the spillover of the drug related violence in Mexico to the US Indeed, the Department of Justice defines drug trafficking organizations as "the greatest organized crime threat to the US" (Seelke et al., 2011). Therefore, the US should come up with a specific policy to combat the illegal drug trade through the US-Mexico border to reduce drug-related violence in the country.

As a result of the increasing violence due to illegal drug trafficking along the US and Mexico border, U.S policymakers have created several counterdrug assistance programs for Mexico and Central America to combat drug trafficking and decrease drug related violence. However, these assistance programs did not stop either problem as they did not target the root of them. Therefore, the Mexican government under the former presidency of Felipe Calderon requested a higher level of cooperation and assistance from the US. In October 22, 2007, the US and Mexico announced the Merida Initiative.

The Merida Initiative was a multi-year plan for US assistance to Mexico and Central America to fight against drug trafficking and organized crime. Since December 2012, the Obama Administration and Mexican President Enrique Peña Nieto have continued US-Mexican security cooperation, which focuses on reducing violent crime in Mexico (Seelke and Finklea, 2014). From FY2008 to FY2014, Congress appropriated about $2.4 billion in the Merida Initiative assistance for Mexico, including some $194.2 million provided in the FY2014 Consolidated Appropriations Act (Seelke and Finklea, 2014). In March 2014, the US delivered more than $1.2 billion of Merida Initiative assistance (Seelke and Finklea, 2014). For the fiscal year 2015, the Obama Administration asked for $115 million for Merida Initiative assistance (Seelke and Finklea, 2014). The policy was an important step towards the solution of the drug related violence and instability in the region. However, today there is debate over the success of this policy and its uneven implementation.

US-Mexican security cooperation has increased as a result of the development and implementation of the Merida Initiative (Seelke and Finklea, 2014). Today, the Obama administration's assistance, known as "Beyond Merida," focuses on training and equipping Mexican counterdrug forces emphasizing the weak institutions and social problems that have allowed the drug trade in Mexico to flourish (Seelke and Finklea, 2014). The current Merida approach focuses on the four pillars: disrupting organized criminal groups, institutionalizing the rule of law, creating a twenty-first century border, and building strong and resilient communities (Seelke and Finklea, 2014).

This paper examines the sustainability of the Merida Initiative as a counterdrug policy in Mexico. The paper begins with an overview of the arguments about the problem and the policy in the literature; then discusses three major policy options that could reduce organized crime and drug trafficking in Mexico and evaluate these possible options through the established criteria. Finally, it proposes the most practical policy option that addresses established criteria the best and would resolve Mexico's problem efficiently.

LITERATURE REVIEW

Maureen Meyer (2007) explains the tragedy in the country: "Since 2005, Mexico has been beset by an increase in drug-related violence. In that year over 1,500 people were killed in drug-related violence; in 2006, the number of victims climbed to more than 2,500." She then explains that despite the military actions of the Mexican government as a response to increased violence, there were 2,113 casualties in 2007 (Meyer, Maureen, 2007). In addition, the *Los Angeles Times* (2014) claims that since 2008, there has been a savage struggle among Mexican drug cartels to control the drug trade across the US border. Los Angeles Times (2014) also states that the conflict has left thousands dead, paralyzed cities with fear, and spawned a culture of corruption reaching the upper levels of the Mexican State (*Los Angeles Times*, 2014).

The problem has also been examined by its negative effect on the society. Diana Villiers Negroponte (2009) argues that drug related violence creates an underlying insecurity within the society. She claims the conflict between organized criminal groups creates distrust in the police force and members of the judiciary, as well as corruption among government bureaucrats (Negroponte, 2009).

The Merida Initiative proposed by former US President George W. Bush and former Mexican President Felipe Calderon was designed to combat drug trafficking, transnational crime, and terrorism. At the meeting in March 2007, the presidents of the two countries agreed to expand bilateral and regional counternarcotic and security cooperation (Cook, 2008). According to the State Department (2010), there were four major goals of this policy:

> (1) Break the power and impunity of criminal organizations; (2) assist the Mexican and Central American governments in strengthening border, air, and maritime controls; (3) improve the capacity of justice systems in the region; and (4) curtail gang activity in Mexico and Central America and diminish the demand for drugs in the region (Seelke, 2010).

Congress approved an initial $400 million for Mexico and $65 million for Central America, the Dominican Republic, and Haiti to assist these nations in their wars against drug cartels. Additionally, Congress approved $300 million for Mexico and $110 million for Central America, the Dominican Republic, and Haiti for the fiscal year 2009 (Fact Sheet, 2009). The initial $400 million of funding for Mexico was to provide helicopters and surveillance aircraft, non-intrusive inspection equipment, technologies and secure communications to improve data collection and storage, technical advice and training to strengthen the institutions of justice (Seelke, 2011).

The Department of State manages the Merida Initiative in cooperation with several other US agencies, and it is responsible for its implementation (US Government Accountability Office Report, 2010). According to the report by the Government Accountability Office (GAO) in July 2010, the US agencies have delivered the funds allocated in Mexico successfully. The report claims that:

> As of March 31, 2010, 46 percent of Merida funds for fiscal years 2008 to 2010 had been obligated, and approximately 9 percent had been expended. In Mexico, US agencies have delivered major equipment including five Bell helicopters, several X-ray inspection devices, law enforcement canines and training for their handlers, and training for over 4,000 police officers (US Government Accountability Office Report, 2010).

Despite successful appropriation of the funds to Mexico under the Merida Initiative, there were some problems with the implementation of the initiative. Most of the funds were not delivered on time. The same report defines these challenges as "an insufficient number of staff to administer the program, negotiations on interagency and bilateral agreements, procurement processes, changes in government, and funding availability" (US Government Accountability Office Report, 2010). To address problems regarding timing of fund availability, agencies have employed alternative methods to expedite the implementation of certain programs in Mexico and some Central American countries. Therefore, the report is optimistic about the implementation timing as agencies improved efforts to expedite the process and claim that the pace of delivery has increased over time (US Government Accountability Office Report, 2010).

The same report by the GAO claims there are several gaps within the US Strategy for Merida Initiative that would improve management of the policy. The report (2010) argues that strategic documents do not include performance measures to show progress in achieving the four strategic goals. They believe that these issues are important to consider because they help evaluate the success of the program and determine whether relevant adjustments are necessary. Therefore, the GAO suggests the outcome-based performance measurements should be involved in the policy strategy to facilitate assessment of progress and the policy itself (US Government Accountability Office Report, 2010).

Indeed, there has been a debate over the efficiency of the Merida Initiative as a counterdrug policy. A Witness for Peace Fact Sheet (2011) criticizes the policy by arguing that Merida Initiative ignores the two major root causes of drug trafficking: high US demand for illicit drugs and poverty in Mexico. The fact sheet argues that widespread drug use in the US makes drug trafficking a profitable initiative and reinforces such an environment. It criticizes the policy in terms of its lack of strategy about drug prevention and rehabilitation programs in the US to decrease the demand for drugs. They further claim that trade policies that US has adopted towards Mexico do not solve the problem of poverty in Mexico. The Witness for Peace Fact Sheet (2011) further claims that the impoverished and unemployed people in Mexico are left without many options to survive, except migration, dangerous work in the informal economy, and finally to engage in criminal activities. Finally, the Witness for Peace Fact Sheet (2011) argues that since a similar military policy has failed to combat drug cultivation and insurgent groups, it is likely the Merida Initiative will fail as well. They point out that although the US has spent millions of dollars on military aid to reduce the cocaine supply through Plan Colombia, farmers in the country are still planting cocaine at increasing levels (Witness for Peace Fact Sheet, 2011). Negroponte (2009) also argues that the initiative failed to promote strategies to deal with social problems caused by drug trafficking and increasing violence. She claims that an increased police and military presence may temporarily curtail violent crime and car theft, but their presence does little to combat the underlying insecurity within society: the lack of trust in the police force and members of the judiciary, as well as pervasive levels of corruption among government bureaucrats. Although she believes that the Merida Initiative was a beneficial approach because it initiated a comprehensive regional program, Negroponte argues that it was projected on a short time plan, which made it insufficient in containing the problems (2009).

POLICY ANALYSIS

Despite all the gaps within the policy proposal, the Merida initiative was an important step towards a common purpose: combating drug trafficking into the US and decreasing organized crime in Mexico (Negroponte, 2009). Throughout the negotiations and implementation process between the 2007 and 2010, the diplomatic relations between Mexico and the US have improved (Negroponte, 2009). US and Mexican policymakers have defined the problem as transnational organized crime and have collaborated on approaches to achieve their goal. (Negroponte, 2009) The US has supplied a large amount of money to assist several programs employed by the Mexican government to promote law enforcement, train and equip its agencies, promote justice reforms, and modernize Mexico's borders (Seelke & Finklea, 2014). Unfortunately, the current violence in Mexico indicates this policy will not achieve its purpose permanently. Policymakers should take further action beyond the Merida Initiative to minimize violence and drug-trafficking in Mexico because it presents a serious threat to the US border and public security.

There are several policy options that could solve the drug-related violence in Mexico. However, a practicable option would be the one that responds to the values of each society. The first policy approach is preserving the status-quo by continuing the Obama Administration's approach, also known as "Beyond Merida" policy, embraces the original purposes of Merida Initiative but focuses on "four pillars" and "institution building" rather than military assistance. The second option is to reduce the allocated funds to Mexico and minimize US involvement in Mexico's domestic affairs. This policy option projects minimal US involvement in the law enforcement process and intelligence operations of the Mexican government, and cuts some funds that will be allocated to Mexico under current Merida Initiative. Finally, the third option suggests a new approach where the US would take more aggressive action to minimize the violence in Mexico. This paper recommends the third option, where there is US-Mexican security cooperation beyond the Obama administration's current policy by employing more determined and aggressive policies regarding drug problems in Mexico.

The criteria that will determine the best plausible policy option among these three options will consist of three values that are significant to the US interests. The first objective for the US is creating stronger border security. The ongoing drug related violence among the criminal groups and illegal arms trade into Mexico threatens both the public security in Mexico and national security of the US The second criterion for the US is to institutionalize law enforcement in Mexico, which would eventually establish a long-term order and judicial system in Mexico and reduce violence. Finally, it is crucial for the US to employ domestic policies decreasing the demand and illegal consumption for illicit drugs in its national borders. Since the US is the main consumer of the drugs produced in Mexico, decreasing demand for illegal drugs in the US is significant factor in reducing the drug related problems in Mexico. Without decreasing the demand for these illegal drugs in its borders, the US cannot achieve its goals because high demand in the US for these illicit drugs creates an incentive for organized criminal groups to engage in intense drug trafficking.

The first policy approach is the continuation of the Obama Administration's current Beyond Merida policy. The current policy that has been employed by the Obama Administration is based on "four pillars" and "institution building" which as Olson and Wilson describe it is: "a new framework for bilateral cooperation" (Olson, Eric L., and Wilson, Christopher E. 2010). This policy aims to focus more on institutional reforms in Mexico rather than military assistance. As Olson and Wilson (2010) explain: "The first two pillars represent a refinement of previous efforts, and the final two represent a new and expanded approach to anti-drug efforts" (Olson and Wilson, 2010). The first pillar of this current policy is disrupting and dismantling criminal organizations. This approach calls for viewing cartels as corporations and understanding their strategy to interrupt their business. It also suggests impeding the arms trade from the US to Mexico to prevent cartel activities (Olson and Wilson 2010). The second pillar of this policy is institutionalizing the rule of law, which suggests allocation of more money for civilian institutions that is responsible for promoting justice, and maintaining the rule of law (Olson and Wilson, 2010). The third pillar suggests building a twenty-first century border. Olson and Wilson describe the approach as "changing the very concept of the border from simply being a geographic line to one of secure flows" (2010). By doing so, the officials working at the border will focus on preventing the entrance of illicit drugs into the USA. Finally, the fourth pillar of this option is to build strong and resilient communities which aim "to reduce the demand for drugs, create jobs, improve local infrastructure, and to build better public spaces" (Olson and Wilson 2010).

The "Beyond Merida" approach was designed as a refinement of the Merida Initiative to make that approach more efficient and successful. Although the "four pillars" point out very significant issues that must be considered to solve the problem, they do not make this approach sufficient. Taking this policy approach will be beneficial in terms of achieving one of the established criteria: institutionalization of law enforcement. The second pillar of the policy suggests that the US government will allocate more money to support development of powerful Mexican institutions. This pillar will succeed if these institutions serve honestly and are managed transparently. But in fact, it is very difficult to control what kind of institutions the Mexican government will establish, and how efficiently they will provide order and justice in the country. Therefore, there should be a strict supervision by the US over the Mexican government and those new institutions. This policy option focuses on disrupting criminal organizations and creating twenty-first century borders which is important for providing border and public security. However, these criminal organizations will invariably develop new strategies to get around the US counter drug and terrorism policies, and the violence will continue. Therefore, focusing on these groups does not guarantee the public and border security. In addition, the new understanding of border of being a place to "focus on preventing entrance of dangerous illicit flows" as Olson (2010) describes also does not secure the borders. Corruption is likely, as the officers at the border can be convinced by the organized criminal groups to cooperate with them in return to monetary benefits. Therefore, the unintended consequences of creating such a border approach will create more vulnerable borders and actually contribute to drug trafficking. Furthermore, this policy option does not address the root causes of the problem and fails to meet one of the established criteria: decreasing demand for illegal drugs in the US In fact, none of the established pillars of the Beyond Merida approach addresses the high demand for illegal drugs in the US and poverty in Mexico. The Obama administration's policy fails to meet one of the most important criteria; the problem requires a more comprehensive approach.

The second policy option for the US is to minimize the funds that have been proposed under Merida Initiative and limit involvement in Mexico's domestic affairs. Since the US's efforts to eliminate drug trafficking and drug-related violence in Mexico have not achieved its goals, it is important to revise the US intervention in Mexican domestic policies As the GAO report (2010) asserts, despite addressing several steps to reduce violence, the Merida Initiative was problematic in terms of its implementation. In fact, the GAO report (2010) points out the large amount of money that was allocated for Mexico has not been spent and the pace of the implementation was slow. If we consider little improvements in the Mexican government's reforms during the policy timelines and increasing criminal activities after the implementation of the Merida Initiative, it is reasonable to argue that the US efforts were neither efficient nor sufficient. Therefore, it is among the plausible policy options for the US to minimize the monetary aid and not intervene in Mexico's domestic issues.

By taking this approach, the US would save millions of dollars that it has to spend for the security cooperation agreement under Merida Initiative. However, this policy does not meet any of the established criteria. Protection of the national security can only be achieved by eliminating drug related violence along the US-Mexico border. In fact, the increasing drug-related violence and drug trafficking into the US poses a great threat to US national security. Moreover, the Mexican government's efforts to combat illicit drugs have proved that the problem requires serious measures to solve it that may not be achieved domestically. The institutions in Mexico, such as the law enforcement and judiciary systems, need to be improved to be able to solve the drug problems in the country. Without strict law enforcement and a justice system, there is not much the Mexican government can do to solve the problems. Therefore, the US, a country with a better judicial and law enforcement mechanisms because of its efficient checks and balances system, might be very effective at leading the Mexican government in an initiative to restore peace and order in the country. The US has to collaborate with the Mexican government to solve these problems through fostering economic growth in Mexico and creating effective institutions in the country.

A third policy option should be considered as a further step to that addresses the problems of the current Obama Administration's approach. This new policy suggests advanced security cooperation between the US and Mexico beyond the current US policy. It requires the US to employ more aggressive policies to combat the drug trade and violence in Mexico because this will expedite the process and create a permanent solution. This new policy recommends much stronger US-Mexican security cooperation by employing more determined and active policies toward a mutual "collaborative action" of both countries against drug trafficking and violence in Mexico. The new approach will require both countries to take decisive actions to prevent illicit drug trafficking and the violence that comes from it. By having the two countries take responsibility to eradicate the problem in Mexico, the established criteria will be satisfied.

Border and public security are very important for the US; therefore, rather than having the police force at the border as proposed by the Obama administration, border control should be done through US military officers. The lack of a military presence at US-Mexico border leaves the border without an effective means to stop the violence. The criminal organizations, therefore, sustain their power in the region. By having US military at the border, the illegal entry of drugs and violence will be reduced since military support has worked in the past. Between the years 2006 and 2008, President G.W. Bush deployed 6,000 National Guard troops along the southern border to support the Border Patrol. The mission, "Operation Jump Start," was successful in terms of its influence on the reduction of illegal drug trafficking and drug related violence across the US-Mexican Border. During the operation the US troops seized more than 321,000 pounds of marijuana and cocaine, apprehended more than 176,000 undocumented aliens, built fences 38 miles long, and 96 miles of vehicle barriers (Mason, 2013).

In addition, the US can prevent illegal arms, received by the criminal groups, from flowing south into Mexico. The strict increase in the use of force at the border by US military officers will deter these groups and decrease their illegal weapons supply coming from the US Thus, the violence and terror will decrease at the border in the long run. In addition to strengthening borders with the US military, the US should encourage and lead the creation of a robust criminal justice system to enforce laws. Rather than just allocating more money to the Mexican government to encourage new institutions as it is suggested in Obama administration's policy, the US should have US government officers and legal experts work with the Mexican government to educate and lead Mexican officers in effective governance and legal issues. By receiving legal and legislative support from the US, the Mexican government would be better off with the decreasing crime and violence rate in the country. Furthermore, this approach will allow the US to control and observe the developments in the government and encourage a better enforcement of law. With strict law enforcement, criminal groups will be tried with rigorous sanctions, thereby weakening the power of the cartels. Furthermore, the US should consider the impact of high demand for illegal drugs on increase drug trafficking and violence. The high demand for illegal drugs generates a great incentive to produce these drugs in Mexico and illegally trade them into the US It is, therefore, very crucial for the US policy-makers to generate specific policies that will aim to the reduce demand for drugs in the US.

Finally, the US should take measures to improve economic growth in Mexico in order to eradicate one of the root causes of the problem, poverty. One approach to decrease poverty in the country might be US foreign direct investment. The federal government should incentivize US corporations and firms to invest in rural areas in Mexico to generate new job opportunities for the rural inhabitants. The US government can subsidize the companies who invest in these areas in Mexico. When companies establish new businesses in Mexico, they can offer higher salaries to their workers that are willing to relocate and work in Mexico. Therefore, both the US companies and their employees can be better off and motivated to run business in Mexico. Once the Mexican economy has become more stable through this strategy, it is likely that foreign investors from other countries will be attracted to investing in Mexico. In addition, the US investors can also use the crops in rural areas as a source of renewable energy through the construction of power plants, and create a comparative advantage for Mexico, which will in the long run enhance their economy. The Mexican and US governments can make an additional agreement upon the usage of the lands eligible for renewable development. Under this mutual agreement, the US government can rent these lands and hand them over to the American companies to establish renewable energy businesses. Thus, with greater economic development, Mexican people will have less incentive to engage in criminal behavior and violence, as their new jobs will pay more than the organized drug trade ever could.

Despite its benefits, there are several challenges for taking this approach. This new approach requires huge human and capital resources to adopt anti-drug policies, and employment of more government officials to assist Mexican government. Modification of Beyond Merida might also increase the risk of tension at the border following its implementation. However, the tension will be much less in the long run as the US military forces and sanctions under the robust law enforcement mechanisms deter the criminal groups. Moreover, temporary assistance may not guarantee a transformation of the Mexican judiciary system. Once the US officials leave, the Mexican government officers might cease following US instruction. Finally, modification of the current Beyond Merida policy requires a long time commitment for the US government to achieve the established goals. However, the benefits of this policy far outweigh its shortcomings because it is more comprehensive and determined than previous policies. If the US vigorously cooperates with the Mexican government and allocates its resources efficiently, drug-traffic and violence will decrease.

CONCLUSION

Drug trafficking problems in Mexico have been a serious concern over the past 20 years. The increased drug related violence has made the problem much more obvious and complex. Although Mexican policymakers have been working hard to solve the problem, the increasing violence is evidence that their efforts are insufficient to address the root causes of the problem. In fact, former Mexican President Calderon explained the difficulty of the problem when he said that "this is not an easy task, nor will it be fast. ... It will take a long time, requiring the use of enormous resources" (Meyer, 2007). It is obvious that policy makers have to work hard and decisively to solve the problem and provide security in the region. Despite all the challenges, Mexico and the US can solve it if they strongly collaborate with each other in the war against illicit drugs in Mexico. Indeed, The Merida Initiative has made progress towards a solving the problem by improving the relations between the two countries, but it was not successful in terms of its implementation.

Among the three practicable options discussed in this paper, the best course of action that meets the established criteria is the third option: modification of the Beyond Merida approach into a more comprehensive approach, which requires an aggressive US assistance and tight implementation. The US should act more decisively and ambitiously to stop drug trafficking and drug related violence in the region. The four pillars of the "Beyond Merida" policy should be transferred to more comprehensive pillars, which would enhance the physical US role in the process. For instance, the US should assign its military officers to secure the US-Mexican border rather than having Mexican or US police. Rather than just focusing on the entrance of dangerous illicit flows, the US should control the illicit gun trafficking from the south to Mexico to weaken the power of the cartels and criminal groups. In addition, the US should institutionalize law enforcement in Mexico rather than only allocating more money to Mexican government. The US judiciary and government officials should work temporarily with the Mexican government to educate and teach Mexican officials effective governance techniques and law enforcement. With a better judicial system, organized crime and violence will be reduced in Mexico. Furthermore, the US should promote economic development in Mexico aiming to diminish poverty in order to reduce drug-related violence in the country. Finally, the US should actively conduct specific counter–drug policies and rehabilitation programs to decrease the domestic demand for those illicit drugs. Without efficient policies to reduce US public demands for illegal drugs, the drug producers in Mexico will continue their production and sell drugs illegally to US consumers. However, reduction in demand for drugs will drop Mexican producers' revenues and lead them to quit excess illicit drug production. Therefore, it is crucial for the US policy makers to develop such policies that will reduce the domestic drug demand and minimize the drug traffic into the country.

The current security cooperation between the US and Mexico shows that both countries are determined to bring peace into the region and in Mexico. If the US and Mexico continue their security cooperation towards a mutual responsibility idea with an aggressive US role in policymaking and implementation, drug trafficking and drug related violence will be successfully diminished. When the drug trafficking is eradicated, the violence that threatens the public security of both countries will vanish as well and peace will be appear.

REFERENCES

Cook, Colleen W., and Claire Ribando Seelke. 2008. "Merida Initiative: Proposed US Anti-crime and Counterdrug Assistance for Mexico and Central America." http://fpc.state.gov/documents/organization/103694.pdf

"Fact Sheet: The Merida Initiative/Plan Mexico" 2011, Witness For Peace http://www.witnessforpeace.org/downloads/Witness%20for%20Peace%20Fact%20Sheet_Merida%20Initiative_2011.pdf

Mason Chuck R. (2013, February 25) "Securing America's Borders: The Role of the Military." http://fas.org/sgp/crs/homesec/R41286.pdf

"The Merida Initiative Fact Sheet." 2009. US Department of State, Bureau of International Narcotics and Law Enforcement Affairs. http://www.state.gov/j/inl/rls/fs/122397.htm

"Merida Initiative the US Has Provided Counternarcotics and Anti-crime Support But Needs Better Performance Measures." 2010. Government Accountability Office. GAO-10-837. http://www.gao.gov/new.items/d10837.pdf

"Mexico Under Siege". 2014. LA Times, http://www.latimes.com/world/drug-war/la-fgsg-drug-war-2014-storygallery.html (state)

Meyer, Maureen. 2007. "At a Crossroads: Drug Trafficking, Violence and the Mexican State." Washington Office on Latin America 13 http://www.beckleyfoundation.org/pdf/BriefingPaper13.pdf

"National Drug Assessment", 2011, US Department of Justice, National Drug Intelligence Center http://www.justice.gov/archive/ndic/pubs44/44849/44849p.pdf

Negroponte, Villiers Diana. 2009. "The Merida Initiative and Central America: The Challenges of Containing Public Insecurity and Criminal Violence." Foreign Policy at Brookings: 3 http://www.brookings.edu/research/papers/2009/05/merida-initiative-negroponte

Olson, Eric L., and Wilson, Christopher E. 2010. "Beyond Merida: the Evolving Approach to Security Cooperation." Wilson Center, University of San Diego, Trans-Border Institute http://wilsoncenter.org/sites/default/files/beyond_merida.pdf

Seelke, C., & Finklea, Kristin. (2014, April 8). "The US-Mexican Security Cooperation: The Mérida Initiative and Beyond." http://fas.org/sgp/crs/row/R41349.pdf

Seelke, Clare R. 2010. "Merida Initiative for Mexico and Central America: Funding and Policy Issues." http://fpc.state.gov/documents/organization/141560.pdf

Seelke, Clare R., Wyler, Liana, S., and Beittel, June. 2011. "Latin America and the Caribbean Illicit Drug Trafficking and US Counterdrug Programs." http://fas.org/sgp/crs/row/R41215.pdf

Drugs: History, Production, and Trade in Latin America

POSTREADING QUESTIONS

1. Describe the ancient symbolism and use of coca plants among the people of Bolivia.
2. How do gender and ethnicity impact the arrest and imprisonment of drug smugglers in the United States and Latin America?
3. Explain the notion of "treadmill of destruction" and its environmental consequences as related to cocaine production, distribution, and trade.
4. What were the goals of the 2010 Merida Initiative? Outline the achievements and failures of this initiative.

SUGGESTED ADDITIONAL READINGS

Chesnut, R. A. (2018). *Devoted to death. Santa Muerte the skeleton saint.* 2nd Edition. New York, NY: Oxford University Press.

Decker, S. H., & Chapman, M. T. (2008). *Drug smugglers on drug smuggling: Lessons from the inside.* Philadelphia, PA: Temple University Press.

Gootenberg, P. (2008). *Andean cocaine: The making of a global drug.* Chapel Hill, NC: University of North Carolina Press.

Jones, N. P. (2016). *Mexico's illicit drug networks and the state's reaction.* Washington DC: Georgetown University Press.

Youngers, C., & Rosin, E. (Eds). (2005). *Drugs and democracy in Latin America: The impact of U.S. policy.* Boulder, CO: Lynne Rienner.

Issues in Latin America: Migration and Transnationalism

LATIN AMERICAN AND Caribbean migrants have become a recurrent topic of today's political discourse. Nevertheless, few understand the push-pull factors involved in the process of migration and the sociocultural effects of transnational migrants when returning to their homelands. The earliest migrations to Latin America can be traced to around 20,000 years ago with dates and migratory flows still being debated as the archaeological record is updated with new findings. The inhabitants of the Caribbean region arrived in multiple waves around 7,000 years ago, departing mostly from the rimland area of Latin America. In the 15th century, the arrival of European colonizers prompted native migratory flows resulting from famine, diseases, the encomienda system, forced labor, and religious persecution. Dwindling native populations led to the subsequent forced migration of African slaves and afterward of Indian indentured laborers in the early 20th century. As a result, the multicultural makeup of Latin American and Caribbean populations was transformed by the influx of a myriad of migrants from Africa, Asia, and Europe to these regions. In modern times, the direction of Latin American and Caribbean migratory flows echoes the geography of political and military struggles, racial and ethnic discrimination, religious persecution, economic inequality, and drug-related conflicts pushing local rural populations searching for safety and opportunity into urban areas or international destinations. In recent times, an influx of migrants from underdeveloped countries is driving the increase of policies, fueled by xenophobia and extreme nationalism, aimed to reduce the migratory flow to developed countries such as the United States. Examples of these policies include the establishment and subsequent overpopulation of temporary migratory camps alongside borders, the parent-children separation at these camps, a surge of deportations, increased funding to expand border walls and resources, rising fees for applications required to legally migrate, and a decrease of approvals for those legally seeking asylum and refugees, as well as for higher-educated workers, to mention some. In particular, undocumented migrants have been the most affected, facing a more dangerous and costly path ridden with crime gangs, diseases, and xenophobia before arriving to the border of their final destination.

Section III gives readers an understanding of the push factors and historical struggles that continue to trouble Latin American and Caribbean immigrants, emigrants, and transnational migrants to these regions. Sued-Badillo's (2011) article provides a brief history of the Caribbean Taíno who, as the native population, struggled along with the African slaves to survive and resist the European colonization of the region. The indentured Indian migration to the Caribbean and rimland area of Latin America is the subject of Roopnarine's (2018) reading. In this article, the author discusses the nature of the migrant population, the reasons behind their recruitment into indentured labor, and the perils of the sea voyage from India to the Caribbean. Return migration to the Caribbean and its transnational impact are the subjects of Brown's (2006) article. Transnationalism, as defined by Basch et al. refers to "a process by which migrants, through their daily life activities create social fields that cross national boundaries" (1994, p. 8). Latapi's (2012) reading focuses on the relationship between poverty and migration among Mexican migrants. The low impact that remittances have to reduce income inequality of the poor and the cost of lost labor to Mexico are some of the high points of Latipi's discussion.

REFERENCES

Basch, L. N., Schiller, G., & Szanton-Blanc, C. (1994). *Nations unbound: Transnational projects and the deterritorialized nation-state*. New York: Gordon and Breach.

KEYWORDS

Amerindian slavery, Antilles, *Arawak, Borinquén, caciques*, Caribbean, *Caribs*, caste defilement, chiefdom, *Cimarrones, conucos, Coolie*, cultural vector, *encomienda*, gold mining, Haiti-Quisqueya, indentured laborers, India, inequality, Jamaica, ladino slaves, Mexico, migration, plantations, poverty, Puerto Rico, push-pull model, *quinto real*, remittances, return migration, sugar, Suriname, *Tainos*, Trinidad, *zamindari*.

From Tainos to Africans in the Caribbean

Labor, Migration, and Resistance

Jalil Sued-Badillo

UNTIL FAIRLY RECENTLY, historians have based their research concerning the native societies and cultures of the Caribbean on two major types of sources—contemporary chronicles and histories, and Spanish administrative documents. While both are still considered invaluable fonts of data, their very nature is deeply problematic—a situation that has shaped traditional portrayals of Amerindian life in the precontact and immediate postcontact periods.

Chronicles have long been considered the starting point for Amerindian history and culture. Beginning with the writings of Christopher Columbus himself, this category of sources comprises wide-ranging observations made by contemporary travelers and other writers. But information from these sources is decidedly partial, contradictory, and problematic, particularly in regard to the native Tainos.

Of equal importance are the voluminous writings of the first "historians of the Indies," who recorded the process of conquest and colonization. One of the earliest, Peter Martyr, author of *De orbe novo* (in two volumes, the first published in 1511), never set foot in America but wrote from a privileged position at the Spanish court with access to important reports. In contrast, Gonzalo Fernández de Oviedo, author of the *General and Natural History of the Indies* (in five volumes, the first of which appeared in 1535), lived most of his life on Hispaniola, served important official positions, and wrote as a champion of Spanish colonial rule. Friar Bartolomé de las Casas, the most prolific of these historians, is best known for his brief *Account of the Destruction of the Indies* (1552), but less so for his major published works *History of the Indies* (1875) and *Apologetic History of the Indies* (1909). Although he was a witness to much of what he wrote about, he drafted much of it late in life, in constant struggle with his memory.

Of particular interest is *An Account of the Antiquities of the Indians*, a brief but significant account of some religious beliefs of the Tainos in Hispaniola, written by Friar Ramón Pané in 1494. This very first "ethnographic" report drafted on American soil has had an erratic history. The Taino *caciques* (chiefs) were interviewed through interpreters, and the work itself was published in an Italian translation only in 1571. Even aside from the great confusion admitted by Pané in the organization of his early notes, or the different versions of key Amerindian names and place names in each subsequent translation or transcription, the reliability of this work is obviously questionable.

The same can be said of all the other chronicles. They were not systematic studies, and they were often based on casual observations. Many are riddled with cultural biases, exaggerations, omissions and, worse yet, contradictions. This becomes obvious when, for example, comparing Oviedo's work with that of Las Casas. These authors were at opposite ends of the political spectrum of their times, yet no serious historian can do without them.

Far more important than the writings of early chroniclers and travelers are the Spanish administrative archives—primarily the Archivo General de Indias in Seville, which remains the most important source of information on Spain's colonial empire. Containing extensive but rigorous records of everyday affairs, judicial documents, official and private correspondence, reports, testimonies, policy papers, census records, and other facts and figures, its holdings include invaluable data on Amerindian cultures, particularly those on Hispaniola. But, like the chronicles, these documents were created by Spanish officials with at best an imperfect understanding of the people whose lives they were documenting, and often with patently ideological motives.

Only recently have archaeologists and ethnohistorians begun to reconstruct Amerindian societies from a perspective aimed to approach that of the natives themselves. Although contemporary knowledge of the Caribbean as it existed in 1492 is becoming more sophisticated and interdisciplinary, it is still one-sided at best.

THE TAINOS

Historians do not know what the native populations of the Caribbean named themselves. The designation *Taino* is a modern label now applied to a variety of ethnic groups coexisting in the Caribbean archipelago at the end of the 15th century. The term, recorded first off the coast of Haiti and later in Guadeloupe as hearsay, is said to have meant "good or noble Indians," but this meaning has not been linguistically confirmed. The application of this term to the original inhabitants of the Greater Antilles has been a recent practice by historians and archaeologists, mainly those in the Spanish-speaking Caribbean; their North American counterparts have usually preferred the term *Arawak,* also a modern label. Whatever its origin, the collective term at least acknowledges that, in spite of their diversity, the people of the Caribbean region had more characteristics in common than differences.

The islands had been inhabited for more than 7,000 years, having been populated initially in several waves of migration from South and Central America. The last of these migrations occurred from 500 BCE to 300 CE, bringing horticulturalists and proficient pottery makers from Amazonian and Andean backgrounds. They introduced lasting cultural essentials such as language (Arawak), religious symbolism, family structure, economic strategies and products, animals, and metallurgy and pottery making, all to be further developed on the islands. The term *Taino* has been reserved for the people of the last stage before the European conquest and limited to the regions where more social and cultural complexity was achieved; their predecessors are referred to in the archaeological literature as *pre-Tainos*. By the middle of the first millennium CE, pre-Tainos were establishing a new cultural scenario reflecting their progress in adapting to the insular environment and its challenges. The ethnic fusion of the new continental horticulturalists with the original and poorly understood "Archaic" population of the islands transformed the latter's cultures and ushered in new social formations.

Perhaps the most conspicuous center for this process of transculturation, as the Cuban scholar Fernando Ortiz was to call it, was the island of Borinquén (today's Puerto Rico). The smallest of the Greater Antilles, Borinquén was the foremost boundary of the last wave of continental migrations to the insular Caribbean. Its territory proved suitable for slowing down migratory expansion and allowing for the effective integration of newcomers with natives. Borinquén thus experienced ethnic admixtures more comprehensively than other islands, and produced the formative social configurations for the future Taino culture. Migration and other forms of influence from Borinquén toward the Greater and Lesser Antilles acted as a cultural vector and induced a basic cultural uniformity throughout the archipelago.

Two islands were the prime centers of Taino social complexity in the Caribbean: Haiti-Quisqueya (today's Hispaniola, including Haiti and the Dominican Republic), whose sphere of cultural influence also included eastern Cuba and Jamaica, and Borinquén, whose social formation extended into eastern Quisqueya and the Lesser Antilles as far back as Guadalupe. The diffusion of pre-Taino cultural traits from Borinquén, probably beginning around 400 CE, was made possible by the emergence of a chiefdom-like political formation on that island. This regional form of government, transcending smaller tribal boundaries, first appeared in the southern coastal valleys of the island, slowly spreading to the mountainous interior and outward to the neighboring islands.

This type of social arrangement is often considered a forerunner to state formation and has been extensively discussed by modern anthropologists, but its operation remains elusive. Agreement seems to exist that among the Tainos and others like them, a chiefdom was a thickly populated region with multiple communities that were organized politically and hierarchically and subordinated to a center. Such political formations are considered to have been geographically expansionist and war-prone while zealous of their formal frontiers; their paramount chiefs are also considered to have acted as high priests, with religion more than force as the basis of their authority. Such chiefs, known as *caciques*, were polygamous (as attested to by most chroniclers) and highly respected figures who mainly acceded to their positions through inheritance. The governed communities paid tribute mainly in the form of services rendered to the chiefs in agricultural labor, occasional ceremonial constructions, and conscription in case of war. But the chiefs did not control productive activities. They had neither standing armies nor permanent bureaucracies, and close family members acted as occasional administrators, envoys, and key allies.

Kinship structure was matrilineal—that is, the succession to inheritance and rank ran through the mother's side in an arrangement that permitted women to participate in public activities and assume political status as *cacicas*. In Puerto Rico, 12 cacicas have been identified in the historical sources. In Hispaniola, dozens are listed in census reports dating from the early years of colonial occupation, and Anacaona, sister of a former high provincial chief from Jaragua, inherited the rank and ruled over a large number of vassal polities. The participation of women in the political and religious realm makes the Tainos heirs to an ancient and conspicuous Andean practice traceable from Peru to the Antilles and abundantly observed and recorded in the 16th century (Sued-Badillo 1985, 2007).

In Puerto Rico, only one chiefdom governing about two-thirds of the island appears to have existed in 1492. Its central enclave, known as Cayabo, was in the modern southern region of Ponce, and the reigning family bore the name of Agüeybana. The rest of the island apparently remained in the hands of local tribal chiefs, who sought Spanish protection from the lead chiefdom's encroachment. In Hispaniola, most of the island was divided among five large polities—Jaragua, Maguá, Maguana, Marién, and Cayacoa or Higüey—while some of its more isolated regions remained locally independent. In the principal islands, then, the chiefdoms apparently had not yet realized the formation of a political status, which would have implied a much wider and more effective integration beyond the immediate region. A permanent bureaucracy and army, a religion with temples and priests engaging in practices beyond traditional shamanic ceremonies, and forced regular tributes on production and on services (beyond occasional ones) were all things that did not yet exist.

In the absence of formal social classes, public inequalities and an elite structure beyond nuclear kinship were beginning to develop in Haiti and Borinquén, and the fabrication and circulation of sumptuary goods were likely controlled by the caciques for prestige and social status. But a state system organized to control and exploit the general population existed only in parts of Mexico and Peru. In Cuba and Jamaica there is evidence not even of chiefdoms, but only of a still-dominant "tribal" (or kinship-based) social structure and a very limited political geography. Most Spanish observers concurred that Hispaniola had a population of more than a million

FIGURE 3.1.1 A cacique on the island of Cuba leads his people in negotiations with Columbus. Engraving by Benjamin West and Francesco Bartolozzi (1794).
Source: The John Carter Brown Library.

inhabitants by 1492. Along with Puerto Rico—perhaps the more densely populated of the two principal islands—it harbored the Tainos' most impressive material and artistic expressions, which validated their political significance.

But the Tainos' main social achievements came in their effective and ingenious management of their environment. Tropical lands are not paradisiacal; the welfare of their inhabitants depends on their ability to utilize diverse resources efficiently. The Tainos had evolved from horticulture or food gardening to intensive and diversified agriculture with strategies including raised fields, mound planting (*conucos*), crop rotation, water canals, fish traps, and slash-and-burn techniques, and they went on to exploit varied ecological niches for different crops, like mangroves and reefs (Newsom and Wing 2004). In Puerto Rico the Spanish observed a Taino preference for cultivation on hillsides, contrary to practices in Hispaniola. The result was a rich and diverse production of staple foods, grains, and vegetables that, coupled with successful hunting and fishing, provided a balanced caloric intake, definitely superior to that of most Europeans.

The Tainos also had varied animal assets, both wild and domesticated. Marine species came to the island mangroves or estuaries and were caught in fish traps for consumption over time. Domesticated animals included guinea pigs, bush rats (*hutías*), dogs, and doves and other exotic birds. Edible wild resources included crabs, shellfish, iguanas, seals, manatees, land and sea turtles, and birds. The forests supplied rich woods for construction and fuel, resins, medicines, fruits, seeds, fibers, narcotics, dyes, and a long list of other resources. Of complementary importance, the islands were rich in all types of rocks: chert and quartz, granite, marble, jadeite, jasper, and a fair share of semiprecious stones. This permitted a long tradition of superb stonework, including unsurpassable religious icons, petroglyphs, and numerous stone artifacts.

The Tainos substantially modified their environment, making the land and sea work for them. In contrast, lack of prior experience in tropical environments greatly limited Spanish agricultural colonization of the islands. Many of Iberia's main native farming techniques and products were not reproduced for decades, and some foods—like wheat, olives, and grapes—would not be introduced successfully for centuries, thus allowing the survival of many Taino food products and even their planting techniques. Taino root crops, as well as cultigens such as maize, tobacco, peanuts, native fruits and herbs, drugs, and beverages, are still common in the modern Caribbean. The Taino world has been an intrinsic part of Caribbean historic memory and modern national identities—if not biologically, then certainly culturally and spiritually. Today it represents the world before colonialism, a kind of idealized, mythical past suggesting that if life was better in the past, it can also be better in the future.

THE ENCOUNTER

Beginning with the conquest of the Caribbean islands, European expansion to the New World was one of the first chapters of modern colonialism. The Tainos were fated to be among the first Amerinidans to be conquered and directly exploited by a distant and culturally distinct power. The political and economic forces responsible for this major thrust naturally transcended the microcosm of Columbus's life and Castilian politics. They encompassed a massive transformation of the Old World itself. In only 60 years after 1492, Europe shifted from a multiplicity of small warring kingdoms into a handful of strong monarchies building competitive nation-states and expanding frontiers. Commercial cities dominated the seas and established ties with hitherto unthinkable partners. The fragmentation of Christianity, the intense rivalry with the emerging Ottoman Empire, population growth, recurrent agricultural crises, and the need for currency to compete commercially—all these factors were involved in the forces in Europe that took Columbus to the land of the Tainos in 1492.

It is no exaggeration to say that the fate of the New World was sealed by the few golden trinkets Columbus found on the necks and ears of the first Amerindians encountered in the Lucayan islands—not because of any unique Spanish obsession with gold, as Black Legend advocates traditionally argued, but because gold and silver were the Old World's commercial lubricants at a time when trade was reshaping economic and political geography. In the 15th century, precious minerals were as important as crude oil is today. The same interest groups that drove Columbus and others to explore far and wide were motivated by an accepted bimetallic monetary system (gold and silver) that permitted trade among the most diverse economies. Europe lacked gold deposits, and depended for them on unreliable intermediaries. The kingdoms of the Spanish Peninsula, notably Castile, had a notably disorganized monetary system supported by too little gold.

Prior to Columbus's voyages, Castile had been bracing to conquer territories in North Africa to obtain the precious mineral then filtering from the interior of that continent into the hands of Italians, Arabs, and Portuguese merchants. The Catholic Monarchs had devoted much effort to monetary reforms and economic enterprises that could assure them a more competitive position. So, when Columbus returned and informed the monarchs of new lands—greatly exaggerating the first amounts of gold found—their response was immediate and positive. A mere nine months after the first voyage, Columbus returned to the islands in command of 17 ships carrying a variegated crew of nearly 1,500 passengers.

The promise of gold determined the fate of the new lands. Ethnic groups were classified according to the mineral importance of their lands and their disposition to collaborate with exploration ventures or hinder them. If lands were labeled as "useless"—that is, with no tangible assets to be obtained—their populations could be removed by force to places where labor was needed. Such were the cases of Jamaica, Aruba, Curaçao and Bonaire, the Bahamas, and large stretches of the Venezuelan coast during the early 16th century. The prior cultural identities of native communities perished under these coerced migrations. The most notorious case of such identity theft was that of the "Caribs," a label that came to be used to criminalize different groups throughout the Caribbean and on the American mainland in order to legally justify violent measures against them.

Beginning in the first years of the 16th century, Hispaniola, Puerto Rico, and Cuba became primary mining centers, their native populations coerced into exploration, porterage, clearing and constructing, extraction, and smelting and shipping of ore. The costs of conquest and exploitation were nearly unmanageable for a poor and distant Catholic kingdom with a weak agricultural tradition that was primarily oriented toward livestock. Although the earlier Spanish conquest of the Canary Islands had set a limited precedent, no kingdom in Spain possessed significant experience with tropical environments or large forced-labor enterprises. Consequently, agriculture and animal husbandry were initially neglected, and food and tools came primarily as cheap imports from Seville—salted sardines, wine, oil—sold at highly inflated prices in the Caribbean.

Some time later, interisland trade slowly began to provide substitutes for some imports. Cassava replaced wheat bread, lard supplanted oil, and local fishing and animal husbandry—mainly swine—supplanted salted meat products. Iberian diets reflected in the early import trade of the islands did not replicate the variegated food-ways of the large, ethnically mixed Andalusian population. Instead, the traditionally sober diet of Christians in the countryside of central and northern Spain—which lacked grains like rice, contained very little meat, and rejected spicy products—was imposed on the insular populations, to their despair and considerable suffering.

Meanwhile, the high cost of metal implements led to the practice of forcing Amerindian workers to till, dig, and labor with their own stone tools, greatly increasing their hardship—a practice denounced by Las Casas and his followers. Finally, the *encomienda* system, which distributed natives as workers among the colonizers, removed them from their traditional food collecting and agricultural activities. When they returned from the mines to their villages nine or ten months later, they had no food available. Rest periods were times of widespread famine. At least during the conquest period, natives also seem to have rejected Spanish salted meat products, and there is no evidence that they raised or consumed animals brought by the Europeans.

After 1508, coinciding with the conquest of Puerto Rico—the second island after Hispaniola to be occupied—private merchants were allowed to trade with the colony, and the encomiendas (also known as *repartimientos*), a system of Indian labor allocation, in essence transferred the administration and care of the natives (including in the spiritual realm) to the private sector. These encomiendas effectively signaled the monarchy's admission of its inability to assume full responsibility for colonial enterprises. With the subsequent conquest of other islands, the task of organizing the economic exploitation of the new territories fell to an ill-equipped assortment of persons and groups, including soldiers of fortune, clergymen, artisans, merchants, part-time urban laborers, and overseers of leading administrators, locally and abroad. The monarchy reduced its required share of benefits to the famous *quinto real* (royal fifth, or 20% of gold minted) and withdrew from directly participating in mining.

Much attention has been given to the study of the encomienda system in the Antilles without rooting it in mining, the primary economic activity of the period. However, subtle differences in its implementation on the different islands were entirely irrelevant to the fate of the natives: all the mining islands experienced significant population decline. When the islands inhabited principally by Tainos were afflicted around 1518–20 by smallpox epidemics, apparently brought into the Caribbean by the first direct slave shipments from Africa, their populations had already dramatically diminished. The census of 1514 on Hispaniola gave ample proof of this, as did the intensity of the slave raids sent from the mining islands to seek replacements.

As the underfed and overworked natives perished, armadas were sent to loot and capture slaves in the region in a way much like the earlier practice of pillage and plunder throughout the Mediterranean. Between 1510 and 1542, tens of thousands of enslaved natives were violently extracted from the Guianas to the region of present-day Colombia, and also from Costa Rica to Florida. The legal excuse covering most of these expeditions was the capture of "Caribs" (a name etymologically equivalent to "cannibals"), who supposedly were a menace to "peaceful" natives and had proven reluctant to accept Christianity. Indians who had resisted relations with the Spaniards were also labeled "Caribs." Slaves were even brought from Mexico in exchange for cattle raised on the islands.

The amount of gold extracted from Hispaniola, Puerto Rico, and Cuba—in that order of importance—and legally exported to Spain between 1500 and 1550 has been estimated at 50 to 60 tons, and it probably represented one-fifth of all the gold shipped from the Spanish empire during the 16th century. But as the first colonial venture of their kind, the islands suffered from metropolitan inexperience, lack of capital, and absence of the infrastructure necessary for mining activities, which Mexico and Peru would both possess decades later. Lack of mining implements, experienced technicians, and roads, along with poor logistics, plagued the mining experience on the islands. Of equal importance was the lack of labor legislation and work regulations that only later were put into practice on the continent. The wealth extracted from the Taino islands by Taino hands, in a relatively short period under such brutal conditions, explains the truly genocidal population decline in the region, openly admitted by Charles V in 1526 when he blamed the repartimiento/encomienda system for its share in that human tragedy and tentatively barred its implementation in Mexico.

Gold mining remained the primary economic activity in the major Taino islands until past the mid-16th century, when it was overshadowed by gold and silver mining in Peru, Colombia, and Mexico. This economic phase lasted much longer than was once believed by historians, who assumed, for example, that with the conquest of Mexico the new territory immediately opened up its mineral wealth. Mexican ores were discovered and exploited only decades after the fall of Tenochtitlan, so that initial conquest did not displace the insular Caribbean as the main gold producer. Nor did the conquest in Central America, from Panama to Guatemala, yield profitable colonies until the second half of that century. Instead, during the initial phase, much of this geographic expanse became rewarding for Amerindian slavers who aimed to supply the labor needs of mining industries in the insular Caribbean. During the late 1530s, Colombia and Peru began to reorient this human traffic away from the islands, forcing gold miners and sugar planters to take recourse in African slavery.

Establishing the factual chronology of conquest and colonization permits a more realistic and holistic understanding of these events and their consequences. Taino societies were subjected to a massive alteration of their existence and culture for nearly half a century. They were victims of forms of violence ranging from forced labor to population displacements; of deliberate dismemberment of communal structures and warfare; and of the often overstated factors of disease, hunger, deprivation, and mistreatment. Their tragedy was not the result of unavoidable forces of nature at play. Dramatic human consequences can come about from natural causes, such as ecological changes triggering population displacements, epidemics, and the like. But the Taino tragedy was the result of an organized economic venture, planned and executed quite consciously by its continental planners, who deliberately took the human costs involved into consideration. The Taino people did not succumb on contact with the first colonizers; their physical and cultural constitution was not as frail as has often been claimed. They perished under the onslaught and callous demands of an internationally ramified economic system, which, while still evolving, was nevertheless proving its capacity to conquer and subdue people and extract significant material benefits. The Tainos were thus the first victims of the social experiment of modern capitalism, and the native Caribbean was where the dynamics between "core" and "peripheral" regions of what became the capitalistic world system were first effectively experienced.

This first capitalistic enterprise in the Antilles was not limited to mining operations, but also generated complementary activities and a well-knit economic network. Pearls were extracted from the fringe islands of the eastern Caribbean—Cubagua, Margarita, and Coche—to which hundreds of Tainos were forcefully removed. The traffic in slaves became an economic enterprise of its own, intermingling dozens of ethnic groups while depopulating vast coastal regions in Venezuela, the Lesser Antilles, the Bahamas, Guyana, Panama, and Nicaragua. Ponce de León's "discovery" of Florida was accomplished during a slaving expedition in which the governor of Cuba, Velázquez, also participated. The need for local food supplies forced large contingents of Tainos to spend their very short periods of rest away from the mines in agricultural tasks or animal husbandry, both of which were very profitable activities for the white elite. Salted fish was traded on the Venezuelan coast, along with slaves. Wooden plates (*bateas*) used to pan gold in the rivers were handmade by natives in Hispaniola and sold in Puerto Rico. Jamaican Tainos ended up on other islands. And of course, an extremely rewarding commerce that involved the coming and going of dozens of ships every year to the Antilles to supply the growing number of colonizers was maintained through Andalusian intermediaries. This was an activity that produced important customs taxes (*almojarifazgo*) for the crown and a large array of goods for the settlers.

BLACKS AND GOLD

Tainos and other Amerindian slaves brought from different parts of the Caribbean region also participated in the first labor-intensive sugar plantations created in Hispaniola around 1520 and in Puerto Rico in the 1540s. The traditional view that mining labor was limited to Amerindians and sugar labor to black slaves is far from correct. Blacks began their ordeal in the Caribbean by working in the mines, and natives lasted long enough to be forced into plantation agriculture, another economic venue that proved as profitable in Europe's progressive accumulation of wealth as it was painful for its coerced labor forces in the New World. By the 1560s, more than 50 sugar mills in Hispaniola and Puerto Rico exported more sugar to Andalusia than did their much larger Mexican counterparts. Being closer to Seville, the islands had a competitive advantage which permitted them to satisfy the demand for sugar in the only legal market in Spain. Aside from this geographical advantage, their greater importance as

FIGURE 3.1.2   Slaves mining for gold under the watch of Spanish soldiers. Engraving from *Americae pars quinta* (1595). *Source*: The John Carter Brown Library.

sugar exporters can be explained only by the intensity of the productive operations that rested on the backs of Africans and Indians.

Although Tainos helped the Spaniards locate the gold-producing regions and became the primary workforce in them, the general logistics associated with placer mining were strained by the Spaniards' inability to communicate effectively with the natives. This factor, more than any other, probably prompted the early introduction of black slaves from the Iberian Peninsula. Being fully assimilated into Christian culture, and fluent in the colonizer's language—many of them having been born in Castile or Portugal—these *ladino* slaves became an important asset in the new colonial scenario. Together with the ladinos also came free blacks (*libertos*), who were not socially different from other poor Spanish Christians migrating to the new frontier in search of a better life. The libertos fared quite well, but for the black slaves life on the islands was a nightmare. Toiling in a harsh tropical environment far from home proved tragic for them.

As early as 1503, ladino slaves were reported to have run away in Hispaniola and were described as exerting a negative influence on the native inhabitants. And in 1514, the first of several ladino uprisings occurred quite unexpectedly in Puerto Rico, where gold production was reaching very high levels. Probably a strong hurricane that year was a precipitating factor. In any case, the event clearly represented the first black slave uprising in the New World. In 1521 another one occurred in Hispaniola, and thus began a tradition of resistance throughout the slaveholding Americas.

Slave labor of the scale and intensity organized in the first Caribbean colonies had no counterpart or antecedents in Europe. Mining and sugar making were both labor-intensive, a fact that imposed a distinctly new style of slavery throughout the Americas—more ruthless, more demanding, and insensitive. The Antilles had not been its first laboratory. The practice of using African slaves to produce sugar in large quantities had originated on Atlantic islands such as Madeira or São Tomé, but the Caribbean islands were where this economic combination acquired much of its historic force and social characteristics.

Modern plantation systems began to take shape in the Spanish Antilles during the 16th century based on enslaved Indians and Africans, who often were intermingled in an ethnic cauldron of hitherto unknown proportions. By 1560, for example, Hispaniola and Puerto Rico had a combined African slave population of some 45,000, not including clandestine groups of Amerindians of various origins. Such numbers of enslaved workers, applied primarily to operations like mining or sugar, were not to be found elsewhere in the hemisphere during that century.

Indians and black slaves—who began to arrive directly from Africa in 1518, according to very exact Spanish documentation—formed a variety of relationships with each other. Some ladinos and enslaved Africans sided with the Tainos and other ethnic groups against the Spaniards; some allied themselves with conquistadors against the Indians. Their life expectancy was terribly short. Few enslaved Africans were able to form families or survive long enough to transform their wretched existence into lasting forms of collective life. Given the high death toll in the mining camps and sugar fields, African slaves were constantly replenished in a vicious transcontinental economic cycle. Nonetheless, personal names of noted maroons (escapees) were always heard throughout the islands, and strong clues about the survival of many black runaways among the "Caribs" (surviving and regrouping Amerindians) of the Lesser Antilles are being uncovered. Only small groups of Creole or mulatto slaves were able to survive, but while they eventually came to constitute an important segment of Caribbean colonial societies during the late 16th century, that process was painfully slow. The overall creolization of Caribbean societies had to wait until almost a century after the conquest, when the dynamic export economies of the larger islands had collapsed and the large cattle ranches (*hatos*) that sprang up throughout the Spanish Greater Antilles significantly attenuated slavery's importance and established a less harsh and demanding life for the enslaved.

RESISTANCE TO CONQUEST

The myth of the easy conquest of the Caribbean islands, the submissive character of their inhabitants, their hospitable nature, and their dire need for protection against invading barbarians bent on devouring their victims has persisted to this day. This colonial version of the events and relations between the European invaders and the Tainos has become entangled with latter-day historical and anthropological accounts to a degree where it has gained widespread acceptance, both abroad and in the Caribbean itself. Yet the original facts of the European-Amerindian encounter have long been distorted and deformed for ideological reasons. This is so because that same period witnessed the forging of the colonial justifications for the conquest of America itself, and the emergence of political discourses used to legitimize European rule in the New World.

The Greater Antilles were the first battleground in the European conquest of the Americas. Many lives were lost in military encounters that lasted for decades. Resistance began with the burning of Columbus's first settlement in Hispaniola, La Navidad, and the killing of all 39 of its residents by warriors of the chief Caonabo in 1492. Most provinces in every island have their tales of local heroic caciques and brave or desperate deeds in defense of their homelands. After Caonabo, the epic figures in Hispaniola are Guarionex, Cotubanama, Guarocuya, Mayobanex, and Enriquillo. In Puerto Rico, where official commemorations have traditionally downplayed Amerindian symbols, popular recognition of local caciques represents an almost intuitive respect for the precolonial past, thus challenging official discourses. For more than 200 years, poets and political dissidents have kept alive a strong sense of admiration for the warring caciques Agüeybana el Bravo, Urayoán, Guarionex, Comerío, Humacao, and others. And long-overlooked, newly discovered documents from the Archivo de Indias in Seville attest to the intense resistance in Borinquén and a high toll of lives on both sides, with evidence of the burning of the first Spanish towns of La Aguada (1511), Caparra (1513), and Santiago (1513), followed by relentless guerilla warfare which, as on the other islands, lasted until the 1530s. In Cuba, meanwhile, Hatuey and Guama have long been recognized as national figures.

Chronicles and administrative documents, furthermore, confirm the conquest's policy of violence, followed from the outset, against the reluctant caciques. Beginning with Columbus's reaction to Caonabo's rebellion in Hispaniola and the subsequent enslavement and shipment to Spain of several thousand Tainos, some native victims of Spanish reprisals were even condemned to row in the infamous galleys of the Mediterranean.

Events such as these reveal the falseness of the image of the Tainos' supposedly docile character and their incapacity to defend their lands—a trait applied to Puerto Ricans in colonial discourse to this very day. But the violent nature of the "encounter"

FIGURE 3.1.3 Spanish conquistadors burning a resistant native at the stake. Engraving based on an account by Friar Bartolomé de las Casas (1620). *Source*: The John Carter Brown Library.

also reveals and dramatizes the intolerance and bigotry of the conquistadores toward culturally different groups, their historical record of hostility to cultural dissidence, and their turbulent religious experience with non-Christians. It dramatizes the limitation of material resources at the onset of their historic entrance to the New World and their inclination to treachery and deceit.

Las Casas denounced the early practice in Hispaniola of killing local chiefs to provoke uprisings that justified punitive and enslaving measures. In 1500, Governor Nicolás de Ovando planned and executed the death of more than 80 caciques in the kingdom of Jaragua (Haiti) who had been assembled by the high chieftainess Anacaona to welcome him, in a deceitful move to reduce Anacaona as a potential threat to the conquest of the island. The event has gone down in history as the Massacre of Jaragua. Anacaona herself was publicly hanged some weeks later. Reports of subsequent strategic slaughter to instantly subdue rebellious natives on other islands are associated with the locations where the events took place: Higüey in Hispaniola, Caonao in Cuba, Daguao and Vieques in Puerto Rico. In 1513, 17 caciques from Puerto Rico were abducted and shipped to Hispaniola without confirmation of their ever having reached the destination. Reports indicate that the practice of killing local chiefs was also carried out in Jamaica.

FIGURE 3.1.4   Natives committing suicide to escape Spanish brutality. Engraving from Theodoro de Bry, *Americae pars quarta* (1594). *Source*: The John Carter Brown Library.

But resistance to conquest followed many paths and involved different events. Every island reported suicides, escapes, and violent behavior. Many women chose to kill their offspring or resort to abortion rather than see their children live as slaves. In Cuba, the chief Anaya hanged himself and his teenage daughter when he was unable to rescue her from a privileged settler. Collective suicide is also reported to have taken place in Cuba. In Puerto Rico, many Tainos escaped to the neighboring "Carib islands," shattering the myth of their traditional enmity with the inhabitants of those islands. In Cuba and Hispaniola *ranchos de indios alzados*, or maroon camps, were reported as early as the 1520s. The first *cimarrones,* a term generally associated with runaway blacks, were actually Taino escapees. But resistance also took nonviolent forms. Refusal to accept the Christian faith was constantly cited by clergymen. And in secret, the outlawed ancestral religions were kept alive.

WORKS CITED

Newsom, Lee A., and Elizabeth S. Wing. 2004. *On Land and Sea: Native American Uses of Biological Resources in the West Indies*. Tuscaloosa, AL: University of Alabama Press.

Sued-Badillo, Jalil. 1985. "Las cacicas indoantillanas." *Revista del Instituto de Cultura Puertorriquena* 87, enero a mayo.

Sued-Badillo, Jalil. 2007. "¿Guadalupe: Caribe o taína? La isla de Guadalupe y su cuestionable identidad Caribe en la época precolonial. Una revisión etnohistórica y arqueológica." *Caribbean Studies* 35, no. 1.

The Migration of Indentured Indians from India to the Caribbean

Lomarsh Roopnarine

THE PREVIOUS SECTION provided an introduction to Indian migration and identity. This chapter examines the movement of Indians from their homeland to various Caribbean colonies. The focus is on the circumstances that led to the arrival of Indians in the Caribbean as well as the factors that made them leave their homeland to work in a distant and unfamiliar environment. Particular attention will be paid to the entire organization of the indenture emigration system, recruitment of Indians in India, and their subsequent experience on the long sea voyage from India to the Caribbean. Statistics will be provided on the number, gender, caste, and religion of Indian emigrants to show the magnitude and diversity of the indenture emigration scheme.

QUESTIONS ON INDENTURED EMIGRATION

The majority of original correspondence or archival records on indenture tends to support the view of the planter class that indentured Indians left their homeland because of the push-pull model of migration; that is, people are pushed out of the sending environment because of deprivation and disadvantaged conditions and pulled to the receiving destination because of opportunities for a better livelihood. This explanation would imply that more Indians would have migrated to the Caribbean, since India was considered a poor colony where millions of Indians lived in hapless conditions. However, only five hundred thousand (0.16 percent) Indian citizens migrated to the Caribbean out of a population of over three hundred million. Why did a large proportion of India's population not migrate? Was it because they did not want to? Or was it because their family ties, jobs, culture, and familiar environment made them feel at home? Or could it be that many more had wanted to migrate but were prevented from migrating because of their own poverty and cultural institutional barriers (caste) that isolated them? Were they simply unaware of indenture emigration? Or did the Caribbean plantations have inadequate accommodation to take in more indentured laborers? Did the planters operate simply on demand rather than on the need for a large surplus of labor? It is therefore crucial that the various aspects of Indian indentured emigration be sorted out before any analyses can be made.

First, Indians were involved in migration before they were brought to the Caribbean. Indian indenture emigration to the Caribbean was a form of migration that was in tandem with other world migration patterns in the mid-nineteenth and twentieth centuries. Like other forms of world migration, Indian migration was built on historical instincts to move, although the specificities were different from other world movements. By the nineteenth century, satisfaction with the once settled, stable, and static way of life in a particular environment gave way to the urge to move. In this regard, Indian migration coincided with the age of migration; that is, people were essentially always on the move. Indians were migrating from rural to urban areas as well as to areas around India looking for seasonal and permanent employment. To be sure, only a small percentage of Indians were involved in indenture emigration. But how they have impacted their new environment is more significant than what would seem to be reflected by their small number. Second, indentured emigration was multifaceted, revealing patterns and practices of regular and irregular, temporary and permanent, and manipulative and voluntary trends. Third, indentured Indians were not from a common background. Sure enough, they were mostly peasants and shared a fundamental indentured status, but they were as diverse as India itself. Moreover, the migrants during the first two decades of indenture were remarkably different from those who left India from the 1870s onward. Fourth, no single theory is sufficient to explain any form of migration. Indenture emigration, however, can be explained by applying the historical-structural perspective, or world system model of migration, followed by the push-pull factors of migration. The world system model is a Marxist approach to migration and argues that migration is caused by uneven socioeconomic global capitalist development (Wallerstein 1974; Wood 1982). The theory is that the forces of capitalism penetrate into underdeveloped regions or colonies of the world and distort social and economic relations, which in turn pushes people in these regions to move. Migration is a natural outgrowth of disruptions and dislocations as well as the structure of the world market system in the process of capitalist accumulation and development. In other words, development in the core simply means underdevelopment in the periphery. The main thought in the historical-structural perspective is that when the capitalist economy grows outward from the core into peripheral regions, migration flows are inevitable because the forces of the capitalist economy provide job opportunities in the core, but they also interfere with material bases of survival (land, labor, wages, jobs, culture, etc.) in peripheral regions. However, internal push factors in the periphery are a consequence of the more powerful external capitalist development structure. Over time, the internal push factors will become so structurally embedded in the periphery that external factors may appear invisible. Nonetheless, and in the case of indenture migration, neither the Caribbean nor India was in the developed or underdeveloped world, respectively. Both places were colonies of the British Empire (except the Dutch and French West Indies) and were treated as such, although for different purposes. The British used the Caribbean mainly for the exploitation of sugar, while India was exploited for cotton. In the constant drive for capital accumulation within the British Empire, inadvertent outcomes emerged, such as the creation of a shortage of labor in one area (the Caribbean) because of slave emancipation and a labor surplus in another (India) because of the internal displacement of the peasantry. The colonial planter class believed that these unexpected outcomes could be beneficial to them if they were channeled wisely from one area of the world to another. For the capitalist class, indentured labor was mobile labor. It is within this context that indentured migration occurred (see Roopnarine 2003).

REASONS FOR INDENTURED MIGRATION: FROM THE CARIBBEAN

Indentured Indians were brought to the Caribbean precisely to supplement rather than substitute the lost slave labor on the sugar plantations. The question of whether or not their arrival was a necessary response to the mass exodus of former slaves from the plantations is an analysis for elsewhere. Long before emancipation, the planters had made up their minds to look for an alternative source of labor because they thought the newly freed slaves would reject or withdraw erratically from labor conditions or even revolt against the planters for injustices inflicted on them as slaves. The planters were also searching for a cheap source of labor that they could import with relative ease to use against and control the newly freed slaves' bargaining power for better wages and other plantation amenities. The continuous influx of indentured Indians was also based on failed experiments with other early postemancipation emigration schemes from Africa, the United States, Europe, Madeira, China, and within the Caribbean islands. These emigration experiments failed in terms of steadily supplying labor to the plantations for reasons related to maladjustment, alcoholism, low wages, poor working conditions, tropical heat, and diseases. By contrast, indentured Indians proved to be reliable laborers.

The eventual reliance on indentured Indian laborers to supplement slave labor did not begin in the Caribbean but in Mauritius. The experiment with indentured Indians in this island in the Indian Ocean caught the attention of private sugar planters in the Caribbean, such as British Guianese planter John Gladstone. In a series of letters to the private recruitment firms Messrs Gillanders, Arbuthnot & Company, Gladstone requested and requisitioned for one hundred Indians from India to work on his plantations in British Guiana. He expressed preference for the Dhangers (the tribal hill people), the very type of indentured Indians who were contracted in Mauritius, to serve his plantation. After some negotiations, Gladstone's request for indentured Indians was accepted (see British Parliamentary Papers 1837–38a, 1837–38b).

The first experiment with 396 indentured Indians in British Guiana was a disaster (see Scoble 1840). More than a third of them perished from abuse and poor working and living conditions. The British government suspended indenture emigration to British Guiana the same year it started (1838) and stated that emigration would resume only when the defects in the system were remedied. The government stopped the private importation of indentured laborers and instead placed all responsibilities under state control and under a series of strict regulations. The British crown and Indian governments emphasized a sound recruitment process, a safe and secure transportation system, and a nonabusive plantation experience. They also insisted that a British agent or a British consular as well as a protector should be stationed at the ports of departure in India and on the Caribbean plantation colonies. Finally, the British and Indian governments reserved the right to suspend and stop indenture emigration to the Caribbean colonies if so needed at any time (British Parliamentary Papers 1874, 29–32). The new state guidelines governing the entire indenture system meant the planters were required to negotiate directly with the British crown and Indian government mainly to avoid abuse and to ensure that indentured Indians would be fairly protected outside the crown's jurisdiction.

In 1845, indenture emigration resumed, but it was suspended in 1848 due to financial difficulties. It resumed again in 1851 and was eventually abolished in 1917. From the 1860s, the British and Indian governments were comfortable with the movement of indentured Indians from India to the Caribbean. Colonial governments in St. Lucia, St. Vincent, Grenada, Jamaica, and St. Kitts—all British Caribbean colonies—were permitted to import indentured laborers. This permission did not go unnoticed by other European governments. The French, Dutch, and Danish governments also saw indentured Indians as a possible solution to alleviate the acute labor shortage in their former slave colonies. During a number of independent conventions and negotiations among the French, Danish, and Dutch governments with the British government following 1860, the British government allowed for the importation of indentured Indians to foreign colonies. These foreign governments who wished to participate in the movement of indentured Indians from India had to comply with a series of regulations designed mainly to safeguard against the ill treatment of indentured Indians.

REASONS FOR INDENTURE MIGRATION: FROM INDIA

A majority of indentured Indians who were taken to the Caribbean did not choose to emigrate willingly, particularly during the first half of the indentureship period (1838–80). A number of them were duped into signing contracts while others felt obligated to go to the Caribbean because they had "eaten their recruiters' salt," meaning that their recruiters had invested in them through feeding, clothing, and housing (British Parliamentary Papers 1910b, 30). Stories abound whereby recruiters would supply the basic needs of intending indentured Indians, such as money, clothing, and food, with the intent of trapping them in debt peonage (see Tinker 1974, 123–26). Indentured Indians' main objection to migration, however, was caste inhibition and obligations. To nineteenth-century Indians, including the peasantry, crossing the *kala pani,* or "black water," was an act to avoid until death. The moment an Indian crossed the *kala pani,* his or her caste was gone and could be reinstated only through excruciating and expensive purification ceremonies. Given the strict caste structure of their close-knit villages, few Indians would have risked caste defilement and ostracism for the unknown Caribbean islands. George Grierson (1883), a colonial official, observed that the main objection of Indians to emigration from their villages was caste restrictions, superstition, and religious beliefs. Around the major recruiting centers in India, stories circulated that Indians were taken away to have *mimiai ka tel* (the oil extracted from a Coolie's head by hanging him upside down). British historian Hugh Tinker (1974) espoused that intending indentured Indians were under the assumption that in the Caribbean they would be converted to Christianity, forced to eat beef and pork, and dispossessed of their holy threads. These Indians were also naturally reluctant to travel to the Caribbean. They would rather have worked in their own familiar environment than venture out to some unknown destination. Agricultural job opportunities existed in India itself, especially in tea gardens and in nearby Assam, Burma, and Mauritius. Grierson noticed that the Assam recruiter could easily outbid the Caribbean recruiter because there was no sea to cross, the distance was shorter, and the pay was better.

The aforementioned factors did not stymie all Indians from indenture emigration. The establishment of British colonialism in India was a divisive factor in the movement of Indians from their homeland to overseas indentured communities. British colonialism transformed the relationship between traditional Indian agriculture and handicraft industries. One critic wrote:

> The demand of the industrial revolution generated an imperial policy and made India productive by transforming it from a producer of manufactured goods to a supplier of raw material (mainly cotton) to the British industrial complex. Subsequently, the East Indian social economy and village community systems were altered and a cash economy was introduced. The ultimate result of British policies in India was that new traders, moneylenders, rent rackers and taxation exacted an enormous toll on the natives. Not only were the natives oblivious to these new developments around them, but vast numbers of them were deceived and became indebted in the process. (Roopnarine 2007, 17)

British colonialism was supported through a land revenue system in Bengal known as *zamindari* in Bombay and *ryotwari* in Madras. Under this system, the British used the *zamindars* (lower echelons of the Indian ruling class) to collect revenues and taxes from the natives, which the latter could not afford. The result was that many natives sold their land to meet their financial burden while others desperately sought new ways of linking life with social and economic justice through migration. Thousands of Indians dealt with their economic hardships by drifting to urban and overseas enclaves looking for employment. These displaced individuals were quite willing to migrate overseas to avoid domestic hardships.

There were myriad other reasons why Indians left their homeland to work overseas. Some Indians migrated because of domestic problems, oppressive personal relationships, and family disputes. Some were even running away from the law. Other Indians migrated because of adventure, like the dancing girls who arrived in Suriname in the 1870s. Some Indians were tied to their landlords like slaves and sought any opportunity to escape their socioeconomic bondage. Natural disasters such as floods and famines added to the pool of migrants in the Caribbean. Civil wars, like the Great Sepoy Mutiny of 1857–58, were another cause for migration. Arguably, some of the above reasons for migrating were domestically derived and driven. But external influence and impact cannot be easily dismissed. Take, for example, the impact of natural disasters. The British colonial system did not create natural disasters, but it certainly did not provide the mechanisms to deal with them. The focus was overwhelmingly on extracting as much revenue as possible rather than providing for the basic needs of protection and survival. When disaster struck, the already desperate situation became even more desperate, forcing thousands to flee to safer grounds, including, perhaps, a trip to the Caribbean to become an indentured laborer. Similarly, British superiority and the lack of respect for Indian religious customs caused the Sepoy Mutiny of 1857–58 in India. The natives' revolt against British colonialism had an enormous impact on India. Thousands of Indians fled their homes in the face of destruction and terror. In 1858, 45,838 Indians migrated out of India. Some migrated to the Caribbean simply to avoid arrest and deportation to the convict settlement of Port Blair (see Laurence 1994). In the final analysis, the demands of the British imperial economy caused socioeconomic upheavals in India and subsequently promoted indenture migration on an unprecedented scale. Internal factors were, however, exacerbated and controlled by the superstructure of the more powerful capitalist development. Whatever might have been the reasons that propelled Indians toward indenture, one factor was constant: there was never a shortage of Indians going to the Caribbean. By the 1870s, the Caribbean planters had become selective in choosing what types of Indians they wanted on their plantations, demonstrating that they did not only have a command over labor but a surplus at their disposal. Table 3.2.1 shows the number of Indians brought to the Caribbean during indenture. Missing from this table are those Indians who were rejected for being too unfit or unreliable to emigrate and perform plantation work. In 1900, for example, of 15,465 Indian emigrants registered for indenture, 3,089, or 19.97 percent, were rejected, and of this figure, 932, or 6.02 percent, were rejected

TABLE 3.2.1   *Destination of Indians Indentured in the Caribbean*

DESTINATION	NO. INDIANS INDENTURED	TIME FRAME
British Guiana	239,960	1838–1917
Trinidad	143,939	1845–1917
Suriname	43,404	1873–1916
Guadeloupe	42,236	1854–1895
Jamaica	37,027	1845–1914
Martinique	25,404	1854–1899
French Guiana	8,500	1862–1885
Grenada	3,200	1857–1885
Belize	3,000	1880–1917
St. Vincent	2,472	1861–1880
St. Lucia	2,300	1858–1895
St. Kitts	361	1860–1861
Nevis	342	1873–1874
St. Croix	325	1863–1868
Total	551,470	

Source: These figures were compiled from a number of sources. See appendix 1 and 2 in Lomarsh Roopnarine, *Indo-Caribbean Indenture: Resistance and Accommodation* (Kingston, Jamaica: University of the West Indies Press, 2007), 122–25.

on account of physical or mental infirmity (see the 1900 *Report on Emigration from the Port of Calcutta to British and Foreign Colonies*). A decade later, the situation had hardly changed. In 1911, of 12,756 Indians waiting in the depots to be shipped to overseas indenture colonies, 1,152 were rejected (see the 1911 *Report on Emigration from the Port of Calcutta to British and Foreign Colonies*). Every year from the 1860s, at least eight hundred Indians were rejected from emigrating while another one hundred deserted the depots and an estimated two hundred changed their minds just before departure. Using these conservative statistics, an estimated sixty thousand to seventy-five thousand Indians probably would have declared their intentions to indenture themselves overseas during the eighty-year period of indenture. But they were either rejected, released owing to their unwillingness to emigrate, or were claimed by their relatives.

The movement of Indians during the aforementioned time period was not fluid. There were a series of commencements, stoppages, and resumptions during the time period for each country (Roopnarine 2007, 124). The figures might not all be accurate, which I have addressed in another article, "A Critique of East Indian Indentured Historiography in the Caribbean" (Roopnarine 2014a). The major problem is to determine who compiled these figures and when. Nonetheless, the figures are important in providing an idea of the size of Indian indenture emigration to the Caribbean. What is new to the emigration statistics is only the shipload of Indians who were brought to Nevis. This is not an error. In 2013, I presented a paper on Indian indenture in the Danish West Indies at the Whim Museum on St. Croix, and a few individuals in the question-and-answer period claimed that their ancestors were brought from India to Nevis (Roopnarine 2014b). The Belize case is unusual. Indians went there in two waves: first from India directly to Belize and then from India to Jamaica and then to Belize. Most Indians were plantation indentures, but those that were taken to French Guiana worked in the gold fields or places deep in the interior region. The death rate among the French Guiana indentures was the highest.

THE ORGANIZATION AND RECRUITMENT OF INDENTURED LABORERS

Caribbean historian Walton Look Lai writes that "indenture experiment embodied many unique features that distinguished it, not only from earlier forms of unfree labour in the region, but even from many other indentured labour experiments taking place simultaneously during the period in other parts of the world, and even in the Americas" (1993, 51). What makes the indenture emigration so unique? The system involved a hierarchy of agencies and officials with duplicating and overlapping responsibilities. Indenture emigration operated in collaboration with the British government, the colonized Indian government, and the colonial government in the colonies. The British government was the most powerful institution in this three-way collaboration. The Dutch, French, and Danish governments were added after the 1860s into the rank of the British government. However, these governments were not only less powerful but were also subject to the indenture immigration rules and regulations established by the British government. The British government could suspend and stop indenture migration immediately in any of the colonies, if so needed. Below these imperial governments were the colonized Indian government and the colonial governments in the Caribbean. The colonized Indian government was genuinely interested in how the indenture system was conducted and at times spoke passionately against injustices and ill treatment of its citizens abroad; but in reality, it was powerless. That is why on many occasions the Indian government stated that it did not want to get mixed up in bargains between the British government and colonial government on pressing indenture issues. The Indian government took a neutral position on indenture whenever it saw fit. The colonial government in the Caribbean actually governed the plantation life of indentured Indians but was largely influenced by the planter class, who had enormous power.

The indenture emigration system functioned in the following way. The government of India appointed protectors of emigration in most regions and districts to monitor the recruitment of Indians. Local judges supervised the judicial aspects of recruitment to ensure that intending indentured Indians understood the terms of their contracts. Medical examinations were conducted to ensure fitness for the long sea journey and plantation work. The respective Caribbean colonial government appointed emigration agents who then employed provincial and district subagents and licensed recruiters. In the Caribbean, each colonial government had an Immigration Department headed by a chief officer (called different names, Protector of Immigrants, Agent-General of Immigrants, or Immigrant Agent-General). The chief immigration officer was assisted by other subimmigration officers, such as inspectors, clerks, and interpreters. The Immigration Department was responsible for the distribution of Indians and the functioning of the indenture system. The distribution of Indian emigrants was determined prior to their arrival through an application specifying the number of emigrants required by the planters. The chief immigration officer and his associates had the right at any time to enter upon any plantation on which indentured Indians were employed and inspect the condition and treatment of emigrants. Finally, the entire indenture system was governed by a series of ordinances.

The first batch of Indians was recruited from Chota Nagpur, the present-day Indian states of West Bengal, Bihar, and Orissa. These recruits were non-Hindu aboriginal tribal people collectively known as "Hill Coolies," or Jangalis. The recruitment of these hill people for labor in the Caribbean was neither substantial nor successful. They preferred to work on the indigo and tea gardens in and around India. They were also ill treated and experienced high death rates in the Caribbean. From the 1860s, recruits were drawn from Bihar and Bengal, the North-West Provinces (currently known as Uttar Pradesh), Oudh, Fyzabad, Gonda, and Basti in the United Province. In 1900, for example, 18,489 Indians were recruited to work overseas, mainly in Mauritius, Fiji, and the Caribbean. Of this number, 2.36 percent came from Bengal; 9.03 percent from Bihar; 54.93 percent from the Northwest Province; 26.34 percent from Oudh; and 7.35 percent from Punjab (see the 1900 *Report on Emigration from the Port of Calcutta to British and Foreign Colonies*). The recruitment of Indians also occurred in South India among the Madras population. While these emigrants were perceived to have done well on the treacherous sea voyage, they simply disliked plantation work. They often resisted plantation work through desertion or engaged in rum drinking until publicly intoxicated. Madras emigrants turned out to be a supplementary source to the whole indenture emigration scheme, constituting a mere 10 percent of all indentured laborers. A smaller number of emigrants were also recruited from the province of Punjab. Like Madras emigrants, the large-scale recruitment of Punjabi emigrants was not encouraged because they were thought to be more militant toward their plantation bosses. Except for unforeseen circumstances in India, such as natural disasters and civil unrest, this pattern of indenture emigration continued more or less until 1917.

On paper at least, the organization of indenture emigration looked sound. In practice, there were weaknesses. While it is difficult to separate how many Indians went willingly and how many involuntarily, unknown numbers were certainly duped and kidnapped into indenture. How many of them were victims of fraudulent recruitment practices is a question of speculation since the statistics on fraudulent practices were never recorded. Tinker claims that there were three responses from the intending indentured Indians with regard to how much they knew about their destinations: (1) some would ask intelligent questions about the conditions; (2) some would not ask questions but listened instead; and (3) some would regard questions with indifference (1974, 120). Surinamese historian Maurits Hassankhan (2011) thinks stories of the recruitment experience from indentured Indians in the Caribbean might be believable but that some are questionable since they might have derived from emotional feelings of missing home and maladjustment to the plantation labor regime. It is safe to say that not more than 10–15 percent of Indians were taken to the Caribbean on fraudulent grounds. What is more accurate is that a majority of Indians did not know what awaited them in the Caribbean, at least during the first two decades of indenture. In the latter stages of the indenture system, Indians had more knowledge of the Caribbean islands because of information filtered back into their villages from time-expired indentured Indians who had returned. Even then, deceitful and romantic methods of recruitment were not altogether eliminated. When resident-based recruiters failed to convince Indians to indenture overseas, newly returned and time-expired indentured Indians from the Caribbean, turned recruiters, were used. These recruiters knew the inner workings of indenture and skillfully used their experience to inveigle intending indentured Indians. The common method was to present a fancy story of easy work, quick money, and religious connection and customs of India in the Caribbean. For instance, recruiters told the intending Indians that they were going to *Sri-Ram* instead of Suriname. To Indians, *Ram* indicates a religious place that sounds like the Ramayana, a Hindu religious text that exemplifies good over evil, duty over self-indulgence, and generosity over selfishness. Likewise, Indians were told they were going to "Chinidad," which means "land of sugar." Chinidad, of course, sounds like China, the country that borders India, thus misrepresenting the long journey they had to endure to the Caribbean. Conversely, the indentured Indians had their own way of defining, discussing, and imagining their new destinations. The islands overseas were called *Tapu*. To the North Indians, Mauritius was known as *Mirich* or *Mirich Desh*. To the South Indians, British Guiana, Demerara, was known as *Damra, Damraila,* or *Doomra;* Trinidad was known as *Chinitat* (Tinker 1974, 120). Fiji was known as *pheegee;* Burbon as *Birboon;* Natal as *Naatal;* Suriname as *Sriram.* Of all these places, Trinidad was the favorite, and Mauritius was the worst because of the land availability and planters' exploitation, respectively.

The British and Indian governments were far too removed from the day-to-day activities to ensure a well-functioning indenture emigration system. The indenture system was too thinly spread out in many colonies in the Indian Ocean and the

Caribbean Sea for effective administration. Subsequently, loopholes and weaknesses in the system were exploited by the recruiters in India and the planters in the Caribbean. In India, the recruiters were merely interested in meeting the quota of emigrants rather than obeying recruitment policies. Women were particularly targeted since about 40 percent of them were needed before a ship could leave the ports in India. The situation became worse when the authorities raised the fee for the recruitment of women with the expectation that more women would be added to the migration pool. Instead, the recruiters began forcing Indian women to labor overseas against their will. The Sanderson Commission reported that the recruiting staffs were very corrupt and that they were paid for results, by the number of recruits they obtained. The consequence was that recruiters were very often successful in enticing single women as well as married women—who left their husbands—to serve indenture. Local magistrates in India often declared that all kinds of riffraff were granted licenses as recruiters. Yearly immigration reports revealed that at least 5 percent of recruiting licenses were revoked. In 1900, for example, 1,088 recruiters were given licenses and twenty-seven were cancelled. The numbers and reasons for cancellation are provided in table 3.2.2.

TABLE 3.2.2   *Reasons for Recruitment License Revocations*

NO. REVOKED	REASON
7	Working for other agencies
4	Fraud
3	Bad character
2	Insufficient accommodation for intending emigrants
2	Kidnapping
1	Theft
1	Detaining unwilling emigrants
1	Wrongfully restraining a woman
1	Found unfit to hold a recruitment license
1	Assaulting emigrants
1	Misconduct
1	Making false statements
1	No permanent residence and no one to certify character
1	Duping a woman into indenture

Source: Report on Emigration from the Port of Calcutta to British and Foreign Colonies, 1900, Protector of Emigrants (Calcutta: Bengal Secretariat Press, 1901).

In the Caribbean, planters had enormous power over most political matters, even over the protectors of emigrants, who were often seen socializing with the planters, indicating that they had more commonality with the planter class than with the laboring class they were supposed to protect. Worst of all was the fact that the laws favored the planter class. Look Lai writes eloquently:

> There was also a systematic institutional deception entrenched in the whole system, in that no one ever informed the intending emigrant ... about the harsh disciplinary laws imposed unilaterally by the planter controlled colonial legislatures contained in the immigration ordinances, the whole apparatus of criminal penalties attached to small and large infractions of the contract or of basic work-discipline. This omission remained basic to the entire immigration experiment and thereby defined the indenture system as a quasi-servile labour system ... (1993, 79)

THE INDIAN EMIGRANTS: GENDER, CASTE, RELIGION, AND LANGUAGE

Perhaps it should be stated that during indenture and even in the modern period, Indians were known as Coolies. The meaning of the word in India was not negative. It was simply used to describe someone who was a porter. In the Caribbean, however, the word meant stupid, backward, uncivilized, and resistant to change. What is interesting is that only the first batches of Indians who went to Mauritius in 1834 and to British Guiana in 1838 were Coolies, but the term was applied to all Indians who served indenture. Unfortunately, the psychological impact of this word on Indians is yet to be fully assessed. Generally, the word was used to make Indians feel inferior and that they were capable only of providing menial labor. The planter class, however, declared openly that they wanted a predominantly young, male, "Coolie" labor force. Two main reasons were given for this preference. First, women were perceived to be a burden rather than a benefit to the patriarchal plantation system due to their role in childbearing and childcare. Second, the colonial officials claimed that it was difficult to entice Indian women to leave their homeland, even when higher commissions were offered to recruiters. These reasons were persuasive, so when indenture began in British Guiana, the ratio of men to women was one hundred to three. This pattern continued until the late 1850s, when social pathologies, in particular abuse and wife murders, started to erupt on the plantations because of the shortage of women. Indian males competed for fewer Indian females. The colonial authorities encouraged the recruitment of more women with good standing to nurture and nourish a stable environment for indentured Indians. Table 3.2.3 provides a sample of the ratio of men to women arriving in 1877, during the middle period of the indenture system.

TABLE 3.2.3 *Male to Female Comparison for Ships from India to British Guiana in 1877*

SHIP NAME	VOYAGE LENGTH (DAYS)	MEN	WOMEN	BOYS	GIRLS
Ailsa	81	296	128	29	11
Ailsa	99	304	125	18	14
Jura	100	337	154	21	8
King Arthur	101	321	93	15	10
Neva	85	275	121	30	15
Pandora	92	300	136	18	14
Rohilla	83	275	100	21	9
Shiela	98	363	117	19	24
Total		2,471	974	171	105

Source: British Guiana, "Immigration Agent General (IAG) Report of the Immigration Agent General for the Year 1877," in *The Argosy* (Georgetown, British Guiana: Demerara, 1888).

The proportion of women to men varies from less than one half to a third or even less. Of the total of eight ships that brought Indians from India to British Guiana in 1877, 2,471 Indians were males while 974 were females. The ratio was two and a half men to one woman (2.5:1.0). Boys and girls comprised 276 individuals. A small number of boys and girls were probably recruited individually like adults, but the high number of individuals who were not adult men and women showed that during the middle years of indenture single emigrants had reduced substantially. Emigrants were going overseas as a family, although some children might have been born out of wedlock. However, more single women than married women were going to the Caribbean. Of the 2,808 women that were dispatched from India to the colonies, including the Indian Ocean islands, in 1906, 1,224 were accompanied by their husbands, and the remaining 1,554, or 56.41 percent, were understood to be single women (see the 1906 *Report on Emigration from the Port of Calcutta to British and Foreign Colonies*). That a majority of single women migrated under whatever circumstances revealed that Indian women in the nineteenth century might have been under less control and social surveillance by their male-dominated social structure than previously thought.

Like gender, a brief assessment of the social structure of Indian emigrants is warranted to show how this once-significant aspect of cultural identity had become meaningless in the Caribbean. Indian emigrants were recruited from the four main castes within Hinduism: Brahmin (priests), Kishatriya (warriors and rulers), Vaishya (business and agricultural caste), and Sudras (menial caste). On the whole, the caste composition of the migrants recruited reflected somewhat the caste composition of India, which meant that more low- and middle-caste Indians were recruited to labor in the Caribbean. D. W. D. Comins (1893c) showed that of 3,072 Indians introduced in Trinidad during the season between 1889 and 1890 there were over forty types of castes. The largest numbers were from Chamar and Muhammadan, while the smallest numbers were from the Sandi and Bostom castes. While it is difficult to say precisely how many different castes were brought to the Caribbean since some Indians gave the immigration authorities the wrong caste to gain upward social mobility, more than two-thirds of the emigrants were from the low caste. Over time, however, the caste structure did not survive in the Caribbean, mainly because of the capitalist nature of the plantation system. Caste doctrines were not considered in the daily routine of work and life. Of all Indian customs, the caste did not survive the crossing from India to the Caribbean plantations.

Like caste, the religious composition of the emigrants also mirrored the religious breakdown of India, with 84 percent of migrants being Hindu and 16 percent being Muslim or other religions. The annual report on emigration for the year 1901 shows in table 3.2.4 that a majority of the emigrants to the Caribbean that year were from a Hindu background. Of all the emigrants, low-caste Hindus constituted 65 percent; high-caste, 12 percent; middle-caste, 7.2 percent; and Muslims, 15 percent, while women made up about a third of emigrants.

These emigrants were recruited from various areas in north and south India and therefore spoke a variety of regional languages. Researcher Steven Vertovec (1992) found that during the indenture period in Trinidad Indians spoke Bengali, Punjabi, Hindu, Urdu, Oriya, Nepali, Gujerati, Telugu, Tamil, Oraons, Santals, Vanga, Radha, Varendra, Rajbangshi, Magahi, Maithili, Shadri, Awadhi, Bhojpuri, Eastern and Western Hindi, Bangaru, Ajmeri, and Tondai Nadu. Over time, however, Bojpuri in Trinidad, Sarnami in Suriname, and various forms of Caribbean Creole became the main languages of communication among Indians. All the other languages have experienced a uniform

TABLE 3.2.4 *Caste and Religion Among Indian Emigrants to the Caribbean in 1901*

CASTE AND RELIGION	DEMERARA	TRINIDAD	SURINAME	TOTAL
Agriculturalist	763	769	309	1,917
Artisan	161	141	109	411
Christians	0	0	2	2
Hindus, Brahmins, High Castes	174	353	228	755
Low caste	524	689	385	1,598
Muslims	352	389	229	970

Source: *Report on Emigration from the Port of Calcutta to British and Foreign Colonies, 1901, Protector of Emigrants* (Calcutta: Bengal Secretariat Press, 1902).

death. The stop of the flow of fresh indentured Indians since 1917, the preference for the English language and Creole in the education system, and prerequisites for secure employment as well as the continuous migration to Europe and North America have marginalized and drowned out the use of Indian languages on a daily basis.

THE SEA JOURNEY FROM INDIA TO THE CARIBBEAN

The sea journey actually began in the depots. Much has been written about the cultural aspects of the depots: caste, religion, the diversity of the emigrants, and how they formed makeshift unions of brotherhood and sisterhood to console, cohere, and coexist in times of hardship. Less known are the physical and psychological conditions. While these conditions improved over time, they were never completely eliminated. Sanitation was poor and diseases and deaths were always present. In 1906, for example, of the twenty thousand intending emigrants in the Calcutta depots waiting to be transported to various overseas colonies, there were three cases of cholera and two deaths; eight cases of small pox; eleven cases of chicken pox; 173 cases of measles and fifteen deaths; 455 admissions for fever and eight deaths; eighty-one cases of cerebrospinal meningitis and forty-one deaths; 261 admissions for respiratory diseases and thirty-five deaths; and twenty-eight infants who died and twenty-six who were born. Women gave birth on every ship that left India to the Caribbean, which indicated that the authorities were not very concerned about the dangers associated with birth on the high seas. Some women who boarded the ships were visibly pregnant since some births happened during the first half of the normal months-long journey. But more importantly, Indian women giving birth on the sea voyages revealed their willingness to take risks. Why were they willing to travel over high seas while pregnant? Were they so desperate for a better life? Were some of them fleeing to conceal their unplanned pregnancy to avoid social expulsion? Were some women leaving on the wishes of the family? Whatever might have been the case, their willingness to travel while pregnant exemplified courage, a cultural characteristic they took with them to the Caribbean plantations (Roopnarine 2010).

The sea voyage from India to the Caribbean is about eleven thousand miles. Nineteenth-century wooden sailing ships would make this journey in about four to five months, or just over one hundred days. After the introduction of iron steamships in the 1870s, the same journey was completed in about three months. In 1877, for example, the ship *Ailsa* left India on November 5 and arrived in British Guiana on January 28, 1878, a total of eighty-one days. Ships normally travelled an average of 1,176 miles per week, 168 miles per day, and seven miles per hour. If the weather was bad, the voyage could potentially be longer. Most ships left India during August and March, when the weather was more favorable. Ships from the Indian Ports of Calcutta and Madras generally travelled through the Bay of Bengal and around the Cape of Good

Hope and stopped at St. Helena to pick up fresh water and food, if needed, before continuing to the Caribbean islands.

The ship crew was a diverse group of individuals from different nationalities and occupational backgrounds. Crew members were ranked according to occupational status. The most important individual on the ship was the surgeon-superintendent, not the captain. He was a male appointed by the protector of immigrants. The surgeon was responsible for the medical inspection of the migrants, proper ventilation and cooking arrangements, hospital space, and food storage. He kept a list of all the passengers, including the crew, and documented all significant events, such as births and deaths, as well as unexpected events (abuse, rape, revolts) that occurred onboard the ship. The surgeon was paid according to how many Indians landed alive. There was also the third mate, who was the surgeon's right-hand man but reported to the captain of the ship. The third mate was customarily the ship's safety officer, responsible for discipline among the emigrants. Below the third mate were the compounders, who were druggists, dispensers of medicine as well as mediators (mainly Indian mediators). They were the intermediaries between European and Indian passengers onboard the ship. They possessed some knowledge of European languages and customs as well as of the Indian passengers. In the lower ranks were the *sirdars* (headmen), *bandharries* (native cooks), and *topazes* (sweepers). These individuals were Indians, but their duties varied. Each *sirdar* was responsible for twenty-five Indian passengers to ensure proper conduct and order onboard the ship, while *bandharries* were drawn from the upper caste to avoid any suspicion of caste contamination. The *topazes* held the lowest rank among the crew and came from a low caste. They were responsible for sweeping and cleaning the ship.

Every sea voyage was guided by nineteen detailed clauses or rules. They were chiefly related to contracts, numbers of emigrants, penalties if contract terms were not carried out, the seaworthiness, staffing, and deck space of ships, the availability of clean water, access to a trained surgeon and medicines, and the proper treatment of migrants. In spite of these regulations, for a majority of Indians the sea voyage was a lonely and uncertain experience. Like in the depots, fear, births, deaths, diseases, depression, suicide, and abuse (especially of women) were common onboard the ships bound for the Caribbean. Cholera, typhoid, dysentery, scurvy, scorbutic diarrhea, and beriberi broke out very often on ships. Although deaths varied from ship to ship and from time to time, they were a common feature on every ship. In 1856–57, 4,094 Indians were taken from Calcutta to the Caribbean in twelve different ships. Of this number, 707 Indians died, an average mortality rate of 17.27 percent. On one ship, the mortality rate was 31.17 percent (British Parliamentary Papers 1874, 23–24). Table 3.2.5 shows that the death rate on ships leaving India for the Caribbean between 1860 and 1861 ranged from 2 percent to 12 percent.

TABLE 3.2.5 *Voyage Mortality Rates from India to the Caribbean, 1860–61*

DESTINATION	NO. SHIPS	NO. EMBARKED	NO. DEATHS	MORTALITY PERCENT
British Guiana	8	3,152	128	4.0
Grenada	2	802	22	2.7
Jamaica	3	1,057	131	12.3
St. Lucia	1	336	17	5.0
St. Vincent	1	308	10	3.2
Trinidad	5	2,023	71	3.4

Source: British Parliamentary Papers, *The Twenty-second General Report of the Colonial Land and Emigration Commissioners* (London: Irish University Press, 1862), 49.

In 1877, of the total of 3,905 emigrants taken to British Guiana, eighty-four perished, including fourteen infants. Deaths on the voyages were reduced toward the end of indenture due to improvements in management and facilities. In 1904, of the 7,135 intending indentured emigrants taken to various colonies on eleven ships, twenty-one, or 0.39 percent, perished, deaths that occurred mainly on ships bound for British Guiana (see the 1904 *Report on Emigration from the Port of Calcutta to British and Foreign Colonies*). Deaths on the sea voyage were inevitable events that accompanied indenture emigration. Why were there so many deaths among the passengers? Newborns, infants, and children were naturally unprepared for the long voyage to the Caribbean. Their parents and guardians were certainly under duress from the tumultuous sea voyage and were not prepared to deal with the additional stress of taking care of younger ones in need. Some young ones died simply from neglect and poor medical attention. Some intending indentured Indians were recruited from impoverished sectors of Indian society and were therefore unfit to endure the long sea voyage. Some were so depressed from the sea voyage that they allowed themselves to die instead of seeking treatment. Others committed suicide. In spite of the dangers associated with the sea voyage, Indian emigrants continued to indenture themselves overseas.

REFERENCES

Notes on the Primary Sources

British Guiana. 1881. 1888. "Immigration Agent General (IAG) Report of the Immigration Agent General for the Year 1877." In *The Argosy*. Georgetown, Guyana: Demara.

British Parliamentary Papers. 1837–38a. "Copy of Letter from John Gladstone, Esq. to Messrs. Gillanders, Arbuthnot & Co." (LII, 180). London: Colonial Record Office.

_____. 1837–38b. "Copy of Letter from Messrs. Gillanders, Arbuthnot & Co. to John Gladstone, Esq." (LII, 232). London: Colonial Record Office.

_____. 1862. *The Twenty-second General Report of the Colonial Land and Emigration Commissioners*. London: Irish University Press.

_____. 1874. *Report by Geoghegan on Immigration from India*. Vol. 47 (C314). London: Colonial Record Office.

_____. 1910b. "Testimony of Mr. Oliver Warner, Minutes of Evidence." In *Report of the Committee on Emigration from India to the Crown Colonies and Protectorates (Sanderson Commission)*. Vol. 27, part 2 (Cd. 5192–94), para. 714. London: HMSO.

Comins, D. W. D. 1893c. *Notes on Emigration from India to Trinidad*. Calcutta: Bengal Secretariat.

Grierson, George A. 1883. *Report on Colonial Emigration from Bengal Presidency*. Calcutta: Bengal Secretariat.

Laurence, Keith. 1994. *A Question of Labor: Indentured Immigration into Trinidad and British Guiana, 1875–1917*. New York: St Martin's Press.

Look Lai, Walton. 1993. *Indentured Labor, Caribbean Sugar: Chinese and Indian Migrants to the British West Indies, 1838–1917*. Baltimore: The John Hopkins University Press.

Report on Emigration from the Port of Calcutta to British and Foreign Colonies, 1900, Protector of Emigrants. 1901. Calcutta: Bengal Secretariat Press.

Report on Emigration from the Port of Calcutta to British and Foreign Colonies, 1901, Protector of Emigrants. 1902. Calcutta: Bengal Secretariat Press

Report on Emigration from the Port of Calcutta to British and Foreign Colonies, 1904, Protector of Emigrants. 1905. Calcutta: Bengal Secretariat Press.

Report on Emigration from the Port of Calcutta to British and Foreign Colonies, 1906, Protector of Emigrants. 1907. Calcutta: Bengal Secretariat Press.

Report on Emigration from the Port of Calcutta to British and Foreign Colonies, 1911, Protector of Emigrants. 1912. Calcutta: Bengal Secretariat Press.

Roopnarine, Lomarsh. 2001. 2003. "Indo-Caribbean Migration: From Periphery to Core." *Caribbean Quarterly* 49 (3, Fall): 30–60.

_____. 2007. *Indo-Caribbean Indenture: Resistance and Accommodation*. Kingston, Jamaica: University of the West Indies Press.

_____. 2010. "The Indian Sea Voyage between India and the Caribbean during the Second Half of the Nineteenth Century." *Journal of Caribbean History* 44 (1): 48–74.

_____. 2014a. "A Critique of East Indian Indentured Historiography in the Caribbean." *Labor History* 55 (3): 389–401.

_____. 2014b. "Lecture on 150th Anniversary of the Arrival of East Indians in Danish St. Croix." Paper presented to the Landmark Society of St. Croix, US Virgin Islands, March 10.

Scoble, John. 1840. *Hill Coolies: A Brief Exposure of the Deplorable Conditions of the Hill Coolies in British Guiana and Mauritius*. London: Harvey & Danton.

Tinker, Hugh. 1974. "A New System of Slavery: Export of Indian Labour Overseas, 1830–1920." London: Oxford University Press.

Vertovec, Steven. 1992. *Hindu Trinidad: Religion, Ethnicity and Socio-Economic Change*. London: Macmillan.

Wallerstein, Immanuel. 1974. *The Modern World-System, Capitalist Agriculture and the Origins of the European World-Economy in the Sixteenth Century*. New York: Academic Press.

Wood, Charles H. 1982. "Equilibrium and Historical-Structural Perspective on Migration." *International Migration Review* 16 (2): 298–319.

Return Migration to the Caribbean

Locating the Concept in Historical Space

Dennis A.V. Brown

THE NEXUS BETWEEN society and migration is often alluded to in the study of the latter phenomenon. However, the ways in which changes in society are mirrored in migration are not always given the centrality of place that they deserve. The recent literature on return migration to the region tends to either herald the existence of a pattern that is related to the most recent historical epoch (Pessar 1997), or point to the existence of distinctive patterns without reference to the socio-historical formations that have led to their existence (De Souza 1998). The integral connection between migration and the evolution of Caribbean society lends a dynamic character to the ways in which people move into and out of the region. If it is accepted that the regions' history can be divided into individual epochs characterized by distinctive political, economic and social configurations locally and internationally, then it is understandable that the character of the migration process associated with these arrangements would evince qualitatively different expressions over time.

The notion of return migration to the region has its material basis in the historical tendency of Caribbean people to venture beyond the regions' shores. Its historical genesis can be associated with the phase of migration that began in the middle to late nineteenth century. The process, however, is best understood to be related to the character of the society and economy of the region. Given that these are subject to change and tend to be greatly influenced by the wider global setting, the character of return migration will be historically specific. This makes it possible to conceive of this phenomenon in mutative or historically sequential terms rather than as an unchanging process with general features that can be understood by being studied at any given point in time.

The central theme of this chapter is that the character of the return migration process to the region is a dynamic one that has evolved in accordance with the changing character of Caribbean society and its relationship to global society. The presumption is made that this interface between processes at the local, regional and global levels is fundamental to what happens within Caribbean society (Brown 2000). Global historical epochs, it is argued, are given form by cycles of technological innovation and diffusion that affect production arrangements in very fundamental ways, leading in turn to a restructuring of socio-economic life within industrial societies and the wider world. This Schumpeterian interpretation of the Kondratiev long waves suggests that there are junctures between historical epochs in which changes in the productive capacities of industrial societies are translated into social change and dislocation throughout the world (Schumpeter 1939; Kondratiev 1935). According to this conceptualization, societies are in a constant state of change in which the features associated with one set of technological innovations begin to dissolve no sooner than they are established, making way for the new institutional forms and arrangements associated with the next wave (Perez 1985).

This means that there will be historical moments in which the patterns associated with one era are complemented by those of another. The moment between historical epochs is therefore distinguished by some degree of indeterminacy—the stamp of one epoch is fading but the other has not yet become dominant. During these periods the migration process is in a state of flux; features of the previous era are still retained even as the new process takes shape. It is argued that, beginning in the last quarter of the twentieth century, technological innovations related to the computer chip and developments in biotechnology began to shape the productive systems of industrial countries. These innovations provided the basis for the transition of these societies from industrial to post-industrial and from modern to postmodern. This has been associated with changes in social relations, patterns of travel and international economic relations, as well as with systems of organization and production within these societies (Kumar 1995; Hoogvelt 1997; Sassen 1998). In keeping with the arguments regarding the relationship between epochal change and migration, this development has been accompanied by fundamental alterations to the pattern of migration affecting the region. If this hypothesis is correct, analysis of empirical data should reveal the co-existence of return migration patterns that can be identified with specific historical epochs. In metaphorical terms, the migration process that characterizes the region during such periods would amount to a kind of image or retinal retention in which one form still lingers even though the eye has found a new object of gaze. Travel into the Caribbean by its people at the present time should therefore not be imagined to be a homogenous process. Rather, it is better understood to be a composite consisting of qualitatively different strands of movement. These are the remnants of previous eras, as well as an emerging pattern of travel that is expressive of the most recent changes in global society and of the ways in which the Caribbean is integrated into this structure.

The view that the nature of return migration is best understood in terms of the changing character of the regions' relationship with the world is based on a nuance in the Caribbean-world interface that is often overlooked (Anderson 1985; Thomas-Hope 1992).[1] Arguments that characterize the contemporary period as a continuation of the capitalist world economy that started five hundred years ago run the risk of overlooking the qualitative differences between this era and all preceding ones (Girvan 2000). In this chapter, the argument is advanced that changes to the character of technological, economic, political and social configurations in the broader world economy lead to qualitative differences in the Caribbean-world interface over time that influence the nature of the migration-return migration process in fundamental ways. This has led to changes in the nature of this process over historical time. In the contemporary period, it is suggested that the distinctive character of the techno-economic-political configuration has meant that the nature of the Caribbean's link with the broader world economy and society is historically new. It has become so complex as to produce historically new forms of movement and to raise questions about the usefulness of traditional notions of the concept, even as the return streams from the previous epoch are about to draw to a close.

In the remainder of this chapter, the analytical framework outlined above is applied to an examination of the historical migration stream that has affected the Caribbean. It is then used to examine migration as it affects the region in the contemporary period.

CARIBBEAN MIGRATION AND THE WIDER WORLD

The close association between migration and Caribbean society is well known. What is less well documented is the association between significant movements of people into and out of the region and changes to the techno-economic-political contours of the industrial world.[2] In broad historical terms, migration as it has affected the region can be divided into two phases: one inward and the other outward, accompanied by return. The first of these consists of the movement that led the region to be populated by those not belonging to an indigenous group. This took the form of the trafficking of West Africans into a system of plantation slavery organized and managed by western Europeans from the sixteenth to the nineteenth centuries. It also took the form of indenture immigration involving, in the main, the movement of people from the Indian subcontinent into servanthood during the period 1838–1917.

The second phase emerged in the mid to late nineteenth century in the form of movement of substantial numbers of persons both within the region and outside of it. It is on the basis of this second phase of travel that return migration to the region became possible. Within the region, movement took the form of travel between the Windward Islands and the "new" colonies of Trinidad and British Guiana. The extra-regional travel took the form of movement to countries such as Panama, the

Dominican Republic, Cuba and the United States. This movement subsided by the end of the second decade of the twentieth century.

After a respite of two decades, the external movement resumed in the form of movement to Britain and subsequently to the United States. The inter-Caribbean movement has also continued into the post–World War II period, shaped by variations in the levels of socio-economic development that have come to characterize the region.[3] See table 3.3.1 for an indication of these trends.

The second phase of travel can be broken down into a number of stages. The first lasted from the middle of the nineteenth century to the second decade of the twentieth century. The second lasted from the immediate post–World War II period to the early 1960s. The third broad phase, from the 1960s to the present, can itself be usefully subdivided into the decades of 1960 and 1970, 1980 to the end of the century, and the post–September 11, 2001, period. These phases of travel are all characterized by particular patterns of return. They ought to be understood against the background of particular social, technological economic and political configurations that lend distinctiveness to, if not determine the character of, the period within which they operate.

TABLE 3.3.1 *Population Movement in the English-Speaking Caribbean 1840–1980*

YEAR OF CENSUS	CENSUS POPULATION	ANNUAL RATE (%)	NATURAL INCREASE	INDENTURED IMMIGRANTS NET TOTAL (1839–1981)	WEST INDIAN EMIGRANTS	MIGRATION BALANCE
1841–44	863,900	–	–	24,500	–	–
1861	1,068,400	1.07	79,700	124,800	–	–
1871	1,238,300	1.49	88,300	81,600	–	–
1881	1,440,000	1.52	130,700	72,400	1,600	70,800
1891	1,607,300	1.11	122,500	45,200	500	44,700
1911	1,951,300	0.97	321,200	64,000	41,200	22,800
1921	1,999,200	0.24	146,100	12,500	110,800	−98,300
1943–46	2,851,000	1.43	832,400	–	–	–
1960	3,766,800	2.00	873,000	–	245,300	–
1970	4,319,500	1.38	1,198,300	–	645,700	–
1980–82	4,845,147	0.96	1,092,310	–	566,663	–
1990–91	5,095,662	0.51	–	–	–	–

Source: Derived in part from Roberts 1981.

The first subdivide of the later phase involved extra-regional movement from the Anglo Caribbean to the Hispanic Caribbean and Central America.[4] This was associated with the penetration of the region by American capital, a waning of the hegemony of the British and an increase in the American sphere of political influence in the region. This period was characterized by the decline of the region's sugar industry, fuelled by the emergence of technology that allowed for the economical extraction of sugar from beet. It took place against the background of changes that had already begun to take place by the middle of the century, which involved an amalgamation of the economies of the world that had not existed previously (Ashworth 1952). These economies associated and interacted on the basis of physical proximity or congruence of political order. Thus, western and central Europe formed one group, Russia and the Baltic comprised another, western Europe and North America formed one more group, and India and the Far East comprised yet another.

The increase in world trade that underlay these coalitions had its genesis in certain changes that were brought to bear on the productive process. The first of these involved its mechanization; the second entailed its division; the third had to do with the bringing of greater complexity to its organization (Ashworth 1952). The greater interaction between the previously unconnected economic groupings took the form of increased levels of migration, movement of capital, and trade in raw materials and finished products.

The state of the international market for the agricultural produce of the colonial territories was a most important factor in determining the state of society and economy within those territories. In terms of the framework presented above, this period of our study can be classified as one in which the techno-economic-political alignments, which had occurred on the globe since the advent of the first industrial revolution, were undergoing fundamental changes. Prior to 1870, innovation centred on the development of the steam engine and its application to the textile and iron industries. The post-1870 period witnessed the emergence of electricity as a major source of energy and the development of the internal combustion engine and new forms of transport. This changed the complexion of world trade by introducing into it a whole new set of goods: railway equipment, steam ships, steel, electrical products and other manufactured products (Kenwood and Lougheed 1971). These changes were transmitted to the British Caribbean via the cost of imported foodstuff and the state of the market for its agricultural produce and as a consequence the availability of employment. Beachey tells us of the distress that this state of affairs caused in the West Indies.

Grenada's production of sugar dropped from ten thousand hogsheads to four thousand hogsheads within the year and a half ending 1884. By 1886, two-thirds of the sugar cultivation in St. Vincent was abandoned (Beachey 1957).

In Jamaica the reduction in the price of sugar coincided with the exodus of labourers to work on the Panama Canal and aggravated the difficulties of the sugar planters who were attempting to economize by reducing wages, which were already very low (Brown 2000).

TRAVEL AND RETURN: THE FIRST PHASE

It is this situation that fuelled the movement out of the territories of the Anglo Caribbean in the closing years of the nineteenth century. The outward movement led to the establishment of overseas Caribbean communities for the first time in the region's history. Some, such as the community of Jamaicans established in Blue Fields, Costa Rica, were to become permanent and represented a loss of population. The vast majority, however, were to return to their countries at the end of their contracts. The movement to Panama perhaps epitomizes the character of the migration in this era. Newton quotes a knowledgeable observer in the early years of the twentieth century as follows:

> We believe it is correct in saying that never before in the history of this colony has such an event taken place; there have been in the past a few spasmodic attempts at emigration, but hitherto, this has been confined to the ordinary labourer from the country district. On this occasion, it is the youth of Kingston that have had to go—lads on whom we have been counting to carry on the duties and responsibilities of citizens. Tailors, shoemakers, carpenters, clerks, they have all gone, and who can blame them for going? There is absolutely nothing for them to do here. ... *We wish them God-speed and a safe return to their native land with a larger portion of this world's goods than they now possess.* (Netwon 1987; my emphasis)

This quotation is illustrative of the character and magnitude of the movement to Panama, the adverse local economic conditions with which it was associated and the social composition of the emigrants. The quotation also points to the sex-selective character of the movement. The typical emigrant we are told was "a black male", usually an agricultural labourer, or unskilled town dweller. He was eager to go to Panama to try to earn enough money to build a house and purchase land on which he could make a living from farming. It also alludes to return to the country of origin (Roberts 1957). This sometimes took the form of an ultimate return, preceded by brief visits following the earning of some amount of monies. The wages offered to labourers in locations such as Panama were much greater than those offered on the local job market (Roberts 1957).[5] This encouraged another pattern of travel involving movement from one labour-contract destination to another in an effort to maximize lifetime job-market earnings (Roberts 1981). Travel out of the region to the job locations was facilitated by the development of trade and shipping links between the United States and the Caribbean (Roberts 1957).[6] This made movement between the Anglo Caribbean, the rest of the region and the United States itself relatively easy and cheap.

Data relating to the magnitude of the return flow during the period 1881–1921 is sketchy. Figures provided by Newton for Barbados and Jamaica indicate that 55 per cent of those who left for Panama from 1881 to 1915 returned during that time. Prior to 1911, Panama was the main destination of emigrants from Jamaica, with smaller numbers going to the United States and other areas such as Cuba and Costa Rica. During the period 1911–21, most travel from Jamaica took place to the United States, with lesser amounts going to Cuba and other destinations within the Caribbean basin. Movement to the United States came to an end in 1924 when travel restrictions were imposed. During the respite of outward movement from 1921 to 1943, some twenty-five thousand of those who had left in the previous decades returned to Jamaica (Roberts 1981).

These then were some of the main features of the return migration movement to the Caribbean as it occurred during the nineteenth and early twentieth centuries. The world was a vastly different place then than it is now, and this was reflected in the Caribbean's position within it and hence, within the features of the travel activities as they occurred. The migration flows with which the return movement was associated took place within the context of a world in which the productive sectors and economies of the industrial countries had been transformed by fundamental techno-economic changes. These changes subsequently had adverse effects on the region's markets for primary produce, while simultaneously facilitating the growth of other kinds of trade and economic activities and the means to conduct them. These changes in effect stymied the attempts to establish anything resembling an independent peasantry in the region and led to an outward flow of young men overseas and women into the urban centres of the territories (Austin-Broos 1985). They also led to the movement of young men with working-class and artisan backgrounds from the urban areas to overseas.

The movement of those who returned was framed and defined by the terms of their labour contract. These migrants viewed the move overseas as something that was being done for a specific time period, for a specific purpose. Interestingly, this stands in marked contrast to the character of the migration process in the wider world that was initiated as a result of the techno-economic changes that have been described. It is also one of the chief markers of the difference in character of return travel to the Caribbean in the historical and contemporary periods. In the wider world, much of the nineteenth and the early twentieth century were characterized by a relaxing of the barriers to the free movement of capital, trade and people. This led to an international migration that was unlike the process taking place in the Caribbean; it was distinguished by the freedom of those migrants from any control on the part of sending or receiving countries. For these migrants, the very promise of freedom from religious and political persecution was what provided impetus for the movement.

The period between World War I and World War II was one in which the old techno-economic arrangements were being replaced by new ones. The new technologies provided the basis for productivity based on the marshalling of abundant supplies of low-cost energy in the form of petroleum and petrochemicals. The need for raw materials to feed this production—and markets in which to convert these resources into profit—fed the intense competition between the West and its European allies and the newly emerging communist empires in eastern Europe and China. One arena in which this competition was acted out was in western Europe, which was devastated by the war. A strong Europe was a necessary bulwark against communism and a pillar for the resurgence of capitalism. These considerations led to the Marshall Plan, in which US$19 billion was provided for the rebuilding of Britain, France and West Germany. The economic activity that this generated called for manpower that was not available in those countries. It also coincided with an economic downturn in the Caribbean that spawned the disturbances of the late 1930s and continued to be a source of distress to the region's people. These circumstances provided the basis for the next wave of movement out of the Anglo-Caribbean region.

TRAVEL AND RETURN: THE SECOND PHASE I

The movement to Britain is well documented.[7] Suffice it to say that in its features it began to resemble the wider-world migration movement that occurred during the nineteenth and early twentieth centuries. Some 63 per cent of the total 31,347 who travelled from Jamaica in the period 1953–55 did so in order to work (Roberts and Mills 1955, 25). Despite the fact that many of these workers were recruited for jobs in Britain while still living in the Caribbean, the restrictive terms of the old labour contracts were no longer present. This wave was less sex-selective, although it resembled the previous one in terms of its socio-economic composition. Large-scale movement from the West Indies to Britain began in the early 1950s and lasted until the mid 1960s (Thompson 1990).[8] At the end of this period there were approximately 450,000 West Indians in Britain. A great deal of the movement occurred in the period 1961–62 when there was a threat of restrictions on travel in the form of the impending Common-wealth Immigration Bill. In this period some 100,000 West Indians migrated to Britain. Nearly two-thirds of these were Jamaicans.

The accounts of the process can be divided into a number of areas. One useful treatment of this literature classifies it in terms of its concerns in the early years with racial harmony and integration and in more recent times with post-colonial consider-ations about diaspora and identity (Chamberlain 1997). The literature on this phase of migration from the region has been critiqued on the grounds of its economic and structural focus. This it is argued provides no insight into the ways in which culture and values influence and shape the migration process (Chamberlain 1997). In terms of the argument that has been put forward in this chapter, this is an interesting proposition.

The author of this argument, Chamberlain, directs our attention to the importance of focusing on the cultural values that inform the migration process across generations of West Indian families. At first glance this argument seems to suggest continuity across generations of motives and values that have influenced and shaped the pro-pensity to migrate within families. While this might seem to contradict the contention that the return migration process is historically specific, this is not the case since Chamberlain goes on to argue for the existence of "periodic differences" and a "structure of feeling". Both of these, she suggests, speak to the existence of a somewhat amorphous historical zeitgeist created on the one hand by the legacy of the past and on the other by the definitions of the future held by the new generation. This blend of past and future, she contends, distinguishes one historical period from another.[9] While not discounting the value of these insights, it should be pointed out that those aspects of the wider setting highlighted in this chapter provide the context within which this intergenerational dialogue takes place. They determine the ways in which these values are given practical expression and, therefore, how they affect migration and return. The values and motivations may or may not change over generations, but the ways in which they inform the *pattern* of travel that takes place will be dependent on the societal-technological context that exists. Thus, the motivation of economic betterment and upward social mobility might not have changed between the migratory streams of the late nineteenth century and the present, but the strategies used to achieve these goals have done so.

By the time of the movement to Britain, migration from the Caribbean had come to mean short-term travel abroad to work and gain resources that were needed to secure one's position at home. In addition to the integration of this conception into the general cultural milieu, many of the emigrants would have had fathers and grandfathers who had been a part of the movement to Central America and the Hispanic islands in the nineteenth century. Growing up with such a legacy would have informed their views on migration. It is therefore no surprise that many of the persons who travelled to Britain during the 1950s and 1960s believed they were leaving the Caribbean only for a brief period (Gmelch 1992).[10]

In practice it turned out quite differently. The historical colonial relationship between Britain and the West Indies meant that the immigrants were regarded as "British subjects" and Britain as something of a "homecoming".[11] By the time large numbers of black people started to arrive a few years later, the underlying prejudices and resentments of the British people came to the fore. In principle, however, apart from the pronouncements of the far Right in the person of Enoch Powell, the right of these immigrants to stay in Britain was never seriously questioned. Furthermore, black workers became an integral part of the British labour market with its chronic need for manpower (Thompson 1990). The right to stay meant that those immigrants who did not meet the success they had anticipated could keep on trying and ultimately had the option of not returning to the Caribbean if they never succeeded. Also among this category of persons were some who had fared so badly that they simply could not afford the cost of a ticket home. For those who were successful, doubts as to whether the standard of living that they enjoyed in the United Kingdom could be replicated in the West Indies deterred many a return to the society of origin. These are the societal circumstances that gave rise to the image of the return migrant as a sojourner, someone who returns home after spending many years abroad. In the contemporary period, this type of migrant forms an important part of the return stream but coexists with other types of return travel that occur within the context of the most recent techno-economic developments and the global societal changes they have spawned. It is to an examination of these that we now turn.

TRAVEL AND RETURN: THE SECOND PHASE II

Beginning in the last quarter of the twentieth century, the world experienced a change in the technological basis of its productive activities. These changes form part of a process that is perhaps best characterized as a multidimensional phenomenon in which developments in the realms of information technology and telecommunications have been associated with the diminished significance of the spatial and temporal barriers to communication and production. This has been accompanied by the dissolution of the global geopolitical arrangements that emerged out of the post–World War II period and the institutionalization of economic neoliberalism as the guiding principle for the conduct of economic activities across the globe. These developments ought not to be seen merely as a continuation of the process of the expansion of the world capitalist economy that started five hundred years ago, rather they should be taken as representing a qualitatively distinct era in the history of relations between the societies of the world (UN 2002).[12] As part of this process, societies and cultures have been brought into juxtaposition as never before. Associated with this, there have been marked increases in the movement of people as tourists and labour. This has been facilitated by the transnationalization of production and the integration of national economies, the increased availability and greater capacity of air transport, and the greater permeability of national borders.

In these circumstances, the nature of international migration and by corollary the process of return has undergone fundamental changes. These changes have included the pattern of outward movement and return. The pattern of travel that we are accustomed to characterizing as "return migration", based on the migratory experiences of the 1950s–1970s, has now been altered by the presence of the pattern of travel associated with the new age. Return migration of today refers to a different phenomenon than it did in the previous era.

In illustrating this point, I draw on data from two Caribbean territories, Grenada and St. Kitts and Nevis. They demonstrate the co-existence of what I refer to as the sojourner model and the circular model. I would argue that, as time goes on, the relative importance of the two patterns of travel will change in favour of the latter.

Table 3.3.2 is compiled from data collected in the Poverty Assessment studies conducted in 1999, in the case of Grenada, and in 2000 in the case of St. Kitts. This is a household-based survey that solicits information from a representative national sample

TABLE 3.3.2 *Pattern of Return Travel During the 1990s, Grenada and St Kitts*

COUNTRY	ONCE	TWICE	THREE TIMES	AT LEAST FOUR TIMES	NS	TOTAL	N
	POPULATION OF TRAVELLERS WHO LIVED ABROAD DURING THE 1990S (%)						
Grenada	60	18	8	5	8	99	360
St. Kitts	77	13	1	7	2	100	148

Source: Caribbean Development Bank Poverty Assessment Report, Grenada and St Kitts, 1999 and 2000.

of householders on consumption, health, education, fertility and migration patterns and experiences. With regard to return migration, the data indicate that the majority of those who have lived abroad during at least the past decade have done so only on one occasion. In the case of both countries, however, 25 per cent of respondents indicated that they intended to do so again. In the case of Grenada, more than half of those who had once lived abroad expressed their intention to do so again. While in St. Kitts, one-quarter of those who had lived abroad once indicated that they intended to do so again. These data seem to indicate the existence of two main categories of return migrants. First, there is a stream made up of those who had once lived abroad and had no intention of doing so again. This amounted to some two fifths of the total migrants in Grenada at the time of the survey and, in the case of St. Kitts, a little less than half. Second, a stream made up of the remainder of travellers who were engaged in a migratory process that involved residence abroad on as many as four occasions.

This latest pattern of travel has been described as a natural accompaniment to the transnationalization of the world that has been made possible by the advent of information and telecommunication technologies. According to Pessar, the contemporary period represents a new phase in global capitalist development. It is characterized by flexible accumulation and a decrease in the significance of national borders as they affect the production and distribution of goods, ideas and people. Against this background, the value of the traditional notion of return migration becomes questionable. In the new pattern that is emerging to match the changing world, return is seen as but one episode in a continuing process of migration. Today's traveller is janusfaced, belonging to no single country, but having active linkages and connections with economic, social and political institutions both at "home" and in "host" societies.[13] The empirical data tell us that in spite of these changes to the wider global setting, the legacy of the past era is reflected in the sizable proportion of travellers in both countries who still fit the profile of the migrant who has gone abroad on one occasion and returned home for good. The transitory character of the Caribbean-world relationship is reflected, however, in the emerging pattern of the circular traveller who has lived in more than one place on a number of occasions.

The destination countries to which Caribbean people travelled in this era are also reflective of the changing character of the relationship of the Caribbean to the wider global society. See table 3.3.3 for an indication of these trends.

For Grenada, the data indicate that the historical pattern of movement to Trinidad has continued. In keeping with the pattern evinced by the region as a whole in the previous decade, as many as two-fifths of the return migrants from Grenada lived in countries outside of the region during the 1990s. This is virtually the same amount that did so during the previous decade. In the 1990s, though, nearly one-third of the migrants travelled to North America, up from 17 per cent in the previous decade. There was a corresponding decline in the proportion travelling to the former colonial power, the United Kingdom.

TABLE 3.3.3 *Countries to Which Grenadian Return Migrants Travelled During the 1980s and 1990s*

	RETURN MIGRANTS FROM GRENADA (%)	
DESTINATION	1980S	1990S
Trinidad	38	34
United States	12	17
Canada	7	12
United Kingdom	22	10
Other	21	27
Total	100	100

Sources: Census of the Commonwealth Caribbean, 1990–91; Country Poverty Assessment, Grenada, 1998.

TABLE 3.3.4 *Countries to Which Kittitian Return Migrants Travelled During the 1990s*

DESTINATION	RETURN MIGRANTS ST KITTS (%) 1990S
Trinidad	5
United States	14
Canada	3
British Virgin Islands	12
United Kingdom	10
St. Thomas	12
Guyana	7
Other Caribbean	37
Total	100

Source: Caribbean Development Bank Poverty Assessment Survey, St Kitts, 2000.

The data for St. Kitts are for one time period only. They are of value to our discussion of the destination countries of Caribbean return travellers insofar as they offer some indication of the extent to which the pattern evinced by Grenada applies to other Caribbean territories as well. The data reveal that North American destinations attracted the largest share of the North Atlantic travellers, as was the case for Grenada. The data also reveal a smaller percentage of total return travellers travelling outside of the geographical region to the countries of the North Atlantic. This amounted to 27 per cent of the return travellers from this country (see table 3.3.4). This proportion of travellers going to countries outside the region is therefore somewhat less than what obtains in Grenada's case. Although, if we consider the British Virgin Islands and St. Thomas as extra-regional destinations, the picture changes somewhat.

CONCLUSION

The propensity to migrate in order to increase available opportunities is an integral part of Caribbean culture and values. The strategies and patterns of travel that follow as a result of this propensity find expression, however, within the context of the techno-economic configuration that happens to dominate the world at any particular time in history. In this chapter, this proposition has provided the framework for an analysis of a return-migration process that has often been conceptualized as an abstraction, devoid of its temporal and historical dimensions. The analysis suggests the existence of a return-migration process that is historically grounded and demarcated by the particular techno-economic configuration that happens to be in ascendance at any particular time. Conceptually, the tendency to abstraction becomes particularly problematic at historical conjunctures in which the term, given meaning based on the experiences of one era, is likely to be used to describe the experiences of another. Recognizing the centrality of variations in quality and patterns of migration to the region over time is, therefore, important to the study of the phenomenon. This chapter has attempted to provide some insight into the basis for this mutability by insisting on the organic linkage between travel and its societal context.

NOTES

1. Anderson, for example, has used the core-periphery framework to argue in favour of a migratory process that is reflective of the dependent economic relationship of the Caribbean to the metropole, but does not speak to the issue of the changing character of this relationship. More recently, Thomas-Hope has used a seemingly immutable notion of globalization to make a similar sort of case.
2. Generally, there is a remarkable association between the three components of population change—mortality, fertility and migration—and techno-economic and institutional change in the industrial

world. Of the three components, migration tends to be most readily responsive to these changes. In the historical epoch, sex-selective migratory movements affected fertility by creating imbalances in the sex ratios (Brown 2000; Marino 1970).

3. The pattern that obtains is one that sees the movement of persons from the poorer countries of the region to a number of relatively prosperous countries. Some of this movement, such as the one from St. Vincent and Grenada to Trinidad and Tobago, represents the continuation of a historical trend. Others, such as the movement of Jamaicans and Guyanese to Antigua, St. Kitts and the Cayman Islands, are associated with developments that have taken place as a result of globalization (Brown 2004).

4. Destination countries included Panama, Cuba, the Dominican Republic and Costa Rica.

5. Roberts (1957) quotes the local rate as 1s 6d, as opposed to the foreign rate of $1.00.

6. This was in keeping with the increased economic and political dominance of the United States in the region. Roberts (1957) quotes figures that indicate that whereas in 1878 the United Kingdom took 79 per cent of Jamaica's exports and the United States 14 per cent, by 1899 a reversal had taken place with the United States taking 79 per cent of the island's trade.

7. See Peach 1986; Roberts and Mills 1955; Davison 1962; Thompson 1990; and Gmelch 1992.

8. Thompson tells us that the movement began in June 1948 with the arrival in London of 492 Jamaicans on board the SS *Empire Windrush* (Thompson 1990; Chamberlain 1997).

9. Chamberlain argues for the distinctiveness of the various migratory streams by suggesting that each of them occurred within a particular pocket of time, closely related to the past but distinguished from it (1998, 36–46).

10. Gmelch points out that less than 10 per cent of the returnees to Barbados that he surveyed believed they were leaving for good at the time of their departure (1997, 285).

11. According to one author, the first immigrants to Britain from the West Indies in 1948 were greeted with a headline in a leading British newspaper that read "Welcome Home" (Thompson 1990).

12. For a similar interpretation, see also Castells 1997–98.

13. This line of reasoning is informed by the notion that concepts are rooted in the social realities that they describe. This reality is deemed to be constantly changing and hence, so are the meanings associated with the concepts.

REFERENCES

Anderson, P. 1985. *Migration and Development in Jamaica*. Kingston: Institute of Social and Economic Research.

Ashworth, W. 1952. *A Short History of the International Economy since 1850*. London: Longman.

Austin-Broos, D. 1985. Religion, Economy and Class in Jamaica: Reinterpreting a Tradition. Mimeograph.

Beachey, R.W. 1957. *The British West India Sugar Industry in the Late Nineteenth Century*. Oxford: Oxford University Press.

Brown, D.A.V. 2000. *The Political Economy of Fertility in the British West Indies 1891–1921*. Kingston: Canoe Press.

_____. 2004. Inbetweenity: Marginalisation, Migration and Poverty Among Haitians in the Turks and Caicos Islands. In *Beyond the Blood, the Beach and the Banana. New Perspectives in Caribbean Studies*, ed. S. Courtman, 135–52. Kingston: Ian Randle.

Castells, M. 1997–98. *La era de la información: economía, sociedad y cultura*. 3 vols. Madrid: Alizana Editores S.A.

Chamberlain, M. 1997. *Narratives of Exile and Return*. New York: St Martin's Press.

_____. 1998. *Caribbean Migration, Globalised Identities*. London: Routledge.

Davison, R.B. 1962. *West Indian Migrants: Social and Economic Facts of Migration from the West Indies.* London: Oxford University Press.

De Souza, R.M. 1998. The Spell of the Cascadura: West Indian Return Migration. In *Globalization and Neoliberalism,* ed. T. Klak, 227–53. Lanham, MD: Rowman and Littlefield.

Girvan, N. 2000. Globalisation and Counter-Globalisation: The Caribbean in the Context of the South. In *Globalisation: A Calculus of Inequality,* ed. D. Benn and K. Hall, 65–87. Kingston: Ian Randle.

Gmelch, G. 1992. *Double Passage: The Lives of Caribbean Migrants Abroad and Back Home.* Ann Arbor: University of Michigan Press.

Hoogvelt, A. 1997. *Globalisation and the Postcolonial World: The New Political Economy of Development.* Baltimore: John Hopkins University Press.

Kenwood, A.G., and A.L. Lougheed. 1971. *The Growth of the International Political Economy, 1820–1960.* London: George Allen and Unwin.

Kondratiev, N. 1935. The Long Waves in Economic Life. *Review of Economic Statistics* 17 (6): 105–15.

Kumar, K. 1995. *From Postindustrial to Postmodern Society: New Theories of the Contemporary World.* Cambridge: Blackwell.

Marino, A. 1970. Family, Fertility and Sex Ratios in the British Caribbean. *Population Studies* 24 (2): 159–72.

Newton, V. 1987. *The Silver Men: West Indian Labour Migration to Panama 1850–1914.* Kingston: Institute of Social and Economic Research.

Peach, C. 1986. *West Indian Migration to Britain: A Social Geography.* London: Oxford University Press.

Perez, C. 1985. Microelectronics, Long Waves and World Structural Change: New Perspectives for Developing Countries. *World Development* 13 (3): 441–63.

Pessar, P., ed. 1997. *Caribbean Circuits: New Directions in the Study of Caribbean Migration.* New York: Center for Migration Studies.

Roberts, G.W. 1957. *The Population of Jamaica.* Cambridge: Cambridge University Press.

———.. 1981. Currents of External Migration Affecting the West Indies: A Summary. *Revista/Review InterAmericana* 11 (3).

Roberts, G.W., and D.O. Mills. 1955. *Study of External Migration Affecting Jamaica, 1953–1955.* Kingston: Institute of Social and Economic Research.

Sassen, S. 1998. *Globalization and Its Discontents: Essays on the New Mobility of People and Money.* New York: The New Press.

Schumpeter, J.S.A. 1939. *Theoretical, Historical and Statistical Analysis of the Capitalist Process.* New York: McGraw Hill.

Thomas-Hope, E. 1992. *Caribbean Migration.* Reprint, Kingston: University of the West Indies Press, 2002.

Thompson, M.E. 1990. Forty and One Years On: An Overview of Afro-Caribbean Migration to the United Kingdom. In *In Search of a Better Life: Perspectives from the Caribbean,* ed. R.W. Palmer, 39–70. New York: Praeger.

United Nations (UN). 2002. Twenty-eighth Session. *Equity, Development and Citizenship: CEPAL.* Mexico City: United Nations.

Migration vs. Development?

The Case of Poverty and Inequality in Mexico

Agustín Escobar Latapi*

INTRODUCTION

The Mexican government and the public remained fundamentally indifferent to international migration until recently, in spite of the fact that emigration absorbed 30% of Mexico's population growth. There are several reasons behind this. First, from 1964 to the late 1990's, international emigration was lower and largely a rural phenomenon. Second, Mexico-US migration seemed harmless.

In terms of public perception, some migrants won and some lost, some stayed and some returned, some remitted large amounts to their families and some did not, but it was hard to find a systematic relationship between migration and national development, other than the fact that, with more and better job opportunities in Mexico, people would stay. In other words, to both the government and the public, the relationship of migration to development was largely neutral, or in any case it was a one-way relationship, going from (insufficient) development in Mexico to (modest levels of harmless) emigration.

In this paper, I argue that the neglect of migration policy in Mexico is mistaken. The migration-development nexus is becoming more perverse in Mexico: The numbers are large, family incomes are lower, and there are negative impacts on the Mexican labour force and economy.

CURRENT MIGRATION AND ITS NEXUS TO DEVELOPMENT

Mexico–U.S. migration slowed considerably with the 2008–09 global recession. The total number of Mexican-born in the U.S. has not increased since 2007, so that, from an average net emigration of approximately 560,000 between 2000 and 2005, net Mexico-US migration fell to zero between 2007 and 2010.

Until 2007, however, the volume of Mexico-US migration was large. Approximately 40% of Mexico's labour force growth was exported every year, and by 2007 about 18% of Mexico's total labour force worked in the U.S.

POSITIVE AND PERVERSE SCENARIOS

Positive scenarios enable migration to foster development through two main channels: remittances and returns. Remittances (and savings) may contribute to development in various ways, as when migrants have learned new skills and are able to practice and develop them upon their return.

But while furthering development through entrepreneurship, new jobs and economic activities, remittances also affect poverty and inequality. Lowering poverty and inequality is itself a component of development, but can have an impact on economic growth through the creation of markets and jobs at the bottom of the economic and social structure. Remittances, usually analysed as a positive financial inflow akin to those derived from exports, in fact differ from them for three reasons. First, most remittances are sent to families, not firms. Second, remittances are mostly used for subsistence, not production. Third, remittances imply the export of labour as opposed to goods and services. Because remittances are mostly sent to families, they are usually analysed as part of income of households, not firms.

Inter-government institutions and initiatives such as the Berne Initiative, the World Bank, the Inter-American Development Bank, the GCIM, the *Puebla* process and others, find that most remittances are directed at poor households. Since remittances are treated as net income, analysts conclude that remittances increase the income of the poor, reduce inequality and promote development. According to this argument, remittances must be protected because they are private transactions, the poor depend on them to survive, and they reduce poverty and inequality.

Remittances are sometimes compared with Official Development Assistance. However, such comparison ignores the fact that remittances are paid for with labour power. The Organization for Economic Cooperation and Development (OECD, 2008) recently concluded that lowest-income countries export mostly high-skilled labour, while middle-income labour countries export mostly low-skill workers. High-skill workers tend to migrate legally, which entitles them to take their family along and significantly reduces remittances. Lower-skilled workers, on the contrary, tend to migrate illegally, leaving their families behind (at least for a certain period) and thus increasing remittances. As a result, very low-income countries would seem to be investing large portions of their GDP in the training of high-skill individuals and then lose these workers in exchange for modest remittances that go mostly to more affluent families, increasing income inequality. As a result, emigration can be a perverse process that slows development through loss of skilled manpower and the capital invested in migrants' skills.

By contrast, medium-income countries export persons in which the country has invested little, and these migrants tend to remit larger relative amounts. These remittances are significant net income for their (poor) families, reducing poverty and possibly accelerating development.

Because of its proximity to the United States, which lessens the cost of migration, and the cumulative, social-networking effect of a century of low-skill emigration, Mexico should be a medium-income country exporting low-skill workers illegally and generating relatively large remittances. As a result, poverty should diminish markedly in Mexico due to migration.

There is a rapidly growing research literature that shows modest, positive impacts of migration on development for two reasons: Total income in poor areas rises, and socio-economic indicators in high-emigration municipalities improve. This paper contributes to this literature by relating the loss in labour force to emigration to the gain in remittances.

The first part of the paper addresses the "migrant-for-remittances exchange" issue in general and its meaning for Mexico to highlight the national interest in migration and remittances. The second part examines the differential propensity to migrate according to socio-economic status, while the third tackles the question of the propensity to remit and the determinants of the amounts remitted. The fourth part asks whether remittances can be considered net positive income for the poor from the point of view of the opportunity cost of emigration and the fifth part provides an overview of recent developments and their impacts on Mexican migrants in the U.S.

THE EXCHANGE OF MIGRANTS FOR REMITTANCES

Labour migration can be analysed as an exchange of labour force for remittances. Although migration can have other benefits and costs, migration involves a loss of population in exchange for remittances (through migrants' families). Mexico is among the three top remittance-receiving countries in the world (World Bank). After a long period of 2-digit growth rates until 2007, remittances have stagnated at $23 billion. Remittances rose much faster than the number of Mexicans in the United States—remittances rose 4.5 times between 1995 and 2005, while the Mexican-born population in the United States expanded by 71 per cent.[1] In social terms, remittances were roughly 7 times the largest government cash transfer programme to aid the poor.

Do migrant remittances exceed what would have been generated if the migrant stayed home? This question tackles the national interest, ignoring the fact that

---

1   Growth may be overestimated because it is generally agreed that there was severe underestimation up to 1995 and that estimates improved afterwards. After 2006, the flow has ceased to grow. It may in fact fall in 2008. The trend for the first seven months of 2008 is for the flow to decrease by approximately 2.9 per cent.

TABLE 3.4.1 *Latin America—Per capita remittances from the United States to GDP per capita ratios, 2003*

RECEIVING COUNTRY	REMITTANCES/ GDP PER CAPITA	RECEIVING COUNTRY	REMITTANCES/ GDP PER CAPITA
Haiti	4.22	Costa Rica	0.74
Bolivia	4.02	Jamaica	0.60
Brazil	3.88	Guyana	0.52
Honduras	2.57	Venezuela	0.49
Colombia	2.24	Argentina	0.40
Guatemala	2.17	Belize	0.39
Ecuador	1.57	Uruguay	0.33
Peru	1.20	Mexico	0.22
El Salvador	1.19	Trinidad & Tobago	0.04
Dominican Republic	0.80		

Source: author's estimates, on the basis of the US Census and US Census bureau estimates of immigrant populations, IMF GDP estimates in dollars, and an IDB survey of remittances by Latin Americans residing in the US in 2003.

migrants may gain from migration by earning immigrant status abroad and unifying their families in places offering better education and more opportunities.

Table 3.4.1 shows the ratio of remittances per capita to GDP per capita in selected Latin American countries, based on an estimation of the sizes of Latin America-born populations in the United States in 2003 and per capita remittances from the United States. The base for this calculation is the entire population from a country in the United States, not just the working population, analogous to the calculation of GDP per capita, which is done on the basis of all residents, not just those gainfully employed.

The per capita remittance to per capita GDP ratio is a function of several factors: the GDP gap between sending and receiving countries, the human capital of the migrants, their age/sex structure and labour participation rates, their incomes abroad, their propensity to remit, and the portion of their income remitted. One could also argue that other factors come into play to define the above. First is the migration pattern itself: Legal migrants can more easily take their families with them which lowers remittances. Attachment of the migrants to their sending families/communities/partners, and their assessment of their long-term prospects at home and abroad are also key, as they influence permanent versus circular migration. Independent of the legality of migration, it is reasonable to suppose that middle class families are less likely to depend on remittances, and they exert less pressure on their migrating relatives, although this may not be the case.

Mexico has one of the lowest migration to remittance ratios, close to Uruguay, Trinidad and Tobago, Belize and Argentina, countries with very different migration patterns. Their migration is mostly old, legal, and higher-skilled, while Mexico's low remittance ratio is the outcome of low skill (which determines low-income jobs), lack of documentation (and less favourable employment conditions abroad), and increasing family reunification in the United States. My conclusion is fairly simple: unless one considers the migrant population as economically redundant to Mexico (i.e., unemployed or of extremely low productivity), migration seems to be a net loss for Mexico.

Who Migrates?

The second question is the differential propensity to migrate and to remit by socio-economic status. Although the poorest Mexicans do not migrate in large numbers (see below), their propensity to migrate is rising because of changes taking place in Mexican agriculture and the inability of Mexico's urban economy to absorb them.

This relates to development because the impact of migration is different according to the socio-economic status of the migrant. Assuming both high and low-socio-economic status migrants share a propensity to remit and return, high-skill migrants may contribute to development through the creation or expansion of small modern enterprises that profit from transnational links for transfer of knowledge, social capital among business persons, and new jobs. Low-skill migrants, on the other hand, mostly contribute to development through poverty alleviation, a reduction of inequality, improvements in poor communities/neighbourhoods, and market integration of the poor. Although the relative loss of high-skill Mexicans to migration is large, the vast majority of the flow consists of low-skill persons.

According to Zenteno's analysis using 2000 census data (2008), the poorest, most marginal municipalities show the lowest emigration rates, and there is no relationship between poverty, marginality and emigration. More recent analyses using 2010 census data show that poorest households have the lowest emigration rates. The highest emigration rates are in poor households, one level above the poorest, and migration rates decline rapidly as income rises. In sum, although the poorest of the poor do not migrate internationally, the poor do migrate at greater rates than the non-poor.

Who Receives Remittances?

The third question refers to the propensity to remit according to socioeconomic status. There are at least two opposing forces shaping the propensity to remit and the amounts remitted. The poor tend to have the lowest skill, lowest-pay, most casual jobs in the United States, often in agriculture where wages are lower, but their families' needs for remittances are greater. Janssen and Escobar (2006) concluded that remittances make up a larger percentage of the total income of poor households, and their importance falls as income rises. National remittances show a more pro-poor distribution, which encourages analysts such as Carton de Grammont (2003) to stress that Mexico's rural poor have become a nomad class, at least from the point of view of their monetary income.

A more precise assessment can be achieved, however, by an estimation of the impact of remittances on income distribution inequality expressed as the Gini index (Table 3.4.2).

TABLE 3.4.2 *Gini coefficient, Mexican household monetary incomes, 2000 and 2002*

	2000	2002
Pre-remittances	0.5391	0.5113
Post-remittances	0.5276	0.5022
Δ=RS	0.0115	0.0111
Kakwani	−0.2144	−0.2739

Source: Janssen and Escobar Latapí (2005).

Remittances reduce monetary income inequality. Since the propensity to receive remittances is higher among rural households, it could be said that inequality is also reduced by remittances. However, there is a substantial difference between 2000 and 2002, since 2002 is less unequal, and remittances, although larger, do less to reduce inequality.

In sum, the poorest among the poor migrate less but poor rural households have a higher propensity to receive remittances. The amount per receiving household grows with a household's other income; in larger settlements it grows less than other income. Dependency on remittances is highest at the bottom of the income ladder. Higher-income households receive larger remittances, but remittances are a smaller portion of their total income. The higher propensity to receive remittances at the bottom of the income structure could be related to the circular migration pattern of the very poor. For decades, poor labourers from Southern Mexico moved to Northwestern Mexico and on to California agriculture before returning home in the winter. This pattern has been altered by fewer US farm jobs among Mexicans in the US and more Mexicans in year-round urban jobs.

Income Inequality in a Non-migration Scenario

The three preceding exercises do not relate the loss in labour power to the gain from remittances. In other words, they assess what would happen if remittances stopped altogether, but say nothing of alternative sources of income for the migrants if they stayed. Do poor households show a higher tendency to receive remittances because their labour loss is higher, or is their loss lower, so that they gain more from migration than non-poor households? We now turn to the hypothetical effect on the Mexican income structure of an alternative allocation of household labour.

Janssen and Escobar (2008) estimated the opportunity cost of migration in terms of the income the migrant would earn if he/she had stayed in the community.[2] The variables are: sex, labour experience, schooling level, occupational strata, indigenous status, the community's marginality level, the size of community, and each individual state.

Table 3.4.3 assesses the impact of migrants staying in Mexico. Note that the actual cost of migration (transport, illegal border crossing, and time lost searching for a job) cannot be estimated, but would reduce the net gain from migration.

TABLE 3.4.3   *Gini index under three scenarios, Mexico, 2000*

(MIGRANT HOUSEHOLDS ONLY)	NO REMITTANCES	OBSERVED	OPPORTUNITY COST
All migrants	0.73	0.53	0.49
Men Only	0.75	0.52	0.50

Source: Janssen and Escobar (2008).

The analysis shows that remittances reduce inequality but non-migration reduces inequality even further. One additional point is that the impact of a sudden halt to remittances would be very large on remittance-receiving households, since the Gini index before remittances is extremely high.[3] A counterfactual has limitations. Suddenly bringing back six million workers to Mexico, especially to rural areas, would severely depress labour markets, although it would also allow employers to increase hiring and production. But this is all hypothetical. The exercise is for all migrants and for men only, because the participation rates of women in rural areas are lower (although they have increased and help to explain the rise in wage income). The counterfactual allows a re-assessment of the relationship between remittances per capita and GDP per capita. Although for Mexico the exchange of migrant labour for remittances yields far less than average GDP, these migrants would not earn the average Mexican GDP in their hometowns because they depart from low-productivity areas and possess little human capital.

---

2   The census provides no data on pre-departure occupations, nor on the migrant's schooling level. We therefore used household average schooling as a proxy for migrant schooling.

3   Although the R2 is low in this final exercise (.438), it was decided that this was preferable to having a higher figure that in our view was less reflective of actual opportunity costs.

CONCLUSIONS

A significant missing piece in this analysis pertains to the migration process of the rural poor. Escobar (2008) argued that the rural poor migrate in specific ways due to three factors: their financial constraints, the recent nature of their migration, and the specific nature of the social capital used to migrate. Poverty and the social organization of the rural poor condition their migration process, which means that the 10:1 earnings ratio between the United States and Mexico does not easily translate into significant economic improvement for migrants and their families. Nevertheless, migration is a process, and the social capital of the poor evolves in ways similar to the social capital of others. Successful migrants often help their families; there is upward mobility, and a few returnees start successful agricultural or other businesses. Good jobs and access to good migration networks can help migrants to overcome poverty and "normalize" their migration process.

The impact of remittances on poverty and inequality can be summarized as follows:

1. Remittances make a significant contribution to GDP.
2. Remittances, however, do not compensate Mexico for the labour lost to migration.
3. Among Mexico's poorest 5%, the propensity to migrate is much lower than average. However, Mexico's 20% poorest households are the most frequent remittance receivers, suggesting a marked difference in migration frequency between the poorest and those just above them.
4. Non-poor households receive larger absolute remittances than poor households, but poor households receive a larger share of their total income from remittances.
5. Remittances reduce income inequality, but poverty and inequality are lower in a no-migration counterfactual scenario.
6. One reason may be the specific social process of migration among the poor, which generates remittances in more difficult conditions than for non-poor migrants.

From a development perspective, we can conclude that, in the current context, migration may represent a net loss for Mexico. Migration has a positive impact on poor, high-emigration areas, but the potential impact on Mexican growth could be greater if these migrants stayed at home.

REFERENCES

Adelman, I., and J.E. Taylor (1990). Is structural adjustment with a human face possible? The case of Mexico. *Journal of Development Studies,* 26(3): 387–407.

Arroyo Alejandre, J., and J. Papail (2004). Los dólares de la migración, Universidad de Guadalajara/IRD/PROFMEX/Casa Juan Pablos, Guadalajara.

Bank of Mexico (2008). Remesas familiars. Available at: http://www.banxico.org.mx/SieInternet/consultarDirectorioInternetAction.do?accion=consultarCuadroAnalitico&idCuadro=CA11&sector=1&locale=es.

Carton de Grammont, H. (2003) Migración y pobreza. In: R. Cordera, et al. (Eds.), *La cuestión social: superación de la pobreza y política social a siete años de Copenhague*, Instituto de Desarrollo Social-Universidad Nacional Autónoma de México/IETD, Mexico City: 57–67.

Cruz, T. (2008). ¿Pueden las remesas abatir la pobreza? Efecto económico y modelos distributivos de las remesas en una comunidad de la región Chatina. In: A. Escobar (Ed.), *Pobreza y migración internacional*. Mexico City: CIESAS, pp. 321–343.

ECLAC (Economic Commission for Latin America and the Caribbean) (2001). *International migration and development in the Americas. Symposium on International Migration in the Americas*, ECLAC, Santiago.

Escobar Latapí, A. (1995). La reestructuración en México y en Estados Unidos y la migración internacional. *Revue Européenne des Migrations Internationales*, 11(2): 73–95.

Escobar Latapí., A. (1998). Migración y desarrollo en Centro y Norteamérica: elementos para una discusión. *CIESAS Occidente, México, Seminario sobre Migración Internacional y Desarrollo en Norte y Centroamérica organizado por la Conferencia Regional de Migración*, Mexico City, May.

Escobar Latapí., A. (Ed.) (2008). *Pobreza y migración internacional*, Mexico City: CIESAS. Escobar Latapí., A. (2008). Mexican policy and Mexico –U.S. migration. In: A. Escobar and S. Martin (Eds.), *Mexico U.S. Migration Management: A binational Approach*, Lanham: Lexington Books, pp. 179–215.

Escobar Latapí., A. and E. Janssen (2006). Migration, the diaspora and development. The case of Mexico. *IILS (ILO) Discussion Paper 167*, Geneva: ILO.

Escobar Latapí,.A. and S. Martin (2008). Introduction. In: L.A. Escobar and S. Martin (Eds.), *Mexico U.S. Migration Management: A Binational Approach*, Lanham: Lexington Books, pp.9–13.

Escobar Latapí,.A. and S. Martin (Eds.) (2008). *Mexico U.S. Migration Management: A binational Approach*, Lanham: Lexington Books.

GCIM (Global Commission on International Migration) (2005). *Migration in an Interconnected World: New Directions for Actions*, GCIM, Geneva, October, http://www.gcim.org/attachements/gcim-complete-report-2005.pdf.

Janssen, E., and A. Escobar Latapí (2005). Remittances, poverty and inequality in Mexico. Paper presented at the *10th International Metropolis Conference*, Toronto, 17–21 October.

Janssen, E., and A. Escobar Latapí (2008). Remesas y costo de oportunidad. El caso Mexicano. In: Escobar, Agustín (ed.), *Pobreza y migración internacional*, Mexico City: CIESAS, pp.345–364.

López, M. (2002). Remesas de mexicanos en el exterior y su vinculación con el desarrollo económico, social y cultural de sus regiones de origen. *Estudios sobre migraciones Internacionales 59*, Geneva: OIT/ILO.

Lowell, L., C. Pederzini, and J. Passel (2008). The demography of Mexico/U.S. migration. In: L.A. Escobar and S. Martin (Eds.), *Mexico U.S. Migration Management: A Binational Approach*, Lanham: Lexington Books, pp.1–31.

Lucas, R.E.B. (2005). International migration and economic development. lessons from low-income countries. *Almqvist & Wiksell International*, Stockholm: Ministry for Foreign Affairs of Sweden.

Martin, P.L. (2008). Managing Mexico-United States migration: economic and labor issues. In: L.A. Escobar and S. Martin (Eds.), *Mexico U.S. Migration Management: A binational Approach*, Lanham: Lexington Books, pp.61–88.

Martin, S., and.A. Escobar Latapí (2008). Conclusion. In: L.A. Escobar and S Martin (Eds.) *Mexico U.S. Migration Management: A binational Approach*, Lanham: Lexington Books, pp.237–258.

Massey, D., and R. Zenteno (1999). The dynamics of mass migration. *Proceedings of the National Academic of Sciences,* 96: 5328–5335.

Nyberg-Sorensen, N., N. Van Hear, and P. Engberg-Pedersen (2002). The migration-development nexus: evidence and policy options: state of the art overview. *International Migration*, 40(5): 3–47.

OECD (2008). *Policy Coherence for Development: Migration and Developing Countries*, The Development Center, Paris: OECD.

Portes, A. (2007). Migration, development, and segmented assimilation: a conceptual review of the evidence. Annals of the American Academy of Political and Social Sciences, 610(1): 73–97.

Portes, A., and L. E. Guarnizo (1991). Tropical capitalists: U.S. bound immigration and small enterprise in the Dominican Republic. In: S. Weintraub and S. Díaz-Briquets (Eds.), *Migration, Remittances and Small Business Development: Mexico and Caribbean Basin Countries*, Boulder: Westview Press, pp.103–131.

Rodríguez, E. (2008). *La Política de Desarrollo Rural: Algunas Reflexiones*. Report, Washington, DC.: Interamerican Development Bank.

Scott, J. (2007). Desarrollo rural en México. *Working paper, CIDE*, April (in Spanish).

Stark, O., and D.E. Bloom (1985). The new economics of labor migration. *The American Economic Review*, Papers and Proceedings of the Ninety-Seventh Annual Meeting of the American Economic Association, May, 75(2): 173–178.

Tuirán, R. (2002). Migración, remesas y desarrollo. In: *La situación demográfica de México 2002*, Mexico City: CONAPO, pp.77–88.

Unger, K. (2005). Regional economic development and Mexican out-migration. *NBER Working Paper no. 11432*, http://www.nber.org/papers/w11432.

Vélez Ibáñez, C. (1995). *Border Visions*, Tucson: University of Arizona Press.

Villa, M. and J. Martínez (2002). Rasgos sociodemográficos y económicos de la migración internacional en América Latina y el Caribe. *Capítulos del SELA*, 65, mayo-agosto, pp. 26–67.

Villa, M. and J. Martínez (1998). *La migración internacional en América Latina y el Caribe. Rasgos sociodemográficos y económicos*, Santiago: CEPAL.

Woodruff, C.M., and R. Zenteno (2001). Remittances and Microenterprises in Mexico. *University of California San Diego, Graduate School of International Relations and Pacific Studies Working Paper*, August 14. Available at: http://ssrn.com/abstract=282019.

Zenteno, R. (2008). Pobreza, marginación y migración mexicana a Estados Unidos. In: L.A.Escobar (Ed.), *Pobreza y migración internacional*, Mexico City: CIESAS, pp.85–130.

STATISTICAL SOURCES

a) Poverty: CONEVAL (2009). *Medición de la Pobreza, 1992–2006*. Available at http://www.coneval.gob.mx.

b) Household Income:
INEGI (2009). *ENIGH 1992, 2000, 2002, and 2006*. Available at: http://www.inegi.gob.mx/inegi/default.aspx?s=est.

c) Population: INEGI (2001). *Estados Unidos Mexicanos. Tabulados básicos. XII Censo General de Población y Vivienda 2000*.

INEGI (1996). *Estados Unidos Mexicanos. Conteo de Población y Vivienda 1995. Resultados definitivos. Tabulados básicos*.

INEGI (2006). *Estados Unidos Mexicanos. Conteo de Población y Vivienda 1995. Resultados definitivos. Tabulados básicos*.

Issues in Latin America

POSTREADING QUESTIONS

1. Discuss the ways that Spanish capitalist enterprises afflicted the Caribbean and Latin America's rimland populations in the 16th century.
2. Compare and contrast the push–pull and world system as explanatory models to Indian indentured migration to the Caribbean.
3. Why is the relationship between migrants' socio-economic status and remittances a nonlinear one? Are poor unskilled Mexicans benefiting from migrating to the United States?
4. How did the global techno-economic configuration influence migratory patterns and travel strategies in the Caribbean? Provide examples.

SUGGESTED ADDITIONAL READINGS

Henderson, T. (2011). *Beyond borders: A history of Mexican migration to the United States*. Hoboken, NJ: Wiley-Blackwell.

Marquardt, M., Steigenga, T., Williams, P., & Vásquez, M. (2011). *Living "illegal": The human face of unauthorized immigration*. New York, NY: The New Press.

Peggy, L. (2001). *The transnational villagers*. Berkeley, CA: University of California Press.

Segura, D. A., & Zavella, P. (2007). *Women and migration in the U.S.-Mexico borderlands: A reader*. Durham, NC: Duke University Press.

Stepick, A. Grenier, G., Castro, M., & Dunn, M. (2003). *This land is our land*. Berkeley, CA: University of California Press.